Honda
VT600 and VT750 Shadow V-Twins Owners Workshop Manual

by Mike Stubblefield
and John H Haynes
Member of the Guild of Motoring Writers

Models covered:

Honda VT600C Shadow VLX. 583cc. (1988 and 1989)
Honda VT600C Shadow VLX. 583cc. (1991 through 2003)
Honda VT600CD Shadow VLX. 583cc. (1993 through 2003)
Honda VT750C/CD Shadow American Classic Edition.
 745cc. (1998 through 2003)
Honda VT750DC Shadow Spirit. 745cc. (2001 through 2003)

(6J3 - 2312)   ABCDE
          FGHIJ
          KLMN

Haynes Publishing
Sparkford Nr Yeovil
Somerset BA22 7JJ England

Haynes North America, Inc
861 Lawrence Drive
Newbury Park
California 91320 USA

Oil 10W-40 SF OR SG Grade   1996
idle speed 1200 RPM +-100
valve lash   IN 0.15 mm
   " "   EX 0.20 mm   cold

gas 91 RON min.
Spark plug + Gap.   NGK DPR8EA-9 ~~~~   ) ~~~
                      ND X24EPR-U9
Gap 0.8 - 0.9 mm

Acknowledgments

Our thanks to Honda of Milpitas, Milpitas, CA, for providing the motorcycles used in these photographs; to Pete Sirett, service manager, for
arranging the facilities and fitting the project into his shop's busy
schedule; and to Bruce Farley, service technician, for doing the
mechanical work and providing valuable technical information. Wiring
diagrams originated exclusively for Haynes North America, Inc. by
George Edward Brodd.

© Haynes North America, Inc. 1999, 2000, 2003

With permission from J.H. Haynes & Co. Ltd.

A book in the Haynes Owners Workshop Manual Series

Printed in the U.S.A.

ISBN 1 56392 516 8

Library of Congress Control Number 2003110305

British Library Cataloguing in Publication Data
A catalogue record for this book is available from the British Library

We take great pride in the accuracy of information given in this
manual, but motorcycle manufacturers make alterations and
design changes during the production run of a particular motorcycle of which they do not inform us. No liability can be accepted by
the authors or publishers for loss, damage or injury caused by any
errors in, or omissions from, the information given.

12,463 miles   10/04/08   Ser.# JH2PC2109TM700832
Eng.# PC21E-2800849

Contents

1999 Honda Shadow 600

About this manual

Its purpose

The purpose of this manual is to help you get the best value from your motorcycle. It can do so in several ways. It can help you decide what work must be done, even if you choose to have it done by a dealer service department or a repair shop; it provides information and procedures for routine maintenance and servicing; and it offers diagnostic and repair procedures to follow when trouble occurs.

We hope you use the manual to tackle the work yourself. For many simpler jobs, doing it yourself may be quicker than arranging an appointment to get the vehicle into a shop and making the trips to leave it and pick it up. More importantly, a lot of money can be saved by avoiding the expense the shop must pass on to you to cover its labor and overhead costs. An added benefit is the sense of satisfaction and accomplishment that you feel after doing the job yourself.

Using the manual

The manual is divided into Chapters. Each Chapter is divided into numbered Sections, which are headed in bold type between horizontal lines. Each Section consists of consecutively numbered paragraphs or steps.

At the beginning of each numbered Section you will be referred to any illustrations which apply to the procedures in that Section. The reference numbers used in illustration captions pinpoint the pertinent Section and the Step within that Section. That is, illustration 3.2 means the illustration refers to Section 3 and Step (or paragraph) 2 within that Section.

Procedures, once described in the text, are not normally repeated. When it's necessary to refer to another Chapter, the reference will be given as Chapter and Section number. Cross references given without use of the word 'Chapter' apply to Sections and/or paragraphs in the same Chapter. For example, 'see Section 8' means in the same Chapter.

References to the left or right side of the vehicle assume you are sitting on the seat, facing forward.

Motorcycle manufacturers continually make changes to specifications and recommendations, and these, when notified, are incorporated into our manuals at the earliest opportunity.

Even though we have prepared this manual with extreme care, neither the publisher nor the authors can accept responsibility for any errors in, or omissions from, the information given.

NOTE

A **Note** provides information necessary to properly complete a procedure or information which will make the procedure easier to understand.

CAUTION

A **Caution** provides a special procedure or special steps which must be taken while completing the procedure where the Caution is found. Not heeding a Caution can result in damage to the assembly being worked on.

WARNING

A **Warning** provides a special procedure or special steps which must be taken while completing the procedure where the Warning is found. Not heeding a Warning can result in personal injury.

Introduction to the Honda VT600 and VT750 Shadow V-Twins

The Honda VT600 Shadow and VT750 Shadow are popular cruiser-style motorcycles. Their light weight, V-twin engines, excellent brakes and good handling have made these machines two of the more popular mid-size bikes.

The engine on all models is a liquid-cooled V-twin with single overhead camshafts and three valves (two intake, one exhaust) per cylinder. Fuel is delivered through one or two carburetors, depending on model.

The front suspension uses telescopic forks. The rear suspension on VT600 models consists of a single shock absorber/spring unit, mounted ahead of the swingarm. VT750 models have a conventional twin-shock setup. The rear spring preload is adjustable on all models.

The front brake on all models is a hydraulically actuated dual-piston caliper. The rear brake on all models is a mechanically-actuated drum brake.

Identification numbers

The vehicle identification number (VIN) is stamped into the left side of the steering head, and/or is located on a label affixed to the right side of the frame, below the exhaust pipe. The frame serial number is stamped into the right side of the steering head and the engine serial number is stamped into the lower right side of the rear cylinder. These numbers should be recorded and kept in a safe place so they can be furnished to law enforcement officials in the event of theft.

The VIN, frame serial number, engine serial number and carburetor identification number should be kept in a handy place (such as your wallet) so they are always available when purchasing or ordering parts for your machine.

Other important identification numbers include the carburetor identification number and the color code. The carburetor identification number is stamped into the intake side of the carburetor. On VT600 models, the color code is located under the seat, on a label affixed to the inner side of the left upper frame tube, next to the fuel filter; on VT750 models, it's on a label affixed to the front side of the left frame tube, right below the ignition switch and just ahead of the left passenger peg. Always refer to the color code when buying painted parts such as the fuel tank, fenders or side covers.

The models covered by this manual are as follows:

VT600C Shadow VLX (1988 and 1989)
VT600CD Shadow VLX Deluxe (1988 and 1989)
VT600C Shadow VLX (1991 through 1996)
VT600CD Shadow VLX Deluxe (1991 through 1996)
VT600C Shadow VLX (1997 through 2003)
VT600CD VLX Deluxe (1997 through 2003)
VT750C Shadow American Classic Edition (1998 through 2003)
VT750CD Shadow Deluxe American Classic Edition
  (1998 through 2003)
VT750DC Shadow Spirit 750, (2001 through 2003)

The Vehicle Identification Number (VIN) is stamped into the left side of the steering head

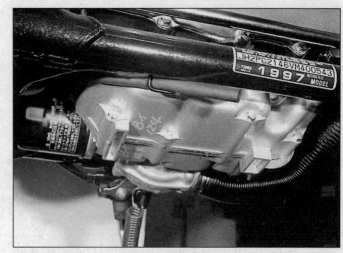

The VIN is also displayed on a label affixed to the right frame rail

The frame serial number is stamped into the right side of the steering head

The engine serial number is stamped into the right side of the crankcase, below the rear cylinder

The following table is a breakdown of the initial frame numbers for each model and year of production:

Year	Model	Initial frame number
1988	VT600	Except California: PC210 JM / California PC211 JM
1989	VT600	Except California: PC210 KM / California: PC211 KM
1991	VT600	Except California: PC210 MM / California: PC211 MM
1992	VT600	Except California: PC210 NM / California: PC211 MM
1993	VT600	Except California: PC210 PM / California: PC211 PM
1994	VT600	Except California: PC210 RM / California: PC211 RM
1995	VT600	Except California: PC210 SM / California: PC211 SM
	VT600D	Except California: PC213 SM / California: PC214 SM
1996	VT600	Except California: PC210 TM / California: PC211 TM
1996	VT600D	Except California: PC213 TM / California: PC214 TM
1997		*Not available at time of printing.*
1998	VT600	*Not available at time of printing.*
	VT750C	Except California: RC440 WM / California: RC441 WM
	VT750CD	Except California: RC443 WM / California: RC444 WM

Year	Model	Initial frame number
	VT750CD2	Except California: RC446 WM / California: RC447WM
1999	VT600	Except California: PC210 XM9 / California: PC211 XM9
	VT600D	Except California: PC213 XM9 / California: PC214 XM9
	VT600D2	Except California: PC216 XM9 / California: PC217 XM9
	VT750C	Except California: RC440 XM1 / California: RC441 XM1
	VT750CD	Except California: RC443 XM1 / California: RC444 XM1
	VT750CD2	Except California: RC446 XM1 / California: RC447 XM1

Year	Model	Initial frame number
2000	VT600	Except California: PC210 YK or YM / California: PC211 YK or YM
	VT600CD	Except California: PC213 YK or YM / California: PC214 YK or YM
	VT600CD2	Except California: PC216 YK or YM / California: PC217 YK or YM
	VT750C	Except California: RC440 YK or YK / California: RC441 YM or YK
	VT750CD	Except California: RC443 YM or YK / California: RC444 YM or YK
	VT750CD2	Except California: RC446 YM or YK / California: RC447 YM or YK
2001	VT600C	Except California: PC210 1K or 1M / California: PC211 1K or 1M
	VT600CD	Except California: PC213 1K or 1M / California: PC214 1K or 1M
	VT750CD	Except California: RC443 1K / California: RC444 1K
	VT750CD2	Except California: RC446 1K / California: RC447 1K
	VT750DC	Except California: RC440 1K / California: RC441 1K
2002	VT600C	Except California: PC210 2K or 2M / California: PC211 2K or 2M
	VT600CD	Except California: PC213 2K or 2M / California: PC214 2K or 2M
	VT750CD, VT750CD2	*Not available at time of printing*
	VT750DC	Except California: RC440 2M / California: RC441 2M
2003	VT600C	Except California: PC210 3K or 3M / California: PC211 3K or 3M
	VT600CD	Except California: PC213 3K or 3M / California: PC214 3K or 3M
	VT750CD, VT750CD2	*Not available at time of printing*
	VT750DCA	Except California: RC440 3M / California: RC441 3M
	VT750DCB	Except California: RC445 3M / California: RC448 3M

Buying parts

Once you have found all the identification numbers, record them for reference when buying parts. Since the manufacturers change specifications, parts and vendors (companies that manufacture various components on the machine), providing the ID numbers is the only way to be reasonably sure that you are buying the correct parts.

Whenever possible, take the worn part to the dealer so direct comparison with the new component can be made. Along the trail from the manufacturer to the parts shelf, there are numerous places that the part can end up with the wrong number or be listed incorrectly.

The two places to purchase new parts for your motorcycle - the accessory store and the franchised dealer - differ in the type of parts they carry. While dealers can obtain virtually every part for your motorcycle, the accessory dealer is usually limited to normal high wear items such as shock absorbers, tune-up parts, various engine gaskets, cables, chains, brake parts, etc. Rarely will an accessory outlet have major suspension components, cylinders, transmission gears, or cases.

Used parts can be obtained for roughly half the price of new ones, but you can't always be sure of what you're getting. Once again, take your worn part to the wrecking yard (breaker) for direct comparison.

Whether buying new, used or rebuilt parts, the best course is to deal directly with someone who specializes in parts for your particular make.

General specifications

600 models

Frame and suspension

Wheelbase	
1988 through1998	1605 mm (63.2 inches)
1999 and later	1600 mm (63.0 inches)
Overall length	2310 mm (90.9 inches)
Overall width	
1988 and 1989, 1991 through 1994	760 mm (29.9 inches)
1995 through 1998	890 mm (35.0 inches)
1999 and later	880 mm (34.6 inches)
Overall height	
1988 through 1998	1125 mm (44.3 inches)
1999 and later	1120 mm (44.1 inches)
Seat height	
1988 through 1998	690 mm (27.2 inches)
1999 and later	650 mm (25.6 inches)
Dry weight	
1988 and 1999, 1991 through 1993	196 kg (432 pounds)
1994	199 kg (439 pounds)
1995 and 1996	
VT600C	199 kg (439 pounds)
VT600CD	202 kg (445 pounds)
1997 and 1998	
VT600C	199 kg (439 pounds)
VT600CD	
Except California	202 kg (445 pounds)
California	203 kg (448 pounds)
1999 and later	
VT600C	
Except California	205 kg (442 pounds)
California	206 kg (454 pounds)
VT600CD	
Except California	208 kg (459 pounds)
California	209 kg (461 pounds)
Front suspension	Telescopic fork
Rear suspension	Single shock absorber/coil spring
Front brake	Single hydraulic disc with 2-piston caliper
Rear brake	Mechanically-actuated drum brake
Fuel capacity	
1988 and 1989, 1991 through 1993	9 liters (2.4 US gallons)
1994 on	11 liters (2.9 US gallons)

Engine

Type	Liquid-cooled, 4-stroke, SOHC 52-degree V-twin
Displacement	583 cc
Compression ratio	9.2 to 1
Ignition system	Transistorized
Carburetor type	
1988 through 1998	Two 34 mm Keihin CV carburetors
1999 on	Single 34 mm Keihin CV carburetor
Transmission	4-speed, constant mesh

750 models

Frame and suspension - VT750C/CD Shadow/Shadow Deluxe American Classic Edition 750

Wheelbase	1615 mm (63.6 inches)
Overall length	2450 mm (96.5 inches)
Overall width	980 mm (38.6 inches)
Overall height	
VT750C	1135 mm (44.7 inches)
VT750CD and CD2	
1998 through 2000	1135 mm (44.7 inches)
2001 and later	1110 mm (43.7 inches)
VT750C3 and CD3	1110 mm (43.7 inches)
Seat height	700 mm (27.6 inches)
Dry weight	229 kg (505 pounds)
Front suspension	Telescopic fork
Rear suspension	Dual shock absorbers/coil springs
Front brake	Single hydraulic disc with 2-piston caliper
Rear brake	Mechanically-actuated drum brake
Fuel capacity	14 liters (3.7 US gallons)

Frame and suspension - VT750DC Shadow Spirit 750

Wheelbase	1645 mm (64.8 inches)
Overall length	2335 mm (91.9 inches)
Overall width	800 mm (31.5 inches)
Overall height	1071 mm (42.1 inches)
Seat height	675 mm (26.6 inches)
Dry weight	
Except California	224.5 kg (494.9 pounds)
California	225.7 kg (497.6 pounds)
Front suspension	Telescopic fork
Rear suspension	Dual shock absorbers/coil springs
Front brake	Single hydraulic disc with 2-piston caliper
Rear brake	Mechanically-actuated drum brake
Fuel capacity	13 liters (3.43 US gallons)

Engine – all 750 models

Type	Liquid-cooled, 4-stroke, SOHC 52-degree V-twin
Displacement	745 cc
Compression ratio	9.0 to 1
Ignition system	Transistorized
Carburetor type	Two 34 mm Keihin CV carburetors
Transmission	5-speed, constant mesh

Maintenance techniques, tools and working facilities

Basic maintenance techniques

There are a number of techniques involved in maintenance and repair that will be referred to throughout this manual. Application of these techniques will enable the amateur mechanic to be more efficient, better organized and capable of performing the various tasks properly, which will ensure that the repair job is thorough and complete.

Fastening systems

Fasteners, basically, are nuts, bolts and screws used to hold two or more parts together. There are a few things to keep in mind when working with fasteners. Almost all of them use a locking device of some type (either a lock washer, locknut, locking tab or thread adhesive). All threaded fasteners should be clean, straight, have undamaged threads and undamaged corners on the hex head where the wrench fits. Develop the habit of replacing all damaged nuts and bolts with new ones.

Rusted nuts and bolts should be treated with a penetrating oil to ease removal and prevent breakage. Some mechanics use turpentine in a spout type oil can, which works quite well. After applying the rust penetrant, let it -work for a few minutes before trying to loosen the nut or bolt. Badly rusted fasteners may have to be chiseled off or removed with a special nut breaker, available at tool stores.

If a bolt or stud breaks off in an assembly, it can be drilled out and removed with a special tool called an E-Z out (or screw extractor). Most dealer service departments and motorcycle repair shops can perform this task, as well as others (such as the repair of threaded holes that have been stripped out).

Flat washers and lock washers, when removed from an assembly, should always be replaced exactly as removed. Replace any damaged washers with new ones. Always use a flat washer between a lock washer and any soft metal surface (such as aluminum), thin sheet metal or plastic. Special locknuts can only be used once or twice before they lose their locking ability and must be replaced.

Tightening sequences and procedures

When threaded fasteners are tightened, they are often tightened to a specific torque value (torque is basically a twisting force). Over-tightening the fastener can weaken it and cause it to break, while under-tightening can cause it to eventually come loose. Each bolt, depending on the material it's made of, the diameter of its shank and the material it is threaded into, has a specific torque value, which is noted in the Specifications. Be sure to follow the torque recommendations closely.

Fasteners laid out in a pattern (i.e. cylinder head bolts, engine case bolts, etc.) must be loosened or tightened in a sequence to avoid warping the component. Initially, the bolts/nuts should go on finger tight only. Next, they should be tightened one full turn each, in a criss-cross or diagonal pattern. After each one has been tightened one full turn, return to the first one tightened and tighten them all one half turn, following the same pattern. Finally, tighten each of them one quarter turn at a time until each fastener has been tightened to the proper torque. To loosen and remove the fasteners the procedure would be reversed.

Disassembly sequence

Component disassembly should be done with care and purpose to help ensure that the parts go back together properly during reassembly. Always keep track of the sequence in which parts are removed. Take note of special characteristics or marks on parts that can be installed more than one way (such as a grooved thrust washer on a shaft). It's a good idea to lay the disassembled parts out on a clean surface in the order that they were removed. It may also be helpful to make sketches or take instant photos of components before removal.

When removing fasteners from a component, keep track of their locations. Sometimes threading a bolt back in a part, or putting the washers and nut back on a stud, can prevent mix-ups later. If nuts and bolts can't be returned to their original locations, they should be kept in a compartmented box or a series of small boxes. A cupcake or muffin tin is ideal for this purpose, since each cavity can hold the bolts and nuts from a particular area (i.e. engine case bolts, valve cover bolts, engine mount bolts, etc.). A pan of this type is especially helpful when working on assemblies with very small parts (such as the carburetors and the valve train). The cavities can be marked with paint or tape to identify the contents.

Whenever wiring looms, harnesses or connectors are separated, it's a good idea to identify the two halves with numbered pieces of masking tape so they can be easily reconnected.

Gasket sealing surfaces

Throughout any motorcycle, gaskets are used to seal the mating surfaces between components and keep lubricants, fluids, vacuum or pressure contained in an assembly.

Many times these gaskets are coated with a liquid or paste type gasket sealing compound before assembly. Age, heat and pressure can sometimes cause the two parts to stick together so tightly that they are very difficult to separate. In most cases, the part can be loosened by striking it with a soft-faced hammer near the mating surfaces. A regular hammer can be used if a block of wood is placed between the hammer and the part. Do not hammer on cast parts or parts that could be easily damaged. With any particularly stubborn part, always recheck to make sure that every fastener has been removed.

Avoid using a screwdriver or bar to pry apart components, as they can easily mar the gasket sealing surfaces of the parts (which must remain smooth). If prying is absolutely necessary, use a piece of wood, but keep in mind that extra clean-up will be necessary if the wood splinters.

After the parts are separated, the old gasket must be carefully scraped off and the gasket surfaces cleaned. Stubborn gasket material can be soaked with a gasket remover (available in aerosol cans) to soften it so it can be easily scraped off. A scraper can be fashioned from a piece of copper tubing by flattening and sharpening one end. Copper is recommended because it is usually softer than the surfaces to be scraped, which reduces the chance of gouging the part. Some gaskets can be removed with a wire brush, but regardless of the method used, the mating surfaces must be left clean and smooth. If for some reason the gasket surface is gouged, then a gasket sealer thick enough to fill scratches will have to be used during reassembly of the components. For most applications, a non-drying (or semi-drying) gasket sealer is best.

Hose removal tips

Hose removal precautions closely parallel gasket removal precautions. Avoid scratching or gouging the surface that the hose mates against or the connection may leak. Because of various chemical reactions, the rubber in hoses can bond itself to the metal spigot that the hose fits over. To remove a hose, first loosen the hose clamps that secure it to the spigot. Then, with slip joint pliers, grab the hose at the clamp and rotate it around the spigot. Work it back and forth until it is completely free, then pull it off (silicone or other lubricants will ease removal if they can be applied between the hose and the outside of the spigot). Apply the same lubricant to the inside of the hose and the outside of the spigot to simplify installation.

If a hose clamp is broken or damaged, do not reuse it. Also, do not reuse hoses that are cracked, split or torn.

Spark plug gap adjusting tool

Feeler gauge set

Control cable pressure luber

Hand impact screwdriver and bits

Tools

A selection of good tools is a basic requirement for anyone who plans to maintain and repair a motorcycle. For the owner who has few tools, if any, the initial investment might seem high, but when compared to the spiraling costs of routine maintenance and repair, it is a wise one.

To help the owner decide which tools are needed to perform the tasks detailed in this manual, the following tool lists are offered: *Maintenance and minor repair*, *Repair and overhaul* and *Special*. The newcomer to practical mechanics should start off with the *Maintenance and minor repair* tool kit, which is adequate for the simpler jobs. Then, as confidence and experience grow, the owner can tackle more difficult tasks, buying additional tools as they are needed. Eventually the basic kit will be built into the *Repair and overhaul* tool set. Over a period of time, the experienced do-it-yourselfer will assemble a tool set complete enough for most repair and overhaul procedures and will add tools from the *Special* category when it is felt that the expense is justified by the frequency of use.

Maintenance and minor repair tool kit

The tools in this list should be considered the minimum required for performance of routine maintenance, servicing and minor repair work. We recommend the purchase of combination wrenches (box end and open end combined in one wrench); while more expensive than

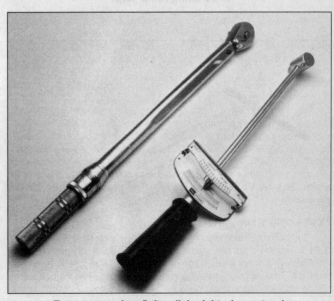

Torque wrenches (left - click; right - beam type)

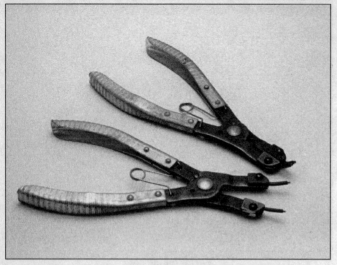

Snap-ring pliers (top - external; bottom - internal)

Allen wrenches (left), and Allen head sockets (right)

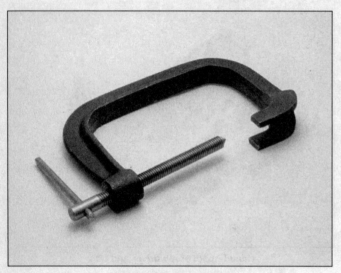

Valve spring compressor

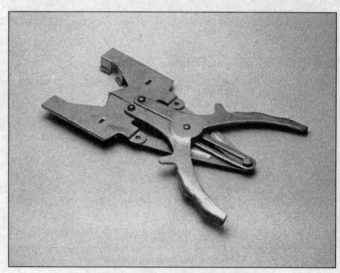

Piston ring removal/installation tool

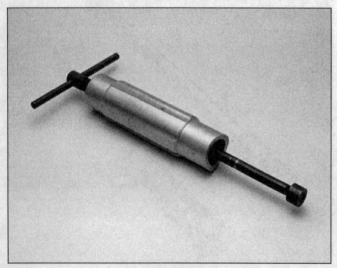

Piston pin puller

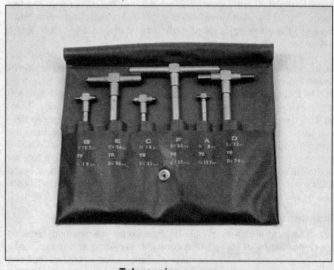

Telescoping gauges

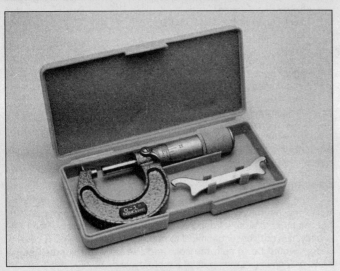

0-to-1 inch micrometer

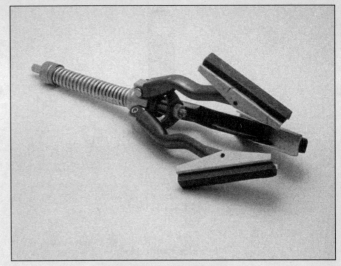

Cylinder surfacing hone

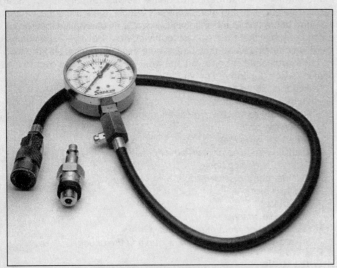

Cylinder compression gauge

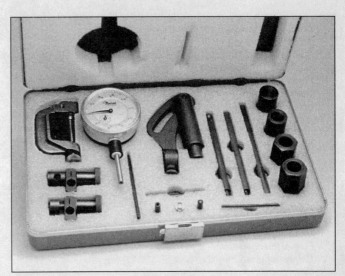

Dial indicator set

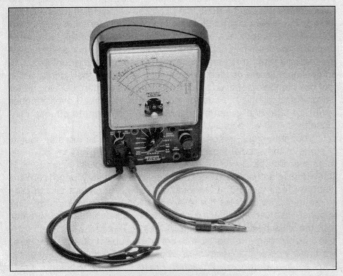

Multimeter (volt/ohm/ammeter)

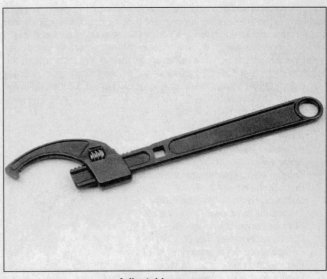

Adjustable spanner

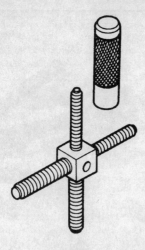

Alternator rotor puller

open-ended ones, they offer the advantages of both types of wrench.

  Combination wrench set (6 mm to 22 mm)
  Adjustable wrench - 8 in
  Spark plug socket (with rubber insert)
  Spark plug gap adjusting tool
  Feeler gauge set
  Standard screwdriver (5/16 in x 6 in)
  Phillips screwdriver (No. 2 x 6 in)
  Allen (hex) wrench set (4 mm to 12 mm)
  Combination (slip-joint) pliers - 6 in
  Hacksaw and assortment of blades
  Tire pressure gauge
  Control cable pressure luber
  Grease gun
  Oil can
  Fine emery cloth
  Wire brush
  Hand impact screwdriver and bits
  Funnel (medium size)
  Safety goggles
  Drain pan
  Work light with extension cord

Repair and overhaul tool set

These tools are essential for anyone who plans to perform major repairs and are intended to supplement those in the Maintenance and minor repair tool kit. Included is a comprehensive set of sockets which, though expensive, are invaluable because of their versatility (especially when various extensions and drives are available). We recommend the 3/8 inch drive over the 1/2 inch drive for general motorcycle maintenance and repair (ideally, the mechanic would have a 3/8 inch drive set and a 1/2 inch drive set).

  Alternator rotor removal tool
  Socket set(s)
  Reversible ratchet
  Extension - 6 in
  Universal joint
  Torque wrench (same size drive as sockets)
  Ball pein hammer - 8 oz
  Soft-faced hammer (plastic/rubber)
  Standard screwdriver (1/4 in x 6 in)
  Standard screwdriver (stubby - 5/16 in)
  Phillips screwdriver (No. 3 x 8 in)
  Phillips screwdriver (stubby - No. 2)
  Pliers - locking
  Pliers - lineman's

  Pliers - needle nose
  Pliers - snap-ring (internal and external)
  Cold chisel - 1/2 in
  Scriber
  Scraper (made from flattened copper tubing)
  Center punch
  Pin punches (1/16, 1/8, 3/16 in)
  Steel rule/straightedge - 12 in
  Pin-type spanner wrench
  A selection of files
  Wire brush (large)

Note: Another tool which is often useful is an electric drill with a chuck capacity of 3/8 inch (and a set of good quality drill bits).

Special tools

The tools in this list include those which are not used regularly, are expensive to buy, or which need to be used in accordance with their manufacturer's instructions. Unless these tools will be used frequently, it is not very economical to purchase many of them. A consideration would be to split the cost and use between yourself and a friend or friends (i.e. members of a motorcycle club).

This list primarily contains tools and instruments widely available to the public, as well as some special tools produced by the vehicle manufacturer for distribution to dealer service departments. As a result, references to the manufacturer's special tools are occasionally included in the text of this manual. Generally, an alternative method of doing the job without the special tool is offered. However, sometimes there is no alternative to their use. Where this is the case, and the tool can't be purchased or borrowed, the work should be turned over to the dealer service department or a motorcycle repair shop.

  Paddock stand (for models not fitted with a centerstand)
  Valve spring compressor
  Piston ring removal and installation tool
  Piston pin puller
  Telescoping gauges
  Micrometer(s) and/or dial/Vernier calipers
  Cylinder surfacing hone
  Cylinder compression gauge
  Dial indicator set
  Multimeter
  Adjustable spanner
  Manometer or vacuum gauge set
  Small air compressor with blow gun and tire chuck

Buying tools

For the do-it-yourselfer who is just starting to get involved in motorcycle maintenance and repair, there are a number of options available when purchasing tools. If maintenance and minor repair is the extent of the work to be done, the purchase of individual tools is satisfactory. If, on the other hand, extensive work is planned, it would be a good idea to purchase a modest tool set from one of the large retail chain stores. A set can usually be bought at a substantial savings over the individual tool prices (and they often come with a tool box). As additional tools are needed, add-on sets, individual tools and a larger tool box can be purchased to expand the tool selection. Building a tool set gradually allows the cost of the tools to be spread over a longer period of time and gives the mechanic the freedom to choose only those tools that will actually be used.

Tool stores and motorcycle dealers will often be the only source of some of the special tools that are needed, but regardless of where tools are bought, try to avoid cheap ones (especially when buying screwdrivers and sockets) because they won't last very long. There are plenty of tools around at reasonable prices, but always aim to purchase items which meet the relevant national safety standards. The expense involved in replacing cheap tools will eventually be greater than the initial cost of quality tools.

It is obviously not possible to cover the subject of tools fully here. For those who wish to learn more about tools and their use, there is a book entitled *Motorcycle Workshop Practice Manual* (Book no. 1454) available from the publishers of this manual. It also provides an introduction to basic workshop practice which will be of interest to a home mechanic working on any type of motorcycle.

Care and maintenance of tools

Good tools are expensive, so it makes sense to treat them with respect. Keep them clean and in usable condition and store them properly when not in use. Always wipe off any dirt, grease or metal chips before putting them away. Never leave tools lying around in the work area.

Some tools, such as screwdrivers, pliers, wrenches and sockets, can be hung on a panel mounted on the garage or workshop wall, while others should be kept in a tool box or tray. Measuring instruments, gauges, meters, etc. must be carefully stored where they can't be damaged by weather or impact from other tools.

When tools are used with care and stored properly, they will last a very long time. Even with the best of care, tools will wear out if used frequently. When a tool is damaged or worn out, replace it; subsequent jobs will be safer and more enjoyable if you do.

Working facilities

Not to be overlooked when discussing tools is the workshop. If anything more than routine maintenance is to be carried out, some sort of suitable work area is essential.

It is understood, and appreciated, that many home mechanics do not have a good workshop or garage available and end up removing an engine or doing major repairs outside (it is recommended, however, that the overhaul or repair be completed under the cover of a roof).

A clean, flat workbench or table of comfortable working height is an absolute necessity. The workbench should be equipped with a vise that has a jaw opening of at least four inches.

As mentioned previously, some clean, dry storage space is also required for tools, as well as the lubricants, fluids, cleaning solvents, etc. which soon become necessary.

Sometimes waste oil and fluids, drained from the engine or cooling system during normal maintenance or repairs, present a disposal problem. To avoid pouring them on the ground or into a sewage system, simply pour the used fluids into large containers, seal them with caps and take them to an authorized disposal site or service station. Plastic jugs (such as old antifreeze containers) are ideal for this purpose.

Always keep a supply of old newspapers and clean rags available. Old towels are excellent for mopping up spills. Many mechanics use rolls of paper towels for most work because they are readily available and disposable. To help keep the area under the motorcycle clean, a large cardboard box can be cut open and flattened to protect the garage or shop floor.

Whenever working over a painted surface (such as the fuel tank) cover it with an old blanket or bedspread to protect the finish.

Safety first!

Professional mechanics are trained in safe working procedures. However enthusiastic you may be about getting on with the job at hand, take the time to ensure that your safety is not put at risk. A moment's lack of attention can result in an accident, as can failure to observe simple precautions.

There will always be new ways of having accidents, and the following is not a comprehensive list of all dangers; it is intended rather to make you aware of the risks and to encourage a safe approach to all work you carry out on your bike.

Essential DOs and DON'Ts

DON'T start the engine without first ascertaining that the transmission is in neutral.

DON'T suddenly remove the pressure cap from a hot cooling system - cover it with a cloth and release the pressure gradually first, or you may get scalded by escaping coolant.

DON'T attempt to drain oil until you are sure it has cooled sufficiently to avoid scalding you.

DON'T grasp any part of the engine or exhaust system without first ascertaining that it is cool enough not to burn you.

DON'T allow brake fluid or antifreeze to contact the machine's paint work or plastic components.

DON'T siphon toxic liquids such as fuel, hydraulic fluid or antifreeze by mouth, or allow them to remain on your skin.

DON'T inhale dust - it may be injurious to health (see *Asbestos* heading).

DON'T allow any spilled oil or grease to remain on the floor - wipe it up right away, before someone slips on it.

DON'T use ill fitting wrenches or other tools which may slip and cause injury.

DON'T attempt to lift a heavy component which may be beyond your capability - get assistance.

DON'T rush to finish a job or take unverified short cuts.

DON'T allow children or animals in or around an unattended vehicle.

DON'T inflate a tire to a pressure above the recommended maximum. Apart from over stressing the carcase and wheel rim, in extreme cases the tire may blow off forcibly.

DO ensure that the machine is supported securely at all times. This is especially important when the machine is blocked up to aid wheel or fork removal.

DO take care when attempting to loosen a stubborn nut or bolt. It is generally better to pull on a wrench, rather than push, so that if you slip, you fall away from the machine rather than onto it.

DO wear eye protection when using power tools such as drill, sander, bench grinder etc.

DO use a barrier cream on your hands prior to undertaking dirty jobs - it will protect your skin from infection as well as making the dirt easier to remove afterwards; but make sure your hands aren't left slippery. Note that long-term contact with used engine oil can be a health hazard.

DO keep loose clothing (cuffs, ties etc. and long hair) well out of the way of moving mechanical parts.

DO remove rings, wristwatch etc., before working on the vehicle - especially the electrical system.

DO keep your work area tidy - it is only too easy to fall over articles left lying around.

DO exercise caution when compressing springs for removal or installation. Ensure that the tension is applied and released in a controlled manner, using suitable tools which preclude the possibility of the spring escaping violently.

DO ensure that any lifting tackle used has a safe working load rating adequate for the job.

DO get someone to check periodically that all is well, when working alone on the vehicle.

DO carry out work in a logical sequence and check that everything is correctly assembled and tightened afterwards.

DO remember that your vehicle's safety affects that of yourself and others. If in doubt on any point, get professional advice.

IF, in spite of following these precautions, you are unfortunate enough to injure yourself, seek medical attention as soon as possible.

Asbestos

Certain friction, insulating, sealing and other products - such as brake pads, clutch linings, gaskets, etc. - contain asbestos. *Extreme care must be taken to avoid inhalation of dust from such products since it is hazardous to health*. If in doubt, assume that they *do* contain asbestos.

Fire

Remember at all times that gasoline (petrol) is highly flammable. Never smoke or have any kind of naked flame around, when working on the vehicle. But the risk does not end there - a spark caused by an electrical short-circuit, by two metal surfaces contacting each other, by careless use of tools, or even by static electricity built up in your body under certain conditions, can ignite gasoline (petrol) vapor, which in a confined space is highly explosive. Never use gasoline (petrol) as a cleaning solvent. Use an approved safety solvent.

Always disconnect the battery ground (earth) terminal before working on any part of the fuel or electrical system, and never risk spilling fuel on to a hot engine or exhaust.

It is recommended that a fire extinguisher of a type suitable for fuel and electrical fires is kept handy in the garage or workplace at all times. Never try to extinguish a fuel or electrical fire with water.

Fumes

Certain fumes are highly toxic and can quickly cause unconsciousness and even death if inhaled to any extent. Gasoline (petrol) vapor comes into this category, as do the vapors from certain solvents such as trichloroethylene. Any draining or pouring of such volatile fluids should be done in a well ventilated area.

When using cleaning fluids and solvents, read the instructions carefully. Never use materials from unmarked containers - they may give off poisonous vapors.

Never run the engine of a motor vehicle in an enclosed space such as a garage. Exhaust fumes contain carbon monoxide which is extremely poisonous; if you need to run the engine, always do so in the open air or at least have the rear of the vehicle outside the workplace.

The battery

Never cause a spark, or allow a naked light near the vehicle's battery. It will normally be giving off a certain amount of hydrogen gas, which is highly explosive.

Always disconnect the battery ground (earth) terminal before working on the fuel or electrical systems (except where noted).

If possible, loosen the filler plugs or cover when charging the battery from an external source. Do not charge at an excessive rate or the battery may burst.

Take care when topping up, cleaning or carrying the battery. The acid electrolyte, even when diluted, is very corrosive and should not be allowed to contact the eyes or skin. Always wear rubber gloves and goggles or a face shield. If you ever need to prepare electrolyte yourself, always add the acid slowly to the water; never add the water to the acid.

Electricity

When using an electric power tool, inspection light etc., always ensure that the appliance is correctly connected to its plug and that, where necessary, it is properly grounded (earthed). Do not use such appliances in damp conditions and, again, beware of creating a spark or applying excessive heat in the vicinity of fuel or fuel vapor. Also ensure that the appliances meet national safety standards.

A severe electric shock can result from touching certain parts of the electrical system, such as the spark plug wires (HT leads), when the engine is running or being cranked, particularly if components are damp or the insulation is defective. Where an electronic ignition system is used, the secondary (HT) voltage is much higher and could prove fatal.

Motorcycle chemicals and lubricants

A number of chemicals and lubricants are available for use in motorcycle maintenance and repair. They include a wide variety of products ranging from cleaning solvents and degreasers to lubricants and protective sprays for rubber, plastic and vinyl.

Contact point/spark plug cleaner is a solvent used to clean oily film and dirt from points, grime from electrical connectors and oil deposits from spark plugs. It is oil free and leaves no residue. It can also be used to remove gum and varnish from carburetor jets and other orifices.

Carburetor cleaner is similar to contact point/spark plug cleaner but it usually has a stronger solvent and may leave a slight oily reside. It is not recommended for cleaning electrical components or connections.

Brake system cleaner is used to remove grease or brake fluid from brake system components (where clean surfaces are absolutely necessary and petroleum-based solvents cannot be used); it also leaves no residue.

Silicone-based lubricants are used to protect rubber parts such as hoses and grommets, and are used as lubricants for hinges and locks.

Multi-purpose grease is an all purpose lubricant used wherever grease is more practical than a liquid lubricant such as oil. Some multi-purpose grease is colored white and specially formulated to be more resistant to water than ordinary grease.

Gear oil (sometimes called gear lube) is a specially designed oil used in transmissions and final drive units, as well as other areas where high-friction, high-temperature lubrication is required. It is available in a number of viscosities (weights) for various applications.

Motor oil, of course, is the lubricant specially formulated for use in the engine. It normally contains a wide variety of additives to prevent corrosion and reduce foaming and wear. Motor oil comes in various weights (viscosity ratings) of from 5 to 80. The recommended weight of the oil depends on the seasonal temperature and the demands on the engine. Light oil is used in cold climates and under light load conditions; heavy oil is used in hot climates and where high loads are encountered. Multi-viscosity oils are designed to have characteristics of both light and heavy oils and are available in a number of weights from 5W-20 to 20W-50.

Gas (petrol) additives perform several functions, depending on their chemical makeup. They usually contain solvents that help dissolve gum and varnish that build up on carburetor and intake parts. They also serve to break down carbon deposits that form on the inside surfaces of the combustion chambers. Some additives contain upper cylinder lubricants for valves and piston rings.

Brake fluid is a specially formulated hydraulic fluid that can withstand the heat and pressure encountered in brake systems. Care must be taken that this fluid does not come in contact with painted surfaces or plastics. An opened container should always be resealed to prevent contamination by water or dirt.

Chain lubricants are formulated especially for use on motorcycle final drive chains. A good chain lube should adhere well and have good penetrating qualities to be effective as a lubricant inside the chain and on the side plates, pins and rollers. Most chain lubes are either the foaming type or quick drying type and are usually marketed as sprays.

Degreasers are heavy duty solvents used to remove grease and grime that may accumulate on engine and frame components. They can be sprayed or brushed on and, depending on the type, are rinsed with either water or solvent.

Solvents are used alone or in combination with degreasers to clean parts and assemblies during repair and overhaul. The home mechanic should use only solvents that are non-flammable and that do not produce irritating fumes.

Gasket sealing compounds may be used in conjunction with gaskets, to improve their sealing capabilities, or alone, to seal metal-to-metal joints. Many gasket sealers can withstand extreme heat, some are impervious to gasoline and lubricants, while others are capable of filling and sealing large cavities. Depending on the intended use, gasket sealers either dry hard or stay relatively soft and pliable. They are usually applied by hand, with a brush, or are sprayed on the gasket sealing surfaces.

Thread cement is an adhesive locking compound that prevents threaded fasteners from loosening because of vibration. It is available in a variety of types for different applications.

Moisture dispersants are usually sprays that can be used to dry out electrical components such as the fuse block and wiring connectors. Some types can also be used as treatment for rubber and as a lubricant for hinges, cables and locks.

Waxes and polishes are used to help protect painted and plated surfaces from the weather. Different types of paint may require the use of different types of wax polish. Some polishes utilize a chemical or abrasive cleaner to help remove the top layer of oxidized (dull) paint on older vehicles. In recent years, many non-wax polishes (that contain a wide variety of chemicals such as polymers and silicones) have been introduced. These non-wax polishes are usually easier to apply and last longer than conventional waxes and polishes.

Troubleshooting

Contents

Engine doesn't start or is difficult to start

1 Starter motor does not rotate

1   Engine kill switch Off.
2   Fuse blown. Check fuse block (Chapter 9).
3   Battery voltage low. Check and recharge battery (Chapter 9).
4   Starter motor defective. Make sure the wiring to the starter is secure. Make sure the starter relay clicks when the start button is pushed. If the solenoid clicks, then the fault is in the wiring or motor.
5   Starter relay faulty. Check it according to the procedure in Chapter 9.
6   Starter button not contacting. The contacts could be wet, corroded or dirty. Disassemble and clean the switch (Chapter 9).
7   Wiring open or shorted. Check all wiring connections and harnesses to make sure that they are dry, tight and not corroded. Also check for broken or frayed wires that can cause a short to ground/earth (see wiring diagram, Chapter 9).
8   Ignition switch defective. Check the switch according to the procedure in Chapter 9. Replace the switch with a new one if it is defective.
9   Engine kill switch defective. Check for wet, dirty or corroded contacts. Clean or replace the switch as necessary (Chapter 9).
10   Faulty sidestand switch. Check the switch circuit and the switch itself according to the procedures in Chapter 9.

2 Starter motor rotates but engine does not turn over

1   Starter motor clutch defective. Inspect and repair or replace (Chapter 9).
2   Damaged starter reduction or idle gear. Inspect and replace the damaged parts (Chapter 9).

3 Starter works but engine won't turn over (seized)

Seized engine caused by one or more internally damaged components. Failure due to wear, abuse or lack of lubrication. Damage can include seized valves, camshafts, pistons, crankshaft, connecting rod bearings, or transmission gears or bearings. Refer to Chapter 2 for engine disassembly.

4 No fuel flow

1 No fuel in tank.
2 Fuel tap turned off or clogged. Disassemble and clean strainer.
3 Fuel tank breather (in cap) clogged. Usually caused by dirt or water. Remove it and clean the cap vent hole.
4 Fuel filter clogged. Inspect and, if necessary, replace the filter (Chapter 4).
5 Fuel line clogged. Pull the fuel line loose and carefully blow through it.
6 Float valve(s) clogged. If the machine has been stored for many months without running, old fuel may can turn into a varnish-like liquid and form deposits on the float valves and jets. Or a bad batch of fuel or an unusual additive may have been used. Try draining the float bowls and cleaning the float valves. It that doesn't alleviate the problem, overhaul the carburetors. Drain and clean the tank too.

5 Engine flooded

1 Float level too high. Check and adjust (Chapter 4).
2 Float valve worn or stuck open. A piece of dirt, rust or other debris can cause the float valve to seat improperly, causing excess fuel to be admitted to the float bowl. Clean the float bowl and inspect the float valve and seat. If the valve and seat are worn, replace them (Chapter 4).
3 Starting technique incorrect. If the carburetors are functioning correctly, the machine should start with little or no throttle. When the engine is cold, the choke should be used and the engine started without opening the throttle. When the engine is at operating temperature, only a very slight amount of throttle should be necessary. If the engine is flooded, turn the fuel tap off and hold the throttle open while cranking the engine. This will allow additional air to reach the cylinders. Remember to turn the fuel back on after the engine starts.

6 No spark or weak spark

1 Ignition switch Off.
2 Engine kill switch turned to the Off position.
3 Battery voltage low. Check and recharge battery as necessary (Chapter 9).
4 Spark plug dirty, defective or worn out. Locate reason for fouled plug(s) using spark plug condition chart and follow the plug maintenance procedures in Chapter 1.
5 Spark plug cap or plug wire faulty. Inspect the plug wires for cracks or deterioration. Make sure that the caps are still firmly attached to the wires. Replace the plug wires if they're worn or damaged (Chapter 5).
6 Spark plug cap not making good contact. Make sure that the plug cap fits snugly over the plug end.
7 Ignition control module defective. Check the module (Chapter 5).
8 Ignition pulse generator(s) defective. Check the ignition pulse generators (Chapter 5).
9 Ignition coil(s) defective. Check the coils, referring to Chapter 5.
10 Ignition or kill switch shorted. This is usually caused by water, corrosion, damage or excessive wear. The switches can be disassembled and cleaned with electrical contact cleaner. If cleaning does not help, replace the switches (Chapter 9).

11 Wiring shorted or broken between:
   a) *Ignition switch and engine kill switch*
   b) *Ignition control module and engine kill switch*
   c) *Ignition control module and ignition coil*
   d) *Ignition coil and spark plug*
   e) *Ignition control module and ignition pulse generator*
Make sure that all wiring connections are clean, dry and tight. Look for chafed and broken wires (Chapters 5 and 9).

7 Compression low

1 Spark plug loose. Remove the plug and inspect the threads. Reinstall and tighten to the specified torque (Chapter 1).
2 Cylinder head not sufficiently tightened down. The head bolts should be tightened to the proper torque in the correct sequence (Chapter 2). If the cylinder head has been loose for awhile, the gasket or head may be damaged, which could cause coolant or oil leaks.
3 Incorrect valve clearance. If the valve is not closing completely, compression pressure is leaking past the valve. Check and adjust the valve clearances (Chapter 1).
4 Cylinder and/or piston worn. Excessive wear will cause compression pressure to leak past the rings. This is usually accompanied by worn rings as well. A top end overhaul is necessary (Chapter 2).
5 Piston rings worn, weak, broken, or sticking. Broken or sticking piston rings usually indicate a lubrication or carburetion problem that causes excess carbon deposits to form on the pistons and rings. Top end overhaul is necessary (Chapter 2).
6 Piston ring-to-groove clearance excessive. This is caused by excessive wear of the piston ring lands. Piston replacement is necessary (Chapter 2).
7 Cylinder head gasket damaged. If the head is allowed to become loose, or if excessive carbon build-up on the piston crown and combustion chamber causes extremely high compression, the head gasket may leak. Retorquing the head is not always sufficient to restore the seal, so gasket replacement is necessary (Chapter 2).
8 Cylinder head warped. This is caused by overheating or improperly tightened head bolts. Machine shop resurfacing or head replacement is necessary (Chapter 2).
9 Valve spring broken or weak. Caused by component failure or wear; the spring(s) must be replaced (Chapter 2).
10 Valve not seating properly. This is caused by a bent valve (from over-revving or improper valve adjustment), burned valve or seat (incorrect carburetion) or an accumulation of carbon deposits on the seat (from carburetion, lubrication problems). The valves must be cleaned and/or replaced and the seats serviced if possible (Chapter 2).

8 Stalls after starting

1 Incorrect choke operation. Make sure the choke knob is all the way out (Chapter 4)
2 Ignition malfunction (Chapter 5).
3 Carburetor malfunction (Chapter 4).
4 Fuel contaminated. The fuel can be contaminated with either dirt or water, or can change chemically if the machine is allowed to sit for several months or more. Drain the tank and float bowls (Chapter 4).
5 Intake air leak. Check for loose carburetor-to-intake manifold connections, loose or missing vacuum gauge access plug, or loose vacuum chamber cover (Chapter 4).
6 Idle speed incorrect. Adjust idle speed (Chapter 1).

9 Rough idle

1 Ignition malfunction (Chapter 5).
2 Idle speed incorrect. Adjust idle speed (Chapter 1).
3 Carburetors not synchronized. Synchronize carburetors (Chapter 1).

4   Carburetor malfunction (Chapter 4.

5   Fuel contaminated. The fuel can be contaminated with either dirt or water, or can change chemically if the machine is allowed to sit for several months or more. Drain the tank and float bowls. If the problem is severe, a carburetor overhaul may be necessary (Chapter 4).

6   Intake air leak (Chapter 4).

7   Air cleaner clogged. Service or replace air filter element (Chapter 1).

Poor running at low speed

10   Spark weak

1   Battery voltage low. Check and recharge battery (Chapter 9).

2   Spark plug fouled, defective or worn out. Clean and inspect the plugs (Chapter 1).

3   Spark plug cap or plug wire defective. Inspect the plug wires (Chapter 5).

4   Spark plug cap not making contact.

5   Incorrect spark plug. Wrong type, heat range or cap configuration. Check and install correct plugs listed in Chapter 1. A cold plug or one with a recessed firing electrode will not operate at low speeds without fouling.

6   Ignition control module defective (Chapter 5).

7   Ignition pulse generator defective (Chapter 5).

8   Ignition coil(s) defective (Chapter 5).

11   Fuel/air mixture incorrect

1   Pilot screw(s) out of adjustment (Chapter 4).

2   Pilot air passage clogged. Remove and overhaul the carburetors (Chapter 4).

3   Air bleed holes clogged. Remove carburetor and blow out all passages (Chapter 4).

4   Air filter element clogged, poorly sealed or missing (Chapter 1).

5   Air cleaner housing, chamber or intake duct loose or damaged. Look for cracks, holes or loose clamps and replace or repair defective parts (Chapter 4).

6   Fuel level too high or too low. Adjust the floats (Chapter 4).

7   Fuel tank breather (in cap) obstructed. Make sure that the air vent passage in the filler cap is open (except California models, on which the vent is plumbed into the EVAP system).

8   Carburetor intake manifolds loose. Check for cracks, breaks, tears or loose clamps or bolts. Repair or replace the rubber boots.

12   Compression low

1   Spark plug loose. Remove the plug and inspect the threads. Reinstall and tighten to the torque listed in the Chapter 1 Specifications.

2   Cylinder head not sufficiently tightened down. If the cylinder head has been loose for awhile, the gasket and head may be damaged. The head bolts should be tightened to the correct torque in the correct sequence (Chapter 2).

3   Incorrect valve clearance. If the valve is not closing completely, compression pressure is leaking past the valve. Check and adjust the valve clearances (Chapter 1).

4   Cylinder and/or piston worn. Excessive wear will cause compression pressure to leak past the rings. This is usually accompanied by worn rings as well. A top end overhaul is necessary (Chapter 2).

5   Piston rings worn, weak, broken, or sticking. Broken or sticking piston rings usually indicate a lubrication or carburetion problem that causes excess carbon deposits to form on the pistons and rings. Top end overhaul is necessary (Chapter 2).

6   Piston ring-to-groove clearance excessive. This is caused by excessive wear of the piston ring lands. Piston replacement is neces-

sary (Chapter 2).

7   Cylinder head gasket damaged. If the head is allowed to become loose, or if excessive carbon build-up on the piston crown and combustion chamber causes extremely high compression, the head gasket may leak. Retorquing the head is not always sufficient to restore the seal, so gasket replacement is necessary (Chapter 2).

8   Cylinder head warped. This is caused by overheating or incorrectly tightened head bolts. Machine shop resurfacing or head replacement is necessary (Chapter 2).

9   Valve spring broken or weak. Caused by component failure or wear; the spring(s) must be replaced (Chapter 2).

10   Valve not seating properly. This is caused by a bent valve (from over-revving or improper valve adjustment), burned valve or seat (incorrect carburetion) or an accumulation of carbon deposits on the seat (from carburetion, lubrication problems). The valves must be cleaned and/or replaced and the seats serviced if possible (Chapter 2).

13   Poor acceleration

1   Carburetors leaking or dirty. Overhaul the carburetors (Chapter 4).

2   Timing not advancing. The ignition pulse generator(s) or the ignition control module may be defective (Chapter 5). If any of these components are defective, they must be replaced; they can't be repaired.

3   Carburetors not synchronized. Synchronize the carburetors (Chapter 1).

4   Engine oil viscosity too high. Using a heavier oil than that recommended in Chapter 1 can damage the oil pump or lubrication system and cause drag on the engine.

5   Brakes dragging. Can be caused by debris which has entered the brake piston sealing boot, by a warped disc, or by a bent axle. Repair as necessary (Chapter 7).

Poor running or no power at high speed

14   Firing incorrect

1   Air filter element restricted. Replace filter (Chapter 1).

2   Spark plug fouled, defective or worn out. Clean or replace the spark plugs (Chapter 1).

3   Spark plug cap or plug wire defective (Chapter 5).

4   Spark plug cap not in good contact (Chapter 5).

5   Incorrect spark plug. Wrong type, heat range or cap configuration. Check and install correct plugs listed in Chapter 1. A cold plug or one with a recessed firing electrode will not operate at low speeds without fouling.

6   Ignition control module defective. Check and, if necessary, replace the module (Chapter 5).

7   Ignition coil(s) defective. Check and, if necessary, replace the coil(s) (Chapter 5).

15   Fuel/air mixture incorrect

1   Main jet clogged. Dirt, water and other contaminants can clog the main jets. Clean the fuel tap filter screen, the float bowl, the jets and the fuel passages (Chapter 4).

2   Incorrect size main jet. The standard jetting is for sea-level atmospheric pressure and oxygen content.

3   Excessive throttle shaft-to-carburetor body clearance. If the throttle shaft of either carburetor is loose, replace the carburetor (Chapter 4).

4   Air bleed holes clogged. Remove and overhaul carburetors (Chapter 4).

5   Air filter element clogged, poorly sealed or missing.

6   Air cleaner-to-carburetor boot poorly sealed. Look for cracks, holes or loose clamps, and replace or repair defective parts.

7   Fuel level too high or too low. Adjust the float(s) (Chapter 4).

8   Fuel tank air vent obstructed. Make sure the air vent passage in the filler cap is open.

9   Carburetor intake manifolds loose. Check for cracks, breaks, tears or loose clamps or bolts. Repair or replace the rubber boots (Chapter 2).

10   Fuel filter clogged. Clean, and if necessary, replace the filter (Chapter 1).

11   Fuel line clogged. Pull the fuel line loose and carefully blow through it.

16   Compression low

1   Spark plug loose. Remove the plug and inspect the threads. Reinstall and tighten to the specified torque (Chapter 1).

2   Cylinder head not sufficiently tightened down. If the cylinder head is suspected of being loose, then there's a chance that the gasket and head are damaged if the problem has persisted for any length of time. The head bolts should be tightened to the proper torque in the correct sequence (Chapter 2).

3   Improper valve clearance. This means that the valve is not closing completely and compression pressure is leaking past the valve. Check and adjust the valve clearances (Chapter 1).

4   Cylinder and/or piston worn. Excessive wear will cause compression pressure to leak past the rings. This is usually accompanied by worn rings as well. A top end overhaul is necessary (Chapter 2).

5   Piston rings worn, weak, broken, or sticking. Broken or sticking piston rings usually indicate a lubrication or carburetion problem that causes excess carbon deposits or seizures to form on the pistons and rings. Top end overhaul is necessary (Chapter 2).

6   Piston ring-to-groove clearance excessive. This is caused by excessive wear of the piston ring lands. Piston replacement is necessary (Chapter 2).

7   Cylinder head gasket damaged. If the head is allowed to become loose, or if excessive carbon build-up on the piston crown and combustion chamber causes extremely high compression, the head gasket may leak. Retorquing the head is not always sufficient to restore the seal, so gasket replacement is necessary (Chapter 2).

8   Cylinder head warped. This is caused by overheating or improperly tightened head bolts. Machine shop resurfacing or head replacement is necessary (Chapter 2).

9   Valve spring broken or weak. Caused by component failure or wear; the spring(s) must be replaced (Chapter 2).

10   Valve not seating properly. This is caused by a bent valve (from over-revving or improper valve adjustment), burned valve or seat (incorrect carburetion) or an accumulation of carbon deposits on the seat (from carburetion, lubrication problems). The valves must be cleaned and/or replaced and the seats serviced if possible (Chapter 2).

17   Knocking or pinging

1   Carbon build-up in combustion chamber. Use of a fuel additive that will dissolve the adhesive bonding the carbon particles to the crown and chamber is the easiest way to remove the build-up. Otherwise, the cylinder head will have to be removed and decarbonized (Chapter 2).

2   Incorrect or poor quality fuel. Old or improper grades of gasoline can cause detonation. This causes the piston to rattle, thus the knocking or pinging sound. Drain old fuel and always use the recommended fuel grade.

3   Spark plug heat range incorrect. Uncontrolled detonation indicates the plug heat range is too hot. The plug in effect becomes a glow plug, raising cylinder temperatures. Install the proper heat range plug (Chapter 1).

4   Improper air/fuel mixture. This will cause the cylinder to run hot, which leads to detonation. Clogged jets or an air leak can cause this imbalance (Chapter 4).

18   Miscellaneous causes

1   Throttle valve doesn't open fully. Adjust the throttle cable (Chapter 1).

2   Clutch slipping. Caused by damaged, loose or worn clutch components. Try adjusting the clutch cable; if that doesn't work, overhaul the clutch (Chapter 2).

3   Ignition timing incorrect and/or not advancing. Ignition timing can be checked, but it is not adjustable. If the timing is incorrect, check the ignition control module and, if necessary, replace it (Chapter 5).

4   Engine oil viscosity too high. Using a heavier oil than the one recommended in Chapter 1 can damage the oil pump or lubrication system and cause drag on the engine.

5   Brakes dragging. Usually caused by debris which has entered the brake piston sealing boot, or by a warped disc, or by a bent axle. Repair as necessary.

Overheating

19   Cooling system not operating properly

1   Coolant level low. Check coolant level as described in Chapter 1. If coolant level is low, the engine will overheat.

2   Leak in cooling system. Check cooling system hoses and radiator for leaks and other damage. Repair or replace parts as necessary (Chapter 3).

3   Thermostat sticking open or closed. Check and replace as described in Chapter 3.

4   Faulty radiator cap. Remove the cap and have it pressure checked at a service station.

5   Coolant passages clogged. Have the entire system drained and flushed, then refill with new coolant.

6   Water pump defective. Remove the pump and check the components.

7   Clogged radiator fins. Clean them by blowing compressed air through the fins from the back side.

20   Firing incorrect

1   Spark plug fouled, defective or worn out. Clean, inspect and, if necessary, replace the spark plugs (Chapter 1).

2   Incorrect spark plug. Wrong type, heat range or cap configuration. Check and install correct plugs listed in Chapter 1.

3   Faulty ignition coil(s) (Chapter 5).

21   Fuel/air mixture incorrect

1   Main jet clogged. Dirt, water and other contaminants can clog the main jets. Clean the fuel tap filter, the float bowl area and the jets and carburetor orifices (Chapter 4).

2   Main jet wrong size. The standard jetting is for sea level atmospheric pressure and oxygen content.

3   Air cleaner poorly sealed or missing.

4   Air cleaner-to-carburetor boot poorly sealed. Look for cracks, holes or loose clamps and replace or repair.

5   Fuel level too low. Adjust the float(s) (Chapter 4).

6   Fuel tank air vent obstructed. Make sure that the air vent passage in the filler cap is open (except California models).

7   Carburetor intake manifolds loose. Check for cracks, breaks, tears or loose clamps or bolts. Repair or replace the rubber boots (Chapter 4).

5   Clutch hub or housing unevenly worn. This causes improper engagement of the discs. Replace the damaged or worn parts (Chapter 2).

28 Clutch not disengaging completely

1   Clutch plates warped or damaged. This will cause clutch drag, which in turn causes the machine to creep. Overhaul the clutch assembly (Chapter 2).
2   Clutch spring tension uneven. Usually caused by a sagged or broken spring. Check and replace the springs (Chapter 2).
3   Engine oil deteriorated. Old, thin, worn out oil will not provide proper lubrication for the discs, causing the clutch to drag. Replace the oil and filter (Chapter 1).
4   Engine oil viscosity too high. Using a heavier oil than recommended in Chapter 1 can cause the plates to stick together, putting a drag on the engine. Change to the correct weight oil (Chapter 1).
5   Clutch housing seized on shaft. Lack of lubrication, severe wear or damage can cause the housing to seize on the shaft. Overhaul of the clutch, and perhaps transmission, may be necessary to repair damage (Chapter 2).
6   Clutch release mechanism defective. Worn or damaged release mechanism parts can stick and fail to apply force to the pressure plate. Overhaul the release mechanism (Chapter 2).
7   Loose clutch hub nut. Causes housing and hub misalignment putting a drag on the engine. Engagement adjustment continually varies. Overhaul the clutch assembly (Chapter 2).

Gear shifting problems

29 Doesn't go into gear or lever doesn't return

1   Clutch cable out of adjustment (Chapter 1) or clutch not disengaging (see Section 27).
2   Shift fork(s) or shift fork shaft bent, worn or jammed. Often caused by dropping the machine or from lack of lubrication. Overhaul the transmission (Chapter 2).
3   Gear(s) stuck on shaft. Most often caused by a lack of lubrication or excessive wear in transmission bearings and bushings. Overhaul the transmission (Chapter 2).
4   Shift drum binding. Caused by lubrication failure or excessive wear. Replace the drum and bearings (Chapter 2).
5   Gearshift spindle bent or damaged. Replace gearshift spindle (Chapter 2).
6   Shift lever broken. Splines stripped out of lever or shaft, caused by allowing the lever to get loose or from dropping the machine. Replace necessary parts (Chapter 2).

30 Jumps out of gear

1   Shift fork(s) or shift fork shaft bent or worn. Overhaul the transmission (Chapter 2).
2   Gear dogs or dog slots worn or damaged. The gears should be inspected and, if necessary, replaced. No attempt should be made to service the worn parts.
3   Shift drum stopper arm broken (Chapter 2).
4   Broken shift linkage return spring (Chapter 2).

Abnormal engine noise

31 Knocking or pinging

1   Carbon build-up in combustion chamber. To remove the build-up, use a fuel additive that will dissolve the layer of carbon on the piston

1   Damaged, kinked or dirty clutch cable. Inspect, lubricate and, if necessary, replace clutch cable (Chapter 2).
2   Faulty clutch lifter plate bearing. Inspect and, if necessary, replace lifter plate bearing (Chapter 2).
3   Damaged clutch lifter mechanism. Inspect and, if necessary, replace lifter mechanism (Chapter 2).
4   Incorrectly routed clutch cable (Chapter 2).

27 Clutch slipping

1   Friction plates worn or warped. Overhaul the clutch assembly (Chapter 2).
2   Metal plates worn or warped (Chapter 2).
3   Clutch springs broken or weak. Old or heat-damaged (from slipping clutch) springs should be replaced with new ones (Chapter 2).
4   Clutch release mechanism defective. Check the mechanism and replace any defective parts (Chapter 2).

crown and combustion chamber. If that doesn't work, the cylinder head will have to be removed and decarbonized (Chapter 2).

2   Old, incorrect or poor quality fuel can cause detonation. This causes the piston to rattle, thus the knocking or pinging sound. Drain the fuel, clean the tank and refill with the recommended grade (Chapter 4).

3   Spark plug heat range incorrect. Uncontrolled detonation indicates that the plug heat range is too hot. The plug in effect becomes a glow plug, raising cylinder temperatures. Install the proper heat range plug (Chapter 1).

4   An incorrect air/fuel mixture can cause the cylinder to run hot and detonate. Clogged jets or an air leak can cause this imbalance (Chapter 4).

32   Piston slap or rattling

1   Cylinder-to-piston clearance excessive. Caused by incorrect assembly. Inspect and overhaul top end parts (Chapter 2).

2   Connecting rod bent. Caused by over-revving, by trying to start a badly flooded engine or by ingesting a foreign object into the combustion chamber. Replace the damaged parts (Chapter 2).

3   Piston pin or piston pin bore worn or seized from wear or lack of lubrication. Replace damaged parts (Chapter 2).

4   Piston ring(s) worn, broken or sticking. Overhaul the top end (Chapter 2).

5   Piston seizure damage. Usually from lack of lubrication or overheating. Replace the pistons and bore the cylinders, as necessary (Chapter 2).

6   Connecting rod bearing and/or piston pin-end clearance excessive. Caused by excessive wear or lack of lubrication. Replace worn parts.

33   Valve noise

1   Incorrect valve clearances. Adjust the valves (Chapter 1).

2   Valve springs broken or weak. Inspect and, if necessary, replace the valve springs (Chapter 2).

3   Camshaft or cylinder head worn or damaged. Lack of lubrication at high rpm is usually the cause of damage. Low oil level or failure to change the oil at the recommended intervals are the chief causes. Since there are no replaceable bearings in the head, the head itself will have to be replaced if there is excessive wear or damage (Chapter 2).

34   Other noise

1   Cylinder head gasket leaking. This will cause compression leakage into the cooling system (which may show up as air bubbles in the coolant in the radiator). Also, coolant may get into the oil (which will turn the oil into a bubbly gray-brown sludge). In either case, have the cooling system pressure-checked by a dealer service department.

2   Exhaust pipe leaking at cylinder head connection. Caused by improper fit of pipe(s) or loose exhaust flange. All exhaust fasteners should be tightened evenly and carefully. Failure to do this will lead to a leak.

3   Crankshaft runout excessive. Caused by a bent crankshaft (from over-revving) or damage from an upper cylinder component failure. Can also be attributed to dropping the machine on either of the crankshaft ends.

4   Engine mounting fasteners loose. Tighten all engine mounting fasteners to the torque listed in Chapter 2 Specifications.

5   Crankshaft bearings worn (Chapter 2).

6   Camshaft chain tensioner worn or broken. Replace the tensioner (Chapter 2).

7   Camshaft chain, sprockets or guides worn (Chapter 2).

Abnormal driveline noise

35   Clutch noise

1   Clutch housing/friction plate clearance excessive (Chapter 2).

2   Loose or damaged clutch pressure plate and/or bolts (Chapter 2).

36   Transmission noise

1   Bearings or shafts are worn. Overhaul the transmission (Chapter 2).

2   Gears are worn or chipped (Chapter 2).

3   Metal chips jammed in gear teeth. Probably pieces from a broken clutch, gear or shift mechanism that were picked up by the gears. This will cause early bearing failure (Chapter 2).

4   Engine oil level too low. Causes a howl from transmission. Also affects engine power and clutch operation (Chapter 1).

37   Chain or final drive noise

1   Chain not adjusted properly (Chapter 1).

2   Sprocket (engine sprocket or rear sprocket) loose. Tighten fasteners (Chapter 6).

3   Sprocket(s) worn. Replace sprocket(s) (Chapter 6).

4   Rear sprocket warped. Replace sprockets and chain as a set (Chapter 6).

5   Wheel coupling worn. Replace coupling (Chapter 6).

Abnormal frame and suspension noise

38   Front end noise

1   Low fluid level or incorrect viscosity oil in forks. This can sound like "spurting" and is usually accompanied by inconsistent fork action (Chapter 6).

2   Fork spring weak or broken. Makes a clicking or scraping sound. Fork oil, when drained, will have metal particles in it (Chapter 6).

3   Steering head bearings loose or damaged. Clunks when braking. Check and adjust or replace as necessary (Chapters 1 and 6).

4   Triple clamp-to-fork tube pinch bolts loose. Make sure all triple-clamp-to-fork tube pinch bolts are tight (Chapter 6).

5   Fork tube bent. Good possibility if machine has been dropped. Replace tube with a new one (Chapter 6).

6   Front axle nut or axle pinch bolts loose. Tighten all axle fasteners to the torque listed in this Chapter's Specifications (Chapter 7).

39   Shock absorber noise

1   Fluid level incorrect. Indicates a leak caused by a defective seal. Shock will be covered with oil. Replace shock (Chapter 6).

2   Defective shock absorber with internal damage. This is in the body of the shock and cannot be remedied. The shock must be replaced (Chapter 6).

3   Bent or damaged shock body. Replace the shock (Chapter 6).

40   Brake noise

1   Squeal caused by dust on brake pads. Usually found in combination with glazed pads. Clean parts with brake cleaning solvent (Chapter 7).

2   Contamination of brake pads. Oil, brake fluid or dirt causing brake

to chatter or squeal. Clean or replace pads (Chapter 7).

3 Pads glazed. Caused by excessive heat from prolonged use or from contamination. Do not use sandpaper, emery cloth, carborundum cloth or any other abrasive to roughen the pad surfaces as abrasives will stay in the pad material and damage the disc. A very fine flat file can be used, but pad replacement is the preferred cure (Chapter 7).

4 Disc warped. Can cause a chattering, clicking or intermittent squeal. Usually accompanied by a pulsating lever and uneven braking. Replace the disc (Chapter 7).

5 Loose or worn wheel bearings. Check and replace as needed (Chapter 7).

Oil pressure indicator light comes on

41 Engine lubrication system

1 Engine oil pump defective (Chapter 2).

2 Engine oil level low. Inspect for leak or other problem causing low oil level and add recommended lubricant (Chapters 1 and 2).

3 Engine oil viscosity too low. Very old, thin oil or an improper weight of oil used in engine. Change to correct lubricant (Chapter 1).

4 Camshaft or journals worn. Excessive wear causing drop in oil pressure. Replace cam and/or head. Abnormal wear could be caused by oil starvation at high rpm from low oil level or improper oil weight or type (Chapter 1).

5 Crankshaft and/or bearings worn. Same problems as above. Check and replace crankshaft and/or bearings (Chapter 2).

42 Electrical system

1 Oil pressure switch defective. Check and, if necessary, replace the switch (Chapter 9).

2 Oil pressure indicator light circuit defective. Check for pinched, shorted, disconnected or damaged wiring (Chapter 9).

Excessive exhaust smoke

43 White smoke

1 Piston oil ring worn. The ring may be broken or damaged, causing oil from the crankcase to be pulled past the piston into the combustion chamber. Replace the rings (Chapter 2).

2 Cylinders worn, cracked, or scored. Caused by overheating or oil starvation. The cylinders will have to be rebored and new pistons installed.

3 Valve guide oil seal(s) damaged or worn. Replace the valve guide seals (Chapter 2).

4 Valve guide(s) worn. Remove the heads, take them to a motorcycle machine shop or a dealer service department and get a valve job (Chapter 2).

5 Engine oil level too high, which causes oil to be forced past the rings. Drain oil to the correct level (Chapter 1).

6 Head gasket broken between oil return passage and cylinder. Causes oil to be pulled into combustion chamber. Replace the head gasket and measure the head for warpage (Chapter 2).

7 Abnormal crankcase pressurization, which forces oil past the rings. Clogged crankcase breather or hoses usually the cause (Chapter 4).

44 Black smoke

1 Air cleaner clogged. Clean or replace the element (Chapter 1).

2 Main jet too large or loose. Compare the jet size to the Specifica-tions (Chapter 4).

3 Choke stuck, causing fuel to be pulled through choke circuit (Chapter 4).

4 Fuel level too high. Check and adjust the float height as neces-sary (Chapter 4).

5 Float valve held off seat. Clean float bowl and fuel line and, if nec-essary, replace float valve and seat (Chapter 4).

45 Brown smoke

1 Main jet too small or clogged. Lean condition caused by wrong size main jet or by a restricted orifice. Clean float bowl and jets and compare jet size to Specifications (Chapter 4).

2 Fuel flow insufficient. Float valve stuck closed due to chemical reaction with old fuel. Float height incorrect. Restricted fuel line. Clean line and float bowl and adjust floats if necessary (Chapter 4).

3 Carburetor intake manifolds loose (Chapter 4).

4 Air cleaner poorly sealed or not installed (Chapter 1).

Poor handling or stability

46 Handlebar hard to turn

1 Steering stem locknut too tight (Chapter 6).

2 Steering head bearings damaged. Roughness can be felt as the bars are turned from side-to-side. Replace bearings and races (Chap-ter 6).

3 Steering head bearing races dented or worn. Dents are the result of wear in only one position (*e.g.*, straight ahead), or can be caused by hitting a curb, expansion joint or hole, or by dropping the machine. Replace the steering head bearings and races (Chapter 6).

4 Steering stem lubrication inadequate. Either because the old grease has gotten hard, or because it has been removed by repeated high-pressure car washes. Disassemble the steering head and repack the bearings (Chapter 6).

5 Steering stem bent. Caused by hitting a curb or hole, or by drop-ping the machine. Replace the stem; do not try to straighten it (Chap-ter 6).

6 Front tire air pressure too low (Chapter 1).

47 Handlebar shakes or vibrates excessively

1 Tires worn or out of balance (Chapter 7).

2 Swingarm bearings worn. Replace worn bearings by referring to Chapter 6.

3 Rim(s) warped or damaged. Inspect wheels for runout (Chapter 7).

4 Wheel bearings worn. Worn front or rear wheel bearings can cause poor tracking. Worn front bearings will cause wobble (Chap-ter 7).

5 Handlebar clamp bolts loose (Chapter 6).

6 Steering stem or fork clamps loose. Tighten them to the specified torque (Chapter 6).

7 Engine mount bolts loose. Will cause excessive vibration with increased engine rpm (Chapter 2).

48 Handlebar pulls to one side

1 Frame bent. Definitely suspect this if the machine has been dropped. May or may not be accompanied by cracking near the bend. Replace the frame (Chapter 6).

2 Wheels out of alignment. Caused by improper location of axle spacers or from bent steering stem or frame (Chapter 6).

3 Swingarm bent or twisted. Caused by age (metal fatigue) or impact damage. Replace the arm (Chapter 6).

4   Steering stem bent. Caused by impact damage or from dropping the motorcycle. Replace the steering stem (Chapter 6).
5   Fork leg bent. Disassemble the forks and replace the damaged parts (Chapter 6).
6   Fork oil level uneven. Replace the fork oil (Chapter 1).

49 Poor shock absorbing qualities

1   Too hard:
a) *Fork oil level excessive (Chapter 6).*
b) *Fork oil viscosity too high. Use a lighter oil (see the Specifications in Chapter 6).*
c) *Fork tube bent. Causes a harsh, sticking feeling (Chapter 6).*
d) *Shock shaft or body bent or damaged (Chapter 6).*
e) *Fork internal damage (Chapter 6).*
f) *Shock internal damage.*
g) *Tire pressure too high (Chapters 1 and 7).*
2   Too soft:
a) *Fork or shock oil insufficient and/or leaking (Chapter 6).*
b) *Fork oil viscosity too light (Chapter 6).*
c) *Fork springs weak or broken (Chapter 6).*

Braking problems

50 Front brakes are spongy, don't hold

1   Air in brake line. Caused by extremely low master cylinder fluid level or by leakage. Locate problem and bleed brakes (Chapter 7).
2   Pad or disc worn (Chapters 1 and 7).
3   Brake fluid leak. See paragraph 1.
4   Contaminated pads. Caused by contamination with oil, grease, brake fluid, etc. Clean or replace pads. Clean disc thoroughly with brake cleaner (Chapter 7).
5   Brake fluid deteriorated. Fluid is old or contaminated. Drain system, replenish with new fluid and bleed the system (Chapter 7).
6   Master cylinder internal parts worn or damaged causing fluid to bypass (Chapter 7).
7   Master cylinder bore scratched from ingestion of foreign material or broken spring. Repair or replace master cylinder (Chapter 7).
8   Disc warped. Replace disc (Chapter 7).

51 Brake lever or pedal pulsates

1   Disc warped. Replace disc (Chapter 7).
2   Axle bent. Replace axle (Chapter 6).

3   Brake caliper bolts loose (Chapter 7).
4   Brake caliper shafts damaged or sticking, causing caliper to bind. Lube the shafts and/or replace them if they are corroded or bent (Chapter 7).
5   Wheel warped or otherwise damaged (Chapter 7).
6   Wheel bearings damaged or worn (Chapter 7).

52 Brakes drag

1   Master cylinder piston seized. Caused by wear or damage to piston or cylinder bore (Chapter 7).
2   Brake lever balky or stuck. Check pivot and lubricate (Chapter 7).
3   Brake caliper binds. Caused by inadequate lubrication or damage to caliper slider pins (Chapter 7).
4   Brake caliper piston seized in bore. Caused by excessive wear, or by a deteriorated piston dust seal, which allows dirt or water to enter piston bore (Chapter 7).
5   Brake pad damaged. Pad material separating from backing plate. Usually caused by faulty manufacturing process or from contact with chemicals. Replace pads (Chapter 7).
6   Pads improperly installed (Chapter 7).

Electrical problems

53 Battery dead or weak

1   Battery faulty. Caused by sulfated plates which are shorted by sedimentation or by low electrolyte level. Also, broken battery terminal making only occasional contact (Chapter 9).
2   Battery cables making poor contact (Chapter 9).
3   Load excessive. Caused by addition of high wattage lights or other electrical accessories.
4   Ignition switch defective. Switch either grounds internally or fails to shut off system. Replace the switch (Chapter 9).
5   Regulator/rectifier defective (Chapter 9).
6   Stator coil open or shorted (Chapter 9).
7   Wiring faulty. Wiring grounded or connections loose in ignition, charging or lighting circuits (Chapter 9).

54 Battery overcharged

1   Regulator/rectifier defective. Overcharging is noticed when battery gets excessively warm or "boils" over (Chapter 9).
2   Battery defective. Replace battery with a new one (Chapter 9).
3   Battery amperage too low, wrong type or size. Install manufacturer's specified amp-hour battery to handle charging load (Chapter 9).

Chapter 1
Tune-up and routine maintenance

Contents

Specifications

Engine

Spark plugs
Type
Standard .... NGK DPR8EA-9 or ND X24EPR-U9
Cold climate .... NGK DPR7EA-9 or ND X22EPR-U9
Extended high-speed riding .... NGK DPR9EA-9 or ND X27EPR-U9
Gap .... 0.8 to 0.9 mm (0.031 to 0.035 inch)

Engine (continued)

Valve clearances (COLD engine)
    Intake.. 0.13 to 0.17 mm (0.005 to 0.007 inch)
    Exhaust.. 0.18 to 0.22 mm (0.007 to 0.009 inch)
Engine idle speed
    VT600 .... 1100 to 1300 rpm
    VT750 .... 900 to 1100 rpm
Cylinder compression pressure
    VT600 .... 12.26 to 14.22 Bars (178 to 206 psi)
    VT750 .... 11.77 to 13.73 Bars (171 to 199 psi)
Carburetor synchronization
    Maximum vacuum difference between cylinders
        VT600
            1988 and 1989, 1991 through 1996 .... 40 mm Hg (1.6 inches Hg)
            1997 on... 20 mm Hg (0.7 inch Hg)
        VT750 .... 20 mm Hg (0.7 inch Hg)
Cylinder numbering
    Rear cylinder 1
    Front cylinder 2

Miscellaneous

Battery electrolyte specific gravity.. 1.280 at 20 degrees C (68 degrees F)
Brake pedal position
    Pedal height (above top of footpeg)
        VT600.. 43 mm (1.7 inches)
        VT750
        VT750C/CD ACE .... 50 mm (2.0 inches)
        VT750DC Spirit .... Not specified
    Pedal freeplay .... 20 to 30 mm (3/4 to 1-1/4 inches)
Clutch lever freeplay .... 10 to 20 mm (3/8 to 3/4 inch)
Drive chain slack
    VT600 .... 20 to 30 mm (3/4 to 1-3/16 inches)
    VT750 .... 15 to 25 mm (5/8 to 1 inch)
Throttle grip freeplay.. 2 to 6 mm (1/8 to 1/4 inch)
Minimum tire tread depth
    Front .... 1.5 mm (0.06 inch)
    Rear .... 2.0 mm (0.08 inch)
Tire pressures (cold)
    Front .... 2 Bars (29 psi)
    Rear
        Up to 90 kg (198 lbs)... 2 Bars (29 psi)
        Above 90 kg (198 lbs) .... 2.5 Bars (36 psi)

Torque specifications

Cooling system drain plugs
    Water pump drain plug... 13 Nm (108 in-lbs)
    Rear cylinder drain plug .... 13 Nm (108 in-lbs)
Oil drain plug
    VT600
        1988 through 1998... 34 Nm (25 ft-lbs)
        1999 on.. 30 Nm (22 ft-lbs)
    VT750 .... 30 Nm (22 ft-lbs)
Spark plugs
    Used .... 14 Nm (120 in-lbs)
    New .... Hand tighten until sealing washer touches seat,
                                  then tighten plug 1/2-turn
Steering head bearing adjustment nut
    VT600 .... 25 Nm (18 ft-lbs)
    VT750 .... 21 Nm (15 ft-lbs)
Valve adjustment screw locknuts .... 23 Nm (17 ft-lbs)
Valve adjustment cover bolts (VT600) .... 12 Nm (108 in-lbs)

Recommended lubricants and fluids

Fuel type	Unleaded
Fuel capacity	
VT600	
1988 and 1989, 1991 through 1993	
Total	9 liters (2.4 gallons)
Reserve	1.9 liters (0.5 gallons)
1994 on	
Total	11 liters (2.9 gallons)
Reserve	3.4 liters (0.9 gallons)
VT750C/CD ACE	
Total	14.0 liters (3.7 gallons)
Reserve	3.6 liters (0.95 gallons)
VT750DC Spirit	
Total	13.0 liters (3.43 gallons)
Reserve	4.0 liters (1.06 gallons)
Engine/transmission oil	
Type	API grade SF or SG
Viscosity	
Most conditions	SAE 10W-40
Cold weather	SAE 10W-30
Hot weather	SAE 20W-40
Very hot weather	SAE 20W-50
Capacity	
VT600	
Oil change only	2.1 liters (2.21 quarts)
With filter change	2.25 liters (2.38 quarts)
VT750	
Oil change only	2.2 liters (2.32 quarts)
With filter change	2.4 liters (2.54 quarts)
Coolant	
Type	50/50 mixture of ethylene glycol-based antifreeze and distilled water
Capacity	
Radiator and engine	
VT600	1.6 liters (1.51 quarts)
VT750	1.75 liters (1.85 quarts)
Reservoir	0.4 liter (0.42 quart)
Brake fluid	DOT 4
Wheel bearings	Medium weight, lithium-based multi-purpose grease
Swingarm pivot bearings	Medium weight, lithium-based multi-purpose grease
Cables and lever pivots	Chain and cable lubricant or 10W30 motor oil
Sidestand pivot	Chain and cable lubricant or 10W30 motor oil
Brake pedal/shift lever pivots	Chain and cable lubricant or 10W30 motor oil
Throttle grip	Multi-purpose grease or dry film lubricant

1 Honda Shadow Routine maintenance intervals

Note: *The pre-ride inspection outlined in the owner's manual covers checks and maintenance that should be carried out on a daily basis. It's condensed and included here to remind you of its importance. Always perform the pre-ride inspection at every maintenance interval (in addition to the procedures listed). The intervals listed below are the shortest intervals recommended by the manufacturer for each particular operation during the model years covered in this manual. Your owner's manual may have different intervals for your model.*

Daily or before riding

Check the engine oil level
Check the fuel level and inspect for leaks
Check the engine coolant level and look for leaks
Check the operation of both brakes - also check the front brake fluid level and look for leakage
Check the tires for damage, the presence of foreign objects and correct air pressure
Check the throttle for smooth operation and correct freeplay
Check the operation of the clutch - make sure the freeplay is correct
Make sure the steering operates smoothly, without looseness and without binding
Check for proper operation of the headlight, taillight, brake light, turn signals, indicator lights and horn
Make sure the sidestand fully returns to its "up" position and stays there under spring pressure
Make sure the engine STOP switch works properly

After the initial 600 miles/1000 km

Perform all of the daily checks plus:
Check/adjust the carburetor synchronization
Adjust the valve clearances
Check/adjust the drive chain slack
Change the engine oil and oil filter
Check the tightness of all fasteners
Check the steering
Check/adjust clutch freeplay
Check the front brake fluid level
Check the cooling system hoses
Inspect brake pads and shoes
Check/adjust the brake pedal position
Check the operation of the brake light
Check the operation of the sidestand switch
Lubricate the clutch cable, throttle cable(s) and speedometer cable

Every 300 miles/500 km

Check/adjust the drive chain slack (if equipped)

Every 4000 miles/6000 km or 6 months

Change the engine oil
Clean the air filter element and replace it if necessary
Adjust the valve clearances
Clean and gap the spark plugs
Lubricate the clutch cable, throttle cable(s) and speedometer cable

Check/adjust throttle cable freeplay
Check/adjust the idle speed
Check/adjust the carburetor synchronization
Check the front brake fluid level
Adjust front brake freeplay
Check the brake disc and pads
Check the rear brake shoes for wear
Check/adjust the brake pedal position
Check the operation of the brake light
Lubricate the clutch and brake lever pivots
Lubricate the shift/brake pedal pivots and the sidestand pivot
Check the steering
Check the front forks for proper operation and fluid leaks
Check the tires, wheels and wheel bearings
Check the battery electrolyte level and specific gravity; inspect the breather tube
Check the exhaust system for leaks and check the tightness of the fasteners
Check the cleanliness of the fuel system and the condition of the fuel lines and vacuum hoses
Inspect the crankcase ventilation system
Check the operation of the sidestand switch
Check and adjust clutch cable freeplay

Every 12,000 km/8,000 miles or 12 months

All of the items above plus:
Change the engine oil and oil filter
Replace the spark plugs

Every 18,000 km/12,000 miles

Repack the swingarm bearings
Inspect the cooling system and replace the coolant

Every 24,000 km/15,000 miles or two years

Clean and lubricate the steering head bearings

Every 50,000 km/30,000 miles

Replace the drive chain

Every two years

Replace the brake master cylinder and caliper seals and change the brake fluid

Every four years

Replace the brake hose

2   Introduction to tune-up and routine maintenance

Refer to illustration 2.3

This Chapter covers in detail the checks and procedures necessary for the tune-up and routine maintenance of your motorcycle. Section 1 includes the routine maintenance schedule, which is designed to keep the machine in proper running condition and prevent possible problems. The remaining Sections contain detailed procedures for carrying out the items listed on the maintenance schedule, as well as additional maintenance information designed to increase reliability.

Since routine maintenance plays such an important role in the safe and efficient operation of your motorcycle, it is presented here as a comprehensive check list. For the rider who does all his own maintenance, these lists outline the procedures and checks that should be done on a routine basis.

Maintenance information is printed on labels attached to the motorcycle **(see illustration)**. If the information on the labels differs from that included here, use the information on the label.

Deciding where to start, or "plug into," the routine maintenance schedule depends on several factors. If the warranty has recently expired, and if the motorcycle has been maintained according to the warranty standards, you may want to pick up routine maintenance as it coincides with the next mileage or calendar interval. If you have owned the machine for some time but have never performed any maintenance on it, then you may want to start at the nearest interval and include some additional procedures to ensure that nothing important is overlooked. If you have just had a major engine overhaul, then you may

want to start the maintenance routine from the beginning. If you have a used machine and have no knowledge of its history or maintenance record, you may desire to combine all the checks into one large service initially and then settle into the maintenance schedule prescribed.

The Sections which outline the inspection and maintenance procedures are written as step-by-step comprehensive guides to the performance of the work. They explain in detail each of the routine inspections and maintenance procedures on the check list. References to additional information in applicable Chapters is also included and should not be overlooked.

Before beginning any maintenance or repair, the machine should be cleaned thoroughly, especially around the oil filter, spark plugs, cylinder head covers, side covers, carburetors, etc. Cleaning will help ensure that dirt does not contaminate the engine and will allow you to detect wear and damage that could otherwise easily go unnoticed.

3   Fluid levels - check

Engine oil

Refer to illustrations 3.3a and 3.3b

1   Run the engine and allow it to reach normal operating temperature. **Caution:** *Do not run the engine in an enclosed space such as a garage or shop.*
2   Stop the engine and allow the machine to sit undisturbed for about five minutes.
3   Hold the motorcycle level. With the engine off, remove the filler cap from the right side of the crankcase and check the oil level on the dipstick. It should be between the Maximum and Minimum level marks on the dipstick **(see illustrations)**.
4   If the level is below the Minimum mark, add enough oil of the recommended grade and type to bring the level up to the Maximum mark. Do not overfill.

Brake fluid

Refer to illustrations 3.7 and 3.9

5   In order to ensure proper operation of the hydraulic disc brake, the fluid level in the master cylinder reservoir must be properly maintained.
6   With the motorcycle held level, turn the handlebars until the top of the master cylinder is as level as possible.
7   Look closely at the inspection window in the master cylinder reservoir. Make sure that the fluid level is above the Lower mark on the reservoir **(see illustration)**.
8   If the level is low, the fluid must be replenished. Before removing the master cylinder cover, cover the fuel tank to protect it from brake fluid spills (which will damage the paint) and remove all dust and dirt from the area around the cover.

2.3 Decals at various locations on the motorcycle include such information as tire pressures and drive chain service procedures

3.3a Remove the filler plug (arrow) . . .

3.3b . . . and add oil, if necessary, to bring the level up to the maximum mark

3.7 The level of the brake fluid in the master cylinder reservoir should be above the Lower line in the window; to remove the cover, remove these two screws (arrows)

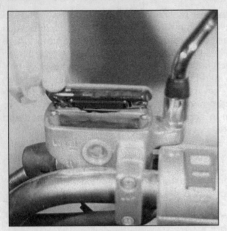

3.9 To add fluid, carefully remove the cover and diaphragm

3.17a On VT600 models, the coolant reservoir filler cap (arrow) is located on the right side of the bike, near the passenger footpeg

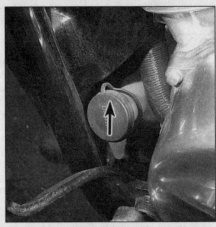

3.17b On VT750 models, the coolant reservoir filler cap (arrow) is located on the left side of the bike, near the shift lever, below the radiator

9   To add brake fluid, remove the reservoir cover screws **(see illustration 3.7)** and lift off the cover and rubber diaphragm **(see illustration)**. **Caution:** *Do not operate the front brake with the cover removed.*
10   Add new, clean brake fluid of the recommended type until the level is above the inspection window. Do not mix different brands of brake fluid in the reservoir, as they may not be compatible.
11   Reinstall the rubber diaphragm and the cover. Tighten the screws evenly, but do not overtighten them.
12   Wipe any spilled fluid off the reservoir body.
13   If the brake fluid level was low, inspect the brake system for leaks.

Coolant

Refer to illustrations 3.17a and 3.17b
14   Warm up the engine and check the coolant level with the engine running at its normal temperature.
15   On VT600 models, the Upper and Lower level marks for the coolant are on the front right corner of the coolant reservoir, right behind the oil filler cap/dipstick **(see illustration 3.3a)**. On VT750 models, the Upper and Lower level marks for the coolant are on the left side of the coolant reservoir, which is located below the radiator, in front of the engine.
16   The reservoir is translucent plastic, so the coolant level is easily visible in relation to the marks. The coolant level should be at the Upper mark on the reservoir.
17   To add coolant, shut off the engine and remove the coolant reservoir filler cap **(see illustrations)**. Using a 50/50 mixture of ethylene glycol and distilled water, bring the coolant level up to the Upper mark on the reservoir. Install the filler cap.
18   If the coolant level in the reservoir was low, or empty, inspect the cooling system (see Section 20). It might be leaking.

4   Battery electrolyte level/specific gravity - check

Refer to illustrations 4.4 and 4.7
Warning: *Be extremely careful when handling or working around the battery. The electrolyte is very caustic and an explosive gas (hydrogen) is given off when the battery is charging.*
1   This procedure applies to conventional batteries with filler caps which can be removed to add water to the battery cells. The original-equipment battery is a sealed, maintenance-free battery; if the motorcycle is still equipped with the original battery, or an OEM replacement, it's unnecessary to check the electrolyte. However, if a conventional battery has been installed, it should be checked as follows.
2   Remove the battery (see Chapter 9).
3   Clean off the battery and place it on a workbench.

4.4 The electrolyte level should be between the marks on the battery case

4   The electrolyte level, which is visible through the translucent battery case, should be between the Upper and Lower level marks **(see illustration)**.
5   If the electrolyte is low, remove the cell caps and fill each cell to the upper level mark with distilled water. Do not use tap water (except in an emergency), and do not overfill. The cell holes are quite small, so it may help to use a plastic squeeze bottle with a small spout to add the water. If the level is within the marks on the case, additional water is not necessary.
6   Next, check the specific gravity of the electrolyte in each cell with a small hydrometer made especially for motorcycle batteries. These are available from most dealer parts departments or motorcycle accessory stores.
7   Remove the caps, draw some electrolyte from the first cell into the hydrometer **(see illustration)** and note the specific gravity. Compare the reading to the Specifications listed in this Chapter. Add 0.004 points to the reading for every 10-degrees F above 20-degrees C (68-degrees F); subtract 0.004 points from the reading for every 10-degrees below 20-degrees C (68-degrees F). Return the electrolyte to the appropriate cell and repeat the check for the remaining cells. When the check is complete, rinse the hydrometer thoroughly with clean water.
8   If the specific gravity of the electrolyte in each cell is as specified,

4.7 Check the specific gravity with a hydrometer

5.2a Using a small flashlight, look at the pads through the small openings at the bottom of the caliper and note whether the pads are worn down to the wear indicator marks parallel to the pad backing plates

5.2b If there are no wear indicator marks on the lower end of the brake pads, inspect the pad rain grooves from the open front side of the caliper; when the grooves in the pads are no longer visible, replace the pads (caliper and pads removed from bike for clarity)

5.3 To check the rear brake shoe thickness, firmly depress the brake pedal; if the pointer on the brake arm points at or near the mark on the brake panel (arrows), replace the brake shoes

the battery is in good condition and is apparently being charged by the machine's charging system.

9   If the specific gravity is low, the battery is not fully charged. This may be due to corroded battery terminals, a dirty battery case, a malfunctioning charging system, or loose or corroded wiring connections. On the other hand, it may be that the battery is worn out, especially if the machine is old, or that infrequent use of the motorcycle prevents normal charging from taking place.

10   Be sure to correct any problems and charge the battery if necessary. Refer to Chapter 9 for additional battery maintenance and charging procedures.

11   Install the battery cell caps, tightening them securely.

12   Install the battery (see Chapter 9). When reconnecting the cables to the battery, attach the positive cable first, then the negative cable. Make sure to install the insulating boot over the positive terminal. Install all components removed for access. Be very careful not to pinch or otherwise restrict the battery vent tube, as the battery may build up enough internal pressure during normal charging system operation to explode.

5   Brake pads and shoes - wear check

Refer to illustrations 5.2a, 5.2b and 5.3

1   The front brake pads and the rear brake shoes should be checked at the recommended intervals and replaced when worn beyond the

limit listed in this Chapter's Specifications. Always replace pads and shoes as complete sets.

2   To check the thickness of the front brake pads, squeeze the front brake lever and look at the pads through the lower "window" of the caliper **(see illustration)**. Note whether the pads are worn down to the wear indicator marks which run parallel to the pad backing plates. If they are, replace the pads (see Chapter 6). If there are no wear indicator marks on the lower ends of the pads, look through the open part of the caliper facing toward the front of the machine and note the small rain grooves cut into each pad **(see illustration)**. If these grooves are still visible, the pads have some service life remaining. If the grooves are gone, replace the pads (see Chapter 6).

3   To check the rear brake shoes, press the brake pedal firmly while you look at the wear indicator mark on the brake panel **(see illustration)**. If the indicator pointer on the brake arm is close to or at the wear indicator mark, replace the shoes (see Chapter 6).

6   Brake system - general check

Refer to illustrations 6.6a and 6.6b

1   A routine general check of the brakes will ensure that any problems are discovered and remedied before the rider's safety is jeopardized.

6.6a The VT600 rear brake light switch (arrow) is located on the right side, below the right passenger footpeg

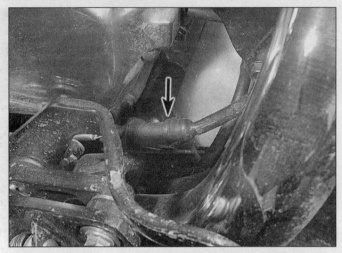

6.6b The VT750 rear brake light switch (arrow) is located on the right side, in front of the engine, near the brake pedal linkage

2   Check the brake lever and pedal for loose connections, excessive play, bends, and other damage. Replace any damaged parts with new ones (see Chapter 7).
3   Make sure all brake fasteners are tight. Check the brake pads and shoes for wear (see Section 5) and make sure the fluid level in the front

brake reservoir is correct (see Section 3). Look for leaks at the hose connections and check for cracks in the hose(s). If the lever or pedal is spongy, bleed the brakes (see Chapter 7).
4   Make sure the brake light operates when the brake lever is depressed.
5   Make sure the brake light is activated just before the rear brake takes effect.
6   If adjustment is necessary, hold the switch so it won't rotate and turn the adjusting nut on the switch body **(see illustrations)** until the brake light is activated when required. If the switch doesn't operate the brake lights, check the switch and circuit (see Chapter 9).
7   The front brake light switch is not adjustable. If it fails to operate properly, replace it (see Chapter 9).

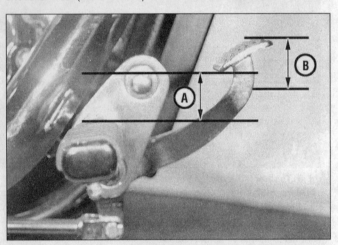

7.1a Brake pedal height (A) and freeplay (B)

7   Rear brake pedal height and freeplay - check and adjustment

Refer to illustrations 7.1a, 7.1b and 7.2
1   The rear brake pedal height, measured from the top of the footpeg to the top of the pedal **(see illustration)**, should be at the height listed in this Chapter's Specifications. If it isn't, adjust the pedal height. Loosen the locknut **(see illustration)**, turn the adjuster bolt to set the pedal height and tighten the locknut.
2   Check pedal freeplay (the distance the pedal travels downward

7.1b To adjust brake pedal height, loosen the locknut (arrow) and turn the adjustment bolt until pedal height is correct, then tighten the locknut

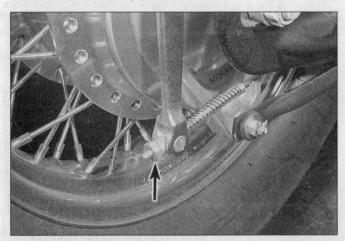

7.2 To adjust brake pedal freeplay, turn this adjusting nut until the pedal freeplay is correct

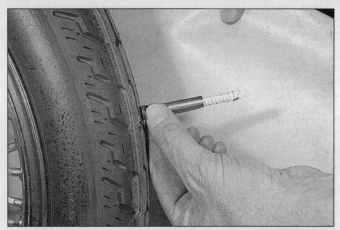

8.2 Measure tread depth at the center of the tire (tread depth gauges are available at most dealerships and motorcycle accessory shops)

8.4 Check tire pressures with an accurate gauge

before the brake shoes contact the drum) and compare it to the value listed in this Chapter's Specifications. If the pedal freeplay isn't within this dimension, adjust it by turning the nut at the rear end of the brake rod **(see illustration)**.

3   If necessary, adjust the brake light switch (see Section 6).

8   Tires/wheels - general check

Refer to illustrations 8.2, 8.4 and 8.5

1   Routine tire and wheel checks should be made with the realization that your safety depends to a great extent on their condition.

2   Check the tires carefully for cuts, tears, embedded nails or other sharp objects and excessive wear. Operation of the motorcycle with excessively worn tires is extremely hazardous, as traction and handling are directly affected. Measure the tread depth at the center of the tire **(see illustration)** and replace worn tires with new ones when the tread depth is less than specified.

3   Repair or replace punctured tires as soon as damage is noted. Do not try to patch a torn tire, as wheel balance and tire reliability may be impaired.

4   Check the tire pressures when the tires are cold and keep them properly inflated **(see illustration)**. Proper air pressure will increase tire life and provide maximum stability and ride comfort. Keep in mind that low tire pressures may cause the tire to slip on the rim or come off, while high tire pressures will cause abnormal tread wear and unsafe handling.

5   Make sure the valve stem locknuts **(see illustration)** are tight. Also, make sure the valve stem cap is tight. If it is missing, install a new one made of metal or hard plastic.

9   Throttle cable and choke operation - check and adjustment

Throttle cable

Refer to illustrations 9.3 and 9.6

1   Make sure the throttle grip rotates easily from fully closed to fully open with the front wheel turned at various angles. The grip should return automatically from fully open to fully closed when released. If the throttle sticks, check the throttle cables for cracks or kinks in the housings and make sure the inner cables are clean and well-lubricated.

2   Start the engine and warm it up. With the engine idling, turn the handlebars all the way to the left, then all the way to the right. The idle speed should not increase. If it does, check throttle grip freeplay.

3   Throttle grip freeplay is the distance the throttle grip can be rotated before resistance is felt, *i.e.* the point at which the throttle cable begins to open the carburetor throttle plates. Measure the throttle grip freeplay **(see illustration)** and compare your measurement to the value listed in this Chapter's Specifications.

4   There are actually *two* throttle cables - an "accelerator" cable and a "decelerator" cable. The accelerator cable opens the throttle plates;

8.5 Make sure the tire valve locknut (arrow) is snug and the valve cap is tight

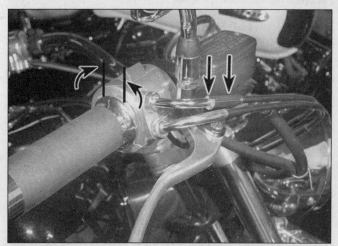

9.3 Rotate the throttle grip to check freeplay; loosen the locknut and turn the adjuster (arrows) to change it (VT750 shown)

9.6 Lower locknuts and adjusters for accelerator cable (lower arrows) and decelerator cable (upper arrows)

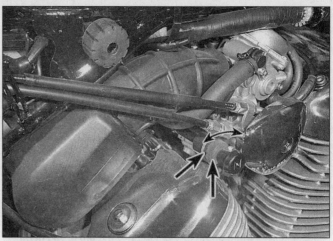

9.12 To adjust the amount of force required to pull out and push in the choke knob, pull back the rubber cover (right arrow) and rotate the friction adjuster (left arrow)

the decelerator cable closes them. If the throttle grip freeplay must be adjusted, it can be adjusted at either end of the accelerator cable, but only at the lower end of the decelerator cable. The upper adjuster at the throttle grip is used to make fine adjustments to the accelerator cable; throttle grip freeplay is usually adjusted here. The lower adjusters at the carburetors are only used to make major adjustments to the cables. Both cables can be adjusted at the carburetors, but the accelerator cable is the one that is adjusted to achieve correct throttle grip freeplay; the decelerator cable is adjusted only to compensate for the amount of freeplay that's added or subtracted from the accelerator cable. There should be no freeplay in the decelerator cable.

5   To adjust freeplay at the throttle grip, loosen the locknut and turn the adjuster until the freeplay is within the specified distance. Tighten the locknut.

6   To adjust freeplay at the carburetors, loosen the cable adjuster locknuts **(see illustration)**, turn the adjuster nut on the decelerator cable to set freeplay to zero, tighten the decelerator cable adjuster locknut, then turn the accelerator cable adjuster nut to bring freeplay at the throttle grip within the range listed in this Chapter's Specifications. Once freeplay is correct, tighten the accelerator cable adjuster locknut.

7   Make sure the throttle grip is now in the fully-closed position.

8   Make sure the throttle linkage lever still contacts the idle adjusting screw when the throttle grip is in the fully-closed position.

9   Again, turn the handlebars all the way through their travel with the engine idling. Idle speed should not change. If it does, either the cables are incorrectly routed or freeplay is still insufficient. **Warning:** *Correct this condition before riding the bike.*

Choke

Refer to illustration 9.12

10   The choke system consists of a pair of starting enrichment (SE) valves - one per carburetor - which control the fuel enrichment circuits in the carburetors. When the choke knob on the left side of the engine is pulled out, the cable-actuated SE valves open the fuel enrichment circuits in the carburetors.

11   Make sure that the choke knob operates smoothly. If the knob is hard to pull out or push in, pull it out and lubricate its sliding surface with cable lubricant or a lightweight oil.

12   If the choke knob is still difficult to pull out or push in, pull back the rubber cover and back off the friction adjuster **(see illustration)**.

13   If adjusting the friction doesn't help, the SE valve cables need to be lubricated (see Chapter 4).

14   If the engine is hard to start when it's cold - but easy to start when it's warmed up - the SE valves are not opening completely. If the idle speed "wanders" up and down, even after the engine is warmed up, the SE valves are not closing completely. In either case, the SE valves should be removed and cleaned, and the valves and valve seats should be inspected (see Chapter 4).

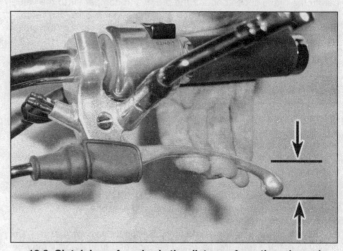

10.2 Clutch lever freeplay is the distance from the released position to the point at which you feel resistance

10   Clutch - check and adjustment

Refer to illustrations 10.2, 10.3 and 10.5

1   Correct clutch freeplay is necessary to ensure proper clutch operation and reasonable clutch service life. Freeplay normally changes because of cable stretch and clutch wear, so it should be checked and adjusted periodically.

2   Clutch cable freeplay is checked at the lever on the handlebar. Slowly pull in on the lever until resistance is felt, measure this distance **(see illustration)** and compare it with the value listed in this Chapter's Specifications. Too little freeplay might result in the clutch not engaging completely. If there is too much freeplay, the clutch might not release fully.

3   Normal freeplay adjustments are made at the clutch lever by loosening the lockwheel and turning the adjuster until the desired freeplay is obtained **(see illustration)**. Always retighten the lockwheel once the adjustment is complete.

4   If freeplay can't be adjusted at the handlebar, major adjustments can be made on the right side of the engine.

5   Loosen the locknuts at the clutch cable bracket on the engine **(see illustration)**. Turn the nuts to achieve the correct freeplay, then tighten them.

6   Recheck freeplay at the clutch lever and make further adjustments (if necessary) with the adjuster at the lever. If freeplay still can't

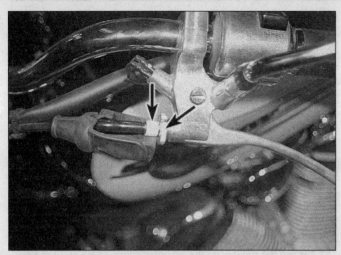

10.3 Normal clutch cable adjustments are made at the handlebar - loosen the clutch cable lockwheel (right arrow) and turn the adjuster (left arrow); tighten the lockwheel after adjustment

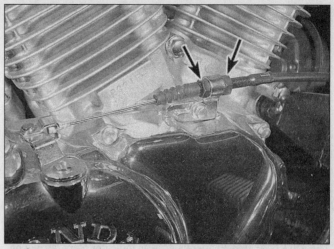

10.5 The clutch cable can also be adjusted at this bracket on the right side of the engine; loosen the locknut (left arrow) and turn the adjusting nut (right arrow) until clutch lever freeplay is correct (on pre-1995 models, the adjuster nut and locknut are on the same side of the bracket)

11.2 Measure chain slack at a point about halfway between the two sprockets on the bottom run

be adjusted within the Specifications, the cable may be stretched or the clutch may be worn. Inspect the clutch cable and the clutch (see Chapter 2).

11 Drive chain and sprockets - check, adjustment and lubrication

Check

Refer to illustration 11.2

1   Make *sure* the ignition switch is off. Shift the transmission into Neutral and place the bike on its sidestand.

2   Push up on the bottom run of the chain and measure the slack at a point about halfway between the two sprockets **(see illustration)**. Compare your measurement to the value listed in this Chapter's Specifications and, if necessary, adjust the chain.

3   The chain should be replaced at the specified mileage interval (see Chapter 5).

Adjustment

Refer to illustrations 11.4, 11.5, 11.6 and 11.7

4   Loosen the rear axle nut **(see illustration)**.

5   Loosen and back off the locknuts on both axle adjuster bolts **(see illustration)**.

11.4 Always loosen the axle nut before adjusting the chain slack

11.5 Loosen both chain adjuster locknuts before turning the adjuster bolts; on VT600 models (shown), note the pointer on top of the adjuster and the adjustment marks on the swingarm

11.6 On VT750 models, there's a single indicator mark (arrow) on each side of the swingarm, and notches in the adjusters themselves

11.7 When the pointer on the adjuster points at the red zone on the chain wear label on VT600 models, replace the chain (on VT750 models, the chain wear label is on the left adjuster; when it reaches the mark on the swingarm, replace the chain)

6   On VT600 models, there is a single index mark on each of the adjusters and a series of marks on each side of the swingarm **(see illustration 11.5)**; on VT750 models, there is a single mark on each side of the swingarm and a series of notches on the adjusters **(see illustration)**.

7   Turn the adjusting nuts on both sides of the swingarm until the proper chain tension is obtained (get the adjuster on the chain side close, then set the adjuster on the opposite side). Be sure to turn the adjusting nuts evenly to keep the rear wheel in alignment. If the index mark on the left adjuster reaches the red zone of the chain wear label on the left side of the swingarm on VT600 models **(see illustration)**, or the red zone on the left adjuster reaches the index mark on the left side of the swingarm on VT750 models, the chain is worn out and must be replaced (see Chapter 7).

8   When the chain has the correct amount of slack, make sure the marks on the adjusters correspond to the same relative marks on each side of the swingarm (VT600 models) or the marks on each side of the swingarm correspond to the same relative notches on the adjusters (VT750 models).

9   Tighten the axle nut to the torque listed in this Chapter's Specifications.

10   Tighten the chain adjuster locknuts securely.

Lubrication

11   Lubricate the chain right after the motorcycle has been ridden. The chain is still warm, so chain lube will penetrate the joints between the side plates, pins, bushings and rollers and reach the internal load bearing surfaces. Use a good quality chain lubricant designed for O-ring type chains. Apply it to the areas where the side plates overlap - not the middle of the rollers. Apply the lube to the top of the lower chain run, so that centrifugal force will work the oil into the chain the next time the bike is ridden. After applying chain lube, let it soak in a few minutes before wiping off any excess.

12   Check the sprockets for wear while lubricating the chain (see Chapter 6).

12 Engine oil/filter - change

Refer to illustrations 12.4, 12.5a and 12.5b

1   Regular oil and filter changes are the single most important maintenance procedure you can perform on a motorcycle. The oil not only lubricates the internal parts of the engine, transmission and clutch, but it also acts as a coolant, a cleaner, a sealant, and a protectant. Because of these demands, the oil takes a terrific amount of abuse and should be replaced often with new oil of the recommended grade and

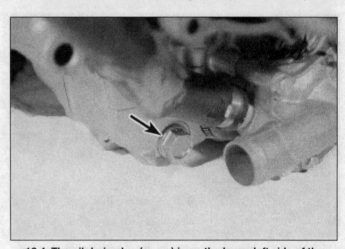

12.4 The oil drain plug (arrow) is on the lower left side of the engine, behind the water pump

type. Saving a little money on the difference in cost between a good oil and a cheap oil won't pay off if the engine is damaged.

2   Before changing the oil and filter, warm up the engine so the oil will drain easily. Be careful when draining the oil; the exhaust pipes, the engine and the oil itself can cause severe burns.

3   Support the motorcycle securely over a clean drain pan. Remove the oil filler cap to vent the crankcase and act as a reminder that there is no oil in the engine.

4   Next, remove the drain plug from the lower left side of the engine **(see illustration)** and allow the oil to drain into the pan. Discard the sealing washer on the drain plug; it should be replaced every time the plug is removed. While the engine is draining, replace the oil filter.

5   The automotive style spin-on oil filter is located at the left lower rear part of the engine; with the bike leaned over to the left on its side-stand, it's easier to access the filter from the right side **(see illustration)**. Remove the filter from the engine with a filter wrench **(see illustration)**. If you don't have this type of filter wrench, use a pair of large water pump pliers to loosen the filter.

6   Coat the threads of the new oil filter and the new filter O-ring with clean engine oil.

7   Install the new filter and tighten it by hand.

8   Check the condition of the drain plug threads and the sealing washer.

9   Slip a new sealing washer over the drain plug, then install and tighten it to the torque listed in this Chapter's Specifications. Avoid

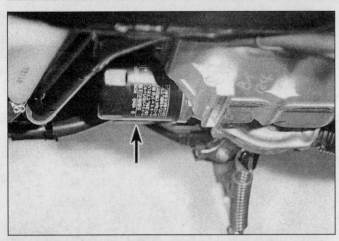

12.5a The oil filter (arrow) is at the lower rear part of the engine; the easiest way to reach it is from the right side, with the bike on its sidestand

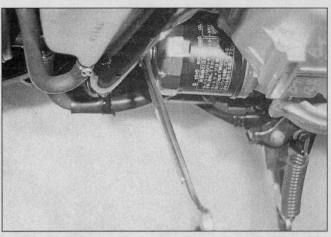

12.5b Use a filter wrench to remove the oil filter (if you don't have this type of filter wrench, use a pair of large water pump pliers)

13.1a To remove the air cleaner housing cover on VT600 models, remove this Allen screw . . .

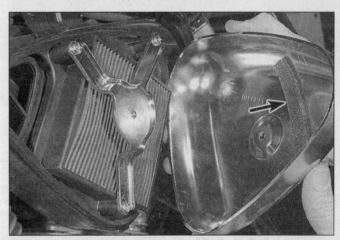

13.1b . . . remove the cover and inspect the foam strip (arrow)

overtightening the drain plug, which can strip the threads in the aluminum engine case.

10   Before refilling the engine, check the old oil carefully. If the oil was drained into a clean pan, small pieces of metal or other material can be easily detected. If the oil is very metallic colored, then the engine is experiencing wear from break-in (new engine) or from insufficient lubrication. If there are flakes or chips of metal in the oil, then something is drastically wrong internally and the engine will have to be disassembled for inspection and repair.

11   If there are pieces of fiber-like material in the oil, the clutch is experiencing excessive wear and should be checked.

12   If the inspection of the oil turns up nothing unusual, refill the crankcase to the proper level with the recommended oil and install the filler cap. Start the engine and let it run for two or three minutes. Shut it off, wait a few minutes, then check the oil level. If necessary, add more oil to bring the level up to the Maximum mark. Check around the drain plug and filter housing for leaks.

13   The old oil drained from the engine cannot be reused in its present state and should be disposed of. Check with your local refuse disposal company, disposal facility or environmental agency to see whether they will accept the used oil for recycling. Don't pour used oil into drains or onto the ground. After the oil has cooled, it can be drained into a suitable container (capped plastic jugs, topped bottles, milk cartons, etc.) for transport to one of these disposal sites.

13   Air filter element - servicing

Refer to illustration 13.1a, 13.1b, 13.1c, 13.2 and 13.3

1   Remove the air cleaner housing cover **(see illustrations)**.

2   On VT600 models, remove the filter element holder **(see illustration)**.

13.1c To remove the air cleaner housing cover on VT750 models, remove the six cover screws (three upper screws shown

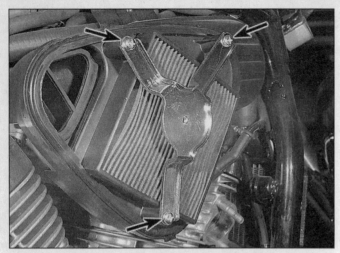

13.2 On VT600 models, remove the filter element holder screws (arrows) and remove the holder

13.3 Remove the filter element (VT600 shown; on VT750 models, simply pull the filter element off the air cleaner housing)

3   Lift out the filter element **(see illustration)**.
4   Tap the filter element on a hard surface to shake out dirt. If compressed air is available, use it to clean the element by blowing from the inside out. If the element is extremely dirty or torn, or if dirt can't be blown or tapped out, replace the element.
5   Installation if the reverse of removal. Make sure the filter element is seated properly in the filter housing before installing the cover.

14   Cylinder compression - check

1   Among other things, poor engine performance may be caused by leaking valves, incorrect valve clearances, a leaking head gasket, or worn pistons, rings and/or cylinder walls. A cylinder compression check will help pinpoint these conditions and can also indicate the presence of excessive carbon deposits in the cylinder heads.
2   The only tools required are a compression gauge and a spark plug wrench. Depending on the outcome of the initial test, a squirt-type oil can may also be needed.
3   Start the engine and allow it to reach normal operating temperature.
4   Support the bike securely so it can't be knocked over during this procedure.
5   Remove *one* spark plug from each cylinder (see Section 15). Work carefully - don't strip the spark plug hole threads and don't burn your hands.
6   Disable the ignition by unplugging the primary wires from the coils (see Chapter 5). Be sure to mark the locations of the wires before detaching them.
7   Install the compression gauge in one of the spark plug holes.
8   Hold or block the throttle wide open.
9   Crank the engine over a minimum of four or five revolutions (or until the gauge reading stops increasing) and observe the initial movement of the compression gauge needle as well as the final total gauge reading. Repeat the procedure for the other cylinder and compare the results to the value listed in this Chapter's Specifications.
10   If the compression in both cylinders built up quickly and evenly to the specified amount, you can assume the engine upper end is in reasonably good mechanical condition. Worn or sticking piston rings and worn cylinders will produce very little initial movement of the gauge needle, but compression will tend to build up gradually as the engine spins over. Valve and valve seat leakage, or head gasket leakage, is indicated by low initial compression which does not tend to build up.
11   To further confirm your findings, add a small amount of engine oil to each cylinder by inserting the nozzle of a squirt-type oil can through the spark plug holes. The oil will tend to seal the piston rings if they are leaking. Repeat the test for the other cylinder.

12   If the compression increases significantly after the addition of the oil, the piston rings and/or cylinders are definitely worn. If the compression does not increase, the pressure is leaking past the valves or the head gasket. Leakage past the valves may be due to insufficient valve clearances, burned, warped or cracked valves or valve seats or valves that are hanging up in the guides.
13   If compression readings are considerably higher than specified, the combustion chambers are probably coated with excessive carbon deposits. It is possible (but not very likely) for carbon deposits to raise the compression enough to compensate for the effects of leakage past rings or valves. Remove the cylinder head and carefully decarbonize the combustion chambers (see Chapter 2).

15   Spark plugs - replacement

Refer to illustrations 15.2a, 15.2b, 15.2c, 15.7a and 15.7b
1   Make sure your spark plug socket is the correct size before attempting to remove the plugs.
2   Disconnect the spark plug caps from the spark plugs **(see illustrations)**. Inspect the caps for damage and wear.
3   Using compressed air, blow any accumulated debris from around the spark plugs. No dirt or debris must be allowed into the combustion chamber. Remove the plugs with a spark plug socket.

15.2a There are two spark plugs per cylinder; this is the spark plug cap for the left plug on the rear cylinder . . .

15.2b . . . and this is the cap (arrow) for the recessed right plug on the rear cylinder (fuel tank removed for clarity)

15.2c On the front cylinder, the open plug is on the right side and the recessed plug (arrow) is in the left front corner of the cylinder head cover (fuel tank removed for clarity)

4   Inspect the electrodes for wear. Both the center and side electrodes should have square edges and the side electrode should be of uniform thickness. Look for excessive deposits and evidence of a cracked or chipped insulator around the center electrode. Compare your spark plugs to the color spark plug reading chart. Check the threads, the washer and the ceramic insulator body for cracks and other damage.

5   If the electrodes are not excessively worn, and if the deposits can be easily removed with a wire brush, the plugs can be regapped and reused (if no cracks or chips are visible in the insulator). If in doubt concerning the condition of the plugs, replace them with new ones, as the expense is minimal.

6   Cleaning spark plugs by sandblasting is permitted, provided you clean the plugs with a high flash-point solvent afterwards.

7   Before installing new plugs, make sure they are the correct type and heat range. Check the gap between the electrodes, as they are not preset. For best results, use a wire-type gauge rather than a flat gauge to check the gap **(see illustration)**. If the gap must be adjusted, bend the side electrode only and be very careful not to chip or crack the insulator nose **(see illustration)**. Make sure the washer is in place before installing each plug.

8   Since the cylinder head is made of aluminum, which is soft and easily damaged, thread the plugs into the heads by hand. Since the plugs are recessed, slip a short length of hose over the end of the plug

to use as a tool to thread it into place. The hose will grip the plug well enough to turn it, but will start to slip if the plug begins to cross-thread in the hole - this will prevent damaged threads and the accompanying repair costs.

9   Once the plugs are finger tight, the job can be finished with a socket. If a torque wrench is available, tighten the spark plugs to the torque listed in this Chapter's Specifications. If you do not have a torque wrench, tighten the plugs finger tight (until the washers bottom on the cylinder head) then use a wrench to tighten them an additional 1/4 to 1/2 turn. Regardless of the method used, do not over-tighten them.

10   Reconnect the spark plug caps and reinstall the air ducts.

16 Lubrication - general

Refer to illustrations 16.2a, 16.2b, 16.3a and 16.3b

1   Since the controls, cables and various other components of a motorcycle are exposed to the elements, they should be lubricated regularly to ensure safe and trouble-free operation.

2   The clutch lever and brake lever pivots, the brake pedal, shift lever and sidestand pivots, the rear brake linkage, the shift linkage and

15.7a Spark plug manufacturers recommend using a wire type gauge when checking the gap - if the wire doesn't slide between the electrodes with a slight drag, adjustment is required

15.7b To change the gap, bend the side electrode only, as indicated by the arrows, and be very careful not to crack or chip the ceramic insulator surrounding the center electrode

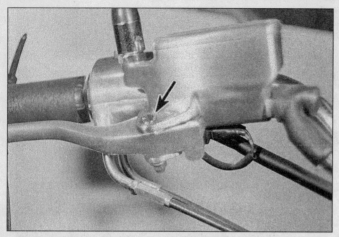

16.2a Lubricate the brake lever pivot (arrow) and clutch lever pivot (not shown, but similar)

16.2b Lubricate the shift lever pivot, the footpeg hinge and the sidestand pivot (arrows)

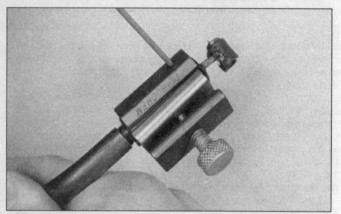

16.3a Lubing a cable with a pressure lube adapter is easier and less messy (they're available at most bike shops)

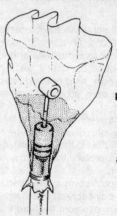

16.3b If you don't have a pressure lube adapter, make a funnel at one end of the cable with a small piece of plastic, tape it to the cable and carefully pour a small amount of oil into the funnel

the footpeg hinges should be lubricated frequently (see illustrations). In order for the lubricant to be applied where it will do the most good, the component should be disassembled. However, if chain and cable lubricant is being used, it can be applied to the pivot joint gaps and will usually work its way into the areas where friction occurs. If motor oil or light grease is being used, apply it sparingly as it may attract dirt (which could cause the controls to bind or wear at an accelerated rate). **Note:** *One of the best lubricants for the control lever pivots is a dry-film lubricant (available from many sources by different names).*

3   To lubricate the throttle cables, disconnect them at the lower end, then lubricate them with a pressure lube adapter (see illustration). If you don't have one, disconnect both ends of the cable and use a funnel (see illustration). It's a good idea to remove and lubricate the throttle twist grip whenever the throttle cables are lubricated (see the handlebar switch removal section of Chapter 9).
4   The choke cables should be lubricated the same way as the throttle cables (see Chapter 4 for the choke cable removal procedure).
5   The speedometer cable should be removed from its housing and lubricated with motor oil or cable lubricant (see Chapter 9 for speedometer cable removal).
6   The swingarm pivot ball and needle bearings should be lubricated with lithium-based multi-purpose grease (see Chapter 6 for the swingarm removal procedure).

17 Valve clearances - check and adjustment

Refer to illustrations 17.5a, 17.5b, 17.5c, 17.7, 17.8, 17.12 and 17.13
1   The engine must be completely cool for this maintenance procedure, so let the machine sit overnight before beginning. Make sure the ignition switch is turned off and the kill switch is in the Off position.
2   Remove the fuel tank (see Chapter 4).
3   On VT600 models, remove the air cleaner housing cover, holder and filter element; on VT750 models, remove the air cleaner housing cover and filter element (see Section 13). On all models, remove the air cleaner chamber and intake duct assembly (see Chapter 4).
4   Remove the spark plugs (see Section 15) so the crankshaft is easier to turn.
5   On VT600 models, remove the valve adjusting covers (see illustrations).

17.5a Remove the two Allen bolts and remove the intake valve adjustment cover from the rear cylinder cover (VT600 models)

17.5b Remove the two Allen bolts (arrow indicates outer bolt; use a long Allen bit on the inner bolt) . . .

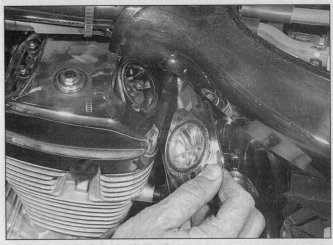

17.5c . . . and remove the exhaust valve adjustment cover from the rear cylinder cover (VT600 models)

6   On VT750 models, remove the cylinder head covers (see Chapter 2).

7   Remove the crankshaft hole cap and the timing hole cap from the left side of the engine **(see illustration)**.

8   Adjust the valves for the front cylinder first. Rotate the crankshaft counterclockwise with a socket **(see illustration)** until the FT mark on the flywheel is aligned with the index mark on the left crankcase cover. This places the front piston at top dead center (TDC). To verify that the front piston is on its compression stroke, wiggle the tip of each front cylinder rocker arm. If the front piston *is* at TDC, the valves will be fully closed; the rocker arms won't be pushing against the valves, so they should feel a little loose. If the rocker arms don't feel loose, the front piston is on its exhaust stroke. Rotate the crankshaft one full turn counterclockwise, so the FT mark again aligns with the index mark.

9   Insert a feeler gauge of the thickness listed in this Chapter's Specifications into the gap between the top of each valve stem and its rocker arm adjuster screw. Pull the feeler gauge out slowly - you should feel a slight drag. If there's no drag, the clearance is too loose. If there's a heavy drag, the clearance is too tight.

10   To adjust the clearance, loosen the rocker arm locknut with a box wrench. Turn the adjusting screw to adjust the clearance, then tighten the locknut.

11   Recheck the clearance with the feeler gauge to make sure it didn't change when you tightened the locknut. Readjust it if necessary.

12   Rotate the crankshaft counterclockwise again until the RT mark

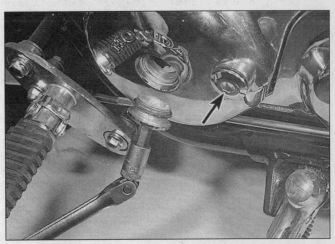

17.7 Remove the crankshaft and timing hole plugs

on the flywheel is aligned with the index mark on the crankcase cover **(see illustration)**. The rear piston should now be at TDC. Verify that it is by wiggling the rear cylinder rocker arms. With the engine in this position, the valves for the rear cylinder can be checked.

17.8 Rotate the crankshaft counterclockwise

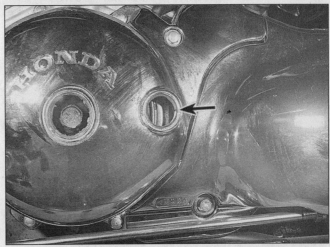

17.12 To bring the rear piston to TDC, align the RT mark on the flywheel with the index mark on the edge of the timing hole

17.13 To measure the valve clearance, insert a feeler gauge of the specified thickness into the gap between each rocker arm and valve stem

18.3 Turn the throttle stop screw (arrow) to set idle speed (throttle link cover, throttle cables and choke knob removed for clarity)

13   Referring to Step 9, insert a feeler gauge of the thickness listed in this Chapter's Specifications between each rocker arm and valve stem **(see illustration)**. Adjust the clearances if necessary as described in Step 10.

14   On VT600 models, inspect the O-rings on the valve adjustment covers. Replace them if they're cracked, torn, flattened or distorted. Install the valve adjustment covers and tighten the Allen bolts to the torque listed in this Chapter's Specifications.

15   On VT750 models, inspect the cylinder head cover O-rings. Replace them if they're cracked, torn, flattened or distorted. Install the cylinder head covers and tighten the cover bolts to the torque listed in the Chapter 2 Specifications (see Chapter 2).

16   Install the spark plugs (see Section 15).

17   Inspect the O-rings for the crankshaft hole and timing hole plugs and replace them if necessary. Install the plugs and tighten them securely.

18   Install the air intake ducts and air chamber (see Chapter 4). Install the air cleaner filter element, holder (VT600 models) and air cleaner housing cover (see Section 13).

19   Install the fuel tank (see Chapter 4).

18   Idle speed - check and adjustment

Refer to illustration 18.3

1   The idle speed should be checked and adjusted before and after the carburetors are synchronized and whenever it is obviously high or low. Before adjusting the idle speed, make sure the valve clearances and spark plug gaps are correct. Also, turn the handlebars back-and-forth and see if the idle speed changes as this is done. If it does, the throttle cables may not be correctly adjusted, or may be worn out. This is a dangerous condition that can cause loss of control of the bike. Be sure to correct this problem before proceeding.

2   The engine should be at normal operating temperature, which is usually reached after 10 to 15 minutes of stop and go riding. Put the transmission in Neutral and place the bike on its sidestand.

3   Turn the throttle stop screw **(see illustration)**, until the idle speed listed in this Chapter's Specifications is obtained.

4   Snap the throttle open and shut a few times, then recheck the idle speed. If necessary, repeat the adjustment procedure.

5   If a smooth, steady idle can't be achieved, the air/fuel mixture may be incorrect. Refer to Chapter 4 for additional carburetor information.

19   Carburetor synchronization - check and adjustment

Refer to illustrations 19.7a, 19.7b and 19.12

Warning: *Gasoline is extremely flammable, so take extra precautions*

when you work on any part of the fuel system. Don't smoke or allow open flames or bare light bulbs near the work area, and don't work in a garage where a natural gas-type appliance (such as a water heater or clothes dryer) is present. Since gasoline is carcinogenic, wear latex gloves when there's a possibility of being exposed to fuel, and, if you get fuel on your skin, wash it off immediately with soap and water. Mop up any spills immediately and do not store fuel-soaked rags where they could ignite. When you perform any kind of work on the fuel system, wear safety glasses and have a class B type fire extinguisher (flammable liquids) on hand.

1   Carburetor synchronization is simply the process of adjusting dual carburetors so they pass the same amount of fuel/air mixture to each cylinder. This is done by measuring the vacuum produced in each cylinder. Carburetors that are out of synchronization will result in decreased fuel mileage, increased engine temperature, less than ideal throttle response and higher vibration levels.

2   To properly synchronize the carburetors, you will need some sort of vacuum gauge setup, preferably with a gauge for each cylinder, or a mercury manometer, which is a calibrated tube arrangement that utilizes columns of mercury to indicate engine vacuum. You'll also need an auxiliary fuel tank, since the bike's fuel tank must be removed for access to the vacuum fittings and synchronizing screws.

3   A manometer can be purchased from a motorcycle dealer or accessory shop and should have the necessary rubber hoses supplied with it for hooking into the vacuum hose fittings on the carburetors.

4   A vacuum gauge setup can also be purchased from a dealer or fabricated from commonly available hardware and automotive vacuum gauges.

5   The manometer is the more reliable and accurate instrument, and for that reason is preferred over the vacuum gauge setup; however, since the mercury used in the manometer is a liquid, and extremely toxic, extra precautions must be taken during use and storage of the instrument.

6   Because of the nature of the synchronization procedure and the need for special instruments, most owners leave the task to a dealer service department or a reputable motorcycle repair shop.

7   Remove the screws from the intake vacuum ports and install vacuum gauge adapters **(see illustrations)**. Connect the vacuum gauges or manometer to the adapters.

8   Start the engine and let it run until it reaches normal operating temperature.

9   Make sure there are no leaks in the vacuum gauge or manometer setup, as false readings will result.

10   Start the engine and make sure the idle speed is correct. If it isn't, adjust it (see Section 18).

11   The carburetor for the rear cylinder is the "base" carburetor. In other words, vacuum at the front carburetor should be compared to vacuum at the rear carburetor. The vacuum readings for both of the cylinders should be within the allowable deviation listed in this Chap-

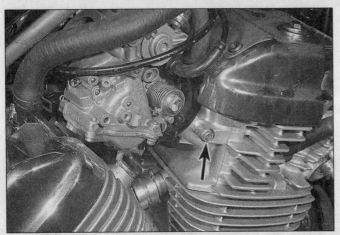

19.7a Remove the vacuum screw (arrow) from the right side of the front cylinder intake port . . .

19.7b . . . remove the other vacuum screw from the left side of the rear cylinder intake port, then install an adapter tube in each vacuum port

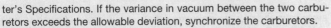

19.12 The carburetor synchronization screw (arrow) is located between the carburetors and can be accessed (with the fuel tank removed) through the space between the intake ducts (carburetors removed for clarity)

20.7 To remove the radiator cap, turn it counterclockwise to the first stop, let any residual pressure escape, then resume turning the cap counterclockwise until it's free and pull it off

ter's Specifications. If the variance in vacuum between the two carburetors exceeds the allowable deviation, synchronize the carburetors.

12   To perform the adjustment, synchronize the carburetors by turning the synchronizing screw **(see illustration)** until the vacuum is identical or within the allowable deviation for both cylinders.

13   Snap the throttle open and shut two or three times, then recheck synchronization and readjust if necessary.

14   When the adjustment is complete, recheck the vacuum readings and idle speed, then stop the engine. Remove the vacuum gauge or manometer and install the intake port screws.

20 Cooling system - check

Refer to illustrations 20.7 and 20.8

Warning: *The engine must be cool before beginning this procedure.*

Note: *Check the coolant level before checking the cooling system (see Section 3).*

1   The cooling system should be checked carefully at the recommended intervals. Look for evidence of leaks, check the condition of the coolant, check the radiator for clogged fins and damage. Make sure the radiator cooling fan operates when the coolant gets hot. If it doesn't, either the fan motor, the fan switch or the circuit is defective (see Chapter 3).

2   Inspect the condition of the coolant hoses. Look for cracks, abrasions and any other damage that might cause a leak. Squeeze the hoses. They should feel firm yet pliable, and should return to their original shape when released. If they feel hard or stiff, replace them.

3   Look for signs of leaks at every cooling system joint (where the hoses are clamped to the radiator, thermostat and water pump). If a hose is leaking at one of these components, tighten the hose clamp. Of course, if a hose is in poor condition, tightening a hose clamp can tear the hose, making the leak worse. Such hoses must be replaced.

4   Inspect the radiator for signs of leaks and other damage. Leaks in the radiator leave tell-tale scale deposits or coolant stains on the outside of the core below the leak. If leaks are noted, remove the radiator and have it repaired or replace it (see Chapter 3). Do not use a liquid leak-stopping additive to try to repair leaks.

5   Inspect the radiator fins for any debris - mud, dirt, insects, etc. - which impedes the flow of air through the radiator. If the fins are dirty, force water or low pressure compressed air through the fins from the backside. If the fins are bent or distorted, carefully straighten them with a small flat-blade screwdriver.

6   Remove the fuel tank (see Chapter 4) and the steering covers (see Chapter 8).

7   Remove the radiator cap **(see illustration)** by turning it counterclockwise until it reaches a stop. If you hear a hissing sound, there's still pressure in the system. Wait until it stops. Then press down on the cap and continue turning it counterclockwise and remove it. Inspect

**20.8 An antifreeze hydrometer is helpful for determining
the condition of the coolant**

**21.3a There are two cooling system drain bolts: this one (arrow)
is on the water pump . . .**

the condition of the coolant in the radiator. If it's rust-colored, or if scale has accumulated inside the radiator, drain, flush and refill the system with a new 50/50 mixture of distilled water and ethylene glycol. Inspect the cap gasket for cracks and any other damage. If any damage is evident, have the cap pressure-tested by a dealer service department or replace it. Install the cap by turning it clockwise until it reaches the first stop, then push it down and continue turning it clockwise until it stops.

8   Check the antifreeze content of the coolant with an antifreeze hydrometer **(see illustration)**. Coolant might appear to be in good condition but might be too weak to offer adequate protection. If the hydrometer indicates a weak mixture, drain, flush and refill the cooling system (see Section 21).

9   Start the engine and let it reach normal operating temperature, then check for leaks again. As the coolant temperature reaches its upper operating temperature, the fan should come on automatically and the coolant temperature should begin to come back down. If it the fan doesn't come on, inspect the fan, the fan switch and the circuit (see Chapter 3).

10   If the coolant level is constantly low, and no evidence of leaks can be found, have the cooling system pressure checked by a Honda dealer service department or by a motorcycle repair shop.

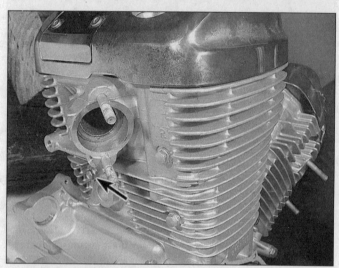

**21.3b . . . the other drain bolt is on the rear side of the rear
cylinder, above the starter motor**

21 Cooling system - draining, flushing and refilling

Warning: *Allow the engine to cool completely before performing this maintenance operation. Also, don't allow antifreeze to come into contact with your skin or painted surfaces of the vehicle. Rinse off spills immediately with plenty of water. Antifreeze is highly toxic if ingested. Never leave antifreeze lying around in an open container or in puddles on the floor; children and pets are attracted by its sweet smell and may drink it. Check with local authorities about disposing used antifreeze. Many communities have collection centers that can dispose of antifreeze safely. Antifreeze is also combustible, so don't store it or use it near open flames.*

Draining

Refer to illustrations 21.3a and 21.3b

1   Remove the fuel tank (see Chapter 4) and the steering covers (see Chapter 8).

2   Remove the radiator cap (see Section 20).

3   To drain the cooling system, remove the drain bolts from the water pump and from the rear side of the rear cylinder, right above the starter motor **(see illustrations)**. Discard the drain bolt sealing washers. Use a funnel to direct the coolant from the rear cylinder drain hole

away from the starter; make sure that no coolant is allowed to spill onto the starter. **Note:** *The coolant will rush out with some force, so be sure to position your drain pan(s) accordingly.*

4   Remove the reservoir (see Chapter 3). Drain the reservoir into the drain pan and wash out the reservoir with clean water. Install the reservoir.

Flushing

5   Flush the system with clean tap water by inserting a garden hose into the radiator filler neck. Allow the water to run through the system until clear water comes out the drain hole. If the radiator is extremely corroded, remove it by referring to Chapter 3 and have it cleaned at a radiator shop.

6   Clean the drain bolt holes and install the drain bolts with new sealing washers. Tighten the drain bolts to the torque listed in this Chapter's Specifications.

7   Fill the cooling system with a mixture of clean water and flushing compound. Make sure that the flushing compound is compatible with aluminum components and follow the manufacturer's instructions carefully.

8   Install the radiator cap (see Section 21), start the engine and allow it to reach normal operating temperature. Let it run for about ten minutes.

22.3 Inspect the condition of the hoses connecting the various EVAP system components (late-model VT600 shown; refer to the vacuum hose routing diagram on the inside of the left side cover for a schematic of the system on your machine)

22.4 The EVAP canister is located down low, right behind the engine, below the swingarm pivot; inspect the condition of the canister and make sure that the hoses and clamps are tight (VT600 model shown; on VT750 models, the canister is in the same location, but is installed transversely instead of longitudinally)

9   Stop the engine. Let the machine cool for awhile, then cover the radiator cap with a heavy rag and turn it counterclockwise to the first stop, wait for it to release any pressure in the system, then push down on the cap and remove it.
10   Drain the system again.
11   Fill the system with clean water, then repeat Steps 8, 9 and 10.

Refilling

12   Fill the system with a 50/50 mixture of distilled water and ethylene glycol. When the system is full (all the way up to the top of the radiator filler neck).
13   Remove the cap from the cooling system reservoir (see Section 3) and fill the reservoir.
14   To bleed the cooling system of air, place the fuel tank in position (it's not necessary to bolt it down), hook up the fuel lines to the carburetors, put the transmission in Neutral, start the engine and let it idle for two to three minutes. Snap the throttle three or four times. Stop the engine and add coolant up to the top of the filler neck again. Install the radiator cap. Check the coolant level in the reservoir and, if necessary, fill it to the upper mark. Install the reservoir filler neck cap.
15   Install the steering head covers (see Chapter 8) and the fuel tank (see Chapter 4).

22 Evaporative emission control system (California models only) - inspection

Refer to illustrations 22.3 and 22.4
1   Remove the fuel tank (see Chapter 4).
2   Remove the left side cover (see Chapter 8) and study the Vacuum Hose Routing Diagram on the inside of the side cover. You can order a new diagram from a Honda dealer if the old one is missing or illegible.
3   Inspect the hoses that connect the fuel tank, the EVAP canister, the EVAP purge control valve and the carburetors **(see illustration)**. Look for loose or detached hoses and weak or missing clamps. Note the condition of the hoses themselves. There should be no cracks, tears or general deterioration. Make sure that none of the hoses are kinked or twisted, which will obstruct the passage of crankcase and fuel system emissions through the system. If any hose is damaged, replace it (see Chapter 4).
4   Lean the bike over to the left on its sidestand and inspect the EVAP canister **(see illustration)**, which is located underneath the

machine, between the engine and the rear wheel, below the swingarm pivot.
5   Install the left side cover and the fuel tank.

23 Exhaust system - check

1   Periodically check all of the exhaust system joints for leaks and loose fasteners. If tightening the clamp bolts fails to stop any leaks, replace the gaskets with new ones (see Chapter 4).
2   The exhaust pipe flange nuts at the cylinder heads are especially prone to loosening, which could cause damage to the head. Check them frequently and keep them tight.

24 Steering head bearings - check, adjustment and lubrication

1   Steering head bearings can become dented, rough or loose as the machine ages. In extreme cases, worn or loose steering head bearings can cause steering wobble that is potentially dangerous.

Check

2   To check the steering hear bearings, support the motorcycle securely and block the machine so the front wheel is in the air.
3   Point the wheel straight ahead and slowly move the handlebars from side-to-side. If there are any dents or rough spots in the bearing races, the front end will feel "rough" as the bearings roll over these spots when the handlebars are turned from side-to-side. If the front end feels rough, replace the steering head bearings and races (see Chapter 6).
4   Facing the bike from the front, grasp the fork legs firmly and try to move them forward and backward. If the steering head bearings are loose, you'll feel a "clunk" (freeplay) as the fork legs are moved back and forth. If there's freeplay in the steering head bearings, adjust the steering head as follows.

Adjustment

Refer to illustration 24.7
5   Remove the headlight (see Chapter 9).
6   Remove the handlebars, the upper triple clamp, the steering stem

24.7 You'll need the right socket to torque the steering head bearing adjustment nut (Honda tool 07916-3710100, or equivalent, available at Honda parts departments)

26.8 Install the fuel filter (left arrow) with its directional arrow pointing toward the fuel pump (right arrow)

locknut and the lock washer (see Chapter 6).
7   Tighten the bearing adjustment nut **(see illustration)** to the torque listed in this Chapter's Specifications.
8   Turn the steering stem from lock to lock five or six times and check for binding.
9   If there is any binding in the steering stem, disassemble the steering stem assembly and inspect the bearings (see Chapter 6).
10   If the steering operates properly, verify that the adjustment nut is still tightened to the correct torque, then reassemble the front end.
11   Install the lock washer, locknut, upper triple clamp and handlebars (see Chapter 6).
12   Install the headlight (see Chapter 9).

Lubrication

13   Periodic cleaning and repacking of the steering head bearings is recommended by the manufacturer. Refer to Chapter 6 for steering head bearing lubrication and replacement procedures.

25 Fasteners - check

1   Since vibration of the machine tends to loosen fasteners, all nuts, bolts, screws, etc. should be periodically checked for proper tightness.
2   Pay particular attention to the following:
  Brake caliper bolts and banjo bolts
  Spark plugs
  Engine oil drain plug
  Oil drain plug
  Cooling system drain plugs
  Gearshift pedal (and linkage, if equipped)
  Footpegs and sidestand
  Engine mounting bolts
  Shock absorber or rear suspension unit mounting bolts
  Front axle (or axle nut) and axle pinch bolt
  Rear axle nut
3   If a torque wrench is available, use it along with the torque specifications at the beginning of this and the other Chapters.

26 Fuel system - check and filter replacement

Warning: *Gasoline is extremely flammable, so take extra precautions when you work on any part of the fuel system. Don't smoke or allow open flames or bare light bulbs near the work area, and don't work in a garage where a natural gas-type appliance (such as a water heater or clothes dryer) is present. Since gasoline is carcinogenic, wear latex*

gloves when there's a possibility of being exposed to fuel, and, if you get fuel on your skin, wash it off immediately with soap and water. Mop up any spills immediately and do not store fuel-soaked rags where they could ignite. When you perform any kind of work on the fuel system, wear safety glasses and have a class B type fire extinguisher (flammable liquids) on hand.
1   Remove the fuel tank (see Chapter 4).
2   Inspect the condition of the fuel tank, the fuel tap, the fuel lines and the carburetors. Look for leaks and signs of damage or wear (see Chapter 4).
3   If the fuel tap is leaking, note whether the fuel tap-to-fuel tank locknut is tight. If leakage persists, the tap should be removed from the fuel tank, disassembled, cleaned and inspected (see Chapter 4).
4   If the fuel lines are cracked or otherwise deteriorated, replace them.
5   If the carburetor gaskets are leaking, the carburetors should be disassembled and rebuilt (see Chapter 4).
6   Install the fuel tank.

Fuel filter replacement

Refer to illustration 26.8
7   Remove the fuel tank (see Chapter 4).
8   Disconnect the lines from the filter **(see illustration)** and remove the filter from its bracket.
9   Install the new filter with the directional arrow on the filter pointing toward the fuel pump.
10   Reconnect the lines. Make sure that the hoses fit tightly on the filter pipes and the clamps are snug.
11   Install the fuel tank.

27 Suspension - check

Refer to illustration 27.3
1   The suspension components must be maintained in top operating condition to ensure rider safety. Loose, worn or damaged suspension parts decrease the vehicle's stability and control.
2   While standing alongside the motorcycle, lock the front brake and push on the handlebars to compress the forks several times. See if the fork tubes move up-and-down smoothly without binding. If the fork tubes stick in the sliders, disassemble and inspect the fork legs (see Chapter 6).
3   Carefully inspect the area around the fork seals for any signs of fork oil leakage **(see illustration)**. If leakage is evident, the seals must be replaced (see Chapter 6).
4   Check the tightness of all suspension nuts and bolts to be sure

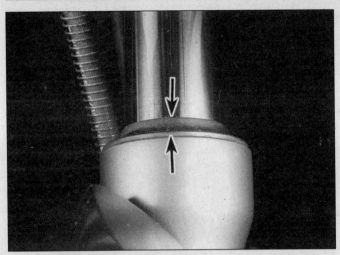

27.3 Inspect each fork seal for oil leaks in the indicated areas (arrows); if oil is leaking past either side of the seal, replace the seal

28.2 To gain access to the spring preload adjuster on VT600 models, remove the left side cover, then use the pin spanner in the bike tool kit to turn the adjuster (arrow)

none have worked loose.

5   Inspect the shock absorber(s) for fluid leakage and tightness of the mounting nuts. If leakage is found, the shock(s) must be replaced.

6   Support the bike securely so it can't be knocked over during this procedure. Grab the swingarm on each side, just ahead of the axle. Rock the swingarm from side to side - there should be no discernible movement at the rear. If there's a little movement or a slight clicking can be heard, make sure the pivot bolt or shafts are tight. If they're tight but movement is still noticeable, remove the swingarm and replace the bearings (see Chapter 6).

7   Inspect the tightness of the rear suspension nuts and bolts (see Chapter 6).

28 Suspension adjustments

Refer to illustrations 28.2 and 28.3

1   Rear spring preload can be adjusted on all models. **Warning:** *The rear shock absorber settings on VT750 models must be even to prevent unstable handling.*

2   On VT600 models, remove the left side cover (see Chapter 8) and adjust rear spring preload with the special pin spanner and expansion bar provided in the tool kit. The pin spanner fits into the holes in the preload collar **(see illustration)**.

3   On VT750 models, adjust rear spring preload by turning the adjuster on the bottom of each shock absorber with the special pin spanner provided in the bike tool kit. The pin spanner fits into the holes

28.3 On VT750 models, insert the pin spanner included in the bike tool kit into the holes (arrows) in the shock body to adjust the spring preload

in the lower part of the shock body **(see illustration)**.

4   The numerically lower settings are for lighter loads and smooth roads. The numerically higher settings are for heavier loads and rough roads. Position 2 is the standard position.

Notes

Chapter 2
Engine, clutch and transmission

Contents

Specifications

VT600 models

General
Bore x stroke	75.0 x 66.0 mm (2.95 x 2.60 inches)
Displacement	583 cc (35.5 cubic inches)
Compression ratio	9.2 to 1

Camshafts
Bearing oil clearance	
Standard	0.050 to 0.111 mm (0.0020 to 0.0044 inch)
Limit	0.130 (0.0051 inch)
Camshaft journal diameter	
Standard	21.959 to 21.980 mm (0.8645 to 0.8654 inch)
Limit	21.90 mm (0.862 inch)
Camshaft runout limit	0.05 mm (0.002 inch)
Camshaft lobe height	
Intake	
Standard	37.930 mm (1.4933 inches)
Limit	37.730 mm (1.4854 inches)
Exhaust	
Standard	37.950 mm (1.4941 inches)
Limit	37.750 mm (1.4862 inches)
Cam chain tensioner wedge height limit	No more than 0.6 mm (0.24 inch)

Rocker arms
Rocker arm inside diameter	
Standard	12.000 to 12.018 mm (0.4724 to 0.4731 inch)
Limit	12.03 mm (0.474 inch)
Rocker arm shaft diameter	
Standard	11.966 to 11.984 mm (0.4711 to 0.4718 inch)

VT600 models (continued)

Rocker arms (continued)

Rocker arm shaft diameter
  Limit
    1988 and 1989, 1991 through 1996.. 11.83 mm (0.466 inch)
    1997 on.. 11.96 mm (0.471 inch)
Rocker arm-to-rocker shaft clearance
  Standard.. 0.016 to 0.052 mm (0.0006 to 0.0020 inch)
  Limit
    1988 and 1989, 1991 through 1996.. 0.20 mm (0.008 inch)
    1997 on.. 0.07 mm (0.003 inch)

Cylinder head, valves and valve springs

Cylinder head warpage limit .... 0.10 mm (0.004 inch)
Valve stem diameter
  Intake
    Standard .... 5.475 to 5.490 mm (0.2156 to 0.2161 inch)
    Limit .... 5.45 mm (0.215 inch)
  Exhaust
    Standard .... 6.555 to 6.570 mm (0.2580 to 0.2587 inch)
    Limit .... 6.55 mm (0.258 inch)
Valve guide inside diameter
  Intake
    Standard .... 5.500 to 5.512 mm (0.2165 to 0.2170 inch)
    Limit .... 5.56 mm (0.219 inch)
  Exhaust
    Standard .... 6.600 to 6.615 mm (0.2598 to 0.2604 inch)
    Limit .... 6.65 mm (0.262 mm)
Stem-to-guide clearance
  Intake
    Standard .... 0.010 to 0.037 mm (0.0004 to 0.0015 inch)
    Limit .... 0.10 mm (0.004 inch)
  Exhaust
    Standard .... 0.030 to 0.060 mm (0.0012 to 0.0024 inch)
    Limit .... 0.11 (0.004 inch)
Valve seat width (intake and exhaust)
  Standard.. 0.90 to 1.10 mm (0.035 to 0.043 inch)
  Limit... 1.50 mm (0.06 inch)
Valve guide projection height
  Intake.. 19.4 to 19.6 mm (0.76 to 0.77 inch)
  Exhaust.. 17.9 to 18.1 mm (0.70 to 0.71 inch)
Valve spring free length
  Outer spring
    Intake
      Standard .... 42.14 mm (1.659 inch)
      Limit... 40.58 mm (1.598 inch)
    Exhaust
      Standard .... 42.83 mm (1.686 inch)
      Limit... 41.25 mm (1.624 inch)
  Inner spring
    Intake
      Standard .... 38.11 mm (1.500 inch)
      Limit... 36.47 mm (1.436 inch)
    Exhaust
      Standard .... 38.81 mm (1.528 inch)
      Limit... 37.51 mm (1.477 inch)

Cylinders

Bore diameter
  Standard.. 75.000 to 75.015 mm (2.9528 to 2.9533 inches)
  Limit... 75.10 mm (2.957 inches)
Warpage (across top of cylinder)... 0.10 (0.004 inch)
Taper and out-of-round limit .... 0.06 mm (0.002 inch)

Pistons

Piston diameter
  Standard.. 74.965 to 74.990 mm (2.9514 to 2.9524 inches)
  Limit... 74.90 mm (2.949 inches)

Piston-to-cylinder clearance
Standard.. 0.010 to 0.050 mm (0.0004 to 0.0020 inch)
Limit.. 0.10 mm (0.004 inch)
Ring side clearance (top and second rings)
Standard.. 0.015 to 0.045 mm (0.006 to 0.0018 inch)
Limit.. 0.10 mm (0.004 inch)
Ring end gap
Top and second rings
Standard.. 0.10 to 0.30 mm (0.004 to 0.012 inch)
Limit.. 0.50 mm (0.020 inch)
Oil ring
Standard.. 0.20 to 0.70 mm (0.008 to 0.028 inch)
Limit.. 0.90 mm (0.035 inch)
Piston pin bore
Standard.. 18.002 to 18.008 mm (0.7087 to 0.7090 inch)
Limit.. 18.05 mm (0.711 inch)
Piston pin diameter
Standard.. 17.994 to 18.000 mm (0.7084 to 0.7087 inch)
Limit.. 17.98 mm (0.708 inch)
Piston-to-piston pin clearance
Standard.. 0.002 to 0.014 mm (0.0001 to 0.0006 inch)
Limit.. 0.040 mm (0.0016 inch)
Piston pin-to-connecting rod small end clearance
Standard.. 0.016 to 0.040 mm (0.0006 to 0.0016 inch)
Limit.. 0.060 mm (0.0024 inch)

Crankshaft, connecting rods and bearings

Connecting rod small end I.D.
Standard.. 18.016 to 18.034 mm (0.7093 to 0.7100 inch)
Limit.. 18.07 mm (0.711 inch)
Main bearing oil clearance
Standard.. 0.025 to 0.041 mm (0.0010 to 0.0016 inch)
Limit.. 0.06 mm (0.002 inch)
Connecting rod side clearance
Standard.. 0.05 to 0.20 mm (0.002 to 0.008 inch)
Limit.. 0.30 mm (0.001 inch)
Connecting rod bearing oil clearance
Standard.. 0.028 to 0.052 mm (0.0011 to 0.0020 inch)
Limit.. 0.07 mm (0.003 inch)
Crankshaft runout limit .... 0.05 mm (0.002 inch)

Oil pump

Rotor tip clearance
Standard.. 0.15 mm (0.006 inch)
Limit.. 0.20 mm (0.008 inch)
Pump body clearance
Standard.. 0.15 to 0.22 mm (0.006 to 0.009 inch)
Limit.. 0.35 mm (0.014 inch)
Rotor-to-pump body end clearance
Standard.. 0.02 to 0.07 mm (0.001 to 0.003 inch)
Limit.. 0.10 mm (0.004 inch)
Oil pump drive sprocket inside diameter
Standard.. 32.000 to 32.025 mm (1.2598 to 1.2608 inches)
Limit.. 32.10 mm (1.264 inches)

Clutch

Friction disc thickness
Plate A
Standard.. 2.62 to 2.78 mm (0.103 to 0.107 inch)
Minimum.. 2.30 mm (0.090 inch)
Plate B
Standard.. 2.92 to 3.08 mm (0.115 to 0.121 inch)
Minimum.. 2.60 mm (0.102 inch)
Steel plate warpage limit .... 0.30 mm (0.012 inch)
Spring free length
1988
Standard.. 39.0 mm (1.54 inches)
Minimum.. 37.4 mm (1.47 inches)
1989 on
Standard.. 43.2 mm (1.70 inches)
Minimum.. 41.6 mm (1.64 inches)

VT600 models (continued)

Clutch (continued)

Mainshaft diameter (at clutch outer guide)
Standard .... 21.967 to 21.980 mm (0.8648 to 0.8654 inch)
Minimum .... 21.92 mm (0.863 inch)
Clutch outer guide
Inside diameter
Standard .... 21.991 to 22.016 mm (0.8658 to 0.8668 inch)
Limit .... 22.09 mm (0.870 inch)
Outside diameter
Standard .... 31.959 to 31.025 mm (1.258 to 1.2589 inches)
Limit .... 31.98 mm (1.259 inches)

Transmission

Gear inside diameter
C1
Standard .... 24.000 to 24.021 mm (0.9449 to 0.9457 inch)
Limit .... 23.94 mm (0.943 inch)
C3, M2, M4
Standard .... 28.000 to 28.021 mm (1.1024 to 1.1032 inches)
Limit .... 28.04 mm (1.104 inch)
Gear bushing
Outside diameter
C1
Standard .... 23.959 to 23.980 mm (0.9433 to 0.9441 inch)
Limit .... 24.94 mm (0.982 inch)
C3, M2, M4
Standard .... 27.959 to 27.980 mm (1.1007 to 1.1016 inches)
Limit .... 27.94 mm (1.100 inches)
Inside diameter
C1
Standard .... 20.016 to 20.037 mm (0.7880 to 0.7889 inch)
Limit .... 20.06 mm (0.790 inch)
M2
Standard .... 25.000 to 25.021 mm (0.9843 to 0.9851 inch)
Limit .... 25.04 mm (0.986 inch)
Bushing-to-shaft clearance
C1
Standard .... 0.023 to 0.057 mm (0.0009 to 0.022 inch)
Limit .... 0.10 mm (0.004 inch)
M2
Standard .... 0.020 to 0.062 mm ((0.0008 to 0.0024 inch)
Limit .... 0.10 mm (0.004 inch)
Gear-to-bushing clearance (C1, C3, M2, M4)
Standard .... 0.020 to 0.062 mm (0.0008 to 0.0024 inch)
Limit .... 0.10 mm (0.004 inch)
Countershaft diameter (C1 bushing)
Standard .... 19.980 to 19.993 mm (0.7866 to 0.7871 inch)
Limit .... 19.96 mm (0.786 inch)
Mainshaft diameter (M2 bushing)
Standard .... 24.959 to 24.980 mm (0.9835 to 0.9826 inch)
Limit .... 24.94 mm (0.982 inch)
Backlash
1st, 2nd, 3rd .... 1.021 to 0.110 mm (0.0008 to 0.0043 inch)
4th .... 1.023 to 0.117 mm (0.0009 to 0.0046 inch)

Shift fork/shift fork shaft/shift drum

Shift fork tip thickness
Standard .... 5.93 to 6.00 mm (0.233 to 0.236 inch)
Limit .... 5.63 mm (0.222 inch)
Shift fork shaft bore inside diameter
Standard .... 13.000 to 13.018 mm (0.5118 to 0.5125 inch)
Limit .... 13.04 mm (0.513 inch)
Shift fork shaft diameter
Standard .... 12.966 to 12.984 mm (0.5105 to 0.5112 inch)
Limit .... 12.90 mm (0.508 inch)
Left shift drum journal diameter
Standard .... 11.966 to 11.984 mm (0.4711 to 0.4718 inch)
Limit .... 11.94 mm (0.470 inch)

Torque specifications

Cam chain tensioner bolt	10 Nm (88 in-lbs)
Cam chain tensioner set plate bolt	12 Nm (106 in-lbs)
Camshaft end holder bolt	
1988 through 1998	9 Nm (78 in-lbs)
1999 on	10 Nm (84 in-lbs)
Camshaft holder	
8 mm bolts and nuts	23 Nm (17 ft-lbs)
6 mm bolts (pre-1997 only)	10 Nm (88 in-lbs)
Camshaft sprocket bolt	23 Nm (17 ft-lbs)
Clutch center locknut	
1988 through 1998	127 Nm (94 ft-lbs)
1999 on	128 Nm (95 ft-lbs)
Clutch lifter plate bolt	12 Nm (106 in-lbs)
Clutch lock nut	130 Nm (96 ft-lbs)
Connecting rod bearing cap nuts	34 Nm (25 ft-lbs)
Countershaft bearing set plate bolt	9 Nm (80 in-lbs)
Crankcase bolts	
1988 and 1989, 1991 through 1996	
8 mm stud bolts	20 to 30 Nm (15 to 22 ft-lbs)
10 mm stud bolts	20 to 50 Nm (15 to 37 ft-lbs)
1997 on	
6 mm bolts (1997 and 1998)	9 Nm (80 in-lbs)
6 mm bolts (1999 on)	12 Nm (108 in-lbs)
8 mm bolts	23 Nm (17 ft-lbs)
Cylinder head	
6 mm bolts	
1989 and 1990, 1991 through 1996	10 Nm (88 in-lbs)
1997 on	12 Nm (106 in-lbs)
8 mm bolts	23 Nm (17 ft-lbs)
8 mm nuts	23 Nm (17 ft-lbs)
10 mm nuts	47 Nm (35 ft-lbs)
Cylinder head cover bolt	10 Nm (88 in-lbs)
Drum stopper plate bolt	12 Nm (106 in-lbs)
Flywheel bolt	127 Nm (94 ft-lbs)
Gearshift cam plate bolt	12 Nm (106 in-lbs)
Gearshift lever pinch bolt	12 Nm (106 in-lbs)
Gearshift drum stopper bolt	23 Nm (17 ft-lbs)
Left crankcase cover bolts	12 Nm (106 in-lbs)
Mainshaft bearing set plate bolt	12 Nm (106 in-lbs)
Oil pipe banjo bolt (1988 and 1989)	23 Nm (17 ft-lbs)
Oil pump driven sprocket bolt	15 Nm (132 in-lbs)
Primary drive gear bolt	88 Nm (65 ft-lbs)
Right crankcase cover bolts	12 Nm (106 in-lbs)
Starter clutch torx bolts	30 Nm (22 ft-lbs)
Stator socket mounting bolt	12 Nm (106 in-lbs)

VT750 models

General

Bore x stroke	79.0 x 76.0 mm (3.11 x 2.99 inches)
Displacement	745 cc (45.4 cubic inches)
Compression ratio	9.0 to 1

Camshafts

Bearing oil clearance	
Standard	0.050 to 0.111 mm (0.0020 to 0.0044 inch)
Limit	0.13 (0.005 inch)
Camshaft journal diameter	
Standard	21.959 to 21.980 mm (0.8645 to 0.8654 inch)
Limit	21.90 mm (0.862 inch)
Camshaft runout (VT750C/CD ACE)	
Standard	0.030 mm (0.012 inch)
Limit	0.05 mm (0.002 inch)
Camshaft runout (VT750DC Spirit)	
Standard	Not specified
Limit	0.03 mm (0.012 inch)

VT750 models (continued)

Camshafts (continued)

Camshaft lobe height
  Intake
    Standard .... 38.381 mm (1.5111 inches)
    Limit .... 38.10 mm (1.500 inches)
  Exhaust
    Standard .... 38.407 mm (1.5121 inches)
    Limit .... 38.20 mm (1.504 inches)
Camshaft lobe height (VT750DC Spirit)
  Intake
    Standard .... 37.188 to 37.348 mm (1.4641 to 1.4704 inches)
    Limit .... 37.16 mm (1.463 inches)
  Exhaust
    Standard .... 37.605 to 37.765 mm (1.4805 to 1.4868 inches)
    Limit .... 37.58 mm (1.480 inches)
Cam chain tensioner wedge height limit .... No more than 0.6 mm (0.24 inch)

Rocker arms

Rocker arm inside diameter
  Standard .... 12.000 to 12.018 mm (0.4724 to 0.4731 inch)
  Limit .... 12.05 mm (0.474 inch)
Rocker arm shaft diameter
  Standard .... 11.966 to 11.984 mm (0.4711 to 0.4718 inch)
  Limit .... 11.83 mm (0.466 inch)
Rocker arm-to-rocker shaft clearance
  Standard .... 0.016 to 0.052 mm (0.0006 to 0.0020 inch)
  Limit .... 0.07 mm (0.003 inch)

Cylinder head, valves and valve springs

Cylinder head warpage limit .... 0.10 mm (0.004 inch)
Valve stem diameter
  Intake
    Standard .... 5.475 to 5.490 mm (0.2156 to 0.2161 inch)
    Limit .... 5.45 mm (0.215 inch)
  Exhaust (VT750C/DC ACE)
    Standard .... 6.555 to 6.570 mm (0.2580 to 0.2587 inch)
    Limit .... 6.55 mm (0.258 inch)
  Exhaust (VT750DC Spirit)
    Standard .... 6.600 to 6.615 mm (0.2598 to 0.2604 inch)
    Limit .... 6.55 mm (0.258 inch)
Valve guide inside diameter
  Intake
    Standard .... 5.500 to 5.512 mm (0.2165 to 0.2170 inch)
    Limit .... 5.56 mm (0.219 inch)
  Exhaust
    Standard .... 6.600 to 6.615 mm (0.2598 to 0.2604 inch)
    Limit .... 6.65 mm (0.262 mm)
Stem-to-guide clearance
  Intake
    Standard .... 0.010 to 0.037 mm (0.0004 to 0.0015 inch)
    Limit .... 0.10 mm (0.004 inch)
  Exhaust
    Standard .... 0.030 to 0.060 mm (0.0012 to 0.0024 inch)
    Limit .... 0.11 (0.004 inch)
Valve seat width (intake and exhaust)
  Standard .... 0.90 to 1.10 mm (0.035 to 0.043 inch)
  Limit .... 1.50 mm (0.06 inch)
Valve guide projection height
  Intake .... 19.5 mm (0.77 inch)
  Exhaust .... 18.0 mm (0.71 inch)
Valve spring free length
  Intake
    Standard .... 42.14 mm (1.659 inch)
    Limit .... 40.58 mm (1.598 inch)
  Exhaust
    Standard .... 42.83 mm (1.686 inch)
    Limit .... 41.25 mm (1.624 inch)

Cylinders

Bore diameter
  Standard .... 79.000 to 79.015 mm (3.1102 to 3.1108 inches)
  Limit .... 79.10 mm (3.114 inches)
Warpage (across top of cylinder) .... 0.10 (0.004 inch)
Taper and out-of-round limit .... 0.06 mm (0.002 inch)

Pistons

Piston diameter
  Standard .... 78.97 to 78.99 mm (3.109 to 3.110 inches)
  Limit .... 78.90 mm (3.106 inches)
Piston-to-cylinder clearance
  Standard .... 0.010 to 0.045 mm (0.0004 to 0.0018 inch)
  Limit .... 0.10 mm (0.004 inch)
Ring side clearance
  Top ring
    Standard .... 0.025 to 0.055 mm (0.0010 to 0.0022 inch)
    Limit .... 0.08 mm (0.003 inch)
  Second ring
    Standard .... 0.015 to 0.045 mm (0.006 to 0.0018 inch)
    Limit .... 0.07 mm (0.003 inch)
Ring end gap
  Top ring (VT750C/CD ACE, 1998 through 2000)
    Standard .... 0.20 to 0.35 mm (0.008 to 0.014 inch)
    Limit .... 0.5 mm (0.02 inch)
  Top ring (VT750C/CD ACE, 2001 on)
    Standard .... 0.025 to 0.055 mm (0.0010 to 0.0022 inch)
    Limit .... 0.08 mm (0.003 inch)
  Top ring (VT750DC Spirit)
    Standard .... 0.025 to 0.055 mm (0.0010 to 0.0022 inch)
    Limit .... 0.08 mm (0.003 inch)
  Second ring (VT750C/CD ACE, 1998 through 2000)
    Standard .... 0.35 to 0.50 mm (0.014 to 0.020 inch)
    Limit .... 0.7 (0.03 inch)
  Second ring (VT750C/CD, 2001 on)
    Standard .... 0.015 to 0.025 mm (0.006 to 0.010 inch)
    Limit .... 0.4 mm (0.020 inch)
  Second ring (VT750DC Spirit)
    Standard .... 0.025 to 0.040 mm (0.0010 to 0.0016 inch)
    Limit .... 0.50 mm (0.020 inch)
  Oil ring
    Standard .... 0.20 to 0.80 mm (0.008 to 0.031 inch)
    Limit .... 1.0 mm (0.04 inch)
Piston pin bore
  Standard .... 18.002 to 18.008 mm (0.7087 to 0.7090 inch)
  Limit .... 18.05 mm (0.711 inch)
Piston pin diameter
  Standard .... 17.994 to 18.000 mm (0.7084 to 0.7087 inch)
  Limit .... 17.98 mm (0.708 inch)
Piston-to-piston pin clearance
  Standard .... 0.002 to 0.014 mm (0.0001 to 0.0006 inch)
  Limit .... 0.04 mm (0.002 inch)
Piston pin-to-connecting rod small end clearance
  Standard .... 0.016 to 0.040 mm (0.0006 to 0.0016 inch)
  Limit .... 0.06 mm (0.002 inch)

Crankshaft, connecting rods and bearings

Connecting rod small end I.D.
  Standard .... 18.016 to 18.034 mm (0.7093 to 0.7100 inch)
  Limit .... 18.07 mm (0.711 inch)
Main bearing oil clearance
  Standard .... 0.030 to 0.046 mm (0.0012 to 0.0018 inch)
  Limit .... 0.07 mm (0.003 inch)
Connecting rod side clearance
  Standard .... 0.05 to 0.20 mm (0.002 to 0.008 inch)
  Limit .... 0.30 mm (0.001 inch)
Connecting rod bearing oil clearance
  Standard .... 0.028 to 0.052 mm (0.0011 to 0.0020 inch)
  Limit .... 0.07 mm (0.003 inch)
Crankshaft runout limit .... 0.03 mm (0.001 inch)

VT750 models (continued)

Oil pump
Rotor tip clearance
   Standard.. 0.15 mm (0.006 inch)
   Limit... 0.20 mm (0.008 inch)
Pump body clearance
   Standard.. 0.15 to 0.22 mm (0.006 to 0.009 inch)
   Limit... 0.35 mm (0.014 inch)
Rotor-to-pump body end clearance
   Standard.. 0.02 to 0.07 mm (0.001 to 0.003 inch)
   Limit... 0.10 mm (0.004 inch)
Oil pump drive sprocket inside diameter
   Standard.. 30.025 to 30.145 mm (1.1821 to 1.1861 inches)
   Limit... 30.15 mm (1.187 inches)

Clutch
Friction plate thickness
   Plate A
      Standard.. 2.62 to 2.78 mm (0.103 to 0.107 inch)
      Minimum.. 2.3 mm (0.09 inch)
   Plate B
      Standard.. 2.92 to 3.08 mm (0.115 to 0.121 inch)
      Minimum.. 2.6 mm (0.10 inch)
Steel plate warpage limit .... 0.30 mm (0.012 inch)
Spring free length
   Standard.. 45.5 mm (1.79 inches)
   Minimum.. 43.9 mm (1.73 inches)
Mainshaft diameter (at clutch outer guide)
   Standard.. 21.967 to 21.980 mm (0.8648 to 0.8654 inch)
   Minimum.. 21.95 mm (0.864 inch)
Clutch outer guide
   Inside diameter
      Standard.. 21.991 to 22.016 mm (0.8658 to 0.8668 inch)
      Limit... 22.03 mm (0.867 inch)
   Outside diameter
      Standard.. 29.994 to 30.007 mm (1.1089 to 1.1814 inches)
      Limit... 29.98 mm (1.180 inches)

Transmission
Gear inside diameter
   C1, C2, C4
      Standard.. 31.000 to 31.025 mm (1.2204 to 1.2215 inches)
      Limit... 31.05 mm (1.222 inches)
   M3, M5
      Standard.. 28.000 to 28.021 mm (1.1024 to 1.1032 inches)
      Limit... 28.04 mm (1.104 inch)
Gear bushing
   Outside diameter
      C1, C2, C4
         Standard.. 30.950 to 30.975 mm (1.2185 to 1.2195 inches)
         Limit... 30.93 mm (1.218 inches)
      M3, M5
         Standard.. 27.959 to 27.980 mm (1.1007 to 1.1016 inches)
         Limit... 27.94 mm (1.100 inches)
   Inside diameter
      C2
         Standard.. 27.995 to 28.016 mm (1.1021 to 1.1030 inches)
         Limit... 28.04 mm (1.104 inches)
      M3
         Standard.. 25.000 to 25.021 mm (0.9843 to 0.9851 inch)
         Limit... 25.04 mm (0.986 inch)
Bushing-to-shaft clearance
   C2
      Standard.. 0.015 to 0.049 mm (0.0006 to 0.0119 inch)
      Limit... 0.08 mm (0.003 inch)
   M3
      Standard.. 0.007 to 0.0049 mm ((0.0003 to 0.0019 inch)
      Limit... 0.08 mm (0.003 inch)

Gear-to-bushing clearance

C1, C2, C4

Standard .... 0.025 to 0.075 mm (0.0010 to 0.0030 inch)

Limit .... 0.11 mm (0.004 inch)

M3, M5

Standard .... 0.020 to 0.062 mm (0.0008 to 0.0024 inch)

Limit .... 0.10 mm (0.004 inch)

Countershaft diameter

At C2 bushing

Standard .... 27.967 to 27.980 mm (1.1011 to 1.1016 inches)

Limit .... 27.95 mm (1.100 inches)

At case journal A

Standard .... 27.972 to 27.990 mm (1.1013 to 1.1020 inches)

Limit .... 27.95 mm (1.100 inches)

At case journal B

Standard .... 19.980 to 19.993 mm (0.7866 to 0.7871 inch)

Limit .... 19.96 mm (0.786 inch)

Mainshaft diameter

At M3 bushing

Standard .... 24.972 to 24.993 mm (0.9831 to 0.9840 inch)

Limit .... 24.95 mm (0.982 inch)

At case journal A

Standard .... 19.980 to 19.993 mm (0.7866 to 0.7871 inch)

Limit .... 19.96 mm (0.786 inch)

At case journal B

Standard .... 21.967 to 21.980 mm (0.8648 to 0.8654 inch)

Limit .... 21.94 mm (0.864 inch)

Shift fork shaft/shift fork/shift drum

Shift fork tip thickness

Standard... 5.93 to 6.00 mm (0.233 to 0.236 inch)

Limit .... 5.6 mm (0.22 inch)

Shift fork shaft bore inside diameter

Standard... 13.000 to 13.021 mm (0.5118 to 0.5126 inch)

Limit... 13.04 mm (0.513 inch)

Shift fork shaft diameter

Standard... 12.966 to 12.984 mm (0.5105 to 0.5112 inch)

Limit... 12.90 mm (0.508 inch)

Left shift drum journal diameter

Standard... 11.966 to 11.984 mm (0.4711 to 0.4718 inch)

Limit.. 11.94 mm (0.470 inch)

Torque specifications

Cam chain tensioner bolt... 10 Nm (88 in-lbs)

Cam chain tensioner set plate bolt.................................. 12 Nm (106 in-lbs)

Camshaft end holder bolt... 10 Nm (88 in-lbs)

Camshaft holder .... 23 Nm (17 ft-lbs)

Camshaft sprocket bolt .... 23 Nm (17 ft-lbs)

Clutch center locknut .... 127 Nm (94 ft-lbs)

Clutch lifter plate bolts... 12 Nm (106 in-lbs)

Clutch lock nut... 130 Nm (96 ft-lbs)

Connecting rod bearing cap nuts .... 34 Nm (25 ft-lbs)

Countershaft bearing set plate bolt .... 9 Nm (80 in-lbs)

Crankcase bolts

6 mm bolts .... 9 Nm (80 in-lbs)

8 mm bolts .... 23 Nm (17 ft-lbs)

Crankcase breather case cover bolt................................... 12 Nm (106 in-lbs)

Cylinder head

6 mm bolts .... 12 Nm (106 in-lbs)

8 mm bolts .... 23 Nm (17 ft-lbs)

8 mm nuts .... 23 Nm (17 ft-lbs)

10 mm nuts .... 47 Nm (35 ft-lbs)

Cylinder head cover bolt... 10 Nm (88 in-lbs)

Cylinder fin socket bolts... 10 Nm (88 in-lbs)

Drum stopper plate bolt.. 12 Nm (106 in-lbs)

Flywheel bolt... 127 Nm (94 ft-lbs)

Gearshift cam plate bolt... 12 Nm (106 in-lbs)

Gearshift lever pinch bolt .... 12 Nm (106 in-lbs)

Gearshift drum stopper bolt .... 23 Nm (17 ft-lbs)

Left crankcase cover bolts .... 12 Nm (106 in-lbs)

VT750 models (continued)

Torque specifications

Mainshaft bearing set plate bolt	12 Nm (106 in-lbs)
Oil pump driven sprocket bolt	15 Nm (132 in-lbs)
Primary drive gear bolt	88 Nm (65 ft-lbs)
Right crankcase cover bolts	12 Nm (106 in-lbs)
Starter clutch torx bolts	30 Nm (22 ft-lbs)
Stator socket mounting bolt	12 Nm (106 in-lbs)

1   General information

The engine/transmission unit is a water-cooled V-twin. The valves are operated by overhead camshafts which are chain driven off the crankshaft. All models have three-valve heads (two intake and one exhaust valve per cylinder). The engine/transmission assembly is constructed from aluminum alloy. The crankcase is divided vertically.

The crankcase incorporates a wet sump, pressure-fed lubrication system which uses a gear-driven oil pump and an oil filter mounted on the rear of the crankcase.

Power from the crankshaft is routed to the transmission via a coil-spring, wet multi-plate type clutch, which is gear-driven off the crankshaft. The transmission on VT600 models is a four-speed, constant-mesh unit; the transmission on VT750 models is a five-speed, constant-mesh unit.

2   Operations possible with the engine in the frame

The following components and assemblies can be serviced with the engine in the frame:

Alternator/flywheel
Camshafts/cam sprockets/cam chains
Carburetors
Front cylinder head/cylinder/piston
Clutch
Gearshift linkage
Ignition pulse generator(s)
Primary drive gear
Starter clutch
Starter motor

3   Operations requiring engine removal

The engine/transmission assembly must be removed from the frame to gain access to the following components:

Rear cylinder head/cylinder/piston
Water pump body

The crankcase halves must be separated to gain access to the following components:

Crankshaft, connecting rods and bearings
Oil pump
Transmission
Shift drum and shift forks

4   Major engine repair - general note

1   It is not always easy to determine when or if an engine should be completely overhauled, as a number of factors must be considered.

2   High mileage is not necessarily an indication that an overhaul is needed, while low mileage, on the other hand, does not preclude the need for an overhaul. Frequency of servicing is probably the single most important consideration. An engine that has regular and frequent oil and filter changes, as well as other required maintenance, will most likely give many miles of reliable service. Conversely, a neglected engine, or one which has not been broken in properly, may require an overhaul very early in its life.

3   Exhaust smoke and excessive oil consumption are both indications that piston rings and/or valve guides are in need of attention. Make sure oil leaks are not responsible before deciding that the rings and guides are bad. Refer to Chapter 1 and perform a cylinder compression check to determine for certain the nature and extent of the work required.

4   If the engine is making obvious knocking or rumbling noises, the connecting rod and/or main bearings are probably at fault.

5   Loss of power, rough running, excessive valve train noise and high fuel consumption rates may also point to the need for an overhaul, especially if they are all present at the same time. If a complete tune-up does not remedy the situation, major mechanical work is the only solution.

6   An engine overhaul generally involves restoring the internal parts to the specifications of a new engine. During an overhaul the piston rings are replaced and the cylinder walls are bored and/or honed. If a rebore is done, then new pistons are also required. The main and connecting rod bearings are generally replaced with new ones and, if necessary, the crankshaft is also replaced. Generally the valves are serviced as well, since they are usually in less than perfect condition at this point. While the engine is being overhauled, other components such as the carburetors and the starter motor can be rebuilt also. The end result should be a like-new engine that will give as many trouble free miles as the original.

7   Before beginning the engine overhaul, read through all of the related procedures to familiarize yourself with the scope and requirements of the job. Overhauling an engine is not all that difficult, but it is time consuming. Plan on the motorcycle being tied up for a minimum of two weeks. Check on the availability of parts and make sure that any necessary special tools, equipment and supplies are obtained in advance.

8   Most work can be done with typical shop hand tools, although a number of precision measuring tools are required for inspecting parts to determine if they must be replaced. Often a dealer service department or motorcycle repair shop will handle the inspection of parts and offer advice concerning reconditioning and replacement. As a general rule, time is the primary cost of an overhaul so it doesn't pay to install worn or substandard parts.

9   As a final note, to ensure maximum life and minimum trouble from a rebuilt engine, everything must be assembled with care in a spotlessly clean environment.

5   Engine - removal and installation

Note: *Engine removal and installation should be done with the aid of an assistant to avoid damage or injury that could occur if the engine is dropped. A hydraulic floor jack should be used to support and lower the engine if possible (they can be rented at low cost).*

Removal

Refer to illustrations 5.12, 5.23a, 5.23b, 5.24a and 5.24b

1   Support the bike securely so it can't be knocked over during this procedure. Place a support under the swingarm pivot and be sure the motorcycle is safely braced.

2   Drain the engine oil and remove the oil filter (see Chapter 1).

3   Drain the coolant (see Chapter 1).

5.12 Drive chain sprocket bolts (left arrows) and gearshift linkage pinch bolt (right arrow)

5.23a To detach the front of the engine from the frame, remove these nuts and bolts (arrows) from the right side . . .

4   Remove the seat and side covers (see Chapter 8).
5   Disconnect the cable from the negative battery terminal (see Chapter 9).
6   Remove the fuel tank (see Chapter 4).
7   Remove the air cleaner housing cover and the filter element (see Chapter 1).
8   Remove the air cleaner chamber and the carburetors (see Chapter 4).
9   Disconnect all four spark plug caps and set the spark plug leads aside.
10   Remove the exhaust pipe protectors and the exhaust pipes (see Chapter 4).
11   Remove the left rear engine cover (see Chapter 7).
12   Detach the gearshift arm from the gearshift spindle **(see illustration)**.
13   Remove the countershaft sprocket and remove the drive chain (see Chapter 7).
14   Disconnect the electrical leads from the oil pressure and neutral switches (see Chapter 9). Detach the switch leads from all clamps on the engine and frame and set the leads safely aside.
15   Disconnect the starter motor cable and ground cable from the starter motor (see Chapter 9).
16   Detach the clutch cable bracket from the engine and disconnect the cable from the clutch lifter arm (see Section 17).
17   Detach the right footpeg, footpeg bracket and brake pedal from the frame (see Chapter 8). Disconnect and remove the middle brake

rod (see Chapter 7).
18   Disconnect the electrical connector for the ignition pulse generator(s) (see Chapter 5) and detach the wire harness from the engine and frame.
19   Disconnect the electrical connector for the alternator (see Chapter 9) and detach the wire harness from the engine and frame.
20   Disconnect and remove the coolant hoses between the radiator and the water pump, and the hoses between the thermostat and the cylinder heads (see Chapter 3).
21   Place a floor jack or a special motorcycle lift beneath the engine. Be sure to place a block of wood between the jack and the engine to protect the aluminum crankcase.
22   On 1988 and 1989 and 1991 through 1996 VT600 models, remove the rear wheel (see Chapter 7) and the swingarm (see Chapter 6).
23   Remove the nuts and bolts from the upper and lower front engine mounting brackets **(see illustrations)** and remove the upper and lower front engine mounting brackets.
24   Remove the nut and bolt that attaches the rear engine mounting bracket to the frame and remove the two bolts that attach the rear mounting bracket to the engine **(see illustrations)** and remove the rear mounting bracket.
25   On 1997 and later VT600 and 1998 and later VT750 models, remove the swingarm pivot cap and remove the swingarm pivot nut, locknut, pivot bolt and collars (see Chapter 6).
26   Remove the engine from the right side of the frame. Protect the frame rails from scratches with duct tape.

5.23b . . . and this bolt (arrow) from the left side

5.24a To detach the rear of the engine from the frame, remove this bolt (arrow) and nut (not visible) . . .

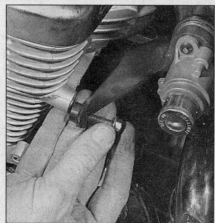

5.24b . . . remove these two bolts (one bolt hidden) and the rear mounting bracket

6.2a A selection of brushes is required for cleaning holes and passages in the engine components

6.2b Type HPG-1 Plastigage is needed to check the connecting rod oil clearances

6.3 An engine stand can be made from short lengths of lumber and lag bolts or nails

Installation

27   Installation is the reverse of removal. Note the following points:

a) *Don't tighten any of the engine mounting bracket nuts and bolts until all of them have been installed.*

b) *Use new gaskets at all exhaust pipe connections.*

c) *Tighten the engine mounting bracket nuts and bolts securely.*

d) *Adjust the rear brake pedal height and freeplay, adjust the clutch cable freeplay and adjust the throttle cable freeplay (see Chapter 1).*

e) *Be sure to add engine oil and coolant (see Chapter 1) before starting the engine.*

6   Engine disassembly and reassembly - general information

Refer to illustrations 6.2a, 6.2b and 6.3

1   Before disassembling the engine, clean the exterior with a degreaser and rinse it with water. A clean engine will make the job easier and prevent the possibility of getting dirt into the internal areas of the engine.

2   In addition to the precision measuring tools mentioned earlier, you will need a torque wrench, a valve spring compressor, oil gallery brushes, a piston ring removal and installation tool, a piston ring compressor and a clutch holder tool (which is described in Section 16). Some new, clean engine oil of the correct grade and type, some engine assembly lube or moly-based grease, and a tube of RTV (silicone) sealant will also be required. Plastigage (type HPG-1) should be used for checking bearing oil clearances **(see illustrations)**.

7.7 Detach the breather hose (arrow) from the cylinder head cover (VT600 models)

3   An engine support stand made from short lengths of lumber bolted together will facilitate the disassembly and reassembly procedures **(see illustration)**. The perimeter of the mount should be just big enough to accommodate the crankcase when it's laid on its side for removal of the crankshaft and transmission components. If you have an automotive-type engine stand, an adapter plate can be made from a piece of plate, some angle iron and some nuts and bolts. The adapter plate can be attached to the engine mounting bolt holes.

4   When disassembling the engine, keep "mated" parts together (including gears, cylinders, pistons, etc.) that have been in contact with each other during engine operation. These "mated" parts must be reused or replaced as an assembly.

5   Engine/transmission disassembly should be done in the following general order with reference to the appropriate Sections.

Remove the cylinder head covers
Remove the rocker arm assemblies
Remove the camshafts and timing chain sprockets
Remove the cylinder heads
Remove the timing chain tensioners
Remove the cylinders
Remove the pistons
Remove the flywheel and starter clutch assembly
Remove the clutch assembly
Remove the primary drive gear
Remove the external gearshift mechanism
Separate the crankcase halves
Remove the crankshaft and connecting rods
Remove the shift drum and forks
Remove the transmission shafts and gears
Remove the oil pump

6   Reassembly is accomplished by reversing the general disassembly sequence.

7   Cylinder head cover - removal and installation

1   Drain the coolant (see Chapter 1).

2   Remove the fuel tank (see Chapter 4).

3   Remove the steering head covers (see Chapter 8).

4   Remove the air cleaner housing cover and filter element (see Chapter 1).

5   Remove the air cleaner chamber and the carburetors (see Chapter 4).

6   Detach the spark plug caps from the spark plugs (see Chapter 1) and set the high tension leads aside.

VT600 models

Refer to illustrations 7.7, 7.8, 7.9a and 7.9b

7   Detach the breather hose from the front or rear cylinder head

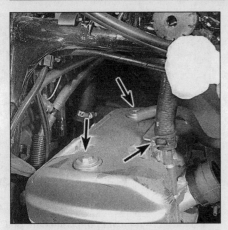

7.8 Remove the coolant hose and cylinder head cover bolts (arrows) (VT600 models)

7.9a To detach a coolant pipe from the cylinder head, remove the hold-down bolt (arrow) . . .

7.9b . . . and pull the pipe straight up (engine removed for clarity) (VT600 models)

cover **(see illustration)**.

8 Detach the coolant hose from the cylinder head **(see illustration)**.

9 Remove the coolant pipe **(see illustrations)**.

10 If you're removing the rear cylinder head cover on a 1995 or later model, remove the exhaust valve adjusting cover (see Section 17 in Chapter 1).

11 If you're removing the rear cylinder head cover on a pre-1995 model, unclamp the wiring harness above the cover and push it aside

to provide sufficient clearance for cover removal. If you're removing the rear cover on a 1995 or later model, align the wire harness above the cover with the valve adjustment hole.

VT750 models

Refer to illustrations 7.14a and 7.14b

12 If you're removing the front cylinder head cover, remove the sub-air cleaner housing (see Chapter 4); if you're removing the rear cylinder head cover, remove the three breather cover bolts and remove the breather cover.

13 Remove the two cylinder head cover outer cover bolts and remove the outer cover. If you're removing the outer cover from the rear cylinder head cover, don't lose the cable guide attached to the right bolt.

14 Remove the cylinder fins from both sides of the cylinder head **(see illustrations)**.

15 If you're removing the front cylinder head cover, remove the thermostat housing mounting bolt (see Chapter 3) and push the thermostat housing up to provide clearance.

All models

Refer to illustrations 7.16a and 7.16b

16 Remove the cylinder head cover bolts **(see illustration 7.8)**. Remove the cylinder head cover and gasket **(see illustration)**. If the cover sticks, gently pry it loose at the prying points **(see illustration)**. **Caution:** *Do NOT pry the cylinder head cover anywhere except the prying points or you may damage the cover, the head or the gasket. Once the cover has been removed, don't drop anything into the cam*

7.14a On VT750 models, the cylinder fins are attached to the cylinder head by four Allen bolts per side, two inner bolts (arrows) (left side of cylinders shown) . . .

7.14b . . . and two outer bolts (arrows) (right side of rear cylinder shown)

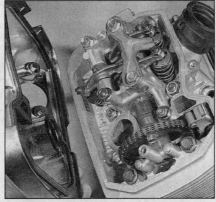

7.16a Try simply lifting the cylinder head cover from the head with your hands (VT600 shown)

7.16b If the cover is stuck to the head, carefully pry it loose at one of the prying points (arrow); the F or R mark indicates front or rear cylinder head

8.4a There are two wedges (arrow) at the upper end of the cam chain tensioner: the thinner wedge is next to the head, the thicker one is nearer the cam chain

8.4b To determine whether the cam chain should be replaced, measure how far the thick wedge projects above the top of the chain tensioner

8.5a Before removing the camshaft, pull up the thin wedge . . .

chain tunnel (the opening below the camshaft sprocket). If you do, it might end up in the crankcase and you might have to split the cases to get it out! Stuff clean shop towels into the cam chain tunnel so nothing accidentally falls into the engine.

17   Pull the old gasket out of its groove in the cylinder head cover and discard it. Clean out the gasket groove, apply a thin coat of Honda Bond A, or a similar contact cement, and install the new gasket into the groove. Apply a thin coat of sealant to the gasket.

18   Separate the rubber grommets from the cylinder head cover bolts and washers and inspect the grommets. Replace them if they're dried out, cracked or torn, or otherwise damaged.

19   Install the cylinder head cover. Make *sure* that the gasket is not pinched, kinked or otherwise distorted. If it is, the cylinder head cover will leak. Install the cylinder head cover bolts and washers and tighten the bolts to the torque listed in this Chapter's Specifications.

20   The remainder of installation is the reverse of removal.

8   Camshaft, sprocket and rocker arms - removal, inspection and installation

Note: *The following procedure applies to the front and rear camshaft and rocker arm assemblies.*

Removal

Refer to illustrations 8.4a, 8.4b, 8.5a, 8.5b, 8.6a, 8.6b, 8.8a, 8.8b, 8.8c, 8.9a and 8.9b

1   Remove the cylinder head cover (see Section 7).

2   Remove the crankshaft hole cap and the timing hole cap (see Section 17 in Chapter 1).

3   Rotate the crankshaft counterclockwise with a socket until the FT mark on the flywheel is aligned with the index mark on the left crankcase cover. This places the front piston at top dead center (TDC) *on its compression stroke.* To verify that the front piston is at TDC on its compression stroke, wiggle the tip of each rocker arm. If the front piston *is* at TDC on its compression stroke, the valves are fully closed, so the rocker arms are not pushing against the valves, so they should feel a little loose. If the front piston is not at TDC on its compression stroke, rotate the crankshaft counterclockwise another 360 degrees and re-align the FT mark on the flywheel with the index mark on the left crankcase cover.

4   Before proceeding, determine cam chain wear as follows. There are two wedges, one behind the other, at the upper end of the cam chain tensioner: a thicker wedge adjacent to the chain and a thinner wedge next to the head **(see illustration)**. To determine whether the cam chain should be replaced, measure the height that the wedge near the chain projects above the top of the tensioner **(see illustration)** and compare your measurement to the maximum allowable height listed in this Chapter's Specifications. If the indicated height exceeds the specified maximum height, replace the cam chain (see Section 21).

5   Holding down the thicker cam chain tensioner wedge with a screwdriver, pull up the thinner cam chain tensioner wedge with a pair of pliers **(see illustrations)** and insert a paper clip through the hole in the thinner wedge to keep it up **(see illustration)**.

6   Remove the bolts from the camshaft end holder (the smaller holder at the sprocket end of the cam), remove the end holder and remove the dowel pins **(see illustrations)**. Put the dowel pins in a plastic bag so you don't misplace them.

7   Remove the camshaft sprocket bolts **(see illustration 8.6b)**. After removing the first bolt, rotate the crankshaft 360 degrees to access the

8.5b . . . and insert a paper clip through the hole in the wedge to keep it up

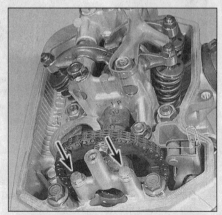

8.6a Remove the camshaft end holder bolts (arrows) . . .

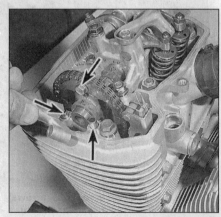

8.6b . . . then remove the end holder and dowel pins (arrows)

8.8a Remove the nut and three bolts (arrows), remove the oil guide plate . . .

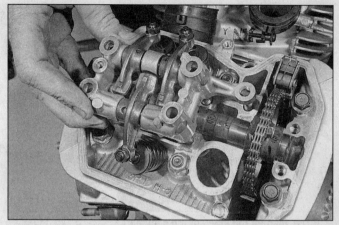

8.8b . . . remove the camshaft holder/rocker arm assembly . . .

8.8c . . . and remove the dowel pins (arrows)

8.9a Remove the camshaft . . .

other bolt (the camshaft will rotate 1/2 turn for each full turn of the crankshaft).

8　Remove the camshaft holder bolts and nut, the oil guide plate, the camshaft holder and the dowel pins **(see illustrations)**.

9　Remove the camshaft and the camshaft sprocket **(see illustrations)**. Secure the cam chain with a piece of wire or string to prevent it from falling into the crankcase. **Caution:** *Do NOT rotate the crankshaft while either or both camshafts are removed.*

Inspection

Camshaft

Refer to illustrations 8.10, 8.12a, 8.12b, 8.14, 8.16a and 8.16b

Note: *Before replacing camshafts because of damage, check with local machine shops specializing in motorcycle engine work. A machine shop might be able to weld, regrind and harden the cam lobes for less than the price of a new camshaft.*

10　Inspect the cam bearing surfaces in the camshaft holder, the cam end holder and the cylinder head **(see illustration)**. Look for signs of

8.9b . . . and remove the camshaft sprocket

8.10 Inspect the camshaft bearing surfaces (arrows) in the cylinder head (and their corresponding upper surfaces in the camshaft holder and end holder) for signs of scoring or spalling

8.12a Inspect the lobes of the camshaft for wear; here's a good example of damage that will require replacement or repair of the camshaft

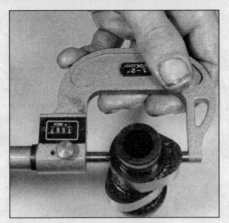

8.12b Measure the height of the cam lobes with a micrometer

8.14 Lay a strip of Plastigage along each camshaft journal, parallel with the centerline but not across an oil hole

scoring (scratches or grooves in the bearing surfaces) and spalling (a pitted appearance), both of which are usually caused by dirty or insufficient oil. If either holder is damaged or worn, replace it; if the cylinder head is worn or damaged, replace it (see Section 10).

11   Support the camshaft on V-blocks and measure the camshaft runout with a dial indicator and compare your measurement to the runout listed in this Chapter's Specifications.

12   Check the camshaft lobes for heat discoloration (blue appearance), score marks, chipped areas, flat spots and spalling **(see illustration)**. Measure the height of each lobe with a micrometer **(see illustration)** and compare the results to the minimum lobe height listed in this Chapter's Specifications. If damage is noted or wear is excessive, replace the camshaft.

13   Measure the camshaft bearing oil clearances. Clean the camshaft, the bearing surfaces in the cylinder head, and the cam holder and end holder, with a clean lint-free cloth, then lay the cam in place in the cylinder head. Secure the cam by installing the cam sprocket and chain so the camshaft doesn't turn as the holder nut and bolts are tightened.

14   Cut strips of Plastigage (type HPG-1) and lay one piece on each bearing journal, parallel with the camshaft centerline **(see illustration)**. Make sure that no oil hole in any journal is facing up; if Plastigage is laid across an oil hole, it will not produce an accurate representation of the actual clearance. Install the cam holder and the end holder in their proper positions and install the nut and bolts. Tighten the nut and bolts evenly in a criss-cross pattern until the specified torque is reached. While doing this, don't let the camshaft rotate.

15   Now unscrew the nut and bolts a little at a time, and carefully lift

off the cam holder and end holder.

16   To determine the oil clearance, compare the crushed Plastigage (at its widest point) on each journal to the scale printed on the Plastigage container **(see illustration)**. Compare the results to this Chapter's Specifications. If the oil clearance is greater than specified, measure the diameter of the cam bearing journal with a micrometer **(see illustration)**. If the journal diameter is less than the specified limit, replace the camshaft and recheck the clearance. If the clearance is still excessive, replace the cylinder head and holders.

17   Inspect the visible portion of the cam chain for obvious wear or damage. Except in cases of oil starvation, the chain wears very little. If the chain has stretched excessively, the tensioner cannot maintain correct chain tension; replace the chain (see Section 21).

18   Inspect the cam sprocket for wear, cracks and other damage. If any damage or wear is evident, replace the sprocket. If the sprocket is severely worn, the cam chain is probably worn too (see Section 21).

19   Using a flashlight, inspect the condition of the cam chain tensioner and the cam chain guide. If either of them looks worn or damaged, remove it for a better look (tensioner, see Section 9; guide, see Section 13).

Camshaft holder/rocker arm assembly

Refer to illustrations 8.20 and 8.23

20   To disassemble the camshaft holder/rocker arm assembly, tap the rocker arm shafts with a soft hammer, separate the shafts from the holders, and remove the rocker arms and wave washers from the shafts **(see illustration)**. Note the location of the wave washers on the shafts; they must be reassembled in this exact order.

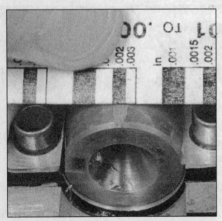

8.16a To calculate the clearance, compare the width of the crushed Plastigage to the scale printed on the Plastigage container

8.16b If cam journal diameter is less than the specified minimum, replace the camshaft

8.20 To disassemble the camshaft holder/rocker arm assembly, tap out the rocker shafts (arrows) with a soft hammer

8.23 Camshaft holder/rocker arm assembly details

1	Camshaft holder	6	Intake rocker arm
2	Intake rocker arm shaft	7	Exhaust rocker arm shaft
3	Intake rocker arm	8	Exhaust rocker arm
4	Wave washer	9	Wave washer
5	Wave washer		

21   Clean the rocker arm components with solvent and dry them off. Blow through the oil passages in the rocker arms with compressed air. Inspect the rocker arm slipper faces (the friction surfaces that ride on the cam lobes) for pits, spalling, score marks and rough spots. Check the rocker arm-to-shaft contact areas and the adjusting screws. Look for cracks in each rocker arm. If the slipper faces are damaged, the rocker arms and the shafts should be replaced as a set. If the slipper faces are worn or damaged, look closely at the corresponding cam lobes; they're probably also worn and they may be damaged.

22   Measure the inside diameter of each rocker arm, then measure the diameter of the rocker arm shafts in the area where each rocker arm rides. Calculate the difference between the inside diameter of each rocker arm and the diameter of the shaft where it rides. The difference is the oil clearance. Compare your measurements with the oil clearance listed in this Chapter's Specifications. If the clearance is beyond the specified limits, replace the rocker arms and shafts as a set.

23   Apply a coat of molybdenum disulfide oil to the rocker arm shafts and install the rocker arm shafts, rocker arms and wave washers in the camshaft holder. Don't mix up the rocker arms: The exhaust rocker arm has a larger slipper face than the intake rocker arms. Don't switch the two rocker arm shafts; they're not interchangeable. The intake

8.26 The front and rear camshafts are identified by an "F" (shown) or "R"; the notch above the F or R indicates TDC when it's upward

rocker shaft has a hole in each end for the cam holder bolts; the exhaust rocker shaft has notches, instead of holes, for the holder bolts **(see illustration)**. The washers for the intake rocker arms go between the rocker arms and the middle boss of the camshaft holder; the washer for the exhaust rocker goes between the right side of the rocker (with the exhaust rocker arm and shaft facing toward you) and the right holder boss (which is marked by a D.) Position the grooves in the rocker arm shafts vertically to align the holes in the intake rocker shaft and the notches in the exhaust rocker shaft (*look* through the bolt holes in the holder to verify that the notches on the exhaust shaft are aligned; if they aren't, rotate the exhaust shaft 180 degrees).

Valve timing and camshaft installation

24   Remove the crankshaft and timing hole caps.

Valve timing

Both camshafts removed
Refer to illustration 8.26

25   If both camshafts were removed, install the front cylinder camshaft first.

26   The camshafts are not interchangeable. Look for the "F" (front cylinder camshaft) or "R" (rear cylinder cam) on the sprocket end of each cam **(see illustration)**. The index notch on the camshaft (right above the F or R) indicates TDC.

27   Turn the crankshaft counterclockwise, align the FT mark on the flywheel with the index mark on the crankcase cover (see Section 17 in Chapter 1) and verify that the front cylinder piston is at TDC.

28   Install the front cylinder camshaft (go to Step 43).

29   Turn the crankshaft counterclockwise 232 degrees and align the RT mark on the flywheel with the index mark on the crankcase cover (see Section 17 in Chapter 1).

30   Install the rear cylinder camshaft (go to Step 43).

Rear camshaft only removed

31   If the rear cylinder camshaft was removed, but the front cam wasn't, remove the front cylinder head cover (see Section 7) and verify that the front cylinder camshaft is correctly positioned as follows. The front cylinder camshaft will be used as a reference for correct installation of the rear cylinder camshaft.

32   Remove the front cylinder camshaft end holder (see Step 6).

33   Turn the crankshaft counterclockwise, align the FT mark on the flywheel with the index mark on the crankcase cover (see Section 17 in Chapter 1) and verify that the camshaft TDC mark is facing up **(see illustration 8.26)**.

34   If the TDC mark is facing up, turn the crankshaft counterclockwise 232 degrees and align the RT mark on the flywheel with the index mark on the crankcase cover.

35   If the TDC mark is facing down, turn the crankshaft counterclockwise 592 degrees (360 degrees + 232 degrees) and align the RT mark on the flywheel with the index mark on the crankcase cover.

36   Install the rear cylinder camshaft (go to Step 43).

Front camshaft only removed

37   If the front cylinder camshaft was removed, but the rear cam wasn't, remove the rear cylinder head cover (see Section 7). Verify that the rear cylinder camshaft is correctly positioned as follows. The rear cylinder camshaft will be used as a reference for correct installation of the front cylinder camshaft.

38   Remove the front cylinder camshaft end holder (see Step 6).

39   Turn the crankshaft counterclockwise, align the RT mark on the flywheel with the index mark on the crankcase cover (see Section 17 in Chapter 1) and verify that the camshaft TDC mark is facing up **(see illustration 8.26)**.

40   If the TDC mark is facing up, turn the crankshaft counterclockwise 488 degrees (360 degrees + 128 degrees) and align the FT mark on the flywheel with the index mark on the crankcase cover.

41   If the TDC mark is facing down, turn the crankshaft counterclockwise 128 degrees and align the FT mark on the flywheel with the index mark on the crankcase cover.

42   Install the camshaft (go to Step 43).

8.43 Install the camshaft sprocket with the "IN" facing toward the valve springs and the timing marks (arrows) aligned with the gasket mating surface

8.45 Make sure the timing marks on the sprocket are still aligned with the gasket mating surface after bolting the sprocket to the camshaft

Camshaft installation

Refer to illustrations 8.43 and 8.45

43   Place the camshaft sprocket in position with the "IN" mark **(see illustration)** facing toward the valve springs and align the timing marks on the sprocket with the gasket mating surface of the cylinder head.

44   Install the camshaft with the TDC mark facing up **(see illustration 8.26)**. Install the camshaft holder dowel pins. Lubricate each rocker arm slipper face with molybdenum oil and install the camshaft holder/rocker arm assembly. Install the oil guide plate. Install the camshaft holder bolts and nut and tighten them to the torque listed in this Chapter's Specifications.

45   Install the camshaft sprocket on the camshaft flange and verify that the timing marks are still aligned with the gasket mating surface of the head **(see illustration)**.

46   Clean the threads of the sprocket bolts, coat them with a thread-locking agent, align the holes in the cam sprocket with the holes in the camshaft sprocket flange and install the upper bolt.

47   Rotate the crankshaft counterclockwise 360 degrees and install the other sprocket bolt. Tighten the second bolt to the torque listed in this Chapter's Specifications.

48   Rotate the crankshaft counterclockwise 360 degrees and tighten the first bolt to the torque listed in this Chapter's Specifications.

49   Remove the paper clip from the cam chain tensioner. Don't drop the paper clip into the cam chain tunnel!

50   Install the dowel pins, the camshaft end holder and the end holder bolts. Tighten the end holder bolts to the torque listed in this Chapter's Specifications.

51   Adjust the valve clearances (see Chapter 1).

52   Install the cylinder head cover (see Section 7).

53   If you removed both camshafts, return to Step 29 to install the remaining camshaft.

---

9   Cam chain tensioner - removal, inspection and installation

---

Refer to illustrations 9.3, 9.4 and 9.5

Note: *The following procedure applies to the front and rear cam chain tensioners.*

1   Remove the cylinder head cover (see Section 7).

2   Remove the camshaft, sprocket and rocker arms (see Section 8).

3   Remove the cam chain tensioner mounting bolts **(see illustration)** and discard the sealing washers.

4   Remove the cam chain tensioner **(see illustration)**.

5   Clean the chain tensioner in solvent and blow dry it with compressed air. Inspect the friction surface of the tensioner **(see illustration)** for wear and damage. If the friction surface is worn or damaged, replace the tensioner.

6   Install the chain tensioner. Using new sealing washers, install the chain tensioner mounting bolts and tighten them to the torque listed in this Chapter's Specifications.

7   Install the camshaft, sprocket and rocker arms (see Section 8).

8   Install the cylinder head cover (see Section 7).

9.3 To remove the chain tensioner, remove these two bolts; discard the old sealing washers

9.4 Remove the chain tensioner from the cam chain tunnel

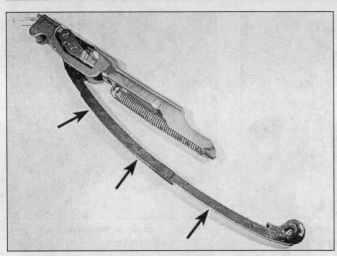

9.5 Replace the chain tensioner if the friction surface is scored or worn

10.6 To detach the cylinder head, remove these four nuts and two bolts (arrows) gradually and evenly, in a criss-cross pattern

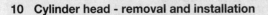

10   Cylinder head - removal and installation

Note: *The following procedure applies to the front and rear cylinder heads. However, if the rear cylinder is to be removed, the engine must be removed from the frame.*

Removal

Refer to illustrations 10.6, 10.7 and 10.8

1   Detach the exhaust pipe from the cylinder head (see Chapter 4).
2   If you are removing the rear cylinder head, remove the engine (see Section 5).
3   Remove the cylinder head cover (see Section 7).
4   Remove the camshaft, sprocket and rocker arms (see Section 8).
5   Remove the cam chain tensioner (see Section 9). Secure the chain so it can't fall into the crankcase.
6   Loosen the cylinder head nuts and bolts evenly in several stages **(see illustration)**. Remove the nuts, bolts and washers.
7   Lift the cylinder head off the studs **(see illustration)**. If it's stuck, tap it gently with a rubber or plastic mallet, being careful not to break the cooling fins. Don't pry against the gasket surfaces or they will be gouged.
8   Remove the dowel pins **(see illustration)** and the old gasket.
9   Inspect the cylinder head gasket and the mating surfaces on the cylinder head and the cylinder for leakage, which could indicate

warpage. Measure the flatness of the cylinder head (see Section 12).
10   Clean all traces of old gasket material from the cylinder head and block. Stuff clean shop rags into the cylinder bore and the cam chain tunnel to prevent gasket material from falling into the engine. Be careful not to let any debris fall into the crankcase, the cylinder bore or the oil passages.
11   Remove and inspect the cam chain guide (see Section 13).
12   Loosen the hose clamp screw and remove the carburetor insulator from the head.

Installation

13   Make sure that all old gasket material is removed from the cylinder head-to-cylinder mating surfaces.
14   Install the cam chain guide (see Section 13).
15   Install the dowel pins and the new cylinder head gasket.
16   Install the carburetor insulator on the head and tighten the hose clamp screw securely. Make sure the slot on the insulator is correctly engaged with the boss on the head. On 1991 and later California VT600 models, make sure that the pin on the outer clamp (the one nearer the carburetor) is aligned with the slot on the insulator. Tighten the clamp screws securely.
17   If you removed both cylinder heads, note the identification mark on the heads: the front cylinder head is marked with an "F" **(see illustration 10.6)** and the rear cylinder head is marked with an "R".
18   Install the cylinder head. Install the cylinder head mounting wash-

10.7 Try to remove the cylinder head with your hands; if it's stuck, tap it loose with a small plastic or rubber mallet

10.8 Remove the dowel pins (arrows) and the cylinder head gasket; if some of the gasket material sticks to the cylinder, carefully scrape it off

12.7a Compress the valve springs and remove the keepers, release the spring compressor . . .

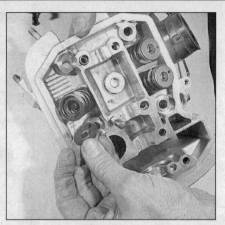

12.7b . . . remove the spring retainer and the spring(s) . . .

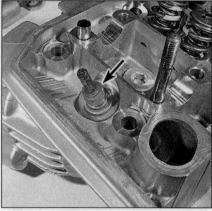

12.7c . . . push on the valve stem . . .

ers, nuts and bolts and hand tighten them. Then tighten them gradually and evenly, in a criss-cross fashion, to the torque listed in this Chapter's Specifications.

19   Install the cam chain tensioner (see Section 9).
20   Install the camshaft, sprocket and rocker arms (see Section 8).
21   Install the cylinder head cover (see Section 7).
22   Install the engine, if removed (see Section 5).
23   Install the exhaust pipe (see Chapter 4).

11 Valves/valve seats/valve guides - servicing

1   Because of the complex nature of this job and the special tools and equipment required, servicing of the valves, the valve seats and the valve guides (commonly known as a valve job) is best left to a professional.
2   The home mechanic can, however, remove and disassemble the head, do the initial cleaning and inspection, then reassemble and deliver the head to a dealer service department or properly equipped motorcycle repair shop for the actual valve servicing.
3   The dealer service department will remove the valves and springs, recondition or replace the valves and valve seats, replace the valve guides, check and, if necessary, replace the valve springs, spring retainers and keepers, install new valve seals and reassemble the valve components.
4   After the valve job has been performed, the head will be in like-new condition. When the head is returned, be sure to clean it again very thoroughly before installation on the engine to remove any metal particles or abrasive grit that may still be present from the valve service operations. Use compressed air, if available, to blow out all the holes and passages.

12 Cylinder head and valves - disassembly, inspection and reassembly

Note: *If the bearing surfaces in the cylinder head are damaged, a shop might be able to repair them. A new cylinder head is expensive, so explore your options before discarding the old head.*

1   Valve servicing and valve guide replacement should be done by a dealer service department or motorcycle repair shop (see Section 11). However, disassembly, cleaning and inspection of the cylinder head and valves can be done at home, with the right tools.
2   To disassemble the valve components safely, a valve spring compressor is absolutely necessary. If you don't own a valve spring compressor, you should be able to rent one at a local tool rental yard. If you're unable to obtain a valve spring compressor, leave the following procedure to a dealer service department or motorcycle repair shop.

Disassembly

Refer to illustrations 12.7a through 12.7e

3   Remove the cylinder head (see Section 10).
4   Before the valves are removed, scrape away any traces of gasket material from the head gasket sealing surface. Work slowly and do not nick or gouge the soft aluminum of the head. Gasket removing solvents, which work very well, are available at most motorcycle shops and auto parts stores.
5   Carefully scrape all carbon deposits out of the combustion chamber area. A hand held wire brush or a piece of fine emery cloth can be used once the majority of deposits have been scraped away. Do not use a wire brush mounted in a drill motor, or one with extremely stiff bristles, as the head material is soft and may be eroded away or scratched by the wire brush.
6   Label three plastic bags, one for each valve spring/valve assembly, so it can be installed in the same valve guide from which it's removed.
7   Compress each valve spring assembly with a spring compressor **(see illustration)** and remove the keepers. Do not compress the spring any more than is absolutely necessary. If the keepers stick to the groove in the valve stem, use a magnet or a pair of tweezers to pull them off. Carefully release the valve spring compressor and remove the retainer **(see illustration)** and the spring(s) (VT600 models have an inner and an outer spring; VT750 models use a single spring). Push on the valve stem **(see illustration)**, pull on the valve head **(see illustration)** and remove the valve from the head. If the valve binds in the guide, push it back into the head and deburr the area around the keeper groove with a very fine file or whetstone **(see illustration)**.

12.7d . . . pull on the valve head and remove the valve from the cylinder head

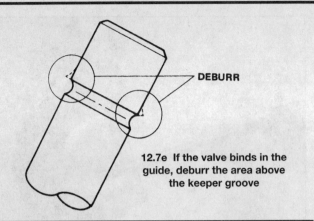

12.7e If the valve binds in the guide, deburr the area above the keeper groove

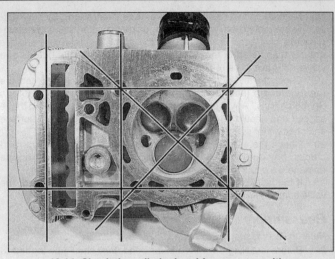

12.14 Check the cylinder head for warpage with a straightedge and feeler gauge

8   Once the valve and valve spring assembly have been removed, labeled and stored, pull off the valve stem seal and discard it (the old seals should never be reused), then remove the lower spring seat and store it with the other valve spring parts.

9   Repeat the previous two Steps for the other two valves. Be sure to keep the parts for each valve assembly in separate plastic bags so they won't be mixed up.

10   Clean the cylinder head with solvent and dry it thoroughly. Compressed air will speed the drying process and ensure that all holes and recessed areas are clean.

11   Clean all of the valve springs, keepers, retainers and spring seats with solvent and dry them thoroughly. Do one valve assembly to keep the original parts together.

12   Scrape off any deposits that may have formed on the valve, then use a motorized wire brush to remove deposits from the valve heads and stems. Again, make sure the valves do not get mixed up.

Inspection

Refer to illustrations 12.14, 12.16, 12.17, 12.18, 12.19a and 12.19b

13   Inspect the head very carefully for cracks and other damage. If cracks are found, a new head will be required. Inspect the cam bearing surfaces for wear and evidence of seizure. Check the camshaft and rocker arms for wear as well (see Section 8).

14   Using a precision straightedge and a feeler gauge, check the head gasket mating surface for warpage **(see illustration).** Lay the straightedge lengthwise, across the head and diagonally (corner-to-corner), intersecting the head bolt holes, and try to slip a feeler gauge under it, on either side of each combustion chamber. The gauge should be the same thickness as the cylinder head warp limit listed in this Chapter's Specifications. If the feeler gauge can be inserted between the head and the straightedge, the head is warped and must either be machined or, if warpage is excessive, replaced with a new

one. Minor surface imperfections can be cleaned up by sanding on a surface plate in a figure-eight pattern with 400 or 600 grit wet or dry sandpaper. Be sure to rotate the head every few strokes to avoid removing material unevenly.

15   Examine the valve seats in each of the combustion chambers. If they are pitted, cracked or burned, the head will require valve service that's beyond the scope of the home mechanic. Measure the valve seat width and compare it to the seat width listed this Chapter's Specifications. If it is not within the specified range, or if it varies around its circumference, valve service work is required.

16   Clean the valve guides to remove any carbon buildup, then measure the inside diameters of the guides (at both ends and the center of the guide) with a small hole gauge and a 0-to-1-inch micrometer **(see illustration).** Record the measurements for future reference. These measurements, along with the valve stem diameter measurements, will enable you to compute the valve stem-to-guide clearance. This clearance, when compared to the Specifications, will be one factor that will determine the extent of the valve service work required. The guides are measured at the ends and at the center to determine if they are worn in a bell-mouth pattern (more wear at the ends). If they are, guide replacement is an absolute must.

17   Carefully inspect each valve face for cracks, pits and burned spots. Check the valve stem and the keeper groove area for cracks **(see illustration).** Rotate the valve and check for any obvious indication that it is bent. Check the end of the stem for pitting and excessive wear and make sure the bevel isn't worn away. The presence of any of the above conditions indicates the need for valve servicing.

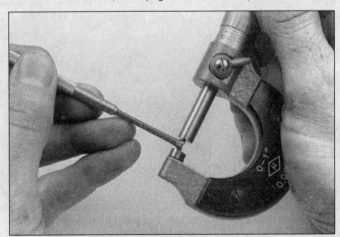

12.16 Measure the valve guide inside diameter with a small hole gauge, then measure the hole gauge with a micrometer

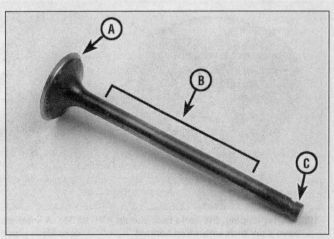

12.17 Check the valve face (A), stem (B) and keeper groove (C) for signs of wear and damage

18   Measure the valve stem diameter **(see illustration)**. By subtracting the stem diameter from the valve guide diameter, the valve stem-to-guide clearance is obtained. If the stem-to-guide clearance is greater than listed in this Chapter's Specifications, the guides and valves will have to be replaced with new ones.

19   Check the end of each valve spring for wear and pitting. Measure the free length **(see illustration)** and compare it to this Chapter's Specifications. Any springs that are shorter than specified have sagged and should not be reused. Stand the spring on a flat surface and check it for squareness **(see illustration)**.

20   Check the spring retainers and keepers for obvious wear and cracks. Any questionable parts should not be reused, as extensive damage will occur in the event of failure during engine operation.

21   If the inspection indicates that no service work is required, the valve components can be reinstalled in the head.

Reassembly

Refer to illustrations 12.23, 12.24, 12.28a and 12.28b

22   Before installing the valves in the head, they should be lapped to ensure a positive seal between the valves and seats. This procedure requires coarse and fine valve lapping compound (available at auto parts stores) and a valve lapping tool. If a lapping tool is not available, a piece of rubber or plastic hose can be slipped over the valve stem (after the valve has been installed in the guide) and used to turn the valve.

23   Apply a small amount of coarse lapping compound to the valve face **(see illustration)**, then slip the valve into the guide. **Note:** *Make sure the valve is installed in the correct guide and be careful not to get*

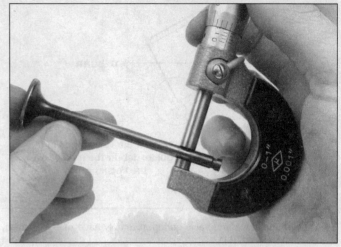

12.18 Measure the valve stem diameter with a micrometer

any lapping compound on the valve stem.

24   Attach the lapping tool (or hose) to the valve and rotate the tool between the palms of your hands. Use a back-and-forth motion rather than a circular motion. Lift the valve off the seat and turn it at regular intervals to distribute the lapping compound properly. Continue the lapping procedure until the valve face and seat contact area is of uni-

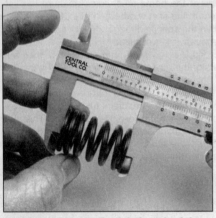

12.19a Measure the free length of the valve springs

12.19b Check the valve springs for squareness

12.23 Apply the lapping compound very sparingly, in small dabs, to the valve face only

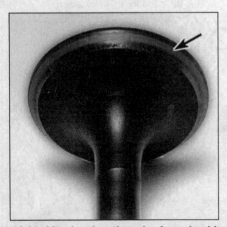

12.24 After lapping, the valve face should have a uniform, unbroken contact pattern (arrow)

12.28a A small dab of grease will hold the keepers in place on the valve while the spring is released

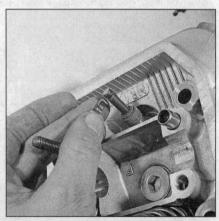

12.28b The small ridge near the top of each keeper locks the keeper into the groove in the valve stem (valve springs removed for clarity)

13.5 Remove the cam chain guide from the cam chain tunnel and inspect it for wear and damage

13.7a Make sure that the cam chain guide tabs are correctly seated in the cylinder . . .

13.7b . . . and that the lower end of the guide is correctly seated against its stop on the crankcase (front cam chain guide shown; rear similar)

form width and unbroken around the entire circumference of the valve face and seat (**see illustration**).

25   Carefully remove the valve from the guide and wipe off all traces of lapping compound. Use solvent to clean the valve and wipe the seat area thoroughly with a solvent soaked cloth.

26   Repeat the procedure with fine valve lapping compound, then repeat the entire procedure for the remaining valves.

27   Lay the spring seats in place in the cylinder head, then install new valve stem seals on each of the guides (**see illustration 12.7c**). Use an appropriate size deep socket to push the seals into place until they are properly seated. Don't twist or cock them, or they will not seal properly against the valve stems. Also, don't remove them again or they will be damaged.

28   Coat the valve stems with assembly lube or moly-based grease, then install one of them into its guide. Next, install the springs and retainers, compress the springs and install the keepers. **Note:** *Install the springs with the tightly wound coils at the bottom (next to the spring seat).* When compressing the springs with the valve spring compressor, depress them only as far as is absolutely necessary to slip the keepers into place. Apply a small amount of grease to the keepers (**see illustration**) to help hold them in place as the pressure is released from the springs. Make certain that the keeper ridges are securely locked in the retaining groove in the valve stem (**see illustration**).

29   Support the cylinder head on blocks so the valves can't contact the workbench top, then very gently tap each of the valve stems with a soft-faced hammer. This will help seat the keepers in their grooves.

30   Once all of the valves have been installed in the head, check for proper valve sealing by pouring a small amount of solvent into each of the valve ports. If the solvent leaks past the valve(s) into the combustion chamber area, disassemble the valve(s) and repeat the lapping procedure, then reinstall the valve(s) and repeat the check. Repeat the procedure until a satisfactory seal is obtained.

13 Cam chain guide - removal, inspection and installation

Refer to illustrations 13.5, 13.7a and 13.7b

Note: *The following procedure applies to the front and rear cam chain guides.*

1   Remove the cylinder head cover (see Section 7).

2   Remove the camshaft, sprocket and rocker arms (see Section 8).

3   Remove the cam chain tensioner (see Section 9).

4   Remove the cylinder head (see Section 10).

5   Remove the cam chain guide (**see illustration**).

6   Inspect the cam chain guide for wear and damage. Replace the guide if it's worn or damaged.

7   Install the guide in the cam chain tunnel. Make sure that the guide mounting tabs are correctly seated in the grooves in the cylinder (**see**

illustration) and the lower end of the guide is correctly seated against the lower guide stop in the crankcase (**see illustration**).

8   Install the cylinder head (see Section 10).

9   Install the cam chain tensioner (see Section 9).

10   Install the camshaft, sprocket and rocker arms (see Section 8).

11   Install the cylinder head cover (see Section 7).

14 Cylinder - removal, inspection and installation

Note: *The following procedure applies to the front and rear cylinders. However, the engine must be removed from the frame before the rear cylinder can be removed.*

Removal

Refer to illustrations 14.5a, 14.5b, 14.5c, 14.6, 14.7a and 14.7b

1   Remove the cylinder head cover (see Section 7).

2   Remove the camshaft, sprocket and rocker arms (see Section 8).

3   Remove the cam chain tensioner (see Section 9).

4   Remove the cylinder head (see Section 10) and the cam chain guide (see Section 13).

5   Coolant passes from the front cylinder to the rear cylinder through a pair of pipes, one on each cylinder, which are connected by a sliding collar locked into position by a pair of retaining clips (**see illustration**). Remove the retaining clips (**see illustration**) and slide the collar away from the cylinder you're removing, far enough to expose the O-ring and the end of the coolant pipe (**see illustration**).

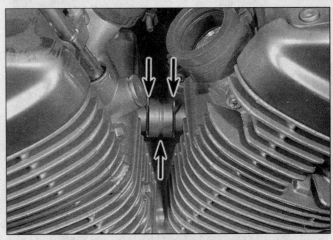

14.5a These two retaining clips (arrows) lock the coolant pipe collar (lower arrow) in position

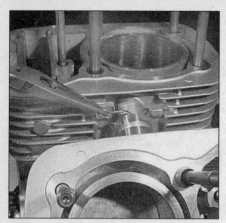

14.5b To unlock the collar, remove the two retaining clips . . .

14.5c . . . and slide the collar away from the cylinder you're removing, until the coolant pipe and O-ring are exposed

14.6 If you're removing the front cylinder, remove these two bolts (arrows) and detach the coolant hose adapter from the cylinder

6   If you're removing the front cylinder, detach the coolant hose adapter **(see illustration)**.

7   Lift the cylinder straight up to remove it **(see illustration)**. If it's stuck, tap around its perimeter with a soft-faced hammer, taking care not to break the cooling fins. Don't attempt to pry between the cylinder and the crankcase, as you will ruin the sealing surfaces. Remove the old base gasket and discard it. Note the location of the dowel pins **(see illustration)**, then remove them. Be careful not to let the dowels drop into the engine.

8   Stuff clean shop towels into the cavity beneath the piston and carefully remove all traces of old gasket material from the mating surfaces of the cylinder and crankcase. Don't allow any gasket material to fall into the crankcase.

Inspection

Refer to illustrations 14.9, 14.10 and 14.13

Note: *If the following inspection indicates that a cylinder is warped, it can be resurfaced or replaced independently of the other cylinder. However, if a rebore is indicated for either cylinder, that cylinder will require an oversize piston, so BOTH cylinders must be rebored to accept the same size pistons, in order to maintain correct balance.*

9   Measure the top of the cylinder for flatness **(see illustration)** and compare your measurements to the allowable warpage listed in this Chapter's Specifications.

10   Inspect the cylinder wall thoroughly for scratches and score marks. Using a cylinder bore gauge or a telescoping snap-gauge and

micrometer, measure the cylinder diameter. Make three pairs of measurements (six in all), parallel and perpendicular to the crankshaft axis, at the top, middle and bottom of the cylinder **(see illustration)**. First, determine cylinder bore diameter. Take the largest measurement and compare it to the cylinder bore diameter listed in this Chapter's Specifications. Next, determine whether the cylinder is round. Compare the readings in one direction to the readings in the other direction, subtract the smaller readings from the larger readings and compare any differences to the allowable out-of-round listed in this Chapter's Specifications. Finally, determine whether the cylinder is tapered. Compare the largest reading to the smallest reading in each direction, subtract the two and compare the difference to the allowable taper listed in this Chapter's Specifications. **Note:** *If you do not have access to a cylinder bore gauge or a three-inch telescoping snap-gauge and three-inch micrometer, have a dealer service department or motorcycle repair shop measure the cylinder(s).*

11   If the cylinder walls are worn, out-of-round or tapered beyond their specified limits, or badly scuffed or scored, have the cylinder rebored and honed by a dealer service department or a motorcycle repair shop. Remember, even if only one cylinder *must* be rebored, the other cylinder will also have to be rebored to the same diameter, so that both cylinders have the same oversize pistons, to maintain balance.

12   If the cylinder is in reasonably good condition and not worn beyond the limits, and if the piston-to-cylinder bore clearance (see Section 15) is still within the allowable range, then the cylinder does

14.7a Lift the cylinder straight up off the studs

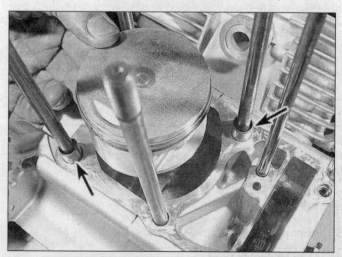

14.7b Note the locations of the dowel pins (arrows), then remove them

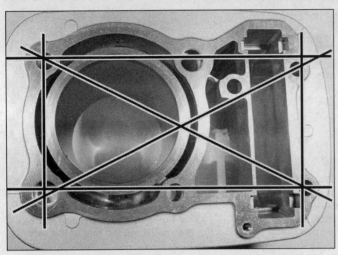

14.9 Measure the top of the cylinder for flatness in the indicated directions

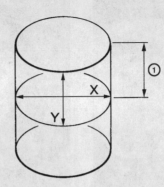

14.10 Measure the cylinder bore at the specified distance from the top of the cylinder (1); measure parallel to the crankshaft centerline, then at right angles to it

not have to be rebored; honing is all that is necessary.

13 To hone the cylinder, you will need the proper size flexible hone with fine stones, or a "bottle brush" type hone, plenty of light oil or honing oil, some shop towels and an electric drill motor. Hold the cylinder block in a vise (cushioned with soft jaws or wood blocks) when performing the honing operation. Mount the hone in the drill motor, compress the stones and slip the hone into the cylinder. Lubricate the cylinder thoroughly, turn on the drill and move the hone up and down in the cylinder at a pace which will produce a fine crosshatch pattern on the cylinder wall with the crosshatch lines intersecting at approximately a 60-degree angle (see illustration). Be sure to use plenty of lubricant and do not take off any more material than is absolutely necessary to produce the desired effect. Do not withdraw the hone from the cylinder while it is running. Instead, shut off the drill and continue moving the hone up and down in the cylinder until it comes to a complete stop, then compress the stones and withdraw the hone. Wipe the oil out of the cylinder and repeat the procedure on the remaining cylinder. Remember, do not remove too much material from the cylinder wall. If you do not have the tools, or do not desire to perform the honing operation, a dealer service department or motorcycle repair shop will generally do it for a reasonable fee.

14 Wash the cylinders thoroughly with warm soapy water to remove all traces of the abrasive grit produced during the honing operation. Be sure to run a brush through the bolt holes and flush them with running water. After rinsing, dry the cylinders thoroughly and apply a coat of light, rust-preventative oil to all machined surfaces.

14.13 Move the hone rapidly up-and-down without stopping

Installation

15 Lubricate the cylinder bore and piston with plenty of clean engine oil. If both cylinders were removed, look for the F or R mark that indicates front or rear cylinder (see illustration 7.16b).

16 Place a new cylinder base gasket on the crankcase. Make sure the two dowel pins are in position (see illustration 14.7b).

17 Attach a piston ring compressor to the piston and compress the piston rings. Or use a large hose clamp; make sure it doesn't scratch the piston and don't tighten it too much.

18 Install the cylinder over the piston and carefully lower it down until the piston crown fits into the cylinder liner. While doing this, pull the camshaft chain up, using a hooked tool or a piece of coat hanger. Also keep an eye on the cam chain guide to make sure it doesn't wedge against the cylinder. Push down on the cylinder, making sure the piston doesn't get cocked sideways, until the bottom of the cylinder liner slides down past the piston rings. A wood or plastic hammer handle can be used to gently tap the cylinder down, but don't use too much force or the piston will be damaged.

19 Remove the piston ring compressor or hose clamp, being careful not to scratch the piston.

20 Install a new O-ring on the coolant pipe, lubricate the O-ring with coolant to allow the collar to slide over it without damaging it. Position the collar in the middle (covering the O-rings of both coolant pipes) and install the retaining clips.

21 If you're installing the front cylinder, install a new O-ring in the groove inside the coolant hose adapter, install the adapter and tighten the adapter bolts securely. If the coolant hose was detached from the adapter, reattach the hose and tighten the hose clamp securely.

22 Install the cam chain guide (see Section 13).

23 Install the cylinder head (see Section 10).

24 Install the cam chain tensioner (see Section 9).

25 Install the camshaft, sprocket and rocker arms (see Section 8).

26 Install the cylinder head cover (see Section 7).

15 Piston - removal, inspection and installation

Note: The following procedure applies to the front and rear pistons.

1 The pistons are attached to the connecting rods with piston pins that are a slip fit in the pistons and rods.

2 Before removing the pistons from the rods, stuff a clean shop towel into each crankcase hole, around the connecting rods. This will prevent the circlips from falling into the crankcase if they are inadvertently dropped.

Removal

Refer to illustrations 15.3a, 15.3b, 15.4a, 15.4b, 15.4c, 15.5a and 15.5b

3 Using a sharp scribe, scratch the location of each piston (front or rear cylinder) into its crown (or use a felt pen if the piston is clean enough). Each piston should also have an IN mark on its crown; this mark faces the intake side of the cylinder when the piston is installed

15.3a The IN mark on the piston must be on the intake side of the cylinder

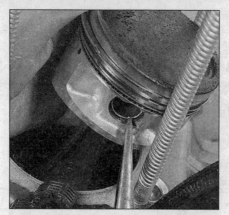

15.3b Wear eye protection when pulling out the circlips; they can pop out of the piston with sufficient force to cause an injury if they hit your eye

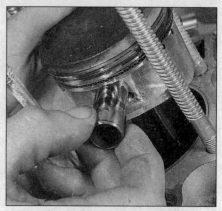

15.4a Push the piston pin partway out, then pull it out the rest of the way

(see illustration). If not, scribe an arrow into the piston crown before removal. Support the first piston, grasp the circlip with a pointed tool or needle-nose pliers **(see illustration)** and remove it from the groove.

4   Push the piston pin out from the opposite end to free the piston from the rod, then pull it out **(see illustration)**; if it's too slippery, jam a pair of snap-ring or needle-nose pliers into the pin and pull it out **(see illustration)**. You may have to deburr the area around the groove for

the circlip to allow the pin to slide out (use a triangular file for this procedure). If the pin won't come out, remove the other circlip. Fabricate a piston pin removal tool from threaded stock, nuts, washers and a piece of pipe **(see illustration)**.

5   Remove the oil jet **(see illustration)**. Pull it straight up **(see illustration)** and discard the old O-ring.

15.4b If the piston pin is slippery or difficult to pull out, insert a pair of needle nose pliers into the pin and work it out of the piston with a back-and-forth twisting motion

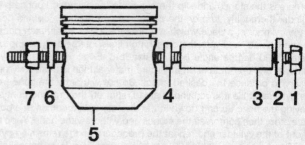

15.4c The piston pins should come out with hand pressure - if they don't, this removal tool can be fabricated from readily available parts

1)	Bolt	7)	Nut (B)
2)	Washer	A	Large enough for piston
3)	Pipe (A)		pin to fit inside
4)	Padding (A)	B	Small enough to fit
5)	Piston		through piston pin bore
6)	Washer (B)		

15.5a There's an oil jet (arrow) for each cylinder inside the crankcase

15.5b To remove an oil jet, pull it straight up; remove and discard the old O-ring and blow out the oil passage in the jet; install the jet with a new O-ring

15.6 Remove the piston rings with a ring removal and installation tool

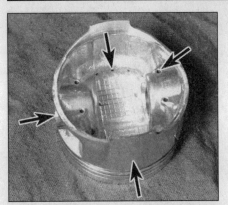

15.11 Check the piston pin bore and the piston skirt for wear, and make sure the internal holes are clear (arrows)

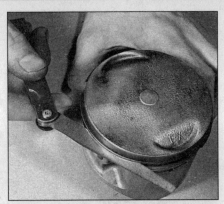

15.13 Measure ring side clearance with a feeler gauge

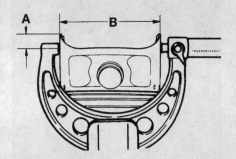

15.14 Measure the piston diameter with a micrometer

A   Specified distance from bottom of piston
B   Piston diameter

Inspection

Refer to illustrations 15.6, 15.11, 15.13, 15.14 and 15.15

6   Using a piston ring installation tool, carefully remove the rings from the pistons **(see illustration)**. Do not nick or gouge the pistons in the process.

7   Clean the piston thoroughly. Scrape all traces of carbon from the top of the piston. A hand-held wire brush or a piece of fine emery cloth can be used once most of the deposits have been scraped away. Do not, under any circumstances, use a wire brush mounted in a drill motor to remove deposits from the piston; the piston material is soft and will be eroded away by the wire brush.

8   Use a piston ring groove cleaning tool to remove any carbon deposits from the ring grooves. If a tool is not available, a piece broken off the old ring will do the job. Be very careful to remove only the carbon deposits. Do not remove any metal and do not nick or gouge the sides of the ring grooves.

9   Once the deposits have been removed, clean the pistons with solvent and dry them thoroughly. Make sure the oil return holes below the oil ring grooves are clear.

10   If the pistons are not damaged or worn excessively and if the cylinders are not rebored, new pistons will not be necessary. Normal piston wear appears as even, vertical wear on the thrust surfaces of the piston and slight looseness of the top ring in its groove. New piston rings, on the other hand, should always be used when an engine is rebuilt.

11   Carefully inspect each piston for cracks around the skirt, at the pin bosses and at the ring lands **(see illustration)**.

12   Look for scoring and scuffing on the thrust faces of the skirt, holes in the piston crown and burned areas at the edge of the crown. If the skirt is scored or scuffed, the engine may have been suffering from overheating and/or abnormal combustion, which caused excessively high operating temperatures. The oil pump should be checked thoroughly. A hole in the piston crown, an extreme to be sure, is an indication that abnormal combustion (pre-ignition) was occurring. Burned areas at the edge of the piston crown are usually evidence of spark knock (detonation). If any of the above problems exist, the causes must be corrected or the damage will occur again.

13   Measure the piston ring-to-groove clearance by laying a new piston ring in the ring groove and slipping a feeler gauge in beside it **(see illustration)**. Check the clearance at three or four locations around the groove. Be sure to use the correct ring for each groove; they are different. If the clearance is greater than specified, new pistons will have to be used when the engine is reassembled.

14   Check the piston-to-bore clearance by measuring the cylinder bore (see Section 14) and the piston diameter. Make sure that the pistons and cylinders are correctly matched. Measure the piston across the skirt on the thrust faces at a 90-degree angle to the piston pin, at the distance from the bottom of the skirt listed in this Chapter's Specifications **(see illustration)**. Subtract the piston diameter from the bore diameter to obtain the clearance. If it is greater than specified, the cylinders will have to be rebored and new oversized pistons and rings

installed. If the appropriate precision measuring tools are not available, the piston-to-cylinder clearances can be obtained, though not quite as accurately, using feeler gauge stock. Feeler gauge stock comes in 12-inch lengths and various thicknesses and is generally available at auto parts stores. To check the clearance, select a feeler gauge of the same thickness as the piston clearance listed in this Chapter's Specifications and slip it into the cylinder along with the appropriate piston. The cylinder should be upside down and the piston must be positioned exactly as it normally would be. Place the feeler gauge between the piston and cylinder on one of the thrust faces (90-degrees to the piston pin bore). The piston should slip through the cylinder (with the feeler gauge in place) with moderate pressure. If it falls through, or slides through easily, the clearance is excessive and a new piston will be required. If the piston binds at the lower end of the cylinder and is loose toward the top, the cylinder is tapered, and if tight spots are encountered as the feeler gauge is placed at different points around the cylinder, the cylinder is out-of-round. Repeat the procedure for the remaining pistons and cylinders. Be sure to have the cylinders and pistons checked by a dealer service department or a motorcycle repair shop to confirm your findings before purchasing new parts.

15   Apply clean engine oil to the pin, insert it into the piston and check for freeplay by rocking the pin back-and-forth **(see illustration)**. If the pin is loose, new pistons and pins must be installed. For a more precise assessment of piston/piston pin wear, measure the diameter of the piston pin and compare your measurement to the piston pin diameter listed in this Chapter's Specifications. Replace the pin if it's excessively worn. Next, measure the inside diameter of the piston pin holes in the piston, subtract the diameter of the piston pin and compare your measurement to the piston pin-to-piston clearance listed in this Chapter's Specifications. If the clearance exceeds the specified maximum, replace the piston and/or the piston pin (depending on whether the pin diameter is acceptable). Finally, measure the inside diameter of the small end of the connecting rod, subtract the diameter of the piston pin and compare your measurement to the piston pin-to-connecting rod clearance listed in this Chapter's Specifications. If the clearance exceeds the specified maximum, replace the piston pin and/or the connecting rod (depending on whether the pin diameter is acceptable).

16   Install the rings on the piston (see Section 16).

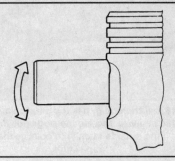

15.15 Slip the pin into the piston and try to wiggle it back-and-forth; if it's loose, replace the piston and pin

15.18a Slip the circlip into its bore with its gap away from the piston cutout . . .

15.18b . . . and push the circlip all the way into its groove; make sure it's securely seated

16.3 Measure ring end gap with a feeler gauge

Installation

Refer to illustrations 15.18a and 15.18b

17   Install a new O-ring on the oil jet and install the oil jet by pushing it firmly back into the crankcase until it's fully seated.

18   Install the piston with the IN mark pointing toward the intake side of the cylinder **(see illustration 15.3a)**. Lubricate the pins and the rod bores with clean engine oil. Install new circlips in the grooves in the inner sides of the pistons (don't reuse the old circlips). Push the pins into position from the opposite side and install new circlips. Compress the circlips only enough for them to fit in the piston. Make sure the circlips are correctly seated in the grooves **(see illustrations)**.

16 Piston rings - installation

Refer to illustrations 16.3, 16.5, 16.9a, 16.9b, 16.11a, 16.11b, 16.12 and 16.15

1   Before installing the new piston rings, the ring end gaps must be checked.

2   Lay out the pistons and the new ring sets so the rings will be matched with the same piston and cylinder during the end gap measurement procedure and engine assembly.

3   Insert the top (No. 1) ring into the bottom of the first cylinder and square it up with the cylinder walls by pushing it in with the top of the piston **(see illustration)**. The ring should be about one inch above the bottom edge of the cylinder. To measure the end gap, slip a feeler

gauge between the ends of the ring and compare the measurement to this Chapter's Specifications.

4   If the gap is larger or smaller than specified, double check to make sure that you have the correct rings before proceeding.

5   If the gap is too small, it must be enlarged or the ring ends may come in contact with each other during engine operation, which can cause serious damage. The end gap can be increased by filing the ring ends very carefully with a fine file **(see illustration)**. When performing this operation, file only from the outside in.

6   Excess end gap is not critical unless it is greater than 0.040 in. (1 mm). Again, double check to make sure you have the correct rings for your engine.

7   Repeat the procedure for each ring that will be installed in the first cylinder and for each ring in the remaining cylinder. Remember to keep the rings, pistons and cylinders matched up.

8   Once the ring end gaps have been checked/corrected, the rings can be installed on the pistons.

9   The oil control ring (lowest on the piston) is installed first. It is composed of three separate components. Slip the expander into the groove, then install the upper side rail **(see illustrations)**. Do not use a piston ring installation tool on the oil ring side rails as they may be damaged. Instead, place one end of the side rail into the groove between the spacer expander and the ring land. Hold it firmly in place and slide a finger around the piston while pushing the rail into the groove. Next, install the lower side rail in the same manner.

10   After the three oil ring components have been installed, check to make sure that both the upper and lower side rails can be turned smoothly in the ring groove.

16.5 If the end gap is too small, clamp a file in a vise and file the ring ends (from the outside in only) to enlarge the gap slightly

16.9a Install the oil ring expander first

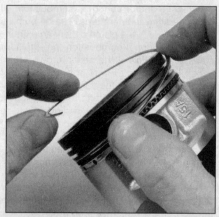

16.9b Installing an oil ring side rail - don't use a ring installation tool to do this

16.11a Install the middle ring with its identification mark up

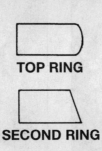

TOP RING

SECOND RING

16.11b The top and middle rings can be identified by their profiles

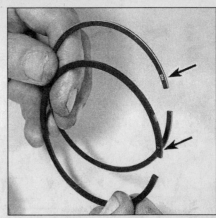

16.12 The top and middle rings have identification marks (arrows); these must be up when the rings are installed

11   Install the second (middle) ring next **(see illustration)**. Do not mix the top and middle rings. They can be identified by their profiles **(see illustration)**, as well as the fact that the top ring is thinner than the middle ring.

12   To avoid breaking the ring, use a piston ring installation tool and make sure that the identification mark is facing up **(see illustration)**. Fit the ring into the middle groove on the piston. Do not expand the ring any more than is necessary to slide it into place.

13   Finally, install the top ring in the same manner. Make sure the

identifying mark is facing up.

14   Repeat the procedure for the remaining piston and rings. Be very careful not to confuse the top and second rings.

15   Once the rings have been properly installed, stagger the end gaps, including those of the oil ring side rails **(see illustration)**.

17 Clutch cable - replacement

Refer to illustrations 17.1, 17.2 and 17.3

1   Push the clutch lifter arm forward and disengage the clutch cable from the lifter arm clevis **(see illustration)**. **Note:** *If necessary, pry open the lifter arm gap slightly with a screwdriver so the cable can pass through it.*

2   Loosen the locknut and adjustment nut **(see illustration)** and disengage the cable from the bracket on the engine.

3   Up at the handlebars, pull back the cable rubber dust boot, back off the locknut and adjuster **(see illustration)** and disengage the cable from the clutch lever.

4   Note the routing of the cable and remove it.

5   Installation is the reverse of removal. Make sure the cable is routed correctly, with no kinks.

6   Adjust the clutch cable freeplay (see Chapter 1).

16.15 Arrange the ring gaps like this

1)   Top compression ring
2)   Oil ring lower rail
3)   Oil ring upper rail
4)   Second compression ring

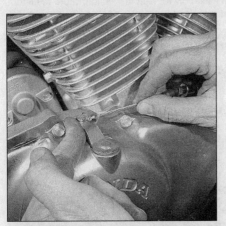

17.1 Push the clutch lifter arm forward and disengage the clutch cable; widen the gap if necessary with a screwdriver

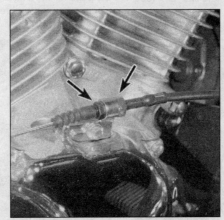

17.2 Loosen the cable locknut and adjuster nut (arrows) and disengage the clutch cable from the bracket

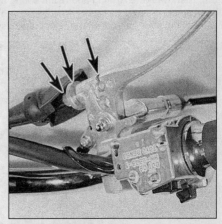

17.3 Peel back the dust boot, back off the locknut (middle arrow), turn the adjuster (left arrow) all the way in (toward the lever), align the slots in the adjuster and locknut with the cable, pull out the cable and disengage the cable plug from the slot in the lever

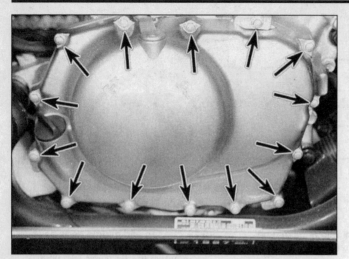

18.4a To separate the right crankcase cover from the engine, loosen the bolts (arrows), 1/4-turn at a time, in a criss-cross pattern; one upper bolt secures the bracket for the clutch cable

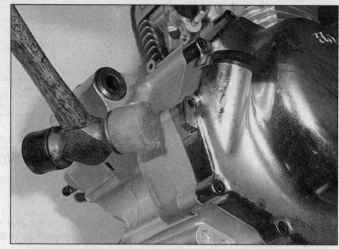

18.4b If the clutch cover sticks to the crankcase, carefully tap it loose at the bosses provided for that purpose; don't pry on the crankcase cover or you will damage the gasket mating surface

18 Clutch - removal, inspection and installation

Removal

Refer to illustrations 18.4a, 18.4b, 18.4c, 18.5a, 18.5b, 18.7, 18.8, 18.9a, 18.9b, 18.10, 18.11, 18.12a, 18.12b, 18.13, 18.14a, 18.14b, 18.14c, 18.15a, 18.15b and 18.17

1   Drain the engine oil (see Chapter 1).

2   Disengage the clutch cable from the clutch lifter arm (see Section 17).

3   On 1988 and 1989 VT600 models, remove the oil pipe bracket and remove the oil pipe banjo bolt and sealing washers from the right crankcase cover.

4   Loosen the right crankcase cover bolts **(see illustration)**. Once they're all loose, remove the bolts and take off the cover. If the cover is stuck, gently tap on one or more of the cover bosses provided for this purpose **(see illustration)**. Don't pry on the cover; prying will damage the gasket surface. Remove the dowel pins **(see illustration)** and store them in a plastic bag. Remove the old gasket and discard it. Carefully remove any gasket material that's stuck to the crankcase or the cover.

5   Remove the clutch lifter piece from the lifter arm **(see illustration)**. Remove the snap-ring and return spring from the lifter arm **(see illustration)**.

6   Pull the lifter arm out of the right crankcase cover and set aside

18.4c Right crankcase dowel pin location

the parts for the lifter arm assembly for later inspection. Store the lifter piece, snap-ring and return spring in a plastic bag so you don't misplace them.

18.5a Remove the clutch lifter piece from the lifter arm

18.5b Remove the snap-ring and return spring (arrow) from the lifter arm

18.7 Place a penny between the gear teeth of the clutch housing and the primary drive gear, then loosen the primary drive gear bolt and the oil pump driven sprocket bolt (arrow)

18.8 Remove the pressure plate bolts (arrows), gradually and evenly, in a criss-cross pattern

18.9a Remove the pressure plate and bearing . . .

18.9b . . . and remove the four clutch springs (arrows)

18.10 Unstake the clutch center locknut

18.11 To loosen the clutch center locknut, immobilize the center with the special Honda tool or a strap wrench

7   If you're planning to remove the oil pump drive chain and sprockets (see Section 19) and/or the primary drive gear (see Section 20), put a penny between the clutch housing gear teeth and the primary drive gear teeth and loosen the primary drive gear bolt and/or the oil pump driven sprocket bolt **(see illustration)**.

8   Remove the clutch lifter plate bolts **(see illustration)**, gradually and evenly, in a crisscross pattern.

9   Remove the clutch lifter plate/bearing and the clutch springs **(see illustrations)**.

10   Unstake the clutch center locknut **(see illustration)**.

11   Using the factory clutch center holder tool or equivalent **(see illustration)**, loosen the clutch center locknut.

12   Remove the clutch center locknut and the spring washer **(see illustrations)**. Discard the old locknut and washer.

13   Remove the clutch center **(see illustration)**.

14   Before disassembling the clutch pack, take a moment to study how it's assembled **(see illustration)**. First, note that the tabs of the

18.12a Remove the clutch center locknut and lockwasher (arrow); the OUT SIDE mark faces outward on installation. . .

18.12b . . . and remove the backup washer (if equipped)

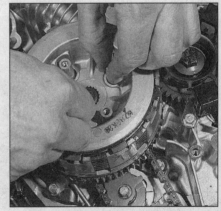

18.13 Remove the pressure plate

18.14a Remove the outer friction disc, judder spring and spring seat (the two narrow metal rings installed concentric with the outer friction disc) . . .

18.14b . . . remove the first metal plate . . .

18.14c . . . then alternately, the remaining friction discs and metal plates

18.15a Remove the washer . . .

18.15b . . . and the clutch housing

outer friction disc are not aligned with the tabs of the other friction discs, but are instead seated in their own cutouts in the clutch housing. Also note that the spring seat and judder spring fit within this outer friction disc, which has a slightly larger diameter than the other friction discs. (This outer friction disc is identified as friction disc "B" in the Specifications.) Remove the outer friction disc, the spring seat and the judder spring. Note that the concave face of the judder spring faces out, toward the spring seat and the clutch center. After removing the outer friction disc, the spring seat and the judder spring, you'll see the first steel plate **(see illustration)**. After removing this steel plate, you'll see the first friction disc **(see illustration)**. Remove all the steel plates

and all the friction discs. On VT600 models, there are six steel plates and six friction discs (not counting the outer friction disc described above); on VT750 models, there are eight steel plates and seven friction discs (not counting the outer friction disc).

15   Remove the clutch housing washer and the clutch housing **(see illustrations)**.

16   Remove and inspect the oil pump drive chain and sprockets (see Section 19).

17   Remove the clutch housing guide **(see illustration)** from the mainshaft.

18   Remove and inspect the primary drive gear (see Section 20).

18.17 Remove the clutch housing guide

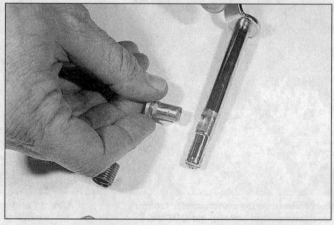

18.19 The clutch lifter piece fits in this notch in the lifter arm

18.20 Inspect the lifter arm seal for cracks, tears and excessive wear; if it's worn or damaged, pry it out with a screwdriver and drive a new seal into place with a socket

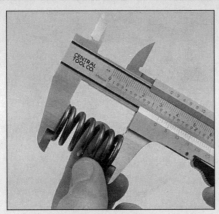

18.22 Measure the clutch spring free length

18.23 Inspect the splines on the clutch center; if any wear is evident, replace the center

Inspection

Refer to illustrations 18.19, 18.20, 18.22, 18.23, 18.24, 18.25a, 18.25b, 18.26 and 18.28

19   Inspect the lifter arm and the clutch lifter piece **(see illustration)** for damage and wear. Make sure the lifter arm isn't bent. The clutch lifter piece should slide in and out of its bore in the right crankcase cover without binding. Inspect the return spring and snap-ring for fatigue and other damage. If any part of the lifter arm assembly is damaged, replace it.

20   Inspect the lifter arm seal **(see illustration)** in the right crankcase cover. If it's cracked, torn or worn, remove it and install a new seal.

21   Inspect the lifter plate bearing for wear and damage. Turn the bearing inner race with your finger; it should turn smoothly and quietly. Make sure that the bearing outer race fits tightly into the lifter plate. If the bearing is damaged or worn, replace the lifter plate and bearing. (The bearing can be replaced separately but it's a good idea to replace the lifter plate and bearing as a set to maintain a tight fit between the two.)

22   Measure the free length of the clutch springs **(see illustration)**. Replace the springs as a set if any one of them is not within the values listed in this Chapter's Specifications.

23   Examine the inner and outer splines on the clutch center **(see illustration)**. If any wear is evident, replace the clutch center.

24   Inspect the judder spring and spring seat **(see illustration)** for distortion, wear and damage. Replace them if necessary.

25   If the lining material of the friction discs is burned or glazed,

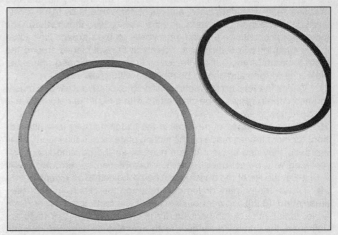

18.24 Inspect the spring seat (left) and the judder spring (right) for distortion and wear; if either of them is damaged or worn, replace it

replace the friction discs. If the metal clutch plates are scored or discolored, replace them. Measure the thickness of each friction disc **(see illustrations)** and compare your measurements to this Chapter's Specifications. If any are near the wear limit, replace the friction discs as a set.

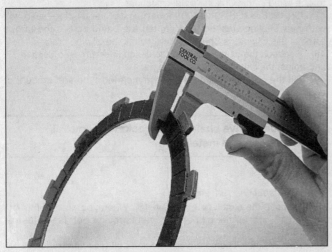

18.25a Measure the thickness of the friction discs

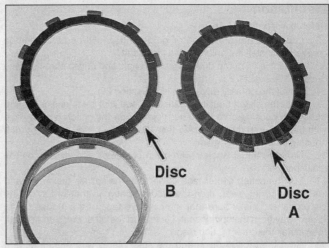

18.25b The friction disc around the judder spring (B) is narrower than the other friction discs (A)

18.26 Check the metal plates for warpage

18.28 Check for wear in the slots, driven gear teeth and center bushing or needle bearing

18.35 Be sure the teeth or pins on the oil pump drive sprocket align with the notches or holes in the clutch housing

26   Lay the metal plates, one at a time, on a perfectly flat surface (such as a piece of plate glass) and check for warpage by trying to slip a gauge between the flat surface and the plate **(see illustration)**. The feeler gauge should be the same thickness as the warpage limit listed in this Chapter's Specifications. Do this at several places around the plate's circumference. If the feeler gauge can be slipped under the plate, it is warped and should be replaced with a new one.

27   Check the tabs on the friction discs for excessive wear and mushroomed edges. They can be cleaned up with a file if the deformation is not severe.

28   Check the edges of the slots in the clutch housing **(see illustration)** for indentations made by the friction plate tabs. If the indentations are deep they can prevent clutch release, so the housing should be replaced with a new one. If the indentations can be removed easily with a file, the life of the housing can be prolonged to an extent.

29   Check the primary driven gear teeth on the clutch housing **(see illustration 18.28)** for wear or damage. If the teeth are worn or damaged, replace the clutch housing. If the primary driven gear teeth are damaged, the primary drive gear teeth may also be damaged. Inspect the primary drive gear and, if necessary, replace it (see Section 20).

30   On VT600 models, inspect the bushing in the clutch housing hub. On VT750 models, inspect the needle bearing in the clutch housing hub. If the bushing or bearing is worn or damaged, have it replaced by a dealer or by a motorcycle machine shop.

31   Measure the inside and outside diameters of the clutch outer guide and compare your measurements to the dimensions listed in this Chapter's Specifications. If the guide inside or outside diameter is worn beyond the specified limit, replace the guide.

Installation

Refer to illustration 18.35

32   Lubricate the clutch outer guide with molybdenum disulfide grease and install the guide on the mainshaft.

33   Install the oil pump drive sprocket, chain and driven sprocket (see Section 19).

34   Install the primary drive gear (see Section 20).

35   Coat the clutch housing bearing surface with clean engine oil, slip the clutch housing onto the outer guide, align the clutch housing hub with the oil pump drive sprocket **(see illustration)** and push the clutch housing onto the outer guide.

36   Coat the thrust washer with clean engine oil and install it on the mainshaft.

37   Lay the clutch center face down, with the splines facing up, and install the spring seat, then the judder spring, in that order, on the clutch center; make sure that the concave face of the judder spring faces away from the spring seat, i.e. toward the other discs and plates, then install the outer friction disc.

38   Coat the friction discs and the steel plates with engine oil and install them on the clutch center, alternating between steel plates and friction discs. Start with a steel plate next to the outer friction disc, then

install a friction disc, then a steel plate, then another friction disc, etc., and, finally, install the pressure plate. On VT600 models, there are six friction discs and six steel plates; on VT750 models, there are seven friction discs and eight steel plates (which means you will begin with a steel plate and end with one too).

39   Install the clutch pack assembly on the mainshaft. The tabs on all the clutch friction discs (except the outer friction disc) should fit into the slots in the clutch housing (the tabs on the outer friction disc fit into their own cutouts between the slots).

40   Install the new spring washer with the OUTSIDE facing out.

41   Install the new clutch center locknut, install the clutch center holder and tighten the locknut to the torque listed in this Chapter's Specifications. Remove the holder and stake the locknut. Be careful not to damage the threads on the mainshaft.

42   Install the clutch springs, the lifter plate and the lifter plate bolts. Tighten the lifter plate bolts to the torque listed in this Chapter's Specifications.

43   If the oil pump driven sprocket or primary drive gear was removed, put a penny between the primary drive gear teeth and the primary driven gear teeth **(see illustration 18.7)** and tighten the sprocket retaining bolt and/or primary drive gear bolt to the torque listed in this Chapter's Specifications.

44   Clean all traces of old gasket material from the right crankcase cover and its mating surface on the crankcase. Install a new gasket on the crankcase and install the dowel pins **(see illustration 18.4c)**.

45   Install the right crankcase cover and install the 14 bolts finger tight. Don't forget to reattach the clutch cable bracket.

46   Tighten the bolts in stages, using a criss-criss pattern, to the torque listed in this Chapter's Specifications.

47   On 1988 and 1989 VT600 models, install the oil pipe banjo bolt with new sealing washers and tighten the banjo bolt to the torque listed in this Chapter's Specifications. Install the oil pipe bracket.

48   Reattach the clutch cable to the clutch lifter arm (see Section 17) and adjust the clutch cable (see Chapter 1).

49   Fill the crankcase with the recommended type and amount of engine oil (see Chapter 1).

19 Oil pump drive chain and sprockets - removal, inspection and installation

Removal

Refer to illustrations 19.2 and 19.3

1   Remove the clutch (see Section 18). When you get to Step 7 in Section 18, loosen the oil pump driven sprocket bolt **(see illustration 18.7)**.

2   Remove the oil pump driven sprocket bolt **(see illustration)**.

3   Remove the oil pump drive sprocket, chain and driven sprocket **(see illustration)**.

Inspection

4   Inspect the drive chain rollers and side plates and the sprocket teeth for damage and wear. If the chain or either sprocket is damaged or worn, replace it. (It's a good idea to replace the sprockets and chain as a set.)
5   Measure the inside diameter of the drive sprocket and compare your measurement to the drive sprocket inside diameter listed in this Chapter's Specifications. If the inside diameter of the sprocket exceeds the limit, replace the drive sprocket. (Again, it's a good idea to replace the sprockets and chain as a set.)

Installation

6   Lubricate the clutch outer guide with clean engine oil, install the driven sprocket first, with the IN facing toward the engine, then slide the driven sprocket onto the guide. Install the driven sprocket retaining bolt and tighten it until the sprocket starts to turn.
7   Install the clutch (see Section 18). When you get to Step 43, tighten the driven sprocket retaining bolt to the torque listed in this Chapter's Specifications. Finish the clutch installation procedure.

---

20   Primary drive gear - removal, inspection and installation

Refer to illustrations 20.3, 20.4 and 20.5
1   Remove the clutch (see Section 18). When you get to Step 7 in Section 18, loosen the primary drive gear bolt **(see illustration 18.7)**.
2   Remove the ignition pulse generator(s) (see Chapter 5).
3   Remove the primary drive gear bolt and washer **(see illustration)**.
4   Remove the ignition pulse generator rotor **(see illustration)**.
5   Remove the primary drive gear **(see illustration)**.
6   On VT600 models, inspect the teeth of the primary drive gear for wear and damage. If the teeth are worn or damaged, replace the primary drive gear.
7   On VT750 models, disassemble the primary drive gear and the sub gear. Note the relationship of the parts to one another as you take the assembly apart. Inspect the teeth on both the primary drive gear and the sub-gear. Inspect the three primary drive gear springs and the friction spring (washer) for wear and damage. If anything is damaged or worn, replace the primary drive gear. Reassemble the primary drive gear and sub-gear. Make sure the three holes on the sub-gear and the primary drive gear are aligned.
8   On VT600 models, install the primary drive gear with the OUT facing out; the gear will only go on one way because of the extra wide spline **(see illustration 20.5)**.
9   On VT750 models, install the primary drive gear with the sub-gear

19.2 Remove the oil pump driven sprocket retaining bolt

19.3 Remove the oil pump drive sprocket, chain and driven sprocket as a set

side facing out. The gear will only go on one way because of an extra wide spline.
10   Install the ignition pulse generator rotor. Again, the rotor will only go on one way because of the extra wide spline.
11   Install the primary drive gear bolt and washer. Install the clutch (see Section 18). When you get to Step 43, tighten the primary drive gear bolt to the torque listed in this Chapter's Specifications. Finish the clutch installation procedure.

20.3 Remove the primary drive gear retaining bolt and washer

20.4 Remove the ignition pulse generator rotor; the extra wide spline (arrow) allows the rotor to be installed only one way

20.5 Remove the primary drive gear; note the OUT, which must face out when the primary drive gear is installed; and again, note the extra wide spline (arrow) which means the primary drive gear can only be installed one way

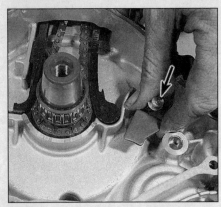

21.8 Loosen the cam chain tensioner set plate bolt (arrow) and swing the plate out of the way (set plate at left end of crank shown; right set plate similar)

21.9 Remove the cam chain from the drive sprocket and pull the chain up through the cam chain tunnel (front cylinder cam chain shown; rear cylinder cam chain similar)

21.10 On VT600 models, the cam chain drive sprocket for the rear cylinder can be removed from the crankshaft (the drive sprocket for the front cylinder cam chain on VT600 models, and both sprockets on VT750 models, are not removable)

21 Cam chains and rear cam chain drive sprocket - removal, inspection and installation

Note: *This procedure applies to the front and rear cam chains and to the rear cam chain drive sprocket on VT600 models (the front cylinder cam chain drive sprocket on VT600 models and both cam chain sprockets on VT750 models are part of the crankshaft.)*

Removal

Refer to illustrations 21.8, 21.9 and 21.10

1   Remove the cylinder head cover (see Section 7).
2   Remove the camshaft, sprocket and rocker arms (see Section 8).
3   Remove the cam chain tensioner (see Section 9).
4   Remove the cylinder head (see Section 10). If you're removing the rear cylinder head, remove the engine first (see Section 5).
5   Remove the chain guide (see Section 13).
6   If you're removing the front cylinder cam chain, remove the left crankcase cover and remove the alternator rotor (see Chapter 9).
7   If you're removing the rear cylinder cam chain, remove the right crankcase cover and the clutch (see Section 18) and remove the primary drive gear (see Section 20).
8   Remove the cam chain tensioner set plate **(see illustration)**.
9   Remove the cam chain from the drive sprocket **(see illustration)** and pull it up through the cam chain tunnel.
10   If you're removing the rear cam chain on a VT600 model, the drive sprocket should be removed from the crankshaft **(see illustration)** and inspected. (The front cam chain drive sprocket on VT600 models and both sprockets on VT750 models are not removable; they're part of the crank.)

Inspection

11   Clean the cam chain in solvent and dry it with compressed air. Inspect the rollers and side plates for wear. Replace the chain if it's worn or damaged.
12   If the cam chain is worn, inspect the drive sprocket on the crankshaft and the driven sprocket on the camshaft (see Section 8). If the drive sprocket for the rear cylinder cam chain on a VT600 is worn, replace it; if any other drive sprocket is worn, replace the crankshaft.

Installation

13   If you removed the drive sprocket for the rear cam chain on a VT600, install it on the crankshaft.
14   Drop the cam chain through the cam chain tunnel and install it on the drive sprocket at the crank. Wire up the cam chain so it can't fall back into the crankcase and install the parts and components removed.
15   If you're installing the front cylinder cam chain, install the alterna-

tor rotor and the left crankcase cover (see Chapter 9).
16   If you're installing the rear cylinder cam chain, install the primary drive gear (see Section 20) and the clutch and the right crankcase cover (see Section 18).
17   Install the chain guide (see Section 13).
18   Install the cylinder head (see Section 10).
19   If you removed the rear cylinder head, install the engine (see Section 5).
20   Install the cam chain tensioner (see Section 9).
21   Install the camshaft, sprocket and rocker arm assembly (see Section 8).
22   Install the cylinder head cover (see Section 7).

22 Gearshift linkage - removal, inspection and installation

Removal

Gearshift linkage

Refer to illustrations 22.3, 22.5a and 22.5b

1   Support the bike securely so it can't be knocked over during this procedure.
2   Remove the left rear cover (see Chapter 7).
3   Look for the index marks on the gearshift lever and the end of the gearshift spindle **(see illustration)**. These marks must be aligned when the shift lever is installed again. If you can't find any marks, make your own punch marks to ensure correct realignment during installation.
4   Remove the lever pinch bolt **(see illustration 22.3)**. Pull the lever off the spindle.
5   Unbolt the left footpeg assembly from the frame and remove the gearshift pedal, shift rod and shift lever as a single assembly **(see illustrations)**.

External shift mechanism

Refer to illustrations 22.8a, 22.8b, 22.9a, 22.9b, 22.10, 22.11a and 22.11b

6   Disconnect the shift lever from the gearshift spindle (Steps 1 through 4).
7   Remove the right crankcase cover and the clutch (see Section 18) and the oil pump drive chain and sprockets (see Section 19).
8   Remove the oil pipe bracket and mainshaft bearing set plate bolts **(see illustration)**. Pull the oil pipe out of the mainshaft bearing set plate and out of the oil pump and remove the oil pipe and bearing set plate **(see illustration)**. Remove and discard the O-ring from the lower end of the oil pipe.
9   Unhook the shifter arm from the gearshift cam plate **(see illustration)** and pull the gearshift spindle out of the crankcase **(see illustration)**.

22.3 Check for alignment marks on the spindle and lever, then remove the pinch bolt (arrow) completely and pull the lever off the spindle

22.5a To detach the footpeg bracket from the frame, remove these bolts (arrows) . . .

22.5b . . . and remove the footpeg/bracket/gearshift pedal, shift rod and shift lever as a single assembly

22.8a To remove the oil pipe bolt, remove the mainshaft bearing set plate bolts (upper arrows) and the oil pipe bracket bolt (lower arrow) . . .

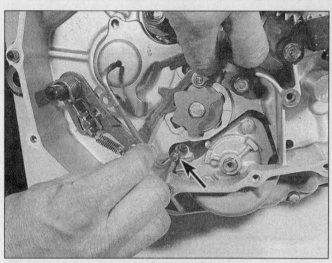

22.8b . . . separate the oil pipe from the set plate and from the oil pump, and remove the O-ring (arrow) from the lower end of the oil pipe

22.9a Unhook the shifter arm from the gearshift cam plate (note how the return spring pin on the crankcase is positioned between the two ends of the return spring) . . .

22.9b . . . and pull the gearshift spindle out of the crankcase

22.10 Remove this bolt (arrow) and remove the washer, gearshift drum stopper, bushing and spring

22.11a Remove this bolt (arrow) . . .

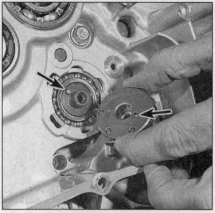

22.11b . . . and remove the gearshift cam plate; the dowel pin (upper arrow) drum and hole (lower arrow) must align when installed

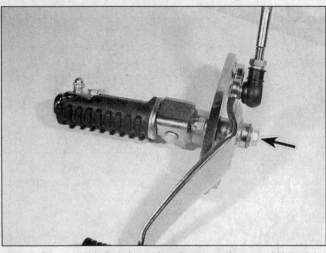

22.12 Remove this bolt (arrow) and remove the gearshift pedal, bushing and dust seals

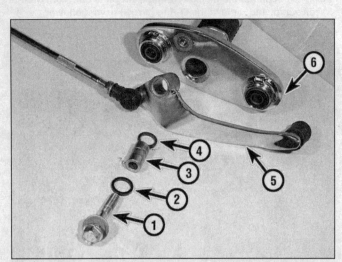

22.13 Clean and inspect the gearshift pedal assembly; if the dust seals or bushing are damaged or worn, replace them

1	Gearshift pedal pivot bolt	5	Gearshift pedal and shift rod
2	Dust seal	6	Footpeg bracket
3	Bushing		
4	Dust seal		

10   Remove the bolt, washer, gearshift drum stopper, bushing and spring **(see illustration)**.

11   Remove the bolt and gearshift cam plate **(see illustrations)**.

Inspection

Gearshift linkage

Refer to illustrations 22.12 and 22.13

12   Unbolt the shift pedal from the footpeg bracket **(see illustration)**.

13   Disassemble the shift pedal assembly, wipe off all grease and dirt and inspect the dust seals and the bushing **(see illustration)** for wear and damage. If any of these parts are worn or damaged, replace them.

14   Inspect the shift rod. Make sure that the rod is straight and the locknuts at both ends are tight. If the shaft is bent, replace it.

15   Lubricate the bushing and the dust seal lips with multipurpose grease and reassemble the shift pedal assembly. Tighten the shift pedal bolt securely.

External shift mechanism

Refer to illustrations 22.16, 22.17, 22.18, 22.19a and 22.19b

16   Inspect the gearshift spindle and return spring **(see illustration)**. If the spindle is damaged, replace the gearshift spindle assembly. If the spring is fatigued, replace it.

17   Inspect the gearshift drum stopper, bushing and spring **(see illustration)**. If the stopper is worn where it contacts the gearshift cam plate, replace the stopper. If the spring is distorted, replace it.

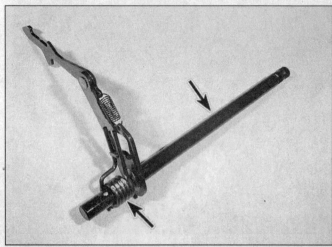

22.16 Inspect the gearshift spindle and return spring (arrows); make sure the spindle is straight and the spring isn't fatigued

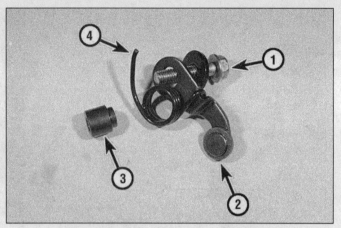

22.17 Shift drum stopper details

1	*Drum stopper bolt*	3	*Bushing*
2	*Drum stopper*	4	*Spring*

22.18 Inspect the cam plate pin holes for wear or damage

18   Remove the three pins from the gearshift cam plate and inspect the pins and the holes for the pins in the cam plate **(see illustration)**. If the pins or holes are worn or damaged, replace the gearshift cam plate. Reassemble the gearshift cam plate assembly.
19   Inspect the gearshift spindle seal. If it's leaking, remove the countershaft sprocket (see Chapter 7), remove the countershaft bearing set plate **(see illustration)** and remove the seal **(see illustration)**. It's a good idea to replace the seal whenever the gearshift spindle is removed. To replace the seal, pry it out with a screwdriver or seal removal tool and tap a new seal into place with a deep socket.

Installation

20   Install the gearshift cam plate. Make sure the positioning hole on the cam plate is aligned with the dowel pin on the shift drum **(see illustration 22.11b)**.
21   Clean the bolt threads of the cam plate bolt, apply a thread locking agent to the threads, install the bolt and tighten it to the torque listed in this Chapter's Specifications.
22   Install the bushing, spring, gearshift drum stopper, washer and bolt. Tighten the gearshift drum stopper bolt to the torque listed in this Chapter's Specifications.
23   Install the gearshift spindle assembly. Make sure that the dowel pin on the crankcase fits between the two ends of the return spring **(see illustration 22.9a)**.
24   Apply clean engine oil to the new oil pipe O-ring and install the O-ring on the oil pipe. Install the mainshaft bearing set plate and the oil

pipe, install the set plate and oil pipe bracket bolts and tighten them securely.
25   Install the gearshift pedal and footpeg bracket and tighten the bracket bolts securely.
26   Install the shift lever on the gearshift spindle. Make sure the punch marks on the shift lever and the spindle are aligned. Install the shift lever pinch bolt and tighten it to the torque listed in this Chapter's Specifications.
27   Install the left rear engine cover (see Chapter 7).

23 Crankcase - disassembly and reassembly

1   To examine and repair or replace the oil pump, crankshaft, connecting rods, bearings, or transmission components, the crankcase must be split into two parts.

Disassembly

Refer to illustrations 23.17, 23.18, 23.19a, 23.19b and 23.20
2   Remove the engine from the frame (see Section 5).
3   Remove the cylinder head covers (see Section 7).
4   Remove the camshafts, sprockets and rocker arms (see Section 8).
5   Remove the cam chain tensioners (see Section 9).
6   Remove the cylinder heads (see Section 10).
7   Remove the cam chain guides (see Section 13).
8   Remove the cylinders (see Section 14).
9   Remove the pistons (see Section 15).

22.19a Replace the gearshift spindle seal if it's leaking

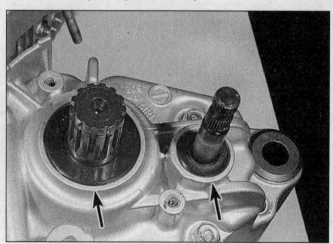

22.19b Gearshift spindle seal (right arrow) and countershaft seal (left arrow)

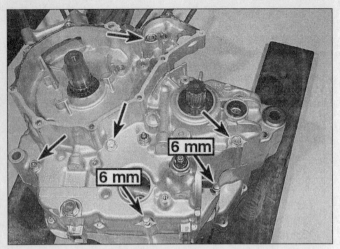

23.17 Remove these bolts (arrows) from the left crankcase half; loosen the two 6 mm bolts first, then loosen the other four (8 mm) bolts, gradually and evenly, in a criss-cross pattern

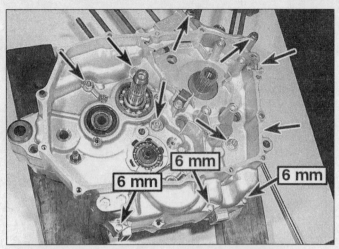

23.18 Remove these bolts (arrows) from the right crankcase half; loosen the three 6 mm bolts first, then loosen the other eight (8 mm) bolts, gradually and evenly, in a criss-cross pattern (two right-hand bolts hidden)

10   Remove the left crankcase cover and the alternator (see Chapter 9). Remove all electrical harnesses from the left side of the engine.
11   Remove the right crankcase cover and the clutch (see Section 18).

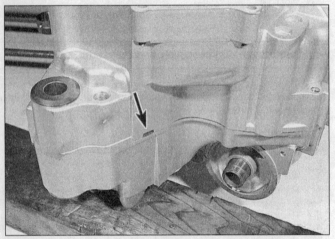

23.19a Locate the prying points (this one on the underside of the cases and two more on the front of the crankcase)

12   Remove the oil pump driven chain and sprockets (see Section 19).
13   Remove the ignition pulse generator(s) (see Chapter 5).
14   Remove the primary drive gear (see Section 20).
15   Remove the cam chains (see Section 21).
16   Remove the oil pipe, mainshaft bearing set plate, gearshift spindle, gearshift drum stopper, gearshift cam plate and countershaft bearing set plate (see Section 22).
17   Remove the bolts from the left crankcase half **(see illustration)**. First, loosen the two 6 mm bolts, then loosen the four 8 mm bolts. Working in a criss-cross pattern, loosen the bolts gradually and evenly.
18   Remove the bolts from the right crankcase half **(see illustration)**. First, loosen the three 6 mm bolts, then loosen the eight 8 mm bolts. Working in a criss-cross pattern, loosen the bolts gradually and evenly.
19   With the engine lying on its left crankcase half, carefully separate the crankcase halves by prying gently and evenly at the pry points around the crankcase seam **(see illustrations)**. Using a soft hammer, tap alternately on the transmission shafts and the engine mounting bosses. If the halves won't separate easily, double check to make sure that all fasteners have been removed. Don't pry against the crankcase mating surfaces or they'll leak.
20   Look for the dowels **(see illustration)**. If they're not in one of the crankcase halves, locate them.

23.19b Once you've broken the seal, carefully separate the crankcase halves

23.20 Remove both dowel pins (arrows) from the left crankcase half (front dowel is missing in this photo; it came off with the other crankcase half) and store them in a plastic bag

25.3a To remove the oil relief pipe, remove its bolt (lower arrow) (the other two bolts are the oil pump mounting bolts) . . .

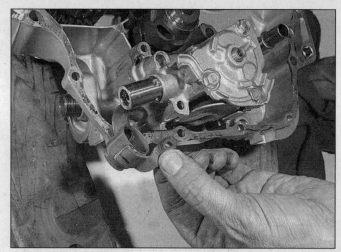

25.3b . . . and lift the pipe off

21   Remove all traces of sealant from the crankcase mating surfaces.
22   Refer to Sections 25 through 30 for information on servicing the internal components of the crankcase.

Reassembly

23   Make sure the oil pump, crankshaft and transmission shafts are correctly installed in the upper crankcase half (see Sections 25, 28 and 29, respectively).
24   Pour some engine oil over the transmission gears, the crankshaft main bearings and the shift drum. Also pour oil into the exposed internal oil passages. Don't get any oil on the crankcase mating surfaces.
25   Make sure the dowels are in place **(see illustration 23.20)**.
26   Apply a thin, even bead of sealant to the crankcase mating surfaces. **Caution:** *Don't apply an excessive amount of sealant. Make sure that no sealant is applied to oil passages.*
27   Carefully assemble the crankcase halves over the dowels. **Caution:** *The crankcase halves should fit together completely without being forced. If they're slightly apart, DO NOT force them together by tightening the crankcase bolts.*
28   Install the right crankcase bolts in their holes **(see illustration 23.18)**. Make sure you don't install a 6 mm bolt in an 8 mm hole, or vice versa. Tighten the bolts gradually and evenly, in a criss-cross fashion, to the torque listed in this Chapter's Specifications. **Note:** *There are different torque settings for the 8 mm bolts and the 6 mm bolts.*
29   Turn the engine over and install the left crankcase bolts in their holes **(see illustration 23.17)**. Make sure you don't install a 6 mm bolt in an 8 mm hole, or vice versa. Tighten the bolts gradually and evenly, in a criss-cross fashion, to the torque listed in this Chapter's Specifications. **Note:** *There are different torque settings for the 8 mm bolts and the 6 mm bolts.*
30   Turn the crankshaft, the mainshaft and the countershaft to make sure they turn freely.
31   Install the gearshift cam plate (see Section 22). Rotate the shift cam by hand to make sure the transmission shifts into the different gear positions.
32   The remainder of assembly is the reverse of disassembly.
33   Be sure to refill the engine oil (see Chapter 1).

24 Crankcase components - inspection and servicing

1   After the crankcases have been separated and the oil pump, the crankshaft, the shift drum and forks, and the transmission shafts have been removed, the crankcases should be cleaned thoroughly with new solvent and dried with compressed air.

2   Remove the oil jets **(see illustrations 15.5a and 15.5b)**. All oil passages should be blown out with compressed air.
3   All traces of old gasket sealant should be removed from the mating surfaces. Minor damage to the mating surfaces can be cleaned up with a fine sharpening stone or grindstone. **Caution:** *Be very careful not to nick or gouge the crankcase mating surfaces or leaks will result.* Check both crankcase halves very carefully for cracks and other damage.
4   If any damage is found that can't be repaired, replace the crankcase halves as a set.

25 Oil pump - removal, inspection and installation

Removal

Refer to illustrations 25.3a, 25.3b, 25.4 and 25.5
1   Remove the engine (see Section 5).
2   Disassemble the engine and separate the crankcase halves (see Section 23).
3   Remove the oil relief pipe bolt and remove the oil relief pipe **(see illustrations)**.
4   Remove the oil pump mounting bolts **(see illustration 25.3a)** and remove the pump **(see illustration)**.

25.4 Remove the oil pump from the crankcase

25.5 The collars, O-rings, and dowel (arrows) may stay in the engine or come out with the oil pump; be sure to remove and install all of them

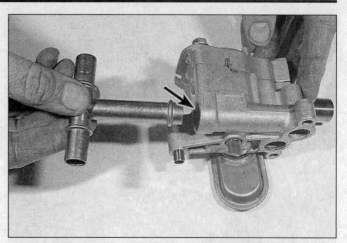

25.6 If the O-ring isn't on the end of the pipe, it's in the pump passage (arrow)

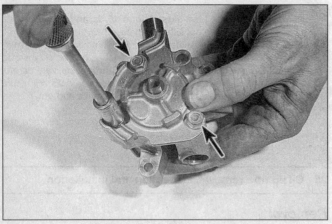

25.7a Remove the cover bolts (arrows) . . .

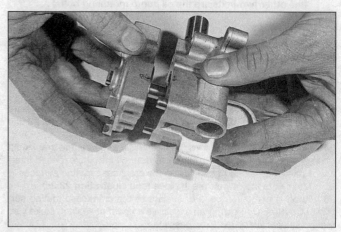

25.7b . . . remove the pump cover . . .

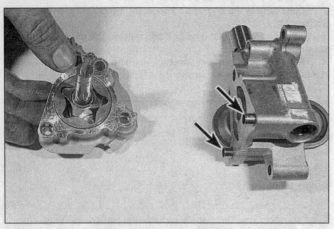

25.7c . . . and locate the dowels

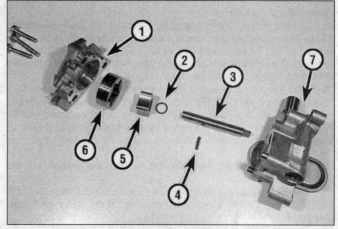

25.8 Oil pump details

1 *Pump cover*	4 *Drive pin*	6 *Outer rotor*
2 *Washer*	5 *Inner rotor*	7 *Pump body*
3 *Driveshaft*		

5   Remove the oil pump collars, O-rings and dowels **(see illustration).**

Disassembly

Refer to illustrations 25.6, 25.7a, 25.7b, 25.7c, 25.8, 25.9, 25.10a, 25.10b and 25.10c

6   Remove the oil pipe and discard the old O-rings and seal **(see illustration).**

7   Remove the pump cover bolts, lift off the cover and remove the dowel pins **(see illustrations).**

8   Remove the washer, the driveshaft, the drive pin, the inner rotor and the outer rotor **(see illustration)** from the pump body.

9   Pull off the strainer **(see illustration).** Discard the old O-ring.

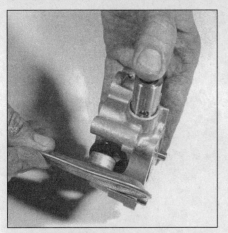

25.9 Pull off the strainer and discard the old O-ring

25.10a Pull out the pressure relief valve and discard the old O-ring

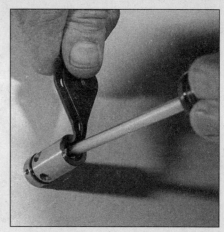

25.10b Remove the snap-ring from the pressure relief valve . . .

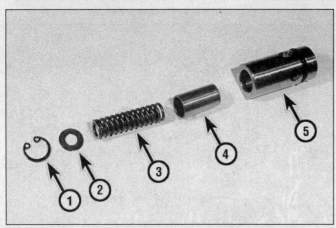

25.10c . . . and disassemble the pressure relief valve

1	Snap-ring	3	Spring	5	Pressure
2	Washer	4	Piston		relief valve

25.13a Measure the clearance between the outer rotor and pump body

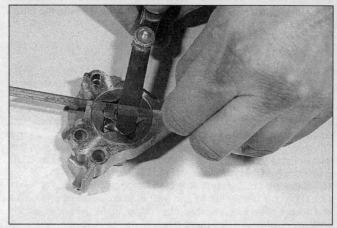

25.13c Measure the clearance between rotors and the cover

25.13b Measure the clearance between the inner and outer rotors

10   Pull out the pressure relief valve (see illustration). Remove the snap-ring and remove the washer, spring and piston from the relief valve (see illustrations). Discard the old O-ring.

Inspection

Refer to illustrations 25.13a, 25.13b and 25.13c

11   Wash the oil pump parts in solvent and dry them off.

12   Check the pump body and rotors for scoring and wear. If any damage or uneven or excessive wear is evident, replace the pump; (individual parts aren't available. (If you are rebuilding the engine, it's a good idea to install a new oil pump anyway.)

13   Measure the clearance between the inner and outer rotors and between the outer rotor and housing (see illustrations). Replace the pump if the clearance is excessive.

14   Inspect the piston and the bore of the relief valve for scoring or other damage. Inspect the spring for fatigue. If any of the relief valve parts are worn or damaged, replace the oil pump.

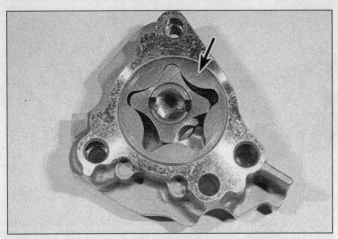

25.16 Install the outer rotor with the punch mark (arrow) facing out (toward the cover)

25.17 Center the drive pin in the driveshaft, then push the driveshaft into the inner rotor until the drive pin is seated in the grooves in the inner rotor

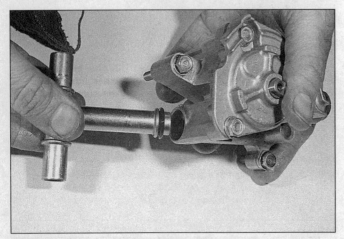

25.22a Install a new seal on the oil pipe before pushing the pipe into the pump body

25.22b Use new O-rings on the ends of the oil pipe which are seated in the cases

Reassembly

Refer to illustrations 25.16 and 25.17

15   If the pump is good, make sure all the parts are spotlessly clean, then lubricate everything with clean engine oil or assembly lube.

16   Install the inner and outer rotors in the pump body. Make sure the outer rotor is installed with the punch mark facing out, toward the cover **(see illustration)**.

17   Install the washer and driveshaft in the inner rotor. Make sure that the pin is centered in the driveshaft so it will align with the slot in the inner rotor **(see illustration)**.

18   Install the pump cover and tighten the cover bolts securely.

19   Install the piston, spring and washer in the pressure relief valve and secure them with the snap-ring. Using a new O-ring, install the pressure relief valve in the pump body.

20   Using a new O-ring, install the strainer in the pump body.

Installation

Refer to illustrations 25.22a and 25.22b

21   Make sure the dowel, collars and O-rings are in position **(see illustration 25.5)**.

22   Make sure that the T-shaped oil pipe has a new seal on the end that fits into the pump and new O-rings on the two ends that fit into the cases **(see illustrations)**. And make SURE that the old oil pipe seal and O-rings are not still in their respective bores in the pump body or the cases (which they sometimes are).

23   Install the pump, install the mounting bolts and tighten them securely.

24   Install the oil relief pipe, install the oil relief pipe bolt and tighten it securely.

25   Installation is otherwise the reverse of removal.

26   Main and connecting rod bearings - general note

1   Even though main and connecting rod bearings are generally replaced with new ones during the engine overhaul, the old bearings should be retained for close examination as they may reveal valuable information about the condition of the engine.

2   Bearing failure occurs mainly because of lack of lubrication, the presence of dirt or other foreign particles, overloading the engine and/or corrosion. Regardless of the cause of bearing failure, it must be corrected before the engine is reassembled to prevent it from happening again.

3   When examining the bearings, remove the rod bearings from the connecting rods and caps and lay them out on a clean surface in the same general position as their location on the crankshaft journals. This will enable you to match any noted bearing problems with the corresponding side of the crankshaft journal. The main bearings are pressed into the crankcase halves and are only removed if they need to be replaced.

4   Dirt and other foreign particles get into the engine in a variety of ways. It may be left in the engine during assembly or it may pass through filters or breathers. It may get into the oil and from there into

27.3 Measure the side clearance between the rods and the crankshaft weights

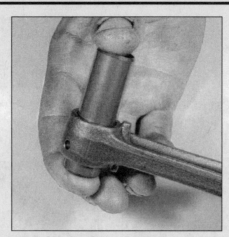

27.7 Slip the piston pin into the rod and rock it back-and-forth to check for looseness

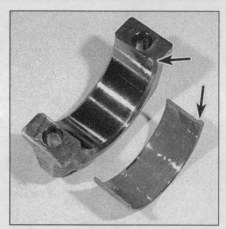

27.12 Make sure the tab (arrow) on the bearing is aligned with the notch (arrow) in the rod or cap

the bearings. Metal chips from machining operations and normal engine wear are often present. Abrasives are sometimes left in engine components after reconditioning operations such as cylinder honing, especially when parts are not thoroughly cleaned using the proper cleaning methods. Whatever the source, these foreign objects often end up imbedded in the soft bearing material and are easily recognized. Large particles will not imbed in the bearing and will score or gouge the bearing and journal. The best prevention for this cause of bearing failure is to clean all parts thoroughly and keep everything spotlessly clean during engine reassembly. Frequent and regular oil and filter changes are also recommended.

5   Lack of lubrication or lubrication breakdown has a number of inter-related causes. Excessive heat (which thins the oil), overloading (which squeezes the oil from the bearing face) and oil leakage or throw off (from excessive bearing clearances, worn oil pump or high engine speeds) all contribute to lubrication breakdown. Blocked oil passages will also starve a bearing and destroy it. When lack of lubrication is the cause of bearing failure, the bearing material is wiped or extruded from the steel backing of the bearing. Temperatures may increase to the point where the steel backing and the journal turn blue from overheating.

6   Riding habits can have a definite effect on bearing life. Full throttle low speed operation, or lugging the engine, puts very high loads on bearings, which tend to squeeze out the oil film. These loads cause the bearings to flex, which produces fine cracks in the bearing face (fatigue failure). Eventually the bearing material will loosen in pieces and tear away from the steel backing. Short trip driving leads to corrosion of bearings, as insufficient engine heat is produced to drive off the condensed water and corrosive gases produced. These products collect in the engine oil, forming acid and sludge. As the oil is carried to the engine bearings, the acid attacks and corrodes the bearing material.

7   Incorrect bearing installation during engine assembly will lead to bearing failure as well. Tight fitting bearings which leave insufficient bearing oil clearances result in oil starvation. Dirt or foreign particles trapped behind a bearing insert result in high spots on the bearing which lead to failure.

8   To avoid bearing problems, clean all parts thoroughly before reassembly, double check all bearing clearance measurements and lubricate the new bearings with engine assembly lube or moly-based grease during installation.

---

27 Connecting rods and bearings - removal, inspection and installation

---

Removal

Refer to illustration 27.3

1   Separate the crankcase halves (see Section 23).

2   Lift the crankshaft out, together with the connecting rods, and set them on a clean surface.

3   Before removing the connecting rods from the crankshaft, measure the connecting rod side clearance. Insert a feeler gauge between each side of the big end of each connecting rod and the crankshaft **(see illustration)** and compare your measurements to the side clearance listed in this Chapter's Specifications. If the side clearance between either rod and the crank is greater than the specified side clearance, replace that rod.

4   Using a center punch or a laundry marker pen with indelible ink, mark the position of each rod and cap, relative to its position on the crankshaft (left or right) to ensure that the same rod removed from each crankpin will be reinstalled on the same crankpin.

5   Unscrew the bearing cap nuts, separate the cap from the rod, then detach the rod from the crankshaft. If a rod cap is stuck, tap on the ends of the rod bolts with a soft-faced hammer to free it.

6   Roll the bearing inserts sideways to separate them from the rods and caps. Keep them in order so they can be reinstalled in their original locations. Wash the parts in solvent and dry them with compressed air, if available.

Inspection

Refer to illustrations 27.7, 27.12, 27.13 and 27.15

7   Check the connecting rods for cracks and other obvious damage. Lubricate the piston pin for each rod, install it in the proper rod and check for play **(see illustration)**. If it wobbles, measure the outside diameter of the piston pin, the inside diameter of the connecting rod, and the inside diameter of the pin bore in the piston (see Section 15). Replace the piston (see Section 15), the pin and/or the connecting rod (see Step 20) as necessary.

8   Examine the connecting rod bearing inserts. If they are scored, badly scuffed or appear to have been seized, new bearings must be installed. Always replace the bearings in the connecting rods as a set. If they are badly damaged, check the corresponding crankshaft journal. Evidence of extreme heat, such as discoloration, indicates lubrication failure. Be sure to inspect the oil pump and pressure relief valve (see Section 25) as well as all oil holes and passages before reassembling the engine.

9   Have the rods checked for twist and bending at a dealer service department or other motorcycle repair shop. If a rod must be replaced, refer to Step 20.

10   If the bearings and journals appear to be in good condition, check the oil clearances as follows:

11   Start with the rod for one cylinder. Wipe the bearing inserts and the connecting rod and cap clean, using a lint-free cloth.

12   Install the bearing inserts in the connecting rod and cap. Make sure the tab on the bearing engages with the notch in the rod or cap **(see illustration)**.

27.13 Lay a strip of Plastigage on the journal, parallel to the crankshaft centerline

27.15 Place the Plastigage scale next to the flattened Plastigage to measure the bearing clearance

13   Wipe off the connecting rod journal with a lint-free cloth. Lay a strip of Plastigage (type HPG-1) across the top of the journal, parallel with the journal axis **(see illustration)**.
14   Referring to the marks you made prior to disassembly, position the connecting rod on the correct journal, then install the rod cap and nuts. Tighten the nuts to the torque listed in this Chapter's Specifica-

tions, but don't allow the connecting rod to rotate at all.
15   Unscrew the nuts and remove the connecting rod and cap from the journal, being very careful not to disturb the Plastigage. Compare the width of the crushed Plastigage to the scale printed in the Plastigage envelope to determine the bearing oil clearance **(see illustration)**.
16   If the clearance is within the range listed in this Chapter's Specifications and the bearings are in perfect condition, they can be reused. If the clearance is greater than the wear limit, replace the bearing inserts with new inserts that have the same color code, then check the clearance once again. Always replace all of the inserts at the same time.
17   If the clearance is greater than the maximum clearance listed in this Chapter's Specifications, measure the diameter of the connecting rod journal with a micrometer. To determine whether the journal is out-of-round, measure the diameter at a number of points around the journal's circumference. Take the measurement at each end of the journal to determine if the journal is tapered.
18   If any journal is tapered or out-of-round or bearing clearance is beyond the maximum listed in this Chapter's Specifications (with new bearings), replace the crankshaft (see Section 28).

Connecting rod bearing selection

Refer to illustrations 27.19a and 27.19b

19   Each connecting rod has a "1" or "2" stamped on it **(see illustration)**; this is the code for the connecting rod inside diameter. Next to that, on the crank weight, is an "A" or a B; this is the code for the crankpin outside diameter. The bearings are color-coded brown, black or blue. To determine the correct bearing color, match the connecting rod I.D. code (left column) to the crankpin O.D. code (upper row) and note the corresponding color code in the following chart. For example,

27.19a The number code on the connecting rod and the letter code on the crankshaft weight are used to determine the color (size) of the rod bearing insert; the code letter on the rod is used to determine the connecting rod weight

Crankpin O.D. code	Code "A" 39.982 to 39.990 mm (1.5741 to 1.5744 inches)	Code "B" 39.974 to 39.981 mm (1.5738 to 1.5741 inches)
Connecting rod I.D. code	Bearing insert thickness	Bearing insert thickness
Code "1" 43.000 to 43.007 mm (1.6929 to 1.6935 inches)	"C" (Brown) 1.487 to 1.491 mm (0.0585 to 0.0587 inch)	"B" (Black) 1.491 to 1.495 mm (0.0587 to 0.0589 inch)
Code "2" 43.008 to 43.016 mm (1.6932 to 1.6935 inches)	"B" (Black) 1.491 to 1.495 mm (0.0587 to 0.0589 inch)	"A" (Blue) 1.495 to 1.499 mm (0.0589 to 0.0590 inch)

27.19b Connecting rod bearing selection chart

27.21 Coat the bearings with assembly lube or moly-based grease

a code 2 on the connecting rod and an A code on the crank weight would indicate a black color-coded rod bearing **(see illustration)**. The color codes are painted on the edges of the bearings.

Matching the connecting rods to the crankshaft

20   The connecting rods and the crankshaft are "select fitted." If a connecting rod must be replaced, make sure you select a new rod with the same weight code as the rod being replaced. Each connecting rod has an "A," a "B" or a "C" stamped on the side of the rod **(see illustration 27.19a)**. This is the connecting rod weight code.

Installation

Refer to illustrations 27.21 and 27.22

21   Wipe off the bearing inserts, connecting rods and caps. Install the inserts into the rods and caps, using your hands only, making sure the tabs on the inserts engage with the notches in the rods and caps **(see illustration 27.12)**. When all the inserts are installed, lubricate them with engine assembly lube or moly-based grease **(see illustration)**. Don't get any lubricant on the mating surfaces of the rod or cap.

22   Install each connecting rod on the correct journal, referring to the marks you made prior to disassembly. Make sure that the connecting rod code number stamped on the side of the rod across the rod/cap seam fits together perfectly when the rod and cap are assembled **(see illustration)**. If it doesn't, the wrong cap is on the rod. Fix this problem before proceeding.

23   When you're sure the rods are positioned correctly, lubricate the threads of the rod bolts and the surfaces of the nuts with molybdenum disulfide grease and tighten the nuts to the torque listed in this Chapter's Specifications. Snug both rod cap nuts evenly, then gradually and evenly tighten them to the specified torque in several steps.

24   Turn the rods on the crankshaft. If either of them feels tight, tap on the bottom of the connecting rod caps with a hammer - this should relieve stress and free them up. If it doesn't, recheck the bearing clearance.

25   As a final step, recheck the connecting rod side clearances (see Step 3). If the clearances aren't correct, find out why before proceeding with engine assembly.

---

28   Crankshaft and main bearings - removal, inspection and installation

Crankshaft removal

1   Separate the crankcase halves (see Section 23).

2   Lift out the crankshaft and connecting rods and set the assembly on a clean surface.

3   Mark, remove and inspect the connecting rods and rod bearings (see Section 27).

Inspection

Refer to illustration 28.6

4   Clean the crankshaft with solvent, using a rifle-cleaning brush to scrub out the oil passages. Dry off the crank with compressed air. Inspect the main and connecting rod journals for uneven wear, scoring and pits. Rub a copper coin across the journal several times - if a journal picks up copper from the coin, it's too rough. Replace the crankshaft.

5   Inspect the teeth on the cam chain drive sprocket(s) on the crankshaft. If the sprocket teeth are damaged or worn, replace the crankshaft. (The rear cylinder cam chain sprocket on VT600 models is removable; the front cylinder cam chain sprocket on VT600 models and both sprockets on VT750 models are part of the crankshaft.) If there's sprocket wear or damage, inspect the cam chains too (see Section 21). Inspect the rest of the crankshaft for cracks and other damage. Have it magnafluxed by a dealer service department or motorcycle machine shop; magnafluxing will reveal any hidden cracks.

6   Set the crankshaft on V-blocks and measure the crank runout at the bearing surfaces with a dial indicator **(see illustration)**. Compare your measurement with the runout listed in this Chapter's Specifications. If the runout exceeds the limit, replace the crank.

27.22 If the halves of the number stamped on the rod and cap don't fit together perfectly, the wrong cap is on the rod (or the cap is on backwards)

28.6 Place the crankshaft in V-blocks or a holding fixture and check for runout with a dial indicator

28.7a Measure journal diameter with a micrometer

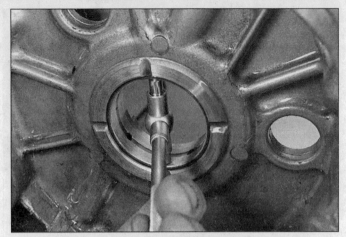

28.7b Measure main bearing diameter with a hole gauge . . .

Main bearing selection

Refer to illustrations 28.7a, 28.7b and 28.7c and 28.10

7   Measure the diameter of the main bearing journals with a micrometer **(see illustration)**. Measure the inside diameter of the main bearings with a hole gauge and micrometer **(see illustrations)**. The difference between these two measurements is the bearing clearance. It should be within the range listed in this Chapter's Specifications.

8   If the clearance is greater than the service limit listed in this Chapter's Specifications but journal diameter is within specifications, press out the old bearings. If you do not have a hydraulic press and the cor-

28.7c . . . then measure the gauge diameter with a micrometer

rect bearing driver, have the main bearings replaced at a dealer service department or a motorcycle machine shop.

9   The main journal outside diameter code number, a "1" or a "2," is stamped on the crankshaft weights **(see illustration 27.19a)**.

10   Measure the inside diameter of the main bearing bores in the crankcase (with the bearings removed). Record your measurements and compare them to the two crankcase I.D. size ranges listed in the accompanying chart to determine whether the crankcase I.D. is a code "A" or a code "B." Cross reference the crankcase I.D. code to the main journal O.D. code to select the correct main bearing color **(see illustration)**.

Matching the crankshaft to the connecting rods

13   The crankshaft and the connecting rods are "select fitted" (see Section 27). Some crankshafts have an "L" or an "H" stamped on the outside face of the right crank weight; this is the crankshaft weight code. On most cranks, you will *not* find an "L" or "H" stamped on the crank weight; that's because most cranks have *no* weight code. To select the correct crankshaft, refer to the accompanying chart. If the front and rear connecting rods have an "A" stamped on them, select an "L" crank; if the rods have a "C" on them, select an "H" crank. Aside from these two combinations, select a crank *with no weight code*. Select the correct crankshaft as follows:

a) *If both connecting rods have an "A" stamped on them, select an "L" crank.*

b) *If both connecting rods have a "C" on them, select an "H" crank.*

c) *If both connecting rods have a "B" on them, select a crank with no weight code.*

d) *If the two connecting rods have different letters, select a crank with no weight code.*

	Main journal O.D. code	Code "1" 44.992 to 45.000 mm (1.7713 to 1.7717 inches)	Code "2" 44.984 to 44.991 mm (1.7710 to 1.7713 inches)
28.10 Main bearing selection chart	Crankcase I.D. code	Bearing insert thickness	Bearing insert thickness
	Code "A" 48.990 to 49.000 mm (1.9287 to 1.9291 inches)	"C" (Brown) 1.993 to 2.003 mm (0.0785 to 0.0789 inch)	"B" (Black) 1.998 to 2.008 mm (0.0787 to 0.0791 inch)
	Code "B" 49.000 to 49.010 mm (1.9291 to 1.9295 inches)	"B" (Black) 1.998 to 2.008 mm (0.0787 to 0.0791 inch)	"A" (Blue) 2.003 to 2.013 mm (0.0789 to 0.0793 inch)

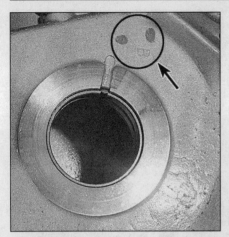

28.14 The main bearing I.D. code (arrow) is stamped into the left case half

29.3a Firmly grasp the end of the shift fork shaft . . .

29.3b . . . and carefully pull it out of the case and out of the shift forks

29.4 Remove the washer and 1st gear from the countershaft and set them aside

29.5 Remove the shift drum

Matching the crankshaft to the crankcase

Refer to illustration 28.14

14   The crankshaft and the crankcase are also select fitted. There is a "1" or a "2" stamped on the crank weights **(see illustration 27.19a)**; this is the main journal outside diameter code number. An "A" or a "B" is stamped into the case **(see illustration)**; this is the main bearing inside diameter code. A "1" crankshaft must be matched with an "A" crankcase; a "2" crankshaft must be matched with a "B" crankcase.

29.6 Remove the mainshaft assembly

Installation

15   Install the connecting rods on the crankshaft (see Section 27).
16   Lubricate the main bearings with engine assembly lube or moly-based grease.
17   Carefully lower the crankshaft/connecting rod assembly into the left crankcase half. Align the connecting rods with the cylinders.
18   Assemble the crankcase halves (see Section 23) and check to make sure the crankshaft and the transmission shafts turn freely.

29   Transmission - removal, inspection and installation

Removal

Refer to illustrations 29.3a, 29.3b, 29.4, 29.5, 29.6, 29.7 and 29.8

1   Remove the engine (see Section 5) and separate the crankcase halves (see Section 23).
2   On 1988 and 1989 and 1991 through 1995 VT600 models, remove the mainshaft, countershaft, shift fork shaft and shift drum as a single assembly.
3   On 1996 and later VT600 models and on all VT750 models, remove the shift fork shaft from the shift fork **(see illustrations)**.
4   Remove the first gear washer and first gear from the countershaft **(see illustration)**.
5   Remove the shift drum **(see illustration)**.
6   Remove the mainshaft assembly **(see illustration)**.

29.7 Remove the shift forks

29.8 Remove the countershaft assembly

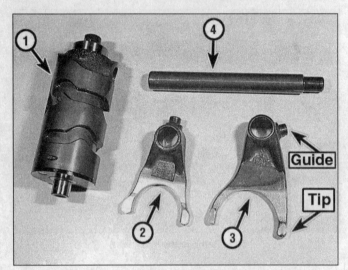

29.10 Inspect the grooves in the shift drum and the tips
and pin guides of the shift forks

1	Shift drum	3	Shift fork
2	Shift fork	4	Shift fork shaft

7 Remove the shift forks **(see illustration)**.
8 Remove the countershaft assembly **(see illustration)**.

Inspection

9 Thoroughly wash the transmission components in clean solvent
and dry them off with compressed air.

Shift drum, shift forks and shift fork shaft

Refer to illustration 29.10

10 Inspect the shift drum **(see illustration)** for evidence of insufficient lubrication and inspect the edges of the grooves in the shift drum
for excessive wear. If the drum is worn or damaged, replace it. Measure the diameter of the left shift drum journal and compare your measurement to the journal diameter listed in this Chapter's Specifications.
If it's smaller than the limit, replace the shift drum.

11 Inspect the shift forks for distortion and wear, especially the fork
tips. If they're discolored or severely worn they are probably bent. If
damage or wear is evident, check the shift fork groove in the corresponding sliding gear as well. Inspect the guide pins too. If the fork tips
or the guide pins are worn or damaged, replace the forks. Measure the
inside diameter of the shift fork shaft bore and the fork tip thickness of
both forks and compare your measurements to the dimensions listed

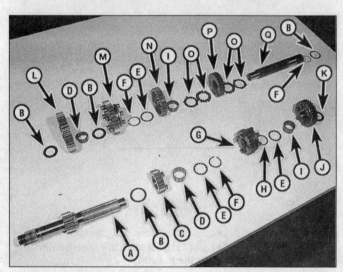

29.13 Transmission details (four-speed shown; five-speed similar)

A	Mainshaft	J	Mainshaft fourth gear
B	Thrust washer	K	Thrust washer
C	Mainshaft second gear	L	Countershaft first gear
D	Bushing	M	Countershaft second gear
E	Splined thrust washer	N	Countershaft third gear
F	Snap-ring	O	Lock washer and stop
G	Mainshaft third gear		washer
H	Snap-ring	P	Countershaft fourth gear
I	Splined thrust washer	Q	Countershaft

in this Chapter's Specifications. If the shift fork shaft bore is bigger
than the limit or the tips are thinner than the limit, replace the shift
fork(s).

12 Inspect the shift fork shaft for excessive wear, evidence of poor
lubrication and straightness (roll it on a flat surface). See if the shift
forks slide freely and smoothly on the shaft. Measure the diameter of
the shaft and compare your measurement to the shift fork shaft diameter listed in this Chapter's Specifications.

Countershaft and mainshaft

*Refer to illustrations 29.13, 29.19, 29.20, 29.21, 29.22a, 29.22b,
29.22c, 29.23a and 29.23b, 29.25 and 29.26*

13 Disassemble the transmission shafts. You'll need snap-ring pliers
to remove some of the parts from the shafts. It's a good idea to discard
all old snap-rings and install new ones when reassembling the transmission. Carefully study each part before removing it from the shaft; if

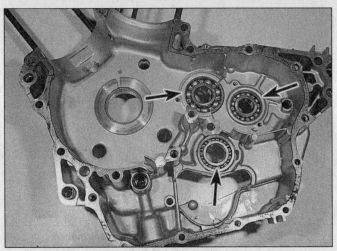

29.19 Inspect the bearings (arrows) for the shift drum, the mainshaft and the countershaft; if a bearing is rough or noisy or loose, replace it (or have it replaced by a dealer or by a machine shop)

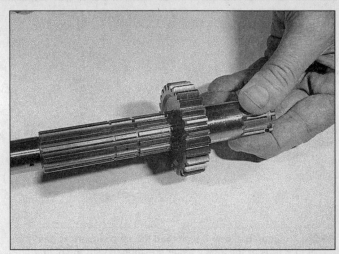

29.20 Install the C4 gear on the countershaft

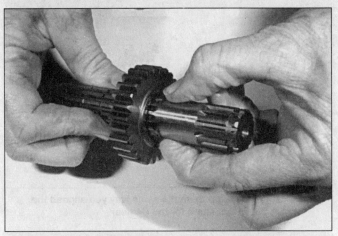

29.21 Install the stopper ring on the countershaft and seat it in its groove in the shaft adjacent to the C4 gear

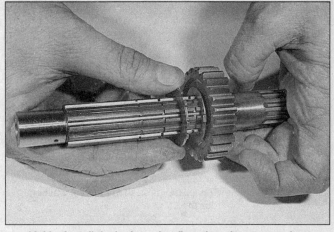

29.22a Install the lock washer first, then the stop washer, on the countershaft

the two sides of a part are not the same, make sure you know which side faces which way before removing that part. There are various ways to do this. One way to ensure that the parts retain their correct relationship to one another is to "stack" them on a long dowel, extension, etc. or to "thread" them on a piece of wire, as they're removed. If you're still in doubt, label the bigger parts to indicate which side faces left or right. Once you're confident that you know how the transmission goes back together, carefully lay out the parts in the order in which they were removed **(see illustration)**.

14   Inspect the gears. Check the gear dogs, gear dog holes and gear teeth for cracks, excessive wear and other obvious damage. If a gear is obviously worn or damaged, replace it, and replace its corresponding gear on the other shaft too. Measure the inside diameter of each gear and compare your measurements to the inside diameters for the various gears listed in this Chapter's Specifications. If the inside diameter of a gear is excessive, replace the gear.

15   Inspect the gear bushings. Check the surface of the inner diameter of each bushing for scoring or heat discoloration or signs of poor lubrication. If a gear or bushing is obviously damaged or worn, replace it. Measure the inside and outside diameters of each bushing and compare your measurements to the I.D. and O.D. dimensions for the bushings listed in this Chapter's Specifications.

16   Inspect the mainshaft and countershaft. Check the splines and sliding surfaces for wear and damage. If either shaft is worn or dam-

aged, replace it. Measure the diameter of each shaft at the gear and bushing sliding surfaces. Compare your measurements to the mainshaft and countershaft diameters listed in this Chapter's Specifications. If either shaft is worn below the limit, replace it.

17   To calculate the gear-to-mainshaft clearance, subtract the shaft diameter from the inside diameter of each gear. Compare your measurements to the gear-to-shaft clearances listed in this Chapter's Specifications. If the clearance is excessive, replace the gear and/or the shaft, depending on which part is causing the excessive clearance. Calculate the bushing-to-shaft clearances the same way and replace the bushing(s) and/or shaft accordingly.

18   Repeat Step 17 for the gear-to-countershaft clearance.

19   Inspect the bearings for the shift drum and the transmission shafts **(see illustration)**. Make sure they rotate smoothly and quietly. If they're rough or noisy or loose, press them out of the cases and press in new bearings, or have them replaced at a dealer service department or motorcycle machine shop.

20   Install the C4 gear on the countershaft **(see illustration)**.

21   Install the stopper ring on the countershaft **(see illustration)**.

22   Install the lock washer and stop washer on the countershaft **(see illustration)**. Position the lock washer and stop washer so that the bigger tabs of the lock washer are aligned with the bigger grooves of the stop washer and so that both washers are located at their groove in the shaft **(see illustrations)**.

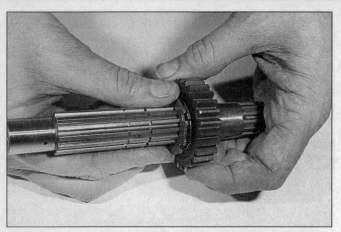

29.22b Position the lock washer and the stop washer so that the bigger tabs of the lock washer are aligned with the bigger grooves of the stop washer . . .

29.22c . . . and so that both washers are in their groove in the shaft

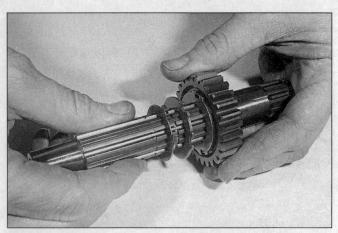

29.23a Install the stop washer first, then the lock washer, for the C3 gear . . .

29.23b . . . and align them the same way you aligned the washers for the C4 gear

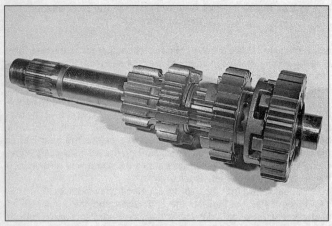

29.25 The mainshaft assembly should look like this when it's reassembled

29.26 The transmission assembly should look like this when it's reassembled

23   Install the stop washer, then the lock washer, for the C3 gear, and align them the same way you aligned the stop washer and lock washer for the C4 gear **(see illustrations)**.

24   Reassembly of the countershaft is otherwise the reverse of disassembly.

25   Reassembly of the mainshaft is the reverse of disassembly **(see illustration)**.

26   When you're done this is how the two assembled shafts should look **(see illustration)**.

Installation

Refer to illustration 29.27

27   Installation of the transmission in the left case half **(see illustration)** is the reverse of removal, noting the following points:

29.27 Install the transmission shafts in the left case half; before installing the other case half, make sure that the shift forks are correctly engaged with their respective shafts

a) *Install a new countershaft seal in the left crankcase half* (see illustration 22.19b).

b) *Lubricate all parts with engine oil before installing them.*

c) *Use the letters on the forks to position them correctly. The forks are identified by a "C" (center) or an "R" (right), starting from the left side of the engine. The letters face the right side of the engine when installed.*

d) *Engage the guide pin on each shift fork with the groove in the shift drum as you insert the shift fork shaft through the forks.*

e) *After reassembling the case halves, make sure that both shafts turn freely and the shift drum and shift forks function correctly.*

30 Initial start-up after overhaul

1   Make sure the engine oil level is correct, then remove the spark plugs from the engine. Place the engine kill switch in the Off position and unplug the primary (low tension) wires from the coils.

2   Turn on the key switch and crank the engine over with the starter several times to build up oil pressure. Reinstall the spark plugs, con-nect the wires and turn the switch to On.

3   Make sure there is fuel in the tank, then turn the fuel tap to the On position and operate the choke.

4   Start the engine and allow it to run at a moderately fast idle until it reaches operating temperature.

5   Check carefully for oil leaks and make sure the transmission and controls, especially the brakes, function properly before road testing the machine. Refer to Section 30 for the recommended break-in procedure.

6   Upon completion of the road test, and after the engine has cooled down completely, recheck the valve clearances (see Chapter 1).

31 Recommended break-in procedure

1   Any rebuilt engine needs time to break-in, even if parts have been installed in their original locations. For this reason, treat the machine gently for the first few miles to make sure oil has circulated throughout the engine and any new parts installed have started to seat.

2   Even greater care is necessary if the engine has been rebored or a new crankshaft has been installed. In the case of a rebore, the engine will have to be broken in as if the machine were new. This means greater use of the transmission and a restraining hand on the throttle until at least 500 miles have been covered. There's no point in keeping to any set speed limit - the main idea is to keep from lugging the engine and to gradually increase performance until the 500 mile mark is reached. These recommendations can be lessened to an extent when only a new crankshaft is installed. Experience is the best guide, since it's easy to tell when an engine is running freely. The following recommendations can be used as a guide:

a) *0 to 90 miles (0 to 150 km): Keep engine speed below 3,000 rpm. Turn off the engine after each hour of operation and let it cool for 5 to 10 minutes. Vary the engine speed and don't use full throttle.*

b) *90 to 300 miles (150 to 500 km): Don't run the engine for long periods above 4,000 rpm. Rev the engine freely through the gears, but don't use full throttle.*

c) *300 to 600 miles (500 to 1000 km): Don't use full throttle for pro-longed periods and don't cruise at speeds above 5,000 rpm.*

d) *At 600 miles (1,000 km): Change the engine oil and filter. Full throttle can be used after this point.*

3   If a lubrication failure is suspected, stop the engine immediately and try to find the cause. If an engine is run without oil, even for a short period of time, severe damage will occur.

Notes

Chapter 3
Cooling system

Contents

Specifications

General

Coolant type	See Chapter 1
Mixture ratio	See Chapter 1
Radiator cap pressure rating	
VT600	88 to 127 kPa (0.9 to 1.3 kgf/cm², 12.8 to 18 psi)
VT750	108 to 137 kPa (1.1 to 1.4 kgf/cm², 16 to 20 psi)
Thermostatic fan switch	
Closes circuit at	98 to 102 degrees C (208 to 216 degrees F)
Opens circuit at	93 to 97 degrees C (199 to 207 degrees F)
Coolant temperature sensor resistance	
VT600 (1988 through 2000), VT750DC	
At 50 degrees C (122 degrees F)	130 to 180 ohms
At 80 degrees C (176 degrees F)	45 to 60 ohms
At 120 degrees C (248 degrees F)	10 to 20 ohms
VT600 (2001 on), VT750C/CD	
112 to 118 degrees C (259 to 270 degrees F)	Starts to close (continuity)
Below 108 degrees C (252 degrees F)	Starts to open (no continuity)

Thermostat rating

Valve opening temperature	80 to 84-degrees C (176 to 183-degrees F)
Valve fully open at	95-degrees C (203-degrees F)
Valve travel (when fully open)	Not less than 8 mm (5/16-inch)

Torque specifications

Coolant temperature sensor	10 Nm (84 in-lbs)
Filler neck flange-to-thermostat housing cover bolts	9 Nm (78 in-lbs)
Thermostat housing cover bolts	
VT600	10 Nm (84 in-lbs)
VT750	9 Nm (78 in-lbs)
Thermostatic fan switch	
VT600, VT750DC	18 Nm (156 in-lbs)
VT750C/CD	8 Nm (70 in-lbs)
Water pump cover bolts	13 Nm (108 in-lbs)

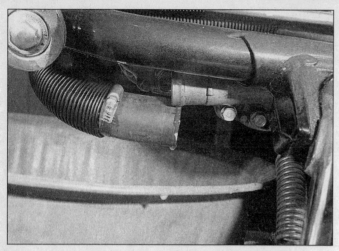

3.2 Loosen the hose clamp and detach the lower radiator hose from the water pump

3.4 The black two-pin connector (upper arrow) for the fan motor is on the left side, just behind the steering head (the lower arrow indicates the white turn signal connector)

1   General information

The models covered by this manual are liquid-cooled. The liquid-cooling system uses a water/antifreeze mixture to carry away excess heat produced during the combustion process. The cylinders are surrounded by water jackets, through which the coolant is circulated by the water pump. The pump is mounted on the left side of the crankcase and is driven by the oil pump shaft. Coolant is pumped through a flexible hose into the front cylinder. There, it flows through the water jacket surrounding the front cylinder. Some coolant exits through a smaller diameter pipe in the head and goes to the thermostat housing; the rest exits the front cylinder through a connecting pipe to the rear cylinder, where it again flows through the rear cylinder water jacket, exits the rear cylinder through another pipe and flows through a flexible hose to the thermostat housing. From the thermostat housing, coolant flows down into the radiator (which is mounted behind the front wheel, on the front of the frame, to take advantage of maximum air flow), where it is cooled by the passing air, through another hose and back to the water pump, where the cycle is repeated.

An electric fan, mounted behind the radiator and automatically controlled by a thermostatic switch, provides a flow of cooling air through the radiator when the coolant temperature exceeds a an upper threshold.

The coolant temperature sending unit, threaded into the thermostat housing, senses the temperature of the coolant and turns on the coolant temperature warning light on the instrument cluster when the coolant temperature reaches a dangerous level.

The entire system is sealed and pressurized. The pressure is controlled by a valve which is part of the radiator cap. By pressurizing the coolant, the boiling point is raised, which prevents premature boiling of the coolant. An overflow hose, connected between the radiator and reservoir tank, directs coolant to the tank when the radiator cap valve is opened by excessive pressure. The coolant is automatically siphoned back to the radiator as the engine cools.

Many cooling system inspection and service procedures are considered part of routine maintenance and are included in Chapter 1.

Warning 1: *Do not allow antifreeze to come in contact with your skin or painted surfaces of the vehicle. Rinse off spills immediately with plenty of water. Antifreeze is highly toxic if ingested. Never leave antifreeze lying around in an open container or in puddles on the floor; children and pets are attracted by its sweet smell and may drink it. Check with local authorities about disposing of used antifreeze. Many communities have collection centers which will see that antifreeze is disposed of safely.*

Warning 2: *Do not remove the radiator cap when the engine and radiator are hot. Scalding hot coolant and steam may be blown out under pressure, which could cause serious injury. To open the radiator cap,* remove the rear screw from the right side panel on the inside of the fairing (if equipped). When the engine has cooled, lift up the panel and place a thick rag, like a towel, over the radiator cap; slowly rotate the cap counterclockwise to the first stop. This procedure allows any residual pressure to escape. When the steam has stopped escaping, press down on the cap while turning counterclockwise and remove it.

2   Radiator cap - check

If problems such as overheating and loss of coolant occur, check the entire system as described in Chapter 1. The radiator cap opening pressure should be checked by a dealer service department or service station equipped with the special tester required to do the job. If the cap is defective, replace it.

3   Radiator - removal and installation

Refer to illustrations 3.2, 3.4, 3.6, 3.7a, 3.7b, 3.8 and 3.10
Warning: The engine must be completely cool before beginning this procedure.
1   Set the bike on its side stand. Disconnect the cable from the negative terminal of the battery.
2   Place a drain pan under the water pump, loosen the lower radiator hose clamp at the pump, detach the hose from the pump **(see illustration)** and drain the coolant.
3   Remove the fuel tank (see Chapter 4) and the steering head covers (see Chapter 8).
4   Follow the wiring harness from the fan motor to the two-pin black electrical connector on the left side, right behind the steering head **(see illustration)**. Unplug this connector and carefully disentangle the fan motor harness so it doesn't snag other wiring when the radiator is removed.
5   On VT600 models, disconnect the horn leads and remove the horn (see Chapter 9).
6   Loosen the hose clamp on the upper radiator hose **(see illustration)** and detach the hose. Loosen the hose clamp on the lower hose too, if you can. On some models it's easier to remove the lower hose with the radiator, because the hose clamp screw is not accessible until the radiator has been removed.
7   Remove the radiator mounting bolt from the bottom of the radiator on VT600 models or from the upper end on VT750 models **(see illustrations)**.
8   Lift up the radiator and disengage the two rubber insulators on the underside of the radiator from the insulator bracket on the frame.

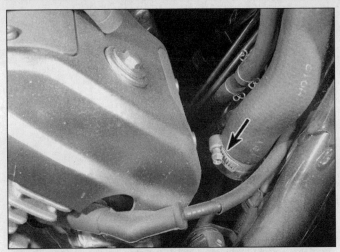

3.6 Loosen the upper radiator hose clamp and detach the upper hose from the radiator (VT600 model shown; on VT750 models, the upper hose is attached to the center of the upper backside of the radiator)

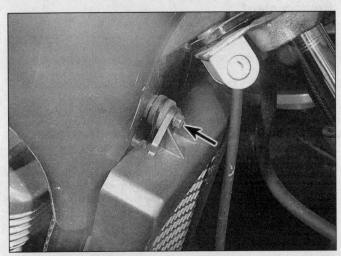

3.7b On VT750 models, the radiator mounting bolt is up top, right above the radiator

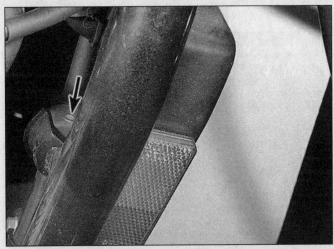

3.8 On VT600 models, seat the two rubber insulators on the upper backside of the radiator in their saddles on the frame when installing the radiator

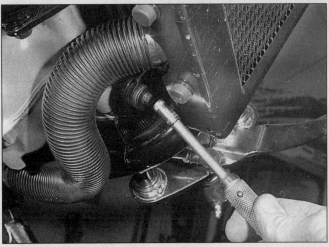

3.7a On VT600 models, the radiator mounting bolt is below the radiator

On VT600 models, there are also two insulators located on the upper backside of the radiator **(see illustration)**.

9   Remove the radiator.

10   Detach the lower radiator hose from the radiator, if you were unable to do so earlier, and remove the grille from the radiator. On VT600 models, the radiator grille is secured to the radiator by a single screw at the upper end of the grille; on VT750 models, the grille is secured by the same bolt that attaches the radiator to the frame **(see illustration)**.

11   If the radiator is to be repaired or replaced, remove the insulators **(see illustration 3.10)** and remove the fan assembly and the thermo-static fan switch (see Section 4).

12   Carefully inspect the radiator for signs of leaks and any other damage. If repairs are necessary, take the radiator to a reputable radiator repair shop. If the radiator is clogged, or if large amounts of rust or scale have formed, the repair shop will also do a thorough cleaning job.

13   Make sure the spaces between the cooling tubes and fins are clear. If necessary, use compressed air or running water to remove anything that may be clogging them. If the fins are bent or flattened, straighten them very carefully with a small screwdriver.

14   Inspect the radiator hoses for cracks, tears and other damage. Be sure to replace the hoses if they are damaged or deteriorated.

15   Installation is the reverse of the removal procedure.

16   Refill the cooling system with the recommended coolant (see Chapter 1).

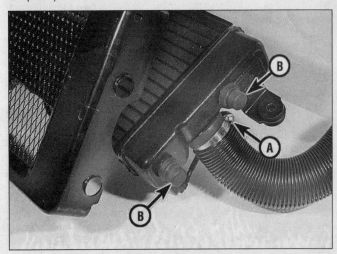

3.10 On VT600 models, detach the lower radiator hose (A); remove the rubber insulators (B) if necessary

4.1 The VT600 fan switch (arrow) is at the lower right rear corner of the radiator (radiator removed for clarity); the VT750 switch is at the lower left side of the radiator

4   Cooling fan and thermostatic fan switch - check and replacement

Check

Refer to illustrations 4.1 and 4.3

1   If the engine is overheating and the cooling fan isn't coming on, remove the right side cover (see Chapter 8) and check the 10A fan motor fuse (see Chapter 9). If the fuse is blown, check the fan motor circuit for a short to ground (see the *Wiring diagrams* at the end of this book). If the fuse is good, locate the fan switch at the lower right rear corner of the radiator on VT600 models **(see illustration)** or at the lower left side of the radiator on VT750 models. Warm up the engine, turn the ignition switch to OFF, unplug the electrical connector from the fan switch, ground the connector with a jumper wire, turn the ignition switch to ON and note whether the fan motor comes on. If the fan motor comes on, the fan switch is defective. If the fan motor still doesn't come on, inspect the wiring and the connectors (see *Wiring diagrams*), then check the fan motor itself.

2   To check the fan motor, remove the fuel tank (see Chapter 4), remove the steering head covers (see Chapter 8), unplug the two-wire black electrical connector **(see illustration 3.4)** and, using a pair of jumper wires connected to the battery terminals, apply battery voltage to the fan-motor side of the connector. If the fan doesn't come on, replace the fan motor. If it does come on, the problem is in the wiring on the switch side of the connector, or the fan switch itself is defective.

3   To check the fan switch, remove the switch (see Step 10), suspend it in a pan of water, heat the water and, using a cooking ther-

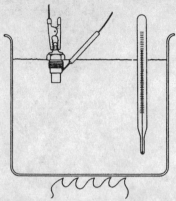

4.3 Thermostatic fan switch test

mometer and an ohmmeter, test the switch as shown **(see illustration)**. **Warning:** *Antifreeze is poisonous. Don't use a cooking pan.* Note the temperature at which the switch closes the circuit and compare this to the temperature listed in this Chapter's Specifications. If the switch doesn't perform as described, replace it.

Replacement

Fan motor

Refer to illustrations 4.6 and 4.7

Warning: The engine must be completely cool before beginning this procedure.

4   Disconnect the cable from the negative terminal of the battery.

5   Remove the radiator (see Section 8).

6   Remove the four bolts securing the fan bracket to the radiator **(see illustration)**. Note how the harnesses for the fan motor and fan switch are routed and how they're clamped to the fan bracket and to the radiator; they must be correctly rerouted before the radiator is installed. Separate the fan and bracket from the radiator.

7   Remove the nut that retains the fan to the motor shaft **(see illustration)** and remove the fan blade assembly from the motor.

8   Remove the three nuts that secure the fan motor to the bracket **(see illustration 4.7)** and detach the motor from the bracket.

9   Installation is the reverse of the removal procedure.

Thermostatic fan switch

Warning: The engine must be completely cool before beginning this procedure.

10   On VT750 models, remove the radiator (see Section 3).

11   Prepare the new switch by wrapping the threads with Teflon tape or by coating the threads with RTV sealant. Make sure there's a new

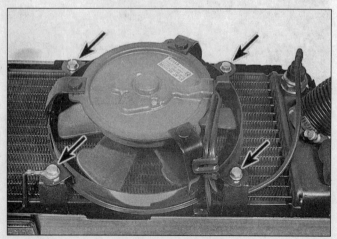

4.6 These are the fan motor bracket bolts; one bolt secures a ground wire

4.7 Here are the fan-to-motor nut (center arrow) and the fan motor-to-bracket nuts (outer arrows)

O-ring on the switch.

12   Place a drain pan under the radiator and have some rags handy to soak up the coolant that will inevitably spill out. Unscrew the switch from the radiator **(see illustration 4.1)** and quickly install the new switch, tightening it to the torque listed in this Chapter's Specifications.

13   Plug the electrical connector into the switch.

14   Check and, if necessary, add coolant to the system (see Chapter 1).

5   Coolant temperature warning system - check and component replacement

Check

System

Note: *Before troubleshooting the coolant temperature warning system, make sure that the coolant is at the correct level (see Chapter 1) and there are no leaks in the system.*

1   The coolant temperature warning light comes on if the engine coolant exceeds its normal operating temperature. If the warning light, or the temperature sensor that turns it on, is defective, you will not know that the engine is overheating until it is too late. To determine whether the system is operating correctly, turn the ignition key to the ON position and watch the coolant temperature warning light (located in the speedometer). It should come on for a few seconds, then go off. This verifies that the coolant temperature warning system is operating correctly on all except 2001 and later VT600 and VT750C/CD models.

2   If the coolant temperature warning light doesn't come on momentarily when the ignition key is turned to ON, or if it stays on all the time, check the system.

VT600 models (1988 through 2000)

3   Remove the fuel tank (see Chapter 4) and the left steering head cover (see Chapter 8).

4   If the coolant temperature warning light isn't coming on briefly when the ignition key is turned to ON, locate the electrical connectors for the black/brown wire and the green/black wire and unplug them. Turn the ignition key to ON and, using a voltmeter or test light, determine whether there's voltage between the black/brown wire and the green/black wires on the harness side of the connectors. If there is, replace the speedometer (see Chapter 9). If there isn't, inspect the harness side of the black/brown and green/black wiring for an open circuit or for loose connections.

5   If the temperature warning light stays on all the time, locate the electrical connector for the green/blue wire and unplug it. Using an ohm-meter, determine whether there is continuity between the harness side of the connector and ground. If there is, look for a short circuit in the green/blue wire. If there isn't, check the coolant temperature sensor.

VT600 and VT750C/CD models (2001 on)

6   Turn the ignition switch to the ON position. The temperature indicator lamp should not light. If it does, follow the wiring harness from the light to the thermosensor, checking for a break or bad connection. Make any necessary repairs and retest.

VT750 C/CD models (1998 through 2000), VT750DC models

7   Remove the headlight lens and reflector (see Chapter 9). (Don't remove the headlight housing, just remove the lens and reflector; the wiring for the coolant temperature sensor and the warning light is inside the headlight housing.)

8   If the coolant temperature warning light isn't coming on briefly when the ignition key is turned to ON, unplug the black six-pin electrical connector for the speedometer. Turn the ignition key to ON and, using a voltmeter or test light, determine whether there's voltage between the black/brown wire and the green/blue wires on the harness side of the connector. If there is, replace the speedometer (see Chapter 9). If there isn't, inspect the harness side of the black/brown and green/blue wires for an open circuit or for loose connections.

9   If the temperature warning light stays on all the time, unplug the black six-pin electrical connector for the speedometer. Using an ohm-

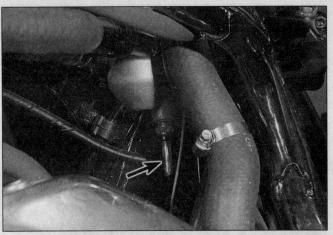

5.14 The coolant temperature sensor (arrow) is installed in the thermostat housing (VT600 shown; VT750 similar)

meter, determine whether there is continuity between the harness side of the green/blue wire and ground. If there is, look for a short circuit in the green/blue wire. If there isn't, check the coolant temperature sensor.

Coolant temperature sensor

10   Remove the coolant temperature sensor (see Step 11).

11   Suspend the temperature sensor in a pan of 50/50 antifreeze/water mixture (plain water will boil before it reaches the maximum test temperature). Heat the water and test the sensor with a cooking thermometer and an ohmmeter **(see illustration 4.3)**. **Warning:** *Antifreeze is poisonous. Don't use the pan or thermometer for cooking after this test.* Note the temperature at which the resistance changes and compare your observations to the sensor resistance listed in this Chapter's Specifications. If the sensor doesn't operate as specified, replace it.

Replacement

Coolant temperature sensor

Refer to illustration 5.14

Warning: The engine must be completely cool before beginning this procedure.

12   Drain the coolant (see Chapter 1).

13   Prepare the new coolant temperature sensor by wrapping the threads with Teflon tape or by coating the threads with RTV sealant.

14   Unscrew the coolant temperature sensor **(see illustration)** from the thermostat housing.

15   Install the new sensor and tighten it to the torque listed in this Chapter's Specifications.

16   Reconnect the electrical connector to the sensor.

17   Refill the cooling system (see Chapter 1).

Speedometer

18   Refer to Chapter 9.

6   Thermostat - removal, check and installation

Removal

Refer to illustrations 6.5a, 6.5b, 6.6 and 6.7

Warning: The engine must be completely cool before beginning this procedure.

1   If the thermostat is functioning correctly, the engine should warm up quickly, within a few minutes (unless the temperature is cold), and should not overheat (indicated by the coolant temperature warning light coming on). If the engine does not reach normal operating temperature quickly, or if it overheats, the thermostat should be removed, checked and, if necessary, replaced.

6.5a Remove the siphon tube (A), the filler neck-to-bracket bolt (B) and the flange-to-cover bolts (C) (one bolt hidden)

2   Remove the fuel tank (see Chapter 4) and the steering head covers (see Chapter 8).
3   On VT600 models, remove the air cleaner housing cover and filter element (see Chapter 1) and remove the air cleaner housing (see Chapter 4).
4   Drain the cooling system (see Chapter 1).

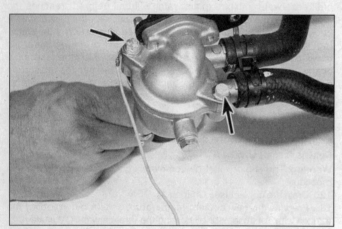

6.6 Remove the thermostat housing cover bolts (arrows) and lift off the cover

6.7 Note how the thermostat is installed, then remove it and discard the old O-ring

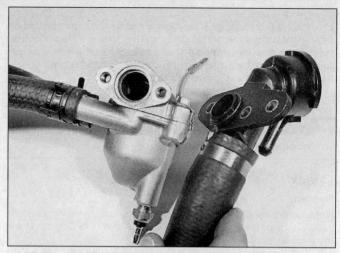

6.5b Detach the radiator filler neck flange from the thermostat housing and remove the O-ring (thermostat housing assembly removed for clarity)

5   Detach the siphon tube **(see illustration)** from the radiator filler neck. Remove the bolt that secures the filler neck flange to the filler neck bracket and the two bolts that secure the flange to the thermostat housing cover. Separate the filler neck flange from the housing cover **(see illustration)** and discard the old O-ring.
6   Remove the thermostat housing cover bolts **(see illustration)** and remove the cover.
7   Note how the thermostat is oriented in the thermostat housing **(see illustration)**, then remove it from the housing and discard the old O-ring.

Check

Refer to illustration 6.9

8   Remove any coolant deposits, then visually check the thermostat for corrosion, cracks and other damage. If it was open when it was removed, it is defective. Check the O-ring for cracks and other damage.
9   To check the thermostat's operation, submerge it in a container of water along with a thermometer **(see illustration)**. **Warning:** *Antifreeze is poisonous. Don't use a cooking pan.* The thermostat should be suspended so it does not touch the container.
10   Gradually heat the water in the container with a hot plate or stove

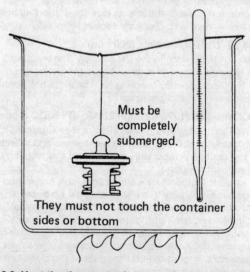

6.9 Heat the thermostat in a pan of water and note the temperatures when it starts to open and when it's fully open

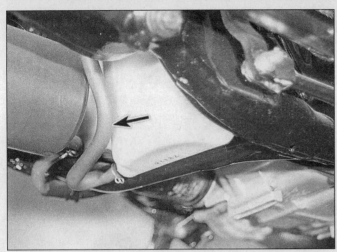

8.2 The VT600 coolant reservoir is under the swingarm, behind the engine; the lower hose (arrow) is the siphon tube . . .

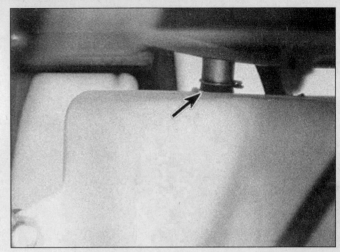

8.6 . . . and the upper hose (arrow) is the overflow tube

and check the temperature when the thermostat first starts to open. Continue heating the water and check the temperature when the thermostat is fully open.

11   Compare your results to the specified thermostat opening temperature range listed in this Chapter's Specifications.

12   If the thermostat does not open as described, replace it.

Installation

13   Install the thermostat into the housing, spring end first **(see illustration 6.7)**.

14   Install a new O-ring in the groove in the thermostat housing.

15   Place the cover on the housing, install the cover screws and tighten them to the torque listed in this Chapter's Specifications.

16   Install a new O-ring on the filler neck flange.

17   Attach the filler neck flange to the thermostat housing cover, install the flange-to-cover bolts and tighten them to the torque listed in this Chapter's Specifications.

18   Reattach the filler neck flange to the frame bracket and tighten the bolt securely.

19   Reattach the siphon tube to the radiator filler neck. If the wire retainer is fatigued, replace it.

20   On VT600 models, install the air cleaner housing (see Chapter 4), the filter element and the air cleaner housing cover (see Chapter 1).

21   Install the steering head covers (see Chapter 8) and the fuel tank (see Chapter 4).

22   Fill the cooling with the recommended coolant (see Chapter 1).

7   Thermostat housing - removal and installation

Warning: The engine must be completely cool before beginning this procedure.

1   Remove the fuel tank (see Chapter 4) and the steering head covers (see Chapter 8).

2   On VT600 models, remove the air cleaner housing cover and filter element (see Chapter 1) and remove the air cleaner housing (see Chapter 4).

3   Drain the cooling system (see Chapter 1).

4   Unplug the electrical lead from the coolant temperature sensor **(see illustration 5.13)**.

5   Detach the siphon tube from the radiator filler neck and remove the bolt that secures the filler neck flange to the filler neck bracket **(see illustration 6.5a)**.

6   Loosen the hose clamps and detach both hoses from the thermostat housing.

7   Remove the thermostat housing.

8   Installation is the reverse of removal.

9   Fill the cooling system with the recommended coolant (see Chapter 1).

8   Coolant reservoir - removal and installation

Refer to illustration 8.2, 8.6, 8.7a, 8.7b and 8.7c

1   Drain the cooling system (see Chapter 1).

2   On VT600 models, the coolant reservoir **(see illustration)** is located behind the engine, below the swingarm pivot bolt and (on California models) in front of the evaporative canister. Raise the motorcycle under the rear part of the frame and support it securely with jack stands.

3   On VT600 California models, remove the evaporative canister (see Chapter 4).

4   On VT750 models, the coolant reservoir is located ahead of the engine, behind and below the radiator.

5   On VT750 models, remove the radiator (see Section 3).

6   Place a container under the reservoir to catch spilled coolant. Detach the siphon tube **(see illustration 8.2)** and the overflow tube **(see illustration)**.

7   On VT600 models, remove the filler neck retaining nut **(see illustration)** and the reservoir retaining bolt **(see illustration)** and detach the

8.7a On VT600 models, remove the filler neck retaining nut (arrow) . . .

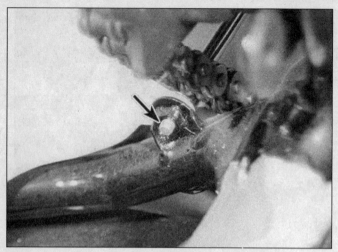

8.7b ... the reservoir retaining bolt (arrow)

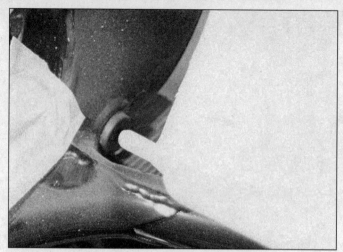

8.7c ... pull this positioning pin out of its grommet in the frame
and remove the reservoir (engine removed for clarity)

9.1 If coolant is leaking from the weep hole (arrow),
replace the water pump

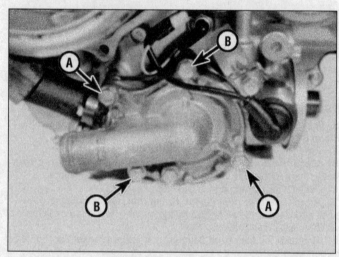

9.5 Remove the hold-down bolts (A) and cover bolts (B)
and lift off the cover

reservoir position pin from the grommet in the frame **(see illustration)**.
8   On VT750 models, remove the reservoir retaining bolt and the filler neck retaining nut.
9   Remove the reservoir.
10   Installation is the reverse of removal. Be sure to fill the cooling system when you're done (see Chapter 1).

9   Water pump - check, removal and installation

Check

Refer to illustration 9.1
Note: *The water pump on these models can't be overhauled - it must be replaced as a unit.*
1   Inspect the area around the water pump for coolant leaks. Try to determine whether the leak is simply the result of a loose hose clamp or deteriorated hose, or whether it's leaking from a damaged pump cover O-ring or from the "weep hole" (coolant drainage passage) in the underside of the pump body **(see illustration)**.
2   If the leak appears to be caused by a loose hose clamp, tighten the clamp, clean up the area, ride the bike and verify that the leak has been fixed. If the leak appears to be caused by a damaged hose, drain the coolant (see Chapter 1) and replace the hose. If the pump is leaking

from a bad cover O-ring, replace the O-ring. If the pump is leaking from the weep hole, replace the pump.
3   If there is any sign of oil in the area around the water pump, the pump housing O-ring may be damaged. Remove the pump and replace the pump housing O-ring.

Removal, inspection and O-ring replacement

Refer to illustrations 9.5, 9.8 and 9.10
4   Remove the engine (see Chapter 2).
5   To inspect the pump cover or the impeller, or to replace the pump cover O-ring, remove the cover bolts **(see illustration)** and separate the cover from the water pump body.
6   Try to wiggle the water pump impeller back-and-forth and in-and-out. If you can feel movement, the water pump must be replaced.
7   Inspect the impeller blades for corrosion. If they are heavily corroded, replace the water pump and flush the system thoroughly (it would also be a good idea to check the internal condition of the radiator).
8   If the cause of the leak was a defective cover O-ring, remove the old O-ring **(see illustration)** and install a new one.
9   Install the pump cover and tighten the pump cover bolts to the torque listed in this Chapter's Specifications.
10   If the pump housing O-ring or the pump itself must be replaced,

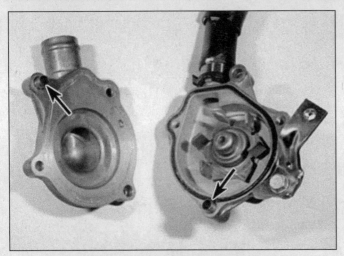

9.8 Locate the cover dowels (arrows); install a new O-ring if the old one is damaged

9.10 Remove the pump hold-down bolts and pull the pump straight out; use a new O-ring (arrow) on installation

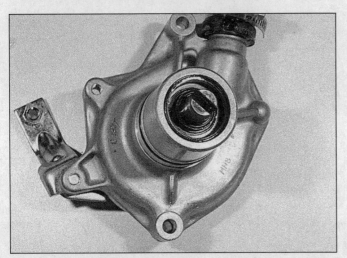

9.12a When installing the water pump, make sure that this slot in the pump shaft . . .

9.12b . . . is aligned with this ridge on the end of the oil pump shaft

remove the pump from the engine by pulling it straight out **(see illustration)**.

Installation

Refer to illustrations 9.12a and 9.12b

11   Before installing the pump, smear a little engine oil on the pump housing O-ring.

12   The water pump is driven off the left end of the oil pump shaft. Make sure the slot in the pump shaft is engaged properly with the ridge on the end of the oil pump shaft **(see illustrations)**.

13   Install the engine (see Chapter 2).

14   Fill the cooling system with the recommended coolant (see Chapter 1), ride the bike and check for leaks.

Notes

Chapter 4
Fuel and exhaust systems

Contents

Specifications

Carburetors

VT600 models (1988 through 1998)

Type	
Except California	VDFDA
California	VDFEA
Float level	7.0 mm (0.28 inch)
Main jet	115
Slow jet	40
Pilot screw adjustment	
Initial opening	1-1/4 turns out
Final opening	1 turn out
High altitude adjustment	1/2 turn in (from low altitude setting)

VT600 models (1999 on)

Type	
Except California	VE5AC
California	VE5AB
Float level	18.5 mm (0.73 inch)
Main jet	125
Slow jet	45
Pilot screw adjustment	
Initial opening	
Except California	3 turns out
California	2-3/4 turns out
Final opening	3/4 turn out

VT750C/CD models

Type	
1998	
49 states	VDFFG
California	VDFEB
Canada (VT750C/CD/CD2)	VDFFG
Canada (VT750C3/CD3)	VDFFJ
1999 on	
Except California	VDFFJ
California	VDFEC
Float level	7.0 mm (0.28 inch)
Main jet	
Front carburetor	105
Rear carburetor	110

Carburetors (continued)

VT750C/CD models (continued)

Slow jet 40
Pilot screw adjustment
    Initial opening .... 2-1/4 turns out
    Final opening .... 1 turn out

VT750DC models

Type
    Except California VDF2D
    California VDF2C
Float level... 7.0 mm (0.28 inch)
Main jet
    Front carburetor 05
    Rear carburetor 108
Slow jet 40
Pilot screw adjustment
    Initial opening .... 2-3/8 turns out
    Final opening .... 1/2 turn out
    High altitude setting .... 1/2 turn in (from low altitude setting)

Fuel pump

Discharge volume (minimum)
    VT600 .... 800 cc (27.1 fl oz) per minute
    VT750 .... 900 cc (30.4 fl oz) per minute

Torque specifications

Fuel tank mounting bolt.. 19 Nm (14 ft-lbs)
Fuel valve nut
    VT600
        1988 through 1998... 23 Nm (17 ft-lbs)
        1999 on .... 35 Nm (26 ft-lbs)
    VT750 .... 34 Nm (25 ft-lbs)

1　General information

The fuel system consists of the fuel tank, the fuel valve, the fuel pump, the fuel filter, the carburetors, the hoses connecting these components, and the accelerator cables.

The carburetors used on these motorcycles are Keihins with butterfly-type throttle valves. All except 1999 and later VT600 models use twin carburetors. VT600 models from 1999 on use a single carburetor equipped with an accelerator pump. For cold starting, an enrichment circuit is actuated by a choke knob mounted on the left side of the bike.

The exhaust system routes the exhaust gases through a pair of exhaust pipes and mufflers on the right side of the bike.

Some of the fuel system service procedures are included in Chapter 1 as routine maintenance items.

2　Fuel tank - removal and installation

Refer to illustrations 2.3, 2.4, 2.5, 2.10, 2.11 and 2.12

Warning: *Gasoline (petrol) is extremely flammable, so take extra precautions when you work on any part of the fuel system. Don't smoke or*

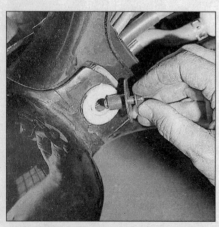

2.3　Remove the fuel tank mounting bolt and bushing; inspect the rubber grommet and replace it if it's damaged

2.4　If you're planning to clean or replace the fuel tank on a VT600, remove the fuel valve knob retaining screw and remove the knob

2.5　Lift the tank slightly, back off the wire retainers and detach the fuel hoses from the fuel valve

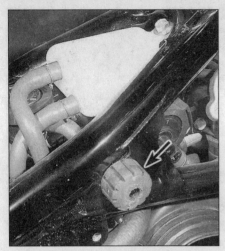

2.10 Inspect the rubber tank insulators; if they're damaged, replace them

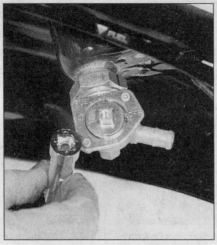

2.11 The square hole in the fuel valve knob aligns with the square lug on the fuel valve shaft

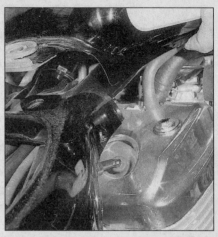

2.12 If the fuel tank is correctly seated on the rubber insulators, the hole in the bracket for the hold-down bolt will be aligned with the bolt hole in the frame

allow open flames or bare light bulbs near the work area, and don't work in a garage where a natural gas-type appliance (such as a water heater or clothes dryer) is present. If you spill any fuel on your skin, rinse it off immediately with soap and water. When you perform any kind of work on the fuel system, wear safety glasses and have a fire extinguisher suitable for class B fires (flammable liquids) on hand.

1   Support the bike securely so it can't be knocked over during this procedure.

2   Remove the seat (see Chapter 8). If the motorcycle has a tank-mounted speedometer, remove it (see Chapter 9).

3   Remove the fuel tank hold-down bolt and bushing **(see illustration)**. Inspect the rubber grommet. If it's cracked, torn or deteriorated, replace it.

4   If necessary, remove the fuel valve knob retaining screw **(see illustration)** and remove the knob.

5   Hold a pan under the fittings to catch drained fuel, lift up the tank and disconnect the fuel hoses from the fuel tap **(see illustration)**.

6   Remove the tank from the bike. **Warning:** *Pour the drained fuel into a safe fuel storage container. Don't leave it in the drain pan.*

7   If you're going to have the tank professionally cleaned, or if you're going to replace it, unscrew the fuel valve nut and remove the fuel valve, the O-ring and the strainer. Discard the old O-ring.

8   Clean the fuel strainer screen thoroughly and inspect it. If the strainer is clogged, torn or otherwise damaged, replace it.

9   Install the strainer, a new O-ring and the fuel valve in the tank and tighten the fuel valve nut securely.

10   Before installing the tank, inspect the fuel hoses and the rubber tank insulators on the frame **(see illustration)**. If the hoses or insulators are cracked, hardened, or otherwise deteriorated, replace them.

11   If you removed the fuel valve knob on a VT600 model, install it and tighten the knob retaining screw securely. Make sure that the square hole in the knob is aligned with the square lug on the fuel valve shaft **(see illustration)**.

12   Installation is the reverse of removal. Make sure the tank is correctly seated on the rubber insulators **(see illustration)** and make sure it doesn't pinch any control cables or wire harnesses.

3   Fuel tank - cleaning and repair

1   All repairs to the fuel tank should be carried out by a professional who has experience in this critical and potentially dangerous work. Even after cleaning and flushing of the fuel system, explosive fumes can remain and ignite during repair of the tank.

2   If the fuel tank is removed from the vehicle, it should not be

placed in an area where sparks or open flames could ignite the fumes coming out of the tank. Be especially careful inside garages where a natural gas-type appliance is located, because the pilot light could cause an explosion.

4   Crankcase emission control system - description, check and component replacement

Description

Refer to illustration 4.1

1   The closed crankcase emission control system prevents crankcase emissions from escaping into the atmosphere by routing blow-by gas from the rear cylinder head through a hose into the crankcase breather separator **(see illustration)**. Blow-by gas is routed from the separator through another hose to the air cleaner housing, where it's mixed with fresh intake air. Finally, the blow-by is drawn into the intake ducts, through the carburetors and into the combustion chamber, where it is burned.

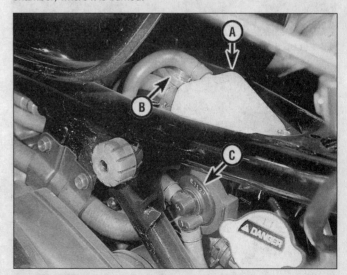

4.1 VT600 emission control components (VT750 similar)

A   Crankcase breather separator
B   Carburetor air vent control valve (California models)
C   Purge control valve (California models)

4.2　Inspect the crankcase emission control system hoses from the rear cylinder head cover to the separator and from the separator to the air cleaner housing (arrows)

Check

Refer to illustration 4.2

2　Inspect the condition of the system hoses **(see illustration)**. Make sure that there are no cuts or tears in the hoses and all connections are tight. If the hoses are worn or damaged, replace them.

4.5　Lift up the separator slightly and detach the drain tube (arrow) from the front of the separator

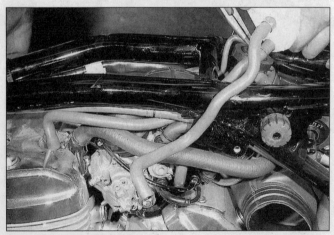

4.6　Detach the hoses from the rear of the separator

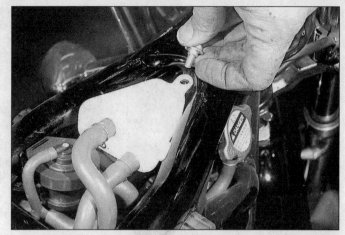

4.4　To detach the crankcase breather separator from the bike, remove this hold-down screw

3　Inspect the condition of the crankcase breather separator **(see illustration 4.1)**. If it's cracked, deteriorated or otherwise damaged, replace it.

Component replacement

Refer to illustrations 4.4, 4.5 and 4.6

4　Remove the crankcase breather separator hold-down screw **(see illustration)** and lift up the separator.
5　Disconnect the drain tube from the separator **(see illustration)**.
6　Disconnect the inlet and outlet hoses from the separator **(see illustration)**.
7　Installation is the reverse of removal.
8　If you're replacing any of the three hoses, carefully note how they're routed before removing them and route the new hose(s) exactly the same way.

5　**Evaporative emission control system (California models) - description, check and component replacement**

Description

Refer to illustration 5.1

1　On California models, an evaporative emission control (EVAP) system captures raw hydrocarbon vapors from the carburetor float bowls and the fuel tank when the engine is not running. The vapors are

5.1　The evaporative emission control (EVAP) system canister (arrow) is located behind and below the engine

5.8a To detach the carburetor air vent control valve, detach the hose from the air vent port . . .

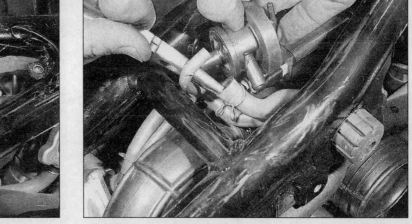

5.8b . . . lift up the valve, label the other hoses and detach them from the valve

stored in a canister located below the swingarm **(see illustration)**. When the engine is started, these vapors are routed from the canister into the combustion chambers and burned.

2   The EVAP system is controlled by the carburetor air vent (CAV) control valve and the purge control valve **(see illustration 4.1)**. When the engine is started, both valves are opened by intake vacuum. Vacuum from the front intake opens the carburetor air vent valve, venting the carburetor float bowls through the air vent valve to the canister; vacuum from the rear intake opens the purge control valve, drawing vapors from the canister through the purge control valve into the intakes. When the engine is turned off, intake vacuum is cut, closing the valves.

3   When the fuel inside the carburetor float bowls heats up, vapors from the float bowls are pushed into the canister. When fuel inside the fuel tank heats up, vapors from the fuel tank are pushed into the canister. These vapors are stored in the canister until the next time the engine is started.

4   Periodically, inspect the hoses connecting the canister, the carburetor air vent control valve and the purge control valve and the intakes.

Check and component replacement

5   Remove the fuel tank (see Section 2).

6   Remove the left side cover (see Chapter 8) and refer to the vacuum hose routing diagram on the inside of the cover for the following inspection and component tests.

7   Make sure that all the hose connections are tight, the hoses are in good condition and none of the hoses are kinked. If any of the hoses are torn, frayed or otherwise deteriorated, replace them.

Carburetor air vent control valve

Refer to illustrations 5.8a, 5.8b and 5.9

Note: *You will need a vacuum pump/gauge and a pressure pump/gauge to do the following test. If you don't have these tools, have the carburetor air vent control valve checked by a dealer service department.*

8   Mark the four hoses attached to the carburetor air vent control valve to ensure correct reassembly, then disconnect all four hoses from the carburetor air vent control valve **(see illustrations)** and remove the valve.

9   Connect a hand-held vacuum pump/gauge to the port for the No. 10 hose **(see illustration)**, which goes to the carburetor for the front cylinder. Apply 250 mm Hg (9.8 in-Hg) and verify that the valve holds vacuum. If it doesn't, replace the valve.

10   Connect the vacuum pump/gauge to the air vent port (on top of the valve), apply 250 mm Hg (9.8 in-Hg) and verify that the valve holds

vacuum. If it doesn't, replace the valve.

11   Reconnect the vacuum pump/gauge to the port for the No. 10 hose and connect a pressure pump/gauge to the air vent port. Plug the port for the No. 4 hose (which goes to the canister), apply 250 mm Hg (9.8 in-Hg) vacuum to the No. 10 port, pump some air into the air vent port and verify that air exits from the port for the No. 6 hose (which goes to the air joint pipe at the carburetors). If it doesn't, replace the valve.

12   If the carburetor air vent control valve fails to perform as described, replace it. Make sure that the hoses are reattached to the valve as indicated by the vacuum hose routing diagram label on the left side cover. Install the left side cover and the fuel tank.

Purge control valve

Refer to illustration 5.14

Note: *You will need a vacuum pump/gauge and a pressure pump/gauge to do the following tests. If you don't have these tools, have the purge control valve checked by a dealer service department.*

13   Mark the three hoses attached to the purge control valve to ensure correct reassembly, then disconnect all three hoses from the purge control valve and remove the valve.

14   Connect a hand-held vacuum pump/gauge to the port for the

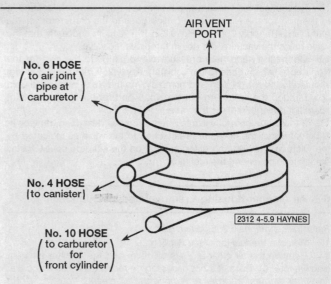

5.9 The carburetor air vent control valve (California models)

AIR VENT PORT

No. 6 HOSE
(to air joint pipe at carburetor)

No. 4 HOSE
(to canister)

No. 10 HOSE
(to carburetor for front cylinder)

2312 4-5.9 HAYNES

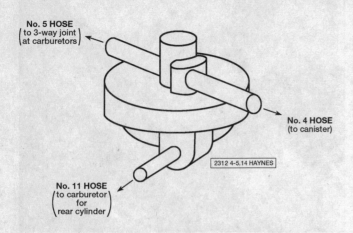

No. 5 HOSE
(to 3-way joint
at carburetors)

No. 4 HOSE
(to canister)

2312 4-5.14 HAYNES

No. 11 HOSE
(to carburetor
for
rear cylinder)

5.14 The purge control valve (California models)

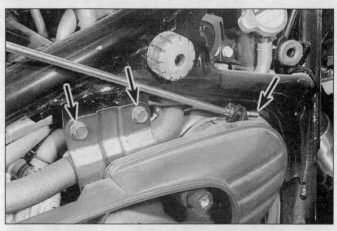

6.3 To detach the air cleaner housing from the air intake chamber on a VT600 model, loosen this hose clamp that secures the housing to the air intake chamber and remove these two bolts (arrows)

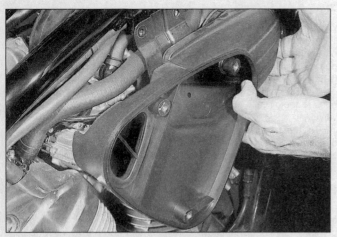

6.5a Pull off the air cleaner housing . . .

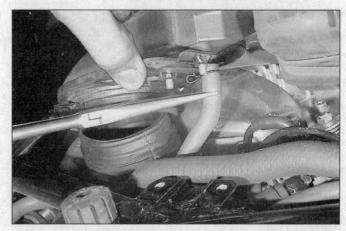

6.5b . . . and detach the crankcase breather separator hose from the backside of the housing (VT600 model shown)

No. 5 hose **(see illustration)**, which goes to the three-way joint. Apply 250 mm Hg (9.8 in-Hg) vacuum and verify that the valve holds this vacuum. If it doesn't, replace the valve.

15   Disconnect the vacuum pump from the No. 5 port and connect it to the port for the No. 11 hose (which goes to the carburetor for the rear cylinder). Apply 250 mm Hg (9.8 in-Hg) vacuum and verify that the valve holds the vacuum. If it doesn't, replace the valve.

16   Connect a hand-held pressure pump/gauge to the port for the No. 4 hose (which goes to the canister). Apply 250 mm Hg (9.8 in-Hg) vacuum to the No. 11 port and pump air into the No. 4 port. Air should flow through the valve and out the No. 5 port for the three-way joint hose. If it doesn't, replace the valve.

17   If the purge control valve fails to perform as described, replace it. Make sure that the hoses are reattached to the valve as indicated by the vacuum hose routing diagram label on the left side cover. Install the left side cover and the fuel tank.

---

6   Air cleaner housing - removal and installation

Refer to illustrations 6.3, 6.5a and 6.5b

1   Remove the fuel tank (see Section 2).

2   Remove the air cleaner housing cover and the air filter element (see Chapter 1). **Note:** *It's not necessary to remove the housing cover and filter element in order to remove the air cleaner housing. But if you're planning to disassemble the air cleaner housing assembly, it's easier to remove the cover and filter while the housing is still installed.*

Of course, if you're simply removing the air cleaner housing assembly in order to reach the sub-air cleaner element, the air cleaner chamber, the carburetors or the engine, then skip this step.

3   Remove the big hose clamp that secures the air cleaner housing to the air cleaner chamber **(see illustrations)**.

4   Remove the air cleaner housing mounting bolts **(see illustrations)**.

5   Pull the air cleaner housing away from the bike and detach the crankcase breather separator hose from the housing **(see illustrations)**.

6   Installation is the reverse of removal. Before reconnecting the air cleaner housing to the air intake chamber on VT600 models, apply a light coat of sealant to the area where the air cleaner housing fits onto the air intake chamber. Before reconnecting the air cleaner housing to the air intake chamber on VT750 models, apply a little grease to the inside of the big hose clamp, and make sure that the positioning pin on the backside of the housing is correctly aligned with the grommet on the front cylinder head fin.

---

7   Sub-air cleaner element (dual-carburetor models) - removal and installation

Refer to illustrations 7.1, 7.3 and 7.4

1   If you're working on a VT600, remove the air cleaner housing (see Section 6). Detach the hose between the carburetor and the sub-air cleaner cover and remove the cover retaining screw **(see illustration)**.

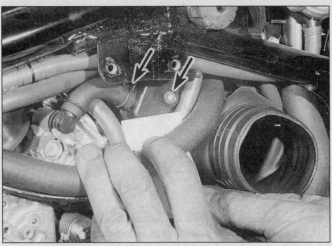

7.1 Pull down this coolant hose to expose the sub-air cleaner cover, then detach the small hose from the carburetor and remove the cover retaining screw (arrows) (VT600 models)

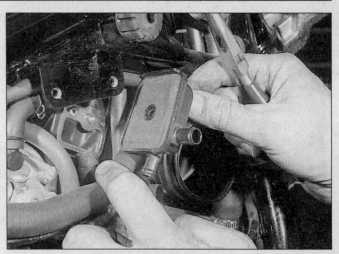

7.3 Pull off the sub-air cleaner cover (VT600 shown; VT750 similar)

7.4 Remove the filter element from the sub-air cleaner cover (VT600 shown; VT750 similar)

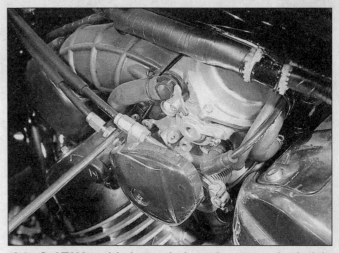

8.4a On VT600 models, loosen the hose clamp screw for the left intake duct at the rear cylinder carburetor . . .

2   If you're working on a VT750, remove the fuel tank (see Section 2).
3   Remove the sub-air cleaner cover **(see illustration)**.
4   Remove the filter element from the sub-air cleaner cover **(see illustration)**.
5   Wash the element thoroughly in non-flammable or high-flashpoint solvent, squeeze it out and allow it to dry thoroughly.
6   Soak the element in gear oil (SAE 80/90) and squeeze out the excess.
7   Installation is the reverse of removal.

8   Air intake chamber and intake ducts - removal and installation

1   Remove the fuel tank (see Section 2).
2   Remove the air cleaner housing (see Section 6).

VT600 models (1988 through 1998)

Refer to illustrations 8.4a, 8.4b, 8.4c, 8.5, 8.6, 8.7, 8.8, 8.9, 8.10a and 8.10b
3   Remove the sub-air cleaner element (see Section 7).
4   Loosen the three intake duct hose clamp screws **(see illustrations)**.

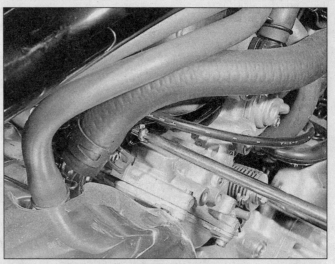

8.4b . . . loosen the hose clamp screw for the right intake duct at the front cylinder carburetor . . .

8.4c . . . and loosen the hose clamp screw for the right intake
duct at the air intake chamber

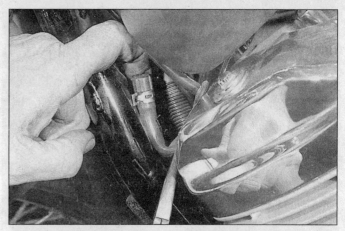

8.5 On VT600 models, detach the air intake chamber drain tube
from the frame

8.6 On VT600 models, detach this sub-air cleaner hose from the
left carburetor to allow more clearance for removing the air
intake chamber

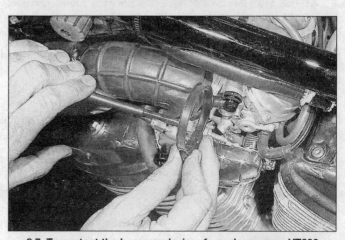

8.7 To protect the hoses and wires from damage on VT600
models, remove the three air intake hose clamps before
removing the air intake chamber

5   Detach the air intake chamber drain tube from the frame **(see
illustration)**.
6   Disconnect the sub-air cleaner hose from the left carburetor to
provide clearance for removing the left intake duct **(see illustration)**.
7   Pull off the hose clamps so they don't cut any hoses or wires or
snag on something when the air intake chamber is removed **(see illustration)**.

8   Disconnect the right air intake duct from the air intake chamber
(see illustration).
9   Remove the air intake chamber and left duct **(see illustration)**.
10   Installation is the reverse of removal. Make sure that the coolant
hoses and the hoses for the crankcase emission control system, the
evaporative emission control system (California models), the air
cleaner housing and the sub-air cleaner element are correctly routed

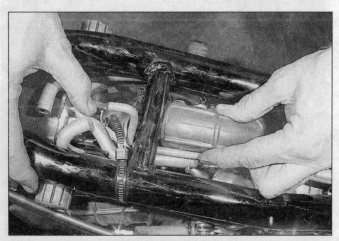

8.8 On VT600 models, detach the right air intake duct from the air
intake chamber

8.9 On VT600 models, remove the air intake chamber from
the left side

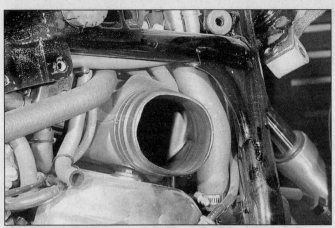

8.10a   When installing the air intake chamber and air intake ducts on VT600 models, make sure that the coolant hoses . . .

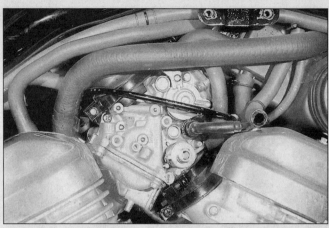

8.10b . . . and emission hoses are routed as shown; make sure none of the hoses are kinked or pinched or accidentally disconnected

around the air intake chamber and intake ducts **(see illustrations)**. Make sure that none of the hoses are kinked, pinched or pulled loose.

VT600 models (1999 on)

11   Remove the air cleaner housing (see Section 6).
12   Disconnect the front cylinder's spark plug wire (see Chapter 1 if necessary).
13   Detach the air cleaner chamber from the mounting boss and remove it from the left side of the frame.
14   Installation is the reverse of the removal steps.

VT750 models

15   Loosen the two intake duct hose clamp screws.
16   Pull out the air intake chamber.
17   Disconnect the breather tube from the air intake chamber.
18   Remove the air intake chamber.
19   Installation is the reverse of removal.

9   Fuel pump system (dual-carburetor models) - check and component replacement

1   On VT600 models, remove the seat; on VT750 models, remove the right side cover (see Chapter 8).

System check

Refer to illustrations 9.3 and 9.9
2   Make sure that the ignition switch is off before proceeding.
3   Locate the white three-pin fuel pump relay connector **(see illustration)**. On VT600 models, the fuel pump relay connector is located to the left of the fuel pump, behind the fuel filter; on VT750 models, it's on the right side of the bike, right above the coil. All fuel pump relay connectors have a black wire, a black/blue wire and either a yellow wire (1988 and 1989 VT600 models) or a yellow/blue wire (all other models). (Neither the yellow nor the yellow/blue wires are part of any of the following tests.)
4   Connect the positive lead of a voltmeter to the terminal for the black wire on the harness side of the fuel pump relay connector and connect the negative voltmeter lead to ground. Turn the ignition switch key to the On position and verify that there is battery voltage.
5   If there is no voltage, check the black wire for a loose connection or an open circuit.
6   If there is voltage, check the black/blue wire for continuity.
7   Connect the leads of an ohmmeter to the terminal for the black/blue wire on the harness side of the fuel pump relay connector and to ground and check for continuity between the black/blue wire and ground.
8   If there is continuity, replace the fuel pump relay.

9   If there is no continuity, jump the terminals for the black and the black/blue wires on the wire harness side of the fuel pump relay connector, unplug the white two-pin fuel pump connector **(see illustration)**. On VT600 models, this connector is located to the right of the fuel pump; on VT750 models, it's located on the right side of the bike (it's the inner connector of a bank of connectors, including a black connector and a green connector). Connect the leads of a voltmeter to the harness side of the fuel pump connector, turn the ignition switch to

9.3   The VT600 fuel pump relay and connector (arrows) are located under the seat, to the left of the fuel pump

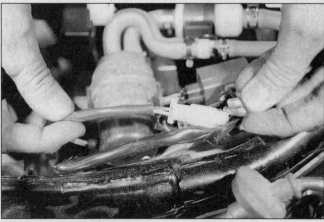

9.9   The VT600 fuel pump connector (white, two-pin) is located to the right of the fuel pump

**9.15 Don't confuse the fuel pump inlet and outlet ports
(VT600 shown; VT750 similar)**

1   Inlet port (marked by IN above port)
2   Outlet port

On and verify that there is voltage at the connector.
10   If there no voltage, check the black/blue wire and the green wire
for a loose connection or an open circuit.
11   If there is voltage, replace the fuel pump.

Fuel pump discharge volume check

Refer to illustration 9.15
12   The fuel pump system may check out okay but still be delivering
poor performance. If the engine lacks power or accelerates poorly, the
fuel pump may be wearing out. Check the fuel pump discharge volume
as follows.
13   Unplug the white three-pin fuel pump relay connector (**see illustration 9.3**).
14   Jump the terminals for the black and the black/blue wires with a
suitable jumper wire.
15   There are two fuel hoses attached to the fuel pump (**see illustration**). Disconnect the *outlet* hose (NOT the hose between the fuel filter
and the fuel pump, but the other hose).
16   Put this hose into a graduated beaker. Turn the ignition switch to
On for five seconds then turn it Off. To determine the fuel pump discharge volume per minute, multiply by 12. Compare your measurement to the minimum fuel pump discharge volume listed in this Chapter's Specifications.
17   If the pump fails to deliver the minimum discharge volume,
replace it.

Replacement

18   On VT600 models, remove the seat; on VT750 models, remove
the right side cover (see Chapter 8).

Fuel pump relay

19   Locate the fuel pump relay. On VT600 models, it's to the left, and
slightly to the rear, of the fuel pump (**see illustration 9.3**). On VT750
models, it's on the right side of the bike, right above the coil for the rear
cylinder.
20   Unplug the fuel pump relay electrical connector (**see illustration 9.3**).
21   Remove the relay from its mounting bracket.
22   Installation is the reverse of removal.

Fuel pump

Refer to illustration 9.25
23   Unplug the fuel pump electrical connector (**see illustration 9.9**).
24   Loosen the fuel line clamps and push the ends of the fuel lines off
the pump fittings (**see illustration 9.15**).

**9.25 To disengage the VT600 fuel pump from its rubber mounting
bracket, simply lift it up, then disconnect the fuel pump tube and
remove the pump**

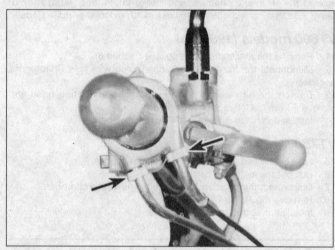

**10.2 Before opening up the switch housing, back off the throttle
cable-to-switch housing locknuts (arrows) (VT600 shown,
VT750 similar)**

25   Disengage the fuel pump from its rubber mounting bracket (**see
illustration**) and lift it up.
26   Disconnect the fuel pump tube from the pump and remove the
pump.
27   Installation is the reverse of removal. Don't forget to reattach the
fuel pump tube before installing the pump in its mounting bracket, and
make sure that the hose between the fuel filter and the pump is
attached to the inlet port, marked IN.

10 Throttle cables and grip - removal, installation and
adjustment

Removal

*Refer to illustrations 10.2, 10.3a, 10.3b, 10.4, 10.5a, 10.5b, 10.5c and
10.7*
1   Loosen the throttle cable adjuster (see Section 9 in Chapter 1).
2   Back off the throttle cable-to-switch housing locknuts (**see illustration**).
3   Remove the handlebar switch retaining screws. Separate the
halves of the handlebar switch and detach the throttle cables from the
throttle grip pulley (**see illustrations**).

10.3a Remove the switch housing retaining screws from the underside of the lower half of the housing, then open up the switch housing

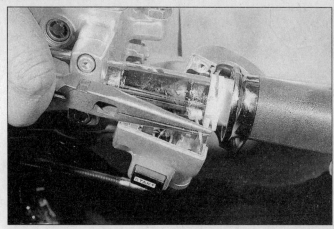

10.3b Disengage the upper ends of both cables from the throttle grip pulley

10.4 On VT600 models, remove the throttle linkage cover screw (arrow) and remove the cover

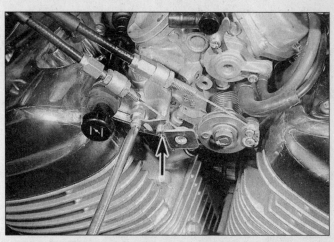

10.5a On VT600 models, remove the two throttle linkage cover screws, remove the bracket . . .

4   On VT600 models, remove the throttle linkage cover **(see illustration)**.

5   On VT600 models, remove the bracket for the throttle linkage cover and detach the throttle cable bracket from the left carburetor **(see illustrations)**. It's not absolutely necessary to detach the throttle cable bracket to replace the cable(s), but it's easier to disengage the cables from the bracket after it's detached. Note also that the choke

knob is attached to the throttle cable bracket. It's not necessary to detach the choke knob from the bracket unless you're removing the carburetors (see Section 12) or servicing the starting enrichment valves (see Section 13).

6   On VT750 models, remove the throttle cable bracket screws and detach the throttle cable bracket from the left carburetor.

7   Detach the throttle cables from the throttle pulley at the carburetors

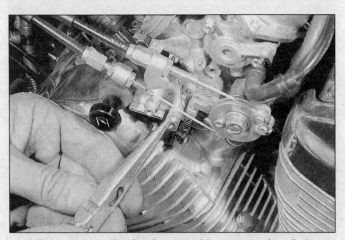

10.5b . . . remove the decelerator cable protector (small clear plastic tube) . . .

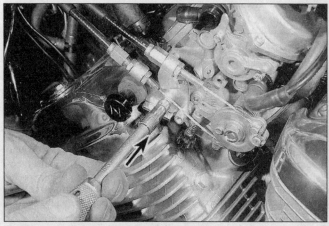

10.5c . . . remove the accelerator cable bracket screws and remove the accelerator cable bracket

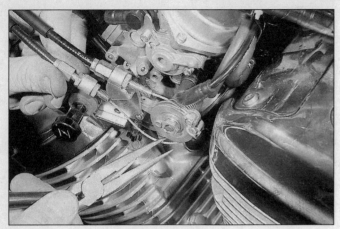

10.7　Disengage the lower ends of both cables from the throttle pulley

10.11　Make sure that the upper cable ends are correctly engaged with the throttle grip pulley

(see illustration). Note how the cables are routed, then remove them.
8　Slide the throttle grip off the handlebar.

Installation

Refer to illustration 10.11

9　Clean the end of the handlebar and the inside of the throttle grip, apply a light coat of multi-purpose grease to both surfaces and install the twist grip on the handlebar. Verify that it turns freely and smoothly with no binding or rough spots.
10　Route the cables exactly the same way they were routed prior to removal. Make sure they don't interfere with other components and are not kinked or sharply angled.
11　Lubricate the ends of the accelerator and decelerator cables with multi-purpose grease and connect them to the throttle pulleys at the carburetors and at the throttle grip. Make sure that the cable ends are correctly engaged with the pulleys **(see illustration)**.
12　On VT600 models, install the throttle cable bracket, the throttle linkage cover bracket and the throttle linkage cover. Tighten the screws securely.
13　On VT750 models, install the throttle cable bracket. Tighten the screws securely.

Adjustment

14　Adjust the throttle cables (see Section 9 in Chapter 1).
15　Turn the handlebars back and forth to make sure the cables don't cause the steering to bind. With the engine idling, turn the handlebars back and forth and make sure idle speed doesn't change. If it does, find and fix the cause before riding the motorcycle.

11　Carburetor overhaul - general information

1　Poor engine performance, hesitation, hard starting, stalling, flooding and backfiring are all signs that major carburetor maintenance may be required.
2　Keep in mind that many so-called carburetor problems are really not carburetor problems at all, but engine mechanical problems or ignition system malfunctions. Try to verify that the carburetors need to be serviced before beginning a major overhaul.
3　Before assuming that a carburetor overhaul is required, inspect the fuel filter; the fuel lines; the crankcase emission control system hoses; the evaporative emission control system hoses (California models); all vacuum hoses; the hose clamps and connections for the air intake chamber and intake ducts; the air filter element; the sub-air cleaner element; the cylinder compression; the spark plugs; the carburetor synchronization; and the fuel pump.
4　Most carburetor problems are caused by dirt particles, varnish and other deposits which accumulate in, and eventually clog, fuel and air passages. Also, gaskets and O-rings shrink or deteriorate, causing

fuel and air leaks which lead to poor performance.
5　A carburetor overhaul consists of disassembly, cleaning, reassembly and adjustments. Completely disassemble both carburetors, clean all parts thoroughly with a carburetor cleaning solvent, then dry them with filtered, unlubricated, compressed air. Blow out the fuel and air passages with compressed air to force out any dirt that may have been loosened but not removed by the solvent. Finally, reassemble the carburetors, using new gaskets, O-rings and, if necessary, a new float valve and seat.
6　Before getting started, make sure that you have the correct carburetor rebuild kit with all the necessary O-rings and other parts, carburetor cleaner, some clean shop rags, an air compressor and a place to work. If you don't have a compressor, buy a couple of cans of compressed air (the type used for cleaning computer keyboards and electronic components, available at any office supply store).
7　Overhaul only one carburetor at a time to avoid mixing up parts.
8　We will show you how to separate the carburetors, but it isn't usually necessary to do so. Don't separate the carburetors unless one of the joints between them is leaking, or one of the carburetors must be replaced. The vacuum chamber, the air cut-off diaphragm, the float assembly and the jets can be serviced without separating the carburetors. Achieving correct synchronization can be tricky after disconnecting and reconnecting the carburetors.

12　Carburetors - removal and installation

Warning: *Gasoline (petrol) is extremely flammable, so take extra precautions when you work on any part of the fuel system. Don't smoke or allow open flames or bare light bulbs near the work area, and don't work in a garage where a natural gas-type appliance (such as a water heater or clothes dryer) is present. If you spill any fuel on your skin, rinse it off immediately with soap and water. When you perform any kind of work on the fuel system, wear safety glasses and have an extinguisher suitable for class B fires (flammable liquids) on hand.*

Removal

VT600 (1988 through 1998) and VT750C/CD models

Refer to illustrations 12.6, 12.10a, 12.10b, 12.12a, 12.12b and 12.12c

1　Remove the fuel tank (see Section 2).
2　Remove the drain screws from both float bowls and drain the carburetors into a suitable container.
3　Remove the air cleaner housing (see Section 6).
4　Remove the sub-air cleaner element (see Section 7).
5　Remove the air intake chamber and intake ducts (see Section 8).
6　Detach the fuel line from the T-fitting located behind the carburetors on VT600 models **(see illustration)** and below the carbs on VT750 models.

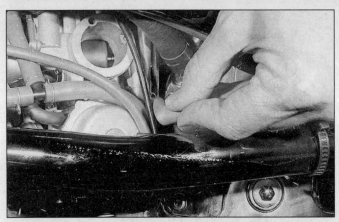

12.6 Detach the fuel hose from the T-fitting behind the carburetors on VT600 models (shown) or below the carbs on VT750 models

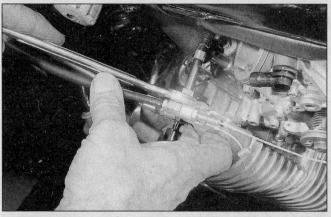

12.10a On VT600 models, back off the choke shaft locknut on the backside of the throttle cable bracket . . .

7   On VT600 models, remove the throttle linkage cover and the cover bracket (see Section 10).
8   On VT750 models, remove the left side cover (see Chapter 8).
9   Detach the throttle cable bracket from the left carburetor and disengage the throttle cables from the pulley (see Section 10). Unless you're replacing the throttle cables, it's not necessary to detach them from the cable bracket; they can remain attached to the bracket.
10   On VT600 models, separate the choke knob and cable from the throttle cable bracket **(see illustrations)**.
11   On VT750 models, remove the cylinder fins from the left side of the rear cylinder (see Section 7 in Chapter 2), detach the choke knob bracket, then detach the choke knob from the bracket.
12   Loosen the carburetor insulator clamp screws **(see illustration)**, carefully work the carbs free from the insulators **(see illustration)**, with a big screwdriver if necessary, pull the carbs from the left side of the engine **(see illustration)**, detach the air hoses and remove the carburetors. (If you're planning to service the cylinder heads, you can also unbolt the insulators from the cylinder heads and remove the carburetor assembly and insulators together.)
13   After the carburetors have been removed, stuff clean rags into the insulators to prevent the entry of dirt or other objects.
14   Inspect the carburetor insulators. If they're cracked or brittle, replace them.

VT600 (1999 and later) models
15   Remove the air cleaner (see Section 6).

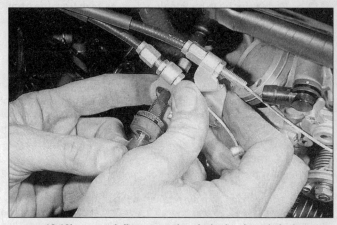

12.10b . . . and disengage the choke knob and shaft from the bracket

16   Loosen the float bowl drain screw and drain the carburetor into a suitable container.
17   Remove the fuel tank (see Section 2).
18   Remove the throttle linkage cover. Loosen the throttle cable adjusters, but don't remove the cables yet.
19   Remove the choke and idle speed knobs.
20   Label and disconnect the fuel line, vacuum hoses and coolant

12.12a Loosen the insulator clamp screws . . .

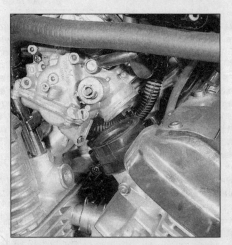

12.12b . . . separate the carburetors from the insulators (if they're hard to pull out of the insulators, use a big screwdriver to gently pry them loose) . . .

12.12c . . . pull the carbs out from the left side of the engine, detach the air tubes (arrow) and remove the carbs

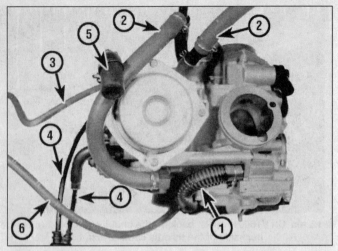

13.2a Carburetor hose routing (top view, as seen from the front)

1 Fuel hose	4 Choke cable/starting
2 Air hoses	enrichment valve
3 Air vent control valve	5 Sub-air cleaner hose
hose	6 Purge valve hose

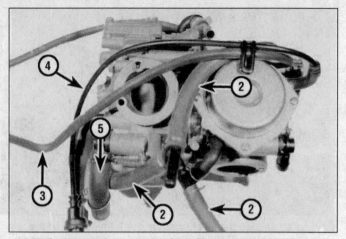

13.2b Carburetor hose routing (top view, as seen from the rear)

2 Air hoses	4 Choke cable/starting
3 Air vent control valve	enrichment valve
hose	5 Sub-air cleaner hose

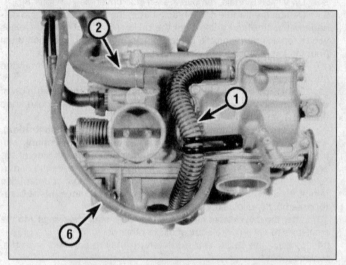

13.2c Carburetor hose routing (front view)

1 Fuel hose	6 Purge valve hose
2 Air hose	

hoses. Plug or cap the coolant hoses so they don't drip.

21   Loosen the clamping band screws and work the carburetor out of the intake manifold. Pull the carburetor out, slip the throttle cables out of the brackets, then disconnect the cable ends from the throttle pulley.

VT750DC models

22   Remove the fuel tank and air cleaner housing (see Sections 2 and 6).

23   Free the fuel line from the retainer on top of the rear cylinder.

24   Remove one screw and take off the throttle cable cover. Working behind the cover, loosen the throttle cable adjuster locknuts, then remove the wiring harness retainer, cover bracket and throttle cable bracket.

25   Slip the throttle cables out of the brackets, then disconnect the cable ends from the throttle pulley.

26   Unbolt the choke cable bracket from the rear cylinder.

27   At the rear carburetor, disconnect the carburetor heater electrical connector, detach the sub-air cleaner tube and loosen the clamping band screw at the cylinder.

28   Repeat Step 27 at the front carburetor.

29   Label and disconnect the vacuum hoses.

30   Work the carburetors and intake tubes free of the cylinders, then lift the assembly, disconnect the fuel line and take it out.

31   Pull back the choke plunger boots, unscrew the nuts and take the plungers out of the carburetors.

Installation

32   Place the carburetor assembly in position on the engine and connect the air intake tube(s), but don't tighten the clamping screws yet.

33   Reverse the removal steps to connect the throttle cables, fuel lines, coolant hoses (if equipped) and emission hoses.

34   Make sure the carburetor(s) and securely seated in the insulator(s), then tighten the clamping screws securely.

35   The remainder of installation is the reverse of the removal steps.

36   Check the idle speed (and carburetor synchronization on dual-carburetor models). Adjust if necessary (see Chapter 1).

---

13 Carburetors - disassembly, inspection, cleaning and reassembly

---

Warning: *Gasoline (petrol) is extremely flammable, so take extra precautions when you work on any part of the fuel system. Don't smoke or*

allow open flames or bare light bulbs near the work area, and don't work in a garage where a natural gas-type appliance (such as a water heater or clothes dryer) is present. If you spill any fuel on your skin, rinse it off immediately with soap and water. When you perform any kind of work on the fuel system, wear safety glasses and have a fire extinguisher suitable for class B type fires (flammable liquids) on hand.
Note: The following procedures are specific to dual carburetors, used on all except 1999 and later VT600 models. Service procedures for the single carburetor used on the 1999 and later VT600 are similar in design to those for dual carburetors, but include an accelerator pump. If you're working on a single carburetor, ignore the steps which don't apply, and service the accelerator pump diaphragm in the same way as the air cut-off diaphragm.

Disassembly

Refer to illustrations 13.2a, 13.2b, 13.2c, 13.2d, 13.2e, 13.2f, 13.3a, 13.3b, 13.3c, 13.5, 13.6, 13.7, 13.8, 13.9, 13.10, 13.11, 13.12a, 13.12b, 13.13, 13.14 and 13.15

Note: Work on one carburetor at a time to avoid mixing up the parts, and to give you a "reference carburetor" to refer to if you can't remember how things go back together. As you disassemble each carburetor,

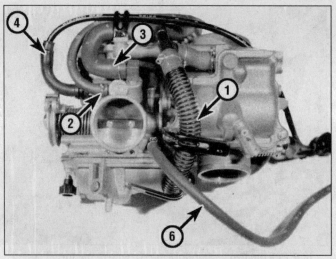

13.2d Carburetor hose routing (rear view)

1	Fuel hose	4	Choke cable/starting
2	Air hose		enrichment valve
3	Air vent control valve hose	6	Purge valve hose

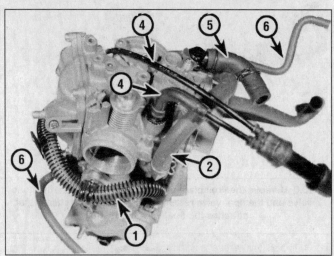

13.2f Carburetor hose routing (right view)

1	Fuel hose	5	Sub-air cleaner hose
2	Air hose	6	Purge valve hose
4	Choke cable/starting		
	enrichment valve		

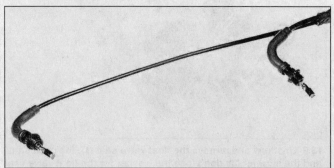

13.3b . . . and pull out the valve

store the parts for each sub-assembly in a clearly labeled plastic bag so you don't lose anything.

1   Remove the carburetors (see Section 12), then place them on a clean working surface.

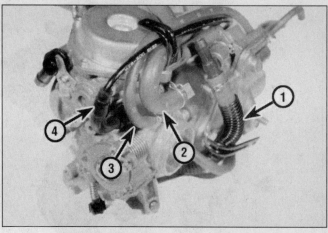

13.2e Carburetor hose routing (left view)

1	Fuel hose	4	Choke cable/starting
2	Air hose		enrichment valve
3	Air vent control valve hose		

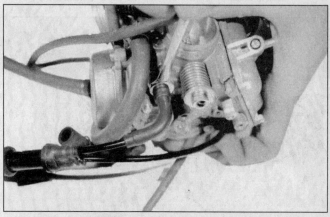

13.3a To remove the starting enrichment valve, loosen it with a wrench . . .

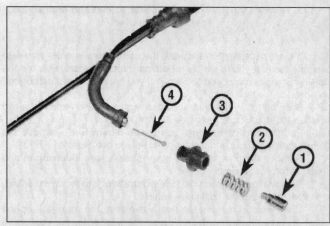

13.3c Each starting enrichment valve assembly consists of the valve itself (1), the spring (2), the collar (3) and the choke cable end (4)

2   Carefully study how the air and fuel hoses are routed **(see illustrations)**, mark them with adhesive labels or colored electrical tape, then detach them from the carburetors. Use the accompanying photos to help you route the hoses correctly during reassembly.

3   Remove the starting enrichment valves **(see illustrations)**.

13.5 Back off the synchronization adjusting screw (right arrow) and remove the two carburetor attaching screws (arrow) (the other attaching screw, not visible in this photo, is in exactly the same location on the side of the other carburetor)

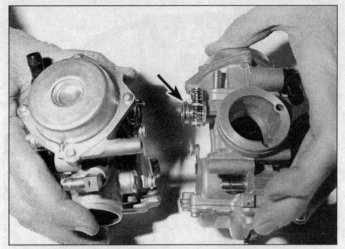

13.6 Pull the two carburetors apart, remove the thrust spring (arrow) and put it in a plastic bag so you don't lose it

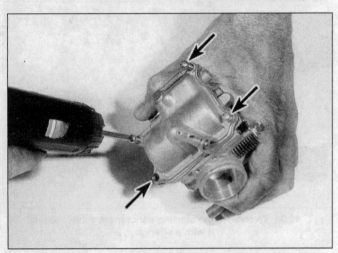

13.7 Remove the float chamber cover screws and remove the float chamber cover

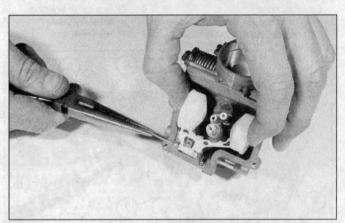

13.8 Remove the float pivot pin and remove the float, the float valve and the float valve retainer (the small metal retainer that attaches the float valve to the float)

4   It's not necessary to separate the carburetors in order to disassemble them. If you're simply rebuilding the carburetors, skip the following Steps and proceed to Step 7. If you are replacing a carburetor, proceed to the next Step.

5   Back off the synchronization adjusting screw and remove the two carburetor attaching screws **(see illustration)**.

6   Pull the two carburetors apart **(see illustration)**, remove the thrust spring and put it in a plastic bag so you don't lose it.

7   Remove the float chamber cover screws **(see illustration)** and remove the float chamber cover.

8   Remove the float pivot pin **(see illustration)** and remove the float, the float valve and the float valve retainer.

9   Unscrew and remove the float valve seat, the main jet and the slow jet **(see illustration)**. Don't lose the washer for the float valve seat.

10   Center punch the plug for the pilot screw, then drill out the plug with a 4 mm (5/32-inch) drill bit **(see illustration)**. To protect the pilot screw from damage, use a drill stop set to prevent the drill bit from going deeper than 3 mm (1/8-inch). Make sure you don't damage the pilot screw.

11   Screw a self-tapping 4 mm screw into the drilled-out plug, grasp the head of the self-tapping screw and pull out the plug **(see illustration)**.

13.9 Unscrew and remove the float valve seat (1), the main jet (2) and the slow jet (3); don't lose the washer for the float valve seat

12   Carefully counting the number of turns, screw in the pilot screw until it seats lightly. **Caution:** *Do NOT keep turning the pilot screw in after you feel it stop; this will damage the screw.* Jot down the number of turns it took to seat the screw; you'll need this number when

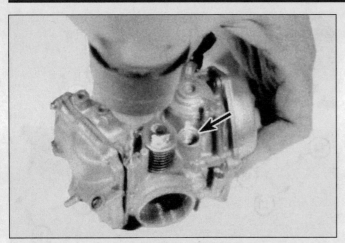

13.10 Center punch the plug for the pilot screw, then drill out the plug with a 4 mm (5/32-inch) drill bit; to protect the pilot screw from damage, use a drill stop set to prevent the drill bit from going deeper than 3 mm (1/8-inch)

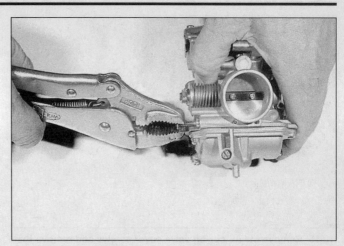

13.11 Screw a self-tapping 4 mm screw into the drilled-out plug, grasp the head of the screw and pull out the plug

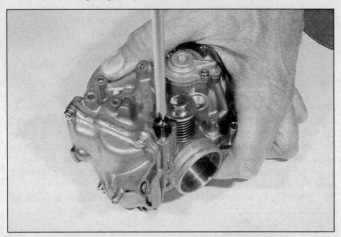

13.12a Carefully counting the number of turns it takes to seat the screw, screw in the pilot screw until it seats lightly and jot down the number for assembly

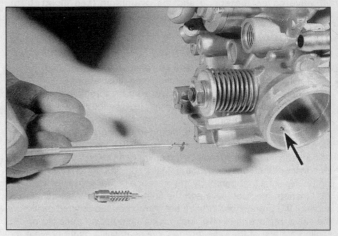

13.12b Remove the pilot screw, washer and O-ring; the bypass hole (arrow) is an alignment mark for throttle adjustment

reassembling the carburetor. Remove the pilot screw, the washer and the O-ring **(see illustrations)**.

13   Remove the vacuum chamber screws and remove the vacuum chamber cover **(see illustration)**. Remove the spring and the piston/diaphragm assembly.

14   Using a Phillips screwdriver, push down on the jet needle holder **(see illustration)**, turn it counterclockwise 90 degrees to unlock it, and remove the jet needle holder, the spring and the jet needle.

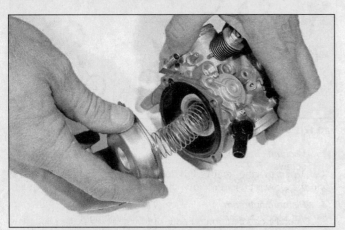

13.13 Remove the vacuum chamber screws and remove the vacuum chamber cover, the spring and the piston/diaphragm assembly

13.14 Using a Phillips screwdriver, push down on the jet needle holder, turn it counterclockwise 90 degrees to unlock it, then remove the jet needle holder, the spring and the jet needle

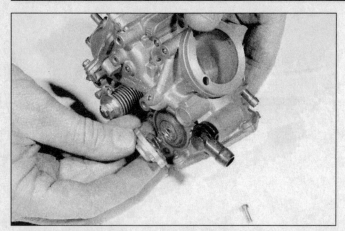

13.15 Remove the air cut-off valve cover screws and remove the air cut-off valve cover, the spring and the diaphragm; remove and discard the old O-ring

15   Remove the air cut-off valve cover screws and remove the air cut-off valve cover, the spring and the diaphragm **(see illustration)**. Remove and discard the old O-ring.

Inspection

Refer to illustrations 13.17a and 13.17b

16   Clean or wipe off all the parts well enough to inspect them.

17   Lay out all the parts for inspection **(see illustrations)**.

18   Operate the throttle shaft to make sure the throttle butterfly valve opens and closes smoothly. If it doesn't, replace the carburetor.

19   Inspect the carburetor body, the float chamber cover and the vacuum chamber cover for cracks, distorted sealing surfaces and other damage. If either cover is damaged, replace it. If the carburetor body is damaged, you'll have to replace the entire carburetor.

20   Inspect the float for damage. Make sure it's not cracked or leaking (this is usually apparent by the presence of fuel inside the float).

21   Inspect the float valve and the float valve seat for scratches and scoring; if a pronounced groove has formed on the tapered portion of the valve, replace the valve. Make sure there are no deposits on the sealing surface of the valve or the valve seat which might prevent the valve from fully closing against the seat. Make sure that no deposits on the bore of the seat are blocking fuel flow through the seat. If any of these parts are damaged, replace them. There's a small filter in the seat; make sure it's not clogged or damaged.

22   Inspect the jets. Make sure that the passages through the jets are clean and free of deposits.

23   Inspect the tapered part of the pilot screw for wear and damage. Make sure the spring is in good shape. Replace any worn or damaged parts.

24   Inspect the spring for the vacuum piston; make sure it's not kinked or distorted. Inspect the vacuum chamber diaphragm for cracks, holes, tears and general deterioration (holding it up to a light will help to reveal problems of this nature). Inspect the surface of the vacuum chamber piston for scratches, scoring and excessive wear. Insert the piston in the piston bore in the carburetor body and note whether it moves up and down smoothly in the piston bore. If it doesn't move smoothly in the bore, replace the carburetor. Inspect the tip of the jet needle for excessive wear. Make sure it's not bent. A good way to check the jet needle for straightness is to roll it on a flat surface, such as a piece of glass. If the jet needle is damaged, replace it.

25   Inspect the spring for the air cut-off diaphragm; make sure it's in good shape. Inspect the air cut-off diaphragm for cracks, holes and tears. If it's damaged, replace it.

Cleaning

Caution: *Use only a petroleum based solvent for carburetor cleaning. Don't use caustic cleaners.*

26   Submerge the metal components in the solvent for about thirty minutes (or longer, if the directions recommend it).

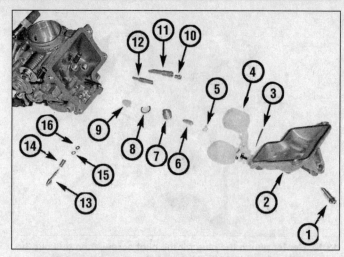

13.17a Float assembly, jets and pilot screw assembly

1	Drain screw	9	Float valve seat filter
2	Float chamber cover	10	Main jet
3	Float valve pin	11	Needle jet holder
4	Float	12	Slow jet
5	Retainer	13	Pilot screw
6	Float valve	14	Spring
7	Float valve seat	15	Washer
8	Float valve seat washer	16	O-ring

27   After the carburetor has soaked long enough for the cleaner to loosen and dissolve most of the varnish and other deposits, use a brush to remove the stubborn deposits. Rinse it again, then dry it with compressed air. Blow out all of the fuel and air passages in the main body. **Caution:** *Never clean the jets or passages with a piece of wire or a drill bit, as they will be enlarged, causing the fuel and air metering rates to be upset.*

28   Thoroughly wash the vacuum chamber diaphragm and the air

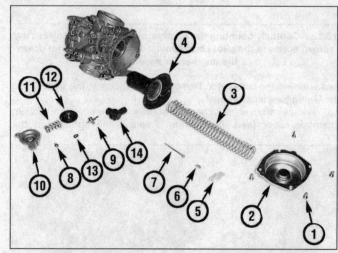

13.17b Vacuum chamber and air cut-off diaphragm assemblies

1	Vacuum chamber cover screws	9	Air cut-off diaphragm cover screw/bracket
2	Vacuum chamber cover	10	Air cut-off diaphragm cover
3	Spring	11	Spring
4	Piston/diaphragm	12	Diaphragm
5	Jet needle holder	13	O-ring
6	Spring	14	Elbow fitting for sub-air cleaner hose
7	Jet needle		
8	Air cut-off diaphragm cover screw		

13.31 Align the positioning tab on the edge of the diaphragm with the notches in the cover and carburetor body

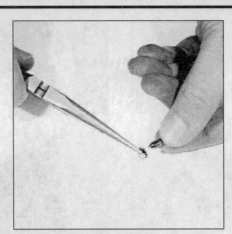

13.35a Reassemble the float valve and the retainer . . .

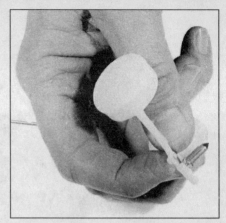

13.35b . . . then attach them to the float

cut-off valve diaphragm with soap and water, then rinse them off with clean water.

Reassembly

Refer to illustrations 13.31, 13.35a, 13.35b, 13.36, 13.45 and 13.47
Note: *When reassembling the carburetors, be sure to use the new O-rings, gaskets and other parts supplied in the rebuild kit.*

29   Install a new O-ring with its flat side toward the carburetor. Install the air cut-off diaphragm, spring and cover. Tighten the cover screws securely.

30   Install the jet needle, spring, and jet needle holder in the vacuum piston. Push down on the jet needle holder and turn it clockwise 90 degrees to lock it into place.

31   Install the vacuum diaphragm/piston assembly in the piston bore. Make sure that the lip on the underside of the diaphragm is seated in the groove in the carburetor casting and the positioning tab on the edge of the diaphragm is aligned with the cavity in the groove **(see illustration)**.

32   Install the spring and the vacuum chamber cover. As you compress the spring, make sure you keep it straight. And don't pinch the diaphragm. Install the cover screws and tighten them securely.

33   Install the needle jet holder, main jet and slow jet. **Caution:** Don't overtighten the jets. Because they're made of soft brass, it's easy to strip the threads.

34   Install the float valve seat/filter. Again, don't overtighten it.

35   Assemble the float valve, retainer and float **(see illustrations)**.

36   Place the float assembly in position and secure it with the float pin. Make sure that the float valve is correctly seated on the float valve seat and the float valve retainer is correctly engaged with the

float **(see illustration)**.

37   Using a carburetor float level gauge (Honda special tool 07401-0010000), check the float level. Place the carburetor(s) on a bench with the float chamber on its side, so that the float is hanging from its pivot pin. Place the gauge so that it's perpendicular to the machined face of the float chamber and position it so that it's aligned with the main jet. Check the float level and compare your measurement to the float level listed in this Chapter's Specifications. If the float level is incorrect, replace the float assembly.

38   Install the float chamber cover with a new O-ring, install the cover screws and tighten them securely.

39   Install the pilot screw, return it to its original position in accordance with your notes and install a new sealing plug. If you're installing a new pilot screw, establish a baseline by setting it at the same position as the old pilot screw, then - after the carburetors are installed and synchronized - adjust it (see Section 14). Don't install a sealing plug at this time if you're using a new pilot screw.

40   Repeat Steps 7 through 39 for the other carburetor.

41   If you separated the carburetors, reattach them as follows. If not, go to Step 50.

42   Back off the synchronizer adjusting screw **(see illustration 13.5)** to remove spring tension.

43   Install the thrust spring **(see illustration 13.6)** between the throttle links.

44   Reattach the carburetors with the two carburetor attaching screws **(see illustration 13.5)** and tighten the screws securely.

45   Make sure the synchronizer spring is correctly positioned **(see illustration)**, then tighten the synchronizer adjusting screw.

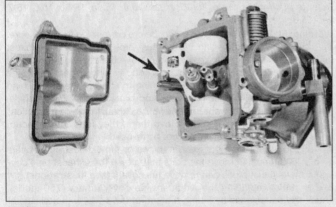

13.36 Place the float assembly in position and secure it with the float pin; make sure that the float valve is correctly seated on the float valve seat and the float valve retainer is correctly engaged with the float

13.45 Make sure that each synchronizer spring is correctly positioned, then tighten the synchronizer adjusting screw

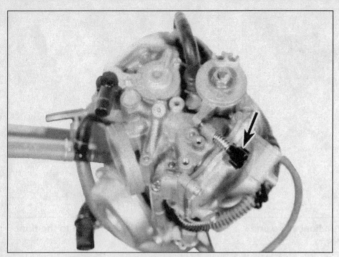

13.47 Use the idle stop screw (arrow) to adjust the throttle valve of the carburetor for the rear cylinder so that it's aligned with the by-pass hole

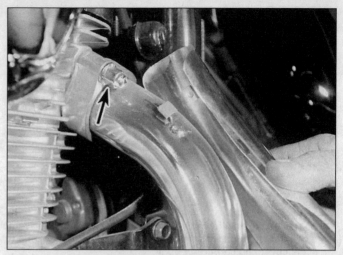

15.2a Unbolt the cover for access to the front exhaust pipe nuts on a VT600 (lower nut hidden)

46   Open the throttle slightly by rotating the throttle valve, then release the throttle. It should close quickly and smoothly, without dragging.
47   Turn the throttle stop screw **(see illustration)** to align the throttle valve in the rear carburetor with the edge of the by-pass hole **(see illustration 13.12b)**.
48   Turn the synchronizer adjusting screw **(see illustration 13.5)** to align the throttle valve in the front carburetor with the edge of the by-pass hole.
49   Operate the throttle and verify that it operates smoothly and that both throttle valves are aligned with their respective by-pass holes.
50   Reattach the starting enrichment valves. Make sure the valve, spring and collar are correctly assembled on the end of each choke cable **(see illustration 13.3c)** and tighten them securely.
51   Referring to the accompanying photos **(see illustrations 13.2a through 13.2f)**, reattach all air and fuel hoses.
52   Install the carburetors (see Section 12).
53   Synchronize the carburetors (see Chapter 1).

14   Idle fuel/air mixture - adjustment

1   Because of emissions regulations of the Environmental Protection Agency (EPA), and the regulatory bodies of some state governments as well, the idle fuel/air mixture is a critical adjustment. In order to comply with these regulations, each carburetor has a sealing plug in the pilot screw hole to prevent tampering. These plugs should only be removed during a complete carburetor overhaul, after which the screws must be returned to their original settings.
2   If you replaced the pilot screws during a carburetor overhaul, adjust the idle fuel/air mixture as follows. Make sure that the carburetors are synchronized (see Chapter 1) before proceeding.
3   Remove each pilot screw plug, if necessary (see Steps 10 and 11 in Section 13).
4   Turn each pilot screw clockwise until it seats lightly, then back it out to the initial opening listed in this Chapter's Specifications. **Caution:** *Do NOT overtighten the pilot screw; overtightening it will damage it.*
5   Start the engine and warm it up to its normal operating temperature.
6   Turn off the engine and hook up a tachometer in accordance with the manufacturer's instructions.
7   Start the engine and adjust the engine idle speed to the idle speed listed in the Chapter 1 Specifications with the throttle stop screw.

8   Back out each pilot screw 1/2-turn from its initial setting.
9   If the engine speed increases by 50 rpm or more, back out each pilot screw another 1/2 turn and continue doing so until the engine speed no longer increases.
10   Adjust the idle speed to the idle speed listed in the Chapter 1 Specifications with the throttle stop screw.
11   Turn in the pilot screw for the rear cylinder carburetor until the engine speed drops 50 rpm.
12   Back out the pilot screw for the rear cylinder carburetor to the final opening listed in this Chapter's Specifications.
13   Adjust the idle speed with the throttle stop screw.
14   Repeat Steps 11, 12 and 13 and adjust the pilot screw for the front cylinder carburetor.
15   Install new sealing plugs into the pilot screw holes with a 7 mm guide driver (Honda special tool 07942-8230000, or equivalent). When each plug is fully seated, its surface is recessed 1 mm (1/32-inch).
16   If the engine runs extremely rough or blows black smoke at idle or continually stalls, and a carburetor overhaul, followed by the preceding adjustment, does not cure the problem, take the motorcycle to a Honda dealer service department, or a motorcycle repair shop, equipped with an exhaust gas analyzer. They will be able to correctly adjust the idle fuel/air mixture to achieve a smooth idle and restore low speed performance.

15   Exhaust system - removal and installation

Refer to illustrations 15.2a, 15.2b, 15.2c, 15.4, 15.5a, 15.5b, 15.6, 15.7 and 15.8
Warning: *Make sure the engine is cool before performing this procedure.*
1   Unless you're replacing the exhaust pipe covers or the exhaust pipes themselves, it's unnecessary to remove the covers. However, at least on VT600 models, this might be a good time to inspect each pipe for corrosion and other damage, including the part of the pipe behind the cover (especially if you live in a damp climate). On VT750 models, however, you do NOT want to remove the exhaust pipe covers unless you're replacing them. If you remove them, they must be replaced; once removed, VT750 covers cannot be re-used.
2   If you're replacing the exhaust pipes or the exhaust pipe covers on a VT600 model, remove the bolts that attach the exhaust pipe covers to the exhaust pipes and remove the covers **(see illustrations)**.
3   If you're replacing the exhaust pipe cover on a VT750 model, knock the cover loose by hitting the end of the cover with a plastic or rubber-tipped mallet. Strike the cover hard enough to break the lock tab, then disengage the cover from the exhaust pipe and discard the cover (once the lock tab is broken, the cover must be replaced).
4   Remove the two nuts that secure the front exhaust pipe to the

15.2b Remove the clamp (arrow) and rear bolt (not shown) to detach the VT600 rear exhaust pipe cover . . .

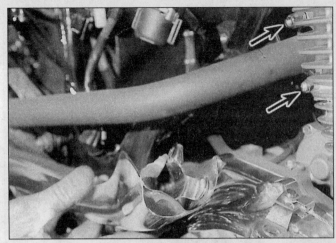

15.2c . . . and lift the cover off

15.4 Remove the two nuts that secure the rear exhaust pipe to the rear cylinder head

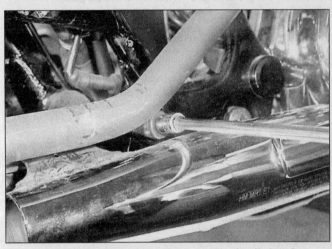
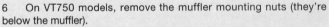

15.5a The VT600 upper muffler is attached to its bracket by this nut . . .

front cylinder head **(see illustration 15.2a)** and the rear pipe to the rear cylinder head **(see illustration)**.

5   On VT600 models, remove the muffler mounting nut and bolt **(see illustrations)**.

6   On VT750 models, remove the muffler mounting nuts (they're below the muffler).

7   Slide back the exhaust pipe joints, pull the pipes out of the cylinder heads, remove the collars **(see illustration)**, disengage the muf-

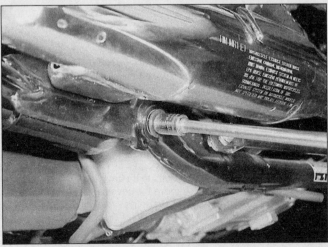

15.5b . . . and the lower muffler is attached to its bracket by this bolt

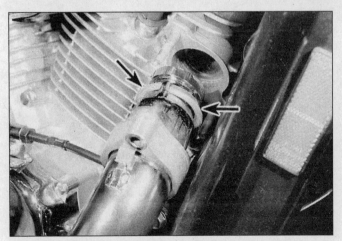

15.7 Slide back the joint, pull the exhaust pipe out of the head and remove the split collar (arrows) (front pipe shown, rear pipe similar)

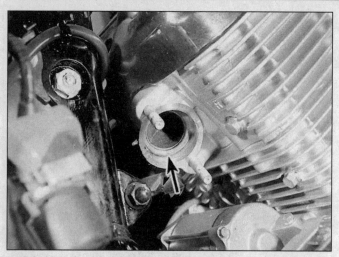

15.8 After the exhaust pipes have been removed, carefully pry out the old gaskets (arrow) (rear exhaust pipe gasket shown, front gasket similar)

flers from their mounting brackets and remove the exhaust pipes and mufflers.

8   Dig out the old gaskets **(see illustration)** from the cylinder heads and discard them.

9   Installation is the reverse of removal. Be sure to use new gaskets and tighten all fasteners securely. If you removed either exhaust pipe cover on a VT750 model, install a new cover: align the slots on the backside of the cover with the tabs on the exhaust pipe and slide the cover into place until the lock tab on the cover locks into place.

Chapter 5
Ignition system

Contents

Specifications

Ignition coil (1988 and 1989, 1991 through 1996 VT600 only*)
Primary resistance .... 1.89 to 2.32 ohms
Secondary resistance
    With plug wires attached .... 23.55 to 30.45 k-ohms
    Without plug wires attached .... 19.8 to 24.2 k-ohms

Ignition pulse generator(s) (1988 and 1989, 1991 through 1996 VT600 only*)
Coil resistance .... 450 to 550 ohms

Ignition timing
VT600
    1988, 1989, 1991 through 1996 .... 6.2 degrees BTDC at idle
    1997 on .... 6.5 degrees BTDC at idle
VT750 .... 8 degrees BTDC at idle
1997 and later VT600 and all VT750 models must be tested by a Honda dealer.

Torque specifications
Ignition pulse generator bolts .... 12 Nm (108 in-lbs)

1   General information

These motorcycles are equipped with a battery-operated, fully transistorized, breakerless ignition system. The system consists of the following components:

Ignition control module
Ignition pulse generator(s) and timing rotor
Battery and fuse
Ignition coils
Spark plugs
Ignition (main) and engine kill (stop) switches
Primary and secondary circuit wiring

The ignition pulse generators are the timing devices that enable the ignition control module to control the primary voltage to the ignition coils. VT600 models are equipped with two ignition pulse generators, one for each cylinder. VT750 models use one pulse generator for both cylinders. Every time a tip of the timing rotor sweeps by the ignition pulse generator, the pulse generator produces a low-voltage output signal to the ignition control module. The module switches primary voltage to the coils on and off in accordance with these signals from the pulse generator(s). With the exception of spark plug replacement, ignition system service is eliminated.

Ignition system components can be checked but they can't be repaired. If ignition system problems occur, the faulty component(s) must be replaced. Most electrical parts cannot be returned, so don't buy anything until you're sure that you have identified the problem.

2   Ignition system - check

Warning: *Because of the very high voltage generated by the ignition system, extreme care should be taken when these checks are performed.*
1   If the ignition system is the suspected cause of poor engine performance or failure to start, a number of checks can be made to isolate the problem.
2   Make sure the engine kill switch is in the Run position.

Engine will not start

3   Disconnect one of the spark plug wires (there are two for each cylinder), connect the wire to a spare spark plug and lay the plug on the engine with the threads of the plug in contact with the engine. If necessary, hold the spark plug with an insulated tool. Crank the engine over and make sure a well-defined, blue spark occurs between the spark plug electrodes. **Warning:** *Don't remove one of the spark plugs from the engine to perform this check - atomized fuel being pumped out of the open spark plug hole could ignite, causing severe injury!*
4   If no spark occurs, repeat the same test on the *other* spark plug lead of the same coil.
5   If the plug sparks when the second lead is attached, then the first plug wire or cap is defective. Install a new wire and cap and retest.
6   If neither plug wire produces a spark on a 1988, 1989 or 1991 through 1996 VT600 model, check and, if necessary, replace the coil (see Section 3).
7   If neither plug wire produces a spark on a 1997 or later VT600 model, or on any VT750 model, try swapping the coils (see Section 3). If the plug wires of the second coil produce a good spark, replace the first coil. No further testing of the ignition coil on these later models is possible without a special diagnostic tester. The coils must be checked by a Honda service department with the necessary diagnostic equipment.
8   Repeat Steps 3 through 5 for the other ignition coil.
9   If both coils are operating satisfactorily, inspect the rest of the ignition system. Make sure that all electrical connectors are clean and tight. Check all wires for shorts, opens and make sure that they're correctly installed.
10   Check the battery voltage with a voltmeter and - on models equipped with batteries having removable filler caps - check the specific gravity with a hydrometer (see Chapter 1). If the voltage is less than 12-volts or if the specific gravity is low, recharge the battery.
11   Check the ignition fuse and the fuse connections (see Chapter 9). If the fuse is blown, replace it; if the connections are loose or corroded, clean or repair them.
12   Check the ignition switch, engine kill switch, neutral switch and sidestand switch.
13   On 1988, 1989 or 1991 through 1996 VT600 models, check the ignition pulse generator resistance (see Section 4).
14   On 1997 and later VT600 models, and on VT750 models, no testing of the ignition pulse generator(s) is possible without a special diagnostic tester. Have the pulse generator(s) checked by a Honda service department with the necessary diagnostic equipment.

2.16 A simple spark gap testing fixture can be made from a block of wood, a large alligator clip, two nails, a screw and a piece of wire

Engine starts but misfires

Refer to illustration 2.16
15   If the engine starts but misfires, make the following checks before deciding that the ignition system is at fault.
16   The ignition system must be able to produce a spark across a six millimeter (1/4-inch) gap (minimum). A simple test fixture **(see illustration)** can be constructed to make sure the minimum spark gap can be jumped. Make sure the fixture electrodes are positioned six millimeters apart.
17   Connect one of the spark plug wires to the protruding test fixture electrode, then attach the fixture's alligator clip to a good engine ground/earth.
18   Crank the engine over (it will probably start and run on the remaining cylinders) and see if well-defined, blue sparks occur between the test fixture electrodes. If the minimum spark gap test is positive, the ignition coil for that cylinder is functioning properly. Repeat the check on one of the spark plug wires connected to the other coil. If the spark will not jump the gap during either test, or if it is weak (orange colored), refer to Steps 3 through 8.

3   Ignition coils - check and replacement

Check

Refer to illustration 3.4
1   Inspect the coils for cracks and other damage. If either coil is obviously damaged, replace it. If the coils are undamaged, proceed to the next Step.
2   The following tests apply only to the ignition coils used on 1988 and 1989 and 1991 through 1996 VT600 models. To determine whether an ignition coil on a 1997 or later VT600 model, or a VT750 model, is defective, have it tested by a Honda dealer service department equipped with the necessary diagnostic equipment.
3   To access the coil for the front cylinder, remove the fuel tank (see Chapter 4) and remove the crankcase breather separator (see Chapter 4). (The separator is the white plastic tank above the coil; it's part of the crankcase emission control system.) To check or replace the coil for the rear cylinder, remove the right side cover (see Chapter 8).
4   To check the primary resistance of a coil, unplug the electrical connectors from the primary terminals and, using an ohmmeter, measure the resistance between these two terminals **(see illustration)**. Compare your measurement to the primary resistance listed in this Chapter's Specifications. If the indicated primary resistance is outside the specified range, replace the coil. If the primary resistance is within range, check the coil secondary resistance.
5   To check the coil secondary resistance, measure the resistance between the two spark plug leads and compare your measurement to

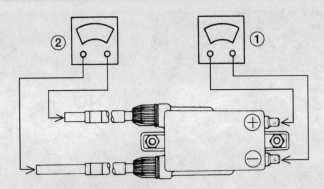

3.4 Test 1: Check coil primary resistance between the primary terminals. Test 2: Check secondary resistance between the two spark plug wire caps, then unscrew the plug leads from the coil and check secondary resistance between the two high tension terminals

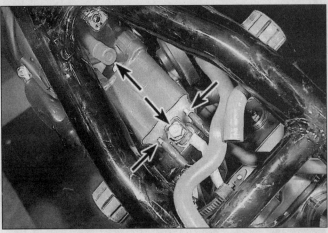

3.6 To remove the coil for the front cylinder, unplug the primary leads (arrows) and remove the coil mounting bolts (arrows); don't forget to reattach the ground wire attached to the rear bolt when installing the coil (VT600 shown, VT750 similar)

the secondary resistance listed in this Chapter's Specifications. If the indicated secondary resistance is outside the specified range, unscrew the spark plug leads from the coil, measure the resistance between the two coil high tension terminals and compare your measurement to the secondary resistance listed in this Chapter's Specifications. If the indicated secondary resistance is now within the specified range, replace the spark plug high tension leads. If the indicated resistance is still not within the specified range, replace the coil.

Replacement

Refer to illustrations 3.6 and 3.7

6   To replace the coil for the front cylinder, remove the fuel tank (see Chapter 4) and remove the crankcase breather separator (see Chapter 4). (The separator is the white plastic tank above the coil; it's part of the crankcase emission control system.) Before detaching the coil, clearly label the primary electrical connectors **(see illustration)**, then unplug them from the primary terminals. Detach the spark plug caps from the front cylinder plugs, remove the two coil mounting bolts, pull back the ground wire eyelet (attached to the rear mounting bolt) and remove the coil. (The accompanying photo depicts the front coil on a VT600 model. The front coil on VT750 models is also located in the same general location; it's bolted to the left side of the upper frame tube.)

7   To replace the coil for the rear cylinder, remove the right side cover (see Chapter 8). The rear coil **(see illustration)** is removed basi-

cally the same way as the front coil. (The accompanying photo depicts the rear coil on a VT600 model. The rear coil on VT750 models is also located behind the right side cover, except that it's mounted vertically.)

8   Installation is the reverse of removal.

4   Ignition pulse generator(s) - check and replacement

Check

Refer to illustration 4.3

1   The following test applies only to the pulse generators used on 1988 and 1989 and 1991 through 1996 VT600 models. In order to determine whether one of the ignition pulse generators on a 1997 or later VT600 model, or the single pulse generator on a VT750 model, is defective, have it tested by a Honda dealer service department equipped with the necessary diagnostic equipment.

2   Remove the fuel tank (see Chapter 4) and the left steering head cover (see Chapter 8).

3   Unplug the white four-pin connector for the ignition pulse generators **(see illustration)**.

4   Using an ohmmeter, measure the resistance between the white/yellow wire and the yellow wire (front ignition pulse generator),

3.7 To remove the coil for the rear cylinder, unplug the primary leads from the rear end of the coil (not visible in this photo) and remove the coil mounting bolts (arrows) (VT600 shown, VT750 similar, except that coil is installed vertically)

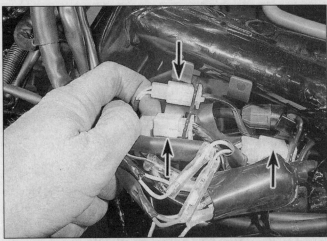

4.3 To check the ignition pulse generators, measure resistance at the white four-pin connector (on the left side, right behind the steering head)

**4.8 To detach either ignition pulse generator, remove the two
retaining bolts (arrows)**

and between the white/blue wire and the blue wire (rear ignition pulse
generator). Compare your measurements to the ignition pulse generator coil resistance listed in this Chapter's Specifications. If the resistance of either coil is outside the specified range, replace that ignition
pulse generator.

Replacement

Refer to illustrations 4.8, 4.9a and 4.9b

5   Remove the fuel tank (see Chapter 4) and the left steering head
cover (see Chapter 8).
6   Unplug the white four-pin connector for the ignition pulse generators **(see illustration 4.3)**. Carefully pull the harness down the right
frame tube. If the connector snags on anything, stop and disengage it
before pulling the harness down.
7   Remove the right crankcase cover (see "Clutch - removal and
installation" in Chapter 2).
8   Remove the ignition pulse generator mounting bolts **(see illustration)** and remove the ignition pulse generator(s).
9   Installation is the reverse of removal. Tighten the pulse generator
mounting bolts to the torque listed in this Chapter's Specifications. The
wires for the ignition pulse generators exit the engine through a hole in
the crankcase, right in front of the pulse generators. Make sure that the
two grommets are correctly installed **(see illustration)** before installing
the right crankcase cover. And before routing the harness up the right

**4.9b Before plugging in the electrical connector for the ignition
pulse generators, make sure that the harness is routed correctly
through this guide, then up the right frame tube**

**4.9a When installing the ignition pulse generator(s), make sure
that the grommets are correctly installed (left grommet); do not
install the right crankcase cover with the grommets unseated
(right grommet), or water will get into the crankcase (and oil
will get out!)**

frame tube and plugging in the electrical connector up top, be sure to
route the harness through the harness guide welded onto the frame
(see illustration).

5   Timing rotor - removal and installation

The timing rotor is attached to the primary drive gear by the primary drive gear retaining bolt. It's removed and installed with the primary drive gear (see Chapter 2).

6   Ignition control module - check and replacement

Check

1   The ignition control module is basically diagnosed by a process of
elimination. It should never even be *checked* until *after absolutely all
other possible causes have been checked and eliminated*. Because a
new module is expensive and cannot be returned, it's a good idea to
have a Honda dealer test the old module before you buy a new unit.

**6.3 To detach the electrical connector plates from the underside
of the tool tray, pull them straight out (VT600 models)**

Replacement

VT600 models

Refer to illustration 6.3

2   Remove the left side cover (see Chapter 8). Locate the six-pin and four-pin electrical connectors for the ignition control module. The module can be identified by its wire colors, referring to wiring diagrams at the end of the book.

3   Disengage the electrical connector plates from the underside of the tool tray **(see illustration)**.

4   Remove the tool tray.

5   Unplug the six-pin and four-pin electrical connectors from the ignition control module.

6   Disengage the module from its mounting stay.

7   Installation is the reverse of removal.

VT750 models

8   Remove the seat (see Chapter 8).

9   Remove the ignition control module from the battery case cover.

10   Unplug the 16-pin or 22-pin connector and remove the module.

11   Installation is the reverse of removal.

---

7   Ignition timing - check

Refer to illustration 7.1

1   Remove the timing hole cap from the left side of the engine **(see illustration)**.

2   Hook up an inductive timing light in accordance with the manufacturer's instructions to one of the rear (No. 1 cylinder) spark plug wires.

3   Warm up the engine to its normal operating temperature.

4   With the engine at its normal idle speed (see Chapter 1), check the timing mark with the timing light. The ignition timing is correct if the firing (F) mark on the flywheel is aligned with the stationary index mark

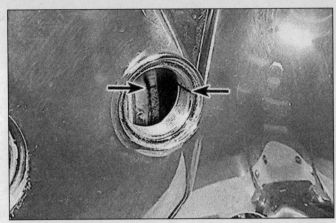

7.1 Align the timing mark (left arrow) with the index mark (right arrow)

on the edge of the timing hole in the left crankcase cover **(see illustration 7.1)**.

5   Increase the engine speed and verify that the advance marks on the flywheel are aligned with the stationary index mark on the edge off the timing hole.

6   Stop the engine, remove the inductive pickup from the rear cylinder spark plug wire and hook it up to one of the front (cylinder No. 2) spark plug wires.

7   Start the engine and allow it to return to its normal idle.

8   Check the timing for the front cylinder the same way (see Steps 4 and 5).

9   The ignition timing is not adjustable. If it's incorrect, either the ignition control module or an ignition pulse generator is defective. Have the system checked out by a Honda dealer with the necessary system diagnostic equipment.

Notes

Chapter 6
Steering and suspension

Contents

Specifications

Front fork

Spring free length	
VT600	
1988 and 1989, 1991 through 1992	305 mm (12 inches)
1993 on	333.9 mm (13-5/32 inches)
VT750	303.4 mm (11-61/64 inches)
Fork oil	
Type	Honda SS-8, or equivalent
Capacity	
VT600	449 cc (16.9 ounces)
VT750	512 cc (17.3 ounces)
Distance from top of fork tube	
VT600	4.4 inches
VT750	4.3 inches

Rear shock absorber and spring

Spring free length	
1988, 1989, 1991 through 1996 VT600	135 mm (5-5/16 inches)
All other models	Do not disassemble shock

Torque specifications

Front forks
  Axle pinch bolts.. 22 Nm (16 ft-lbs)
  Fork caps
    VT600... 23 Nm (17 ft-lbs)
    VT750... 22 Nm (16 ft-lbs)
  Damper rod bolts .... 29 Nm (22 ft-lbs)
Handlebar brackets
  Upper bracket bolts
    VT600... 30 Nm (22 ft-lbs)
    VT750... 23 Nm (17 ft-lbs)
  Lower bracket-to-upper triple clamp nuts .... 23 Nm (17 ft-lbs)
Rear shock absorber
  Upper and lower mounting bolts/nuts
    VT600... 45 Nm (33 ft-lbs)
    VT750... 26 Nm (19 ft-lbs)
  Damper rod locknut (pre-1997 VT600).. 70 Nm (52 ft-lbs)
Steering stem head nut .... 103 Nm (76 ft-lbs)
Triple clamp/fork tube pinch bolts
  VT600
    Upper .... 11 Nm (96 in-lbs)
    Lower .... 50 Nm (37 ft-lbs)
  VT750
    Upper .... 26 Nm (19 ft-lbs)
    Lower .... 50 Nm (37 ft-lbs)
Swingarm pivot bolt/nut
  VT600 .... 88 Nm (65 ft-lbs)
  VT750
    Pivot adjusting bolt .... 25 Nm (18 ft-lbs)
    Pivot locknut .... 64 Nm (47 ft-lbs)

1   General information

The front forks are a conventional coil-spring, hydraulically-damped telescopic type, designed to run at atmospheric pressure, *i.e.* they're not pressurized.

The rear suspension on VT600 models consists of a single nitrogen-charged shock absorber/coil spring assembly and a swingarm. The rear suspension on VT750 models consists of two shock absorbers and a swingarm.

The single shock on VT600 models and the twin shocks on VT750 models have spring preload adjusters which allow seven spring preload settings. Setting one is for light loads and/or good roads; setting seven is for heavy loads and/or bad roads. Setting two is the standard setting.

2   Handlebar - removal and installation

Refer to illustrations 2.1, 2.2 and 2.3

1   If the handlebar is being removed only to service other components, such as the steering head or the fork tubes, simply pry out the caps from the handlebar brackets **(see illustration)**, remove the Allen bolts and the upper halves of the brackets, and set the handlebar aside. It isn't necessary to disconnect the brake hose, the clutch or throttle cables, or the wire harnesses for the handlebar switches, but it is a good idea to support the handlebar assembly with a piece of wire or rope, to avoid excessive strain on the brake hose, the cables and the harnesses.

2   If the handlebar itself is being replaced, disconnect the clutch cable (see Chapter 2), remove the clutch lever bracket **(see illustra-**

2.1 To get to the handlebar bracket bolts, pry out these four caps (arrows) with a small screwdriver

2.2 To remove the clutch lever bracket, remove these bolts (arrows)

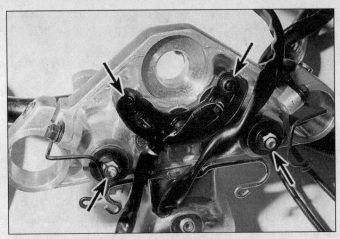

2.3 To detach the lower halves of the handlebar brackets from the upper triple clamp, remove these nuts (arrows)

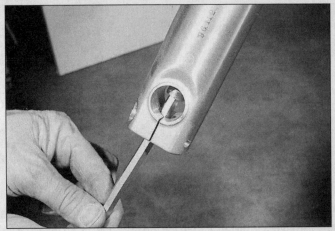

3.3a Back out the damper rod bolt from the lower end of the fork leg . . .

3.3b . . . remove the bolt, discard the sealing washer and drain the fork oil

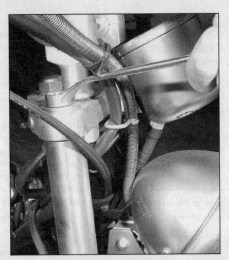

3.4 Remove the fork cap

3.8 Add the specified type and amount of fork oil (fork removed from bike for clarity; it's not necessary to remove the forks to add new fork oil)

tion), remove the switch housings (see Chapter 9), disconnect the throttle cables (see Chapter 4), remove the brake master cylinder (see Chapter 7), and unbolt the handlebar (see Step 1).

3   To remove the lower halves of the handlebar brackets from the upper triple clamp, remove the bracket nuts from the underside of the upper triple clamp **(see illustration)** and pull the brackets out of the triple clamp. Remove the rubber bushings.

4   Inspect the rubber bushings for cracks and distortion. If they're damaged or worn, replace them.

5   Inspect the handlebar for cracks and distortion and replace it if any damage is found.

6   Installation is the reverse of removal. Be sure to tighten the handlebar bracket bolts to the torque listed in this Chapter's Specifications.

3   Fork oil change

Refer to illustrations 3.3a 3.3b, 3.4, 3.8 and 3.9

Note: *The following procedure applies to a fork oil change unassociated with rebuilding the front forks. If you are going to rebuild the forks, it's much easier to simply pour out the old fork oil after the forks have been removed from the bike.*

1   Support the bike securely so it can't be knocked over during this procedure. The front wheel must be raised off the ground using a hydraulic lift, a shop stand, a jack and wood support under the crankcase, axle stands, etc.

2   Remove the front wheel (see Chapter 7).

3   Place a drain pan under the fork legs and remove the damper rod bolts **(see illustrations)**. Discard the old sealing washers. Damper rod bolts can be difficult to remove, because the damper rod turns with the bolt. If this happens, use an air wrench to back out the bolt. If you don't have air tools, have an assistant compress the fork while you loosen the damper rod bolt (compressing the fork makes it harder for the damper rod to turn with the bolt). If you still can't loosen the bolt, remove the fork (see Section 4), put it in a bench vise (be sure to protect the fork with brass or plastic jaw protectors) and, again, have an assistant compress the fork while you loosen the damper rod bolt (it's easier to compress the fork when it's in a bench vise than when it's on the bike).

4   Remove the fork caps **(see illustration)**.

5   After most of the oil has drained, alternate between *slowly* compressing and releasing the forks to pump out the remaining oil. Don't try to compress the forks too quickly or you will squirt oil everywhere!

6   Clean the threads of the damper rod bolts with solvent, dry them off with compressed air, install the bolts with new sealing washers, and tighten the bolts to the torque listed in this Chapter's Specifications.

7   Remove the fork springs from the forks.

8   Pour the type and amount of fork oil listed in this Chapter's Specifications into the fork tube through the opening at the top **(see illustration)**.

9   Measure the level of the oil in the fork with the fork fully compressed and without the spring in position **(see illustration)**. Compare

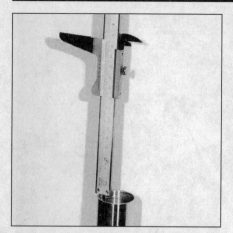

3.9 Measure the distance from the top of the fork tube to the fork oil with the spring removed and the fork fully compressed

4.6a To detach a fork tube from the triple clamps, remove each plug (arrow) (lower triple clamp shown) . . .

4.6b . . . and remove each fork tube pinch bolt (arrow) (upper triple clamp shown)

it to the value listed in this Chapter's Specifications. Add or remove oil as necessary.

10   Install the springs with their more closely-wound coils at the top.

11   Install the fork caps and tighten them to the torque listed in this Chapter's Specifications.

12   The remainder of installation is the reverse of the removal steps.

4   Forks - removal and installation

Removal

Refer to illustrations 4.6a and 4.6b

1   The front end of the bike must be off the ground for this procedure. Raise the bike on a hydraulic lift or shop stand, or put it on a milk crate or some other suitable support. Make sure that whatever you use is strong enough to support the bike securely.

2   Remove the front wheel (see Chapter 7).

3   Remove the front fender (see Chapter 8).

4   If you're planning to remove the left fork, disconnect the brake hose clamp and unbolt the brake caliper (see Chapter 7). Hang the caliper with a piece of wire or rope to protect the brake hose. This is a good time to inspect the caliper and brake pads for wear (see Chapter 7).

5   The tops of the fork tubes are flush with the top surface of the upper triple clamp. The tube(s) must be reinstalled in exactly the same position.

6   Loosen the fork upper and lower triple clamp bolt caps and bolts **(see illustrations)**.

VT600 models

7   Remove the fork(s) from the triple clamps with a twisting motion.

VT750CD models

8   Remove the upper triple clamp (see Section 5).

9   Pull the fork tube(s) down slightly and remove the O-ring(s) between the upper fork cover(s) and the fork tube(s).

10   Remove the upper fork cover bolts and remove the upper fork cover(s).

11   Remove the fork(s) from the triple clamps with a twisting motion.

12   Remove the lower fork cover(s).

Installation

13   Installation is the reverse of removal. On VT750CD models, don't forget to install the lower and upper fork cover(s); be sure to use new O-rings with the upper cover(s). Do NOT torque any of the triple clamp bolts until the front wheel is installed.

14   After removing the bike from the lift, milk crate, etc., pump the front brake lever several times to bring the pads into contact with the disc.

5   Forks - disassembly, inspection and reassembly

Disassembly

Refer to illustrations 5.6, 5.7, 5.8, 5.9a, 5.9b, 5.11a, 5.11b and 5.11c

Note: *Work on one fork leg at a time to avoid mixing up the parts.*

1   *Loosen* (do NOT remove), the damper rod bolts **(see illustration 3.3a)** and the fork tube caps **(see illustration 3.4)**.

2   Remove the forks (see Section 3).

3   Place a fork leg in a bench vise (clamp the vise jaws onto the slider; do not clamp onto the friction surface of the fork tube itself) and remove the fork cap and O-ring, the spacer, the spring seat and the fork spring. Discard the old fork cap O-ring.

4   Remove the fork from the bench vise and pour out the fork oil.

5   Place the fork leg back in the bench vise again. To finish disassembling the fork, you must remove the damper rod bolt (it's a large Allen bolt) from the bottom of the slider **(see illustration 3.3b)**. This bolt attaches the damper rod to the fork slider. When removing the Allen bolt, retrieve the old copper sealing washer and discard it. This washer must be replaced when the fork is reassembled. Sometimes, the damper rod bolt is so tight that the damper rod turns when you try to loosen the bolt. If this happens, try removing the bolt with an air tool, if you have it. If not, have an assistant push the inner fork tube firmly into the slider; compressing the fork spring is usually sufficient to lock the damper rod cylinder into place while the damper rod bolt is loosened. If that doesn't work, try compressing the fork spring *and* loosening the bolt with an air tool. And if that doesn't work? There are aftermarket tools designed to hold the damper rod; see your dealer parts department or an aftermarket motorcycle accessory shop. If you can't

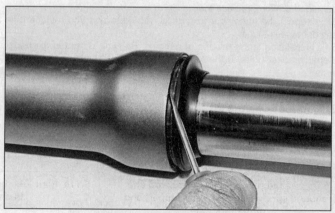

5.6 Pry the dust seal from the fork slider

5.7 Carefully pry the stopper ring out of its groove in the fork slider without distorting it

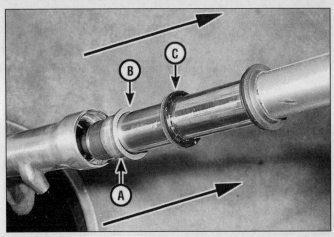

5.8 Pull the slider and fork tube in opposite directions with a few sharp jerks (like a slide hammer); the slider bushing (A), back-up ring (B) and oil seal (C) will pop out of the slider with the tube

find a suitable special tool, have a dealer service department loosen the bolt.

6   Pry the dust seal out of the fork slider with a small screwdriver and slide it up the fork tube, so it's out of the way (see illustration). **Caution:** *If you plan to reuse the dust seal, make sure you don' slide it over rust spots or spots where the chrome is flaking off, or you'll ruin it.*

7   Slide the dust seal up the fork tube and pry out the stopper ring (see illustration).

8   To separate the fork tube from the slider, hold the slider and yank the tube upward repeatedly (like a slide hammer) until the seal, back-up ring and slider bushing pop loose from the slider (see illustration). Remove the dust seal, stopper ring, seal and back-up ring from the fork tube. Discard the dust seal and fork seal. If the stopper ring is fatigued, replace it too.

9   Remove the oil lock piece from the damper rod (see illustrations). If it's not there, it's probably still in the bottom of the fork slider.

10   Invert the tube and remove the damper rod and rebound spring (see illustration).

11   The smaller-diameter fork tube bushing and the larger-diameter slider bushing are on the lower end of the fork tube (see illustration). The fork tube bushing fits tightly around the end of the fork tube and is seated against a shoulder on the end of the tube, while the slider bush-ing slides freely up and down the fork tube and is seated against a shoulder inside the fork slider. You need not remove either bushing unless it appears worn or scratched. If it's necessary to replace the

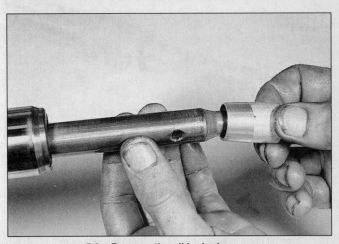

5.9a Remove the oil lock piece . . .

fork tube bushing (the lower bushing on the tube, the one that doesn't slide up and down), pry it apart at the slit and slide it off (see illustration). To remove the slider bushing, simply slide it off the fork tube (see illustration).

5.9b . . . and remove the damper rod and rebound spring from the other (upper) end of the fork tube

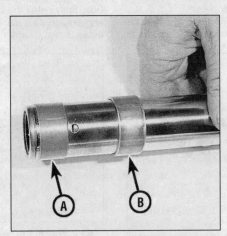

5.11a Fork tube bushing (A) and slider bushing (B)

5.11b Pry the fork tube bushing apart at the slit and slide it off; don't pry the bushing apart any more than necessary, to avoid distorting it

5.11c The slider bushing can be removed by simply sliding it off

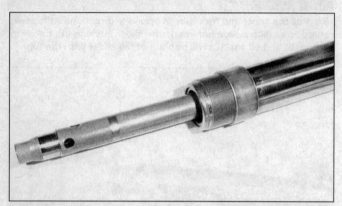

5.19 Insert the damper rod (with its rebound spring) into the upper end of the fork tube and let it drop through the smaller opening in the lower end

Inspection

Refer to illustration 5.12

12   Clean all parts in solvent and blow them dry with compressed air, if available. Lay out the parts for inspection **(see illustration)**.

13   Inspect the fork tube and slider, the bushings and the damper rod for score marks and scratches. Inspect the chrome surface of the fork tube for flaking and excessive wear. Look for dents in the tube. If the fork tube is damaged or worn, replace it.

14   Have the fork tube checked for runout at a dealer service department or other repair shop. **Warning:** *If the fork tube is bent, replace it; don't try to have it straightened.*

15   Measure the overall length of the fork spring and check it for cracks and other damage. Compare the length to the minimum length

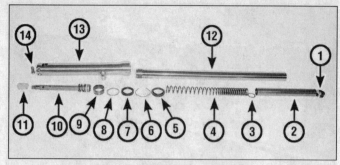

5.12 The front fork assembly:

1	Fork cap and O-ring	10	Damper rod and rebound
2	Spacer		spring
3	Spring seat	11	Lock piece
4	Fork spring	12	Fork tube and fork tube
5	Dust seal		bushing
6	Stopper ring	13	Fork slider
7	Fork seal	14	Damper rod bolt and
8	Back-up ring		sealing washer
9	Slider bushing		

listed in this Chapter's Specifications. If it's defective or sagged, replace both fork springs. Never replace only one spring.

Reassembly

Refer to illustrations 5.19, 5.20, 5.22, 5.23, 5.24a, 5.24b, 5.24c, 5.25a, 5.25b, 5.25c, 5.25d, 5.25e, 5.26 and 5.27

16   Lightly lubricate all parts with clean fork oil as they're reassembled.

17   Install the new fork tube bushing, if the old bushing was removed. Do not pry open the bushing any more than necessary to install it. Be extremely careful not to damage the bushing friction surface. Make sure the bushing is seated at the bottom of the fork tube, against the shoulder.

18   Install the slider bushing on the fork tube.

19   Install the rebound spring on the damper rod. Install the damper rod into the fork tube, then let it slide slowly down until it protrudes from the bottom of the fork tube **(see illustration)**.

20   Install the oil lock piece over the end of the damper rod that protrudes from the fork tube **(see illustration)**.

21   Holding the fork slider upside down (so the lock piece doesn't fall off the lower end of the damper rod), insert the fork tube and damper rod into the slider.

22   Apply a non-permanent thread-locking agent to the damper rod bolt, then install the bolt and a new sealing washer **(see illustration)** and tighten it as much as you can. (Don't try to tighten to the torque listed in this Chapter's Specifications at this time unless you have a

5.20 Install the lock piece on the lower end of the damper rod

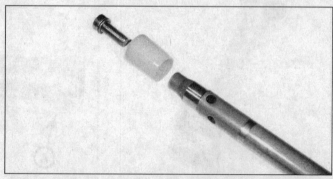

5.22 This is the relationship of the damper rod bolt to the lock piece and damper rod when the damper rod bolt is installed through the bottom end of the slider, into the lower end of the damper rod; if the damper rod isn't aligned correctly with the hole in the slider, the bolt won't thread into it

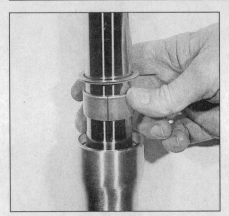

5.23 Install the back-up ring on the fork tube

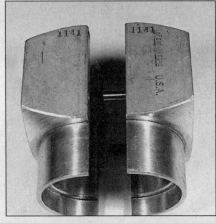

5.24a Using a split-type seal driver (this is a Kent-Moore, but any suitable equivalent will work) . . .

5.24b . . . tap down gently and repeatedly to seat the slider bushing; make sure the bushing is fully seated against the shoulder inside the slider

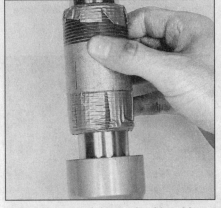

5.24c If you don't have a bushing driver, use a section of pipe instead; be sure to tape the ends of the pipe so it doesn't scratch the fork tube

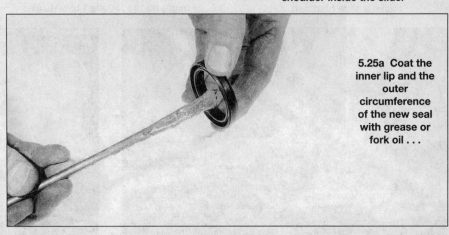

5.25a Coat the inner lip and the outer circumference of the new seal with grease or fork oil . . .

suitable tool for holding the damper rod.) If the bolt won't "catch," *i.e.* it won't tighten up, the damper rod is not correctly aligned with the bolt. Using a flashlight and a Phillips screwdriver with a taped tip, align the threaded bore in the lower end of the damper rod with the bore in the bottom of the slider.

23   Slide the back-up ring down the fork tube **(see illustration)**.

24   Using a suitable bushing driver **(see illustrations)**, drive the slider bushing into place until it's fully seated. If you don't have one of these tools, drive the bushing into place with a section of pipe and an old guide bushing **(see illustration)**. Wrap tape around the ends of the pipe to prevent it from scratching the fork tube. If you're unable to fabricate a suitable bushing driver, take the fork assembly to a Honda dealer service department or a motorcycle machine shop or repair shop to have the bushing installed.

25   Lubricate the lip and the outer circumference of the new oil seal with the fork oil listed in this Chapter's Specifications and slide the seal

5.25b . . . and install the seal on the fork tube; be careful not to damage the seal lip on the upper edge of the fork tube

5.25c Tap the seal gently and repeatedly with a seal driver until it's fully seated into the fork slider (but don't keep hitting it after it bottoms)

5.25d You can also use a bushing driver to tap the seal into place (one half of the bushing driver has been removed for clarity)

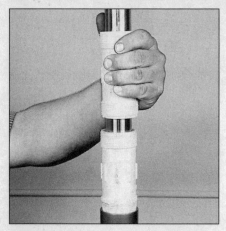

5.25e You can even drive the seal into place with two PVC plumbing fittings of the correct diameter; place one fitting on the seal and strike it with the other fitting (like a slide hammer)

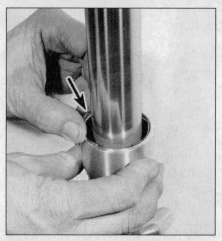

5.26 Compress the stopper ring and fit it securely into its groove in the fork slider (if the stopper doesn't "snap" into place, it might be too fatigued to re-use)

5.27 Use any of the tools previously shown to drive the dust seal into place

6.4a Remove the steering stem nut . . .

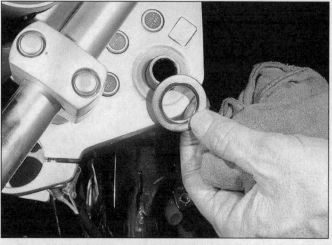

6.4b . . . and remove the washer

down the fork tube with the part number side of the seal facing up **(see illustrations)**. Drive the seal into place with a seal driver (or use the same tool used to drive in the slider bushing) **(see illustrations)** or make something that will do the job **(see illustration)**. Again, if you don't have a suitable tool for this job, take the fork assembly to a Honda dealer service department or other motorcycle repair shop to have the seal installed. If you're extremely careful, the seal can even be installed with a hammer and a drift punch. Work around the circumference of the seal, tapping gently on the outer edge of the seal until it's seated. Be careful! If you distort or damage the seal, you'll have to dig it out, which might mean disassembling the fork again (and taking it to a dealer!).

26   Install the stopper ring **(see illustration)**. Make sure the ring is correctly seated in its groove in the fork slider.

27   Install the dust seal and drive it into place with the same tool used to install the oil seal **(see illustration)**, or use the tool used to install the slider bushing driver. Make sure the dust seal is fully seated.

28   Add the recommended type and amount of fork oil (see Section 3).

29   Install the fork spring, with the closer-wound coils at the top.

30   Install the spring seat, the spacer and the fork cap. Use a new O-ring on the fork cap.

31   Install the fork assembly (see Section 4). If you won't be installing the fork right away, store it in an upright position.

32   Repeat this procedure for the other fork.

6   Steering stem and bearings - removal, inspection and installation

Removal

Refer to illustrations 6.4a, 6.4b, 6.5, 6.6a, 6.6b, 6.7, 6.8 and 6.9

1   If the steering head bearing check/adjustment (see Chapter 1) does not remedy excessive play or roughness in the steering head bearings, the entire front end must be disassembled and the bearings and races replaced.

2   Remove the fuel tank (see Chapter 4) and the steering head covers (see Chapter 8).

3   Remove the front forks (see Section 3).

4   Remove the steering stem nut and washer **(see illustrations)**, then lift off the upper triple clamp (sometimes called the fork bridge or crown). Unless you plan to replace the upper triple clamp, it isn't necessary to remove the handlebars - just set the upper triple clamp aside with everything attached. **Caution:** *If any of the electrical harnesses for the handlebar switches are pulled tight, unplug them (see Chapter 9). It isn't necessary to disconnect the brake hydraulic hose, but make sure that the handlebar/triple clamp assembly is neither hanging by the hose or putting any strain on the hose.*

5   The locknut is secured by four lockwasher tabs. Straighten these tabs with a screwdriver **(see illustration)**.

6.5 Straighten the tabs on the lockwasher with a small screwdriver

6.6a Loosen the locknut with ring nut wrench (also known as a C-spanner)

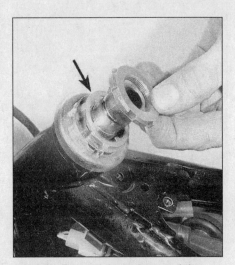

6.6b Remove the locknut and the lockwasher (arrow)

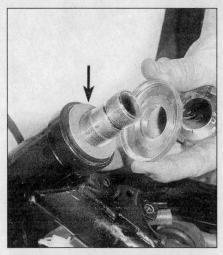

6.7 Remove the bearing adjustment nut and the upper bearing dust seal (arrow)

6.8 Remove the upper bearing inner race

6   Using a ring nuts wrench (also known as a C-spanner wrench), remove the locknut and the lockwasher **(see illustrations)**. There should be a suitable spanner in the bike's tool kit; if not, you can obtain the right wrench from a dealer or motorcycle accessory shop.

7   Remove the bearing locknut and the dust seal **(see illustration)**.

8   Remove the upper bearing inner race **(see illustration)** and remove the upper bearing assembly.

9   Pull down on the lower triple clamp and remove the steering stem/lower bearing/lower triple clamp assembly **(see illustration)**. If it's stuck, gently tap on the top of the steering stem with a plastic mallet or a hammer and a wood block.

Inspection

Refer to illustrations 6.12a, 6.12b, 6.13a, 6.13b, 6.13c, 6.13d, 6.14, 6.16, 6.18a and 6.18b

10   Clean all the parts with solvent and dry them thoroughly, using compressed air, if available. Wipe the old grease out of the steering head and bearing races.

11   Examine the outer races in the steering head for cracks, dents, and pits. If even the slightest amount of wear or damage is evident, the races should be replaced.

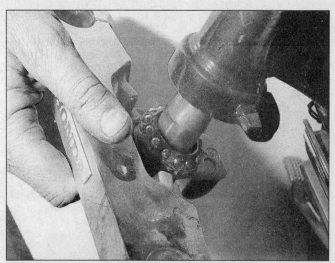

6.9 Carefully pull the steering stem/lower triple clamp assembly from the steering head

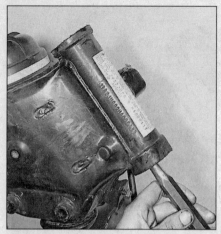

6.12a Insert a long punch or rod from below to tap out the upper steering head outer race . . .

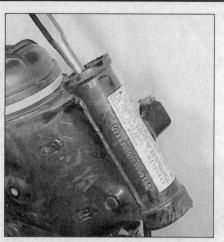

6.12b . . . and from above to tap out the lower bearing outer race

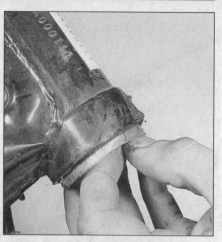

6.13a Position the lower bearing outer race in the steering head . . .

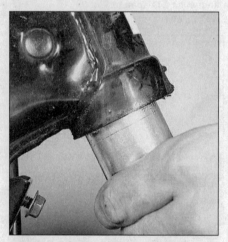

6.13b . . . and tap it into position with a socket slightly smaller in diameter than the race

6.13c Tap the upper bearing outer race into position with the same tools

6.13d . . . the upper bearing outer race should look like this when installed

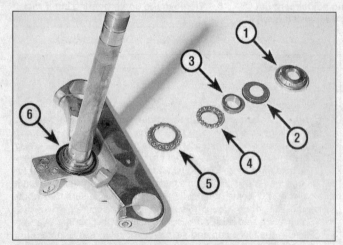

6.14 The steering stem/lower triple clamp assembly

  1   Bearing adjustment nut
  2   Dust seal
  3   Upper steering head bearing inner race
  4   Upper steering head bearing assembly
  5   Lower steering head bearing assembly
  6   Lower steering head bearing inner race

12   To remove the outer races from the steering head, drive them out with a hammer and drift punch **(see illustrations)**. A slide hammer with the right internal-jaw puller will also work.

13   Since the outer races are an "interference-fit" in the frame, installation will be easier if the new races are left overnight in a refrigerator freezer. The frozen races will contract slightly, and slip into place in the frame with very little effort. When installing the races, tap them gently into place with a hammer and punch or a large socket **(see illustrations)**. Do not strike the bearing surface or the race will be damaged.

14   Inspect the bearings **(see illustration)** for wear. Look for cracks, dents, and pits in the races and flat spots on the bearings. If either bearing assembly is damaged or worn, replace both the upper or lower steering head bearings as a set.

15   Inspect the lower bearing inner race (the one that's pressed onto the steering stem) for cracks, dents, and pits. If even the slightest amount of wear or damage is evident, replace the lower inner race. Examine the dust seal under the lower bearing; if it's damaged, replace it.

16   To remove the lower bearing inner race, use a bearing puller (available at tool rental yards, if you don't have one). A hammer and drift punch will also work **(see illustration)**. Don't remove this race unless it, or the dust seal, must be replaced. Removing the race will damage the dust seal, so replace the seal if the bearing is removed.

17   Inspect the steering stem/lower triple clamp assembly for cracks and other damage. Do not attempt to repair this component. If any damage is evident, replace the steering stem/lower triple clamp assembly.

18   Install a new dust seal and the lower bearing inner onto the steer-

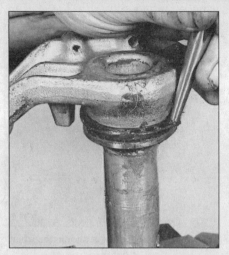

6.16 Tap the seal and lower bearing bottom race off the steering stem

6.18a Install a new seal with its concave side down . . .

6.18b . . . then install the lower bearing inner race with its bearing surface facing up, and press the race onto the stem with a section of pipe (taped to protect the bearing surface)

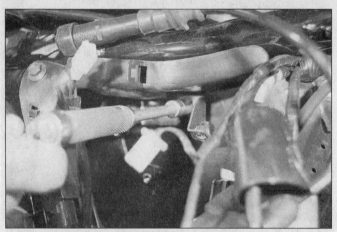

7.6 Remove the front bolt from the rear ignition coil bracket

7.7 Remove the fuel pump bracket mounting nut (on the left side of the bike, right above the rear end of the ignition control module)

ing stem **(see illustrations).** Drive the lower bearing onto the steering stem using a bearing driver. If you don't have access to these tools, a section of pipe with the same diameter as the inner race can be used. Drive the bearing on until it's fully seated.

Installation

19   Pack the bearings with high-quality grease (preferably a moly-based grease). Coat the outer races in the steering head with grease also.

20   Install the lower steering head bearing assembly on the steering stem, then insert the steering stem/lower triple clamp into the lower end of the steering head. Install the upper bearing, inner race, dust seal and bearing adjustment nut. Using the spanner wrench (C-spanner), tighten the adjuster nut while moving the lower triple clamp back and forth. Continue to tighten the nut, 1/8-turn at a time, until all play has been removed from the steering head bearings. However, don't over-tighten the adjustment nut, or the steering will be too firm and the new bearings and/or races will wear out prematurely.

21   Once the adjustment nut is tight and all bearing play has been removed, install the lockwasher and the locknut. Bend up the tabs on the lockwasher to secure the locknut, then install the upper triple clamp on the steering stem. Install the washer and steering stem nut and tighten the stem nut to the torque listed in this Chapter's Specifications.

22   Install the handlebar assembly, if removed (see Section 2).

23   Install the front forks (see Section 3).

24   Install the steering head covers (see Chapter 8) and fuel tank (see Chapter 4).

7   Rear shock absorber (VT600 models) - removal, inspection and installation

Removal

Refer to illustrations 7.6, 7.7, 7.8, 7.9a, 7.9b and 7.10

Warning: *Do not attempt to disassemble this shock absorber. It is nitrogen-charged under high pressure. Improper disassembly could result in serious injury. Instead, take the shock to a dealer service department with the proper equipment to do the job.*

1   The bike must be supported with the rear wheel off the ground for this procedure. Raise the bike on a hydraulic lift or shop stand, or put it on a milk crate or some other suitable support. Make sure that whatever you use is strong enough to support the bike securely.

2   Remove the seat and both side covers (see Chapter 8).

3   Remove the fuel pump and the fuel pump relay (see Chapter 4).

4   Remove the rear ignition coil mounting bolts (see Chapter 5).

5   Remove the turn signal relay from the fuel pump bracket (see Chapter 9).

6   Remove the front bolt from the rear ignition coil bracket **(see illustration).**

7   Locate the fuel pump bracket mounting nut on the left side of the bike, right above the rear end of the ignition control module and remove it **(see illustration).**

7.8 Remove the fuel pump bracket

7.9a Remove the upper shock absorber nut and bolt

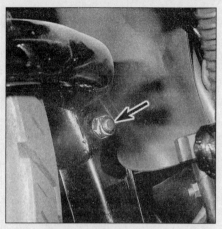

7.9b Remove the lower shock absorber nut and bolt

7.10 Remove the shock absorber from the top

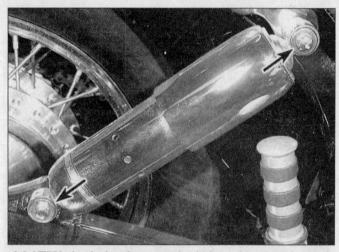

8.2 VT750 shock absorber mounting bolts and washers (arrows)

8   Remove the fuel pump bracket **(see illustration)**.
9   Remove the upper and lower shock absorber nuts and bolts **(see illustrations)**.
10   Remove the shock absorber from the top **(see illustration)**.

Inspection

11   Inspect the shock absorber for obvious physical damage, such as a worn damper rod seal or a bent damper rod. Inspect the coil spring for looseness or signs of fatigue. Inspect the shock for evidence that it's leaking shock oil or nitrogen gas.
12   If the shock absorber or the coil spring is damaged or obviously worn, replace the shock and coil spring as a single assembly. On 1988 and 1989 and 1991 through 1996 VT600 models, either component could be replaced separately at one time. Check with your dealer for availability. Unless the parts department has the older separate parts in stock, you will probably discover that older models are being fitted with the newer unit, which is only available as a single assembly. Even if you do find the parts separately, however, special tools are needed to disassemble the shock/coil spring assembly. Have the unit disassembled and the coil spring or shock absorber replaced by a dealer service department with the right tools.

Installation

13   Installation is the reverse of removal. Be sure to tighten the shock absorber nuts and bolts to the torque listed in this Chapter's Specifications.

8   Rear shock absorbers (VT750 models) - removal, inspection and installation

Warning: *Do not attempt to disassemble this shock absorber. It is nitrogen-charged under high pressure. Improper disassembly could result in serious injury. Instead, take the shock to a dealer service department with the proper equipment to do the job.*

Removal

Refer to illustration 8.2
1   The bike must be supported with the rear wheel off the ground for this procedure. Raise the bike on a hydraulic lift or shop stand, or put it on a milk crate or some other suitable support. Make sure that whatever you use is strong enough to support the bike securely.
2   Remove the upper and lower mounting bolts and the washers from *one* shock absorber **(see illustration)**. Do NOT remove both shocks at the same time!

Inspection

3   Inspect the shock for oil leaks and obvious external damage. Inspect the upper and lower mounting bolt bushings for cracks and excessive wear. If any damage is evident, replace the shock. It cannot be overhauled.

Installation

4   Install the shock absorber, install the washers and mounting bolts

10.8a To detach the VT600 swingarm from the frame, remove the pivot bolt caps from both ends, remove the nut . . .

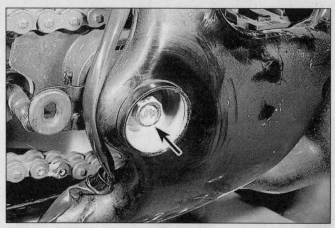

10.8b . . . and remove the pivot bolt (arrow)

and tighten the bolts to the torque listed in this Chapter's Specifications.
5 Repeat Steps 2 through 4 for the other shock.
6 Remove the bike from its support.

9 Swingarm bearings - check

1 Remove the rear wheel (see Chapter 7).
2 Remove the rear shock absorber(s) (VT600 models, see Section 7; VT750 models, see Section 8).
3 Grasp the rear of the swingarm with one hand and place your other hand at the junction of the swingarm and the frame. Try to move the rear of the swingarm from side-to-side. Any wear (play) in the bearings should be felt as movement between the swingarm and the frame at the front. The swingarm will actually be felt to move forward and backward at the front (not from side-to-side).
4 Move the swingarm up and down through its full travel. It should move freely, without any binding or rough spots. If it doesn't move up and down freely, either the swingarm pivot is too tight or the swingarm bearings and/or bushings are damaged.
5 If the swingarm has too much play or is stiff, remove the swingarm (VT600 models, see Section 10; VT750 models, see Section 11) and replace the swingarm bearings and/or bushings (see Section 12).

10 Swingarm (VT600 models) - removal, inspection and installation

Removal

Refer to illustrations 10.8a and 10.8b
1 The bike must be supported with the rear wheel off the ground for this procedure. Raise the bike on a hydraulic lift or shop stand, or put it on a milk crate or some other suitable support. Make sure that whatever you use is strong enough to support the bike securely.
2 Remove the gearshift arm from the gearshift spindle (see Chapter 2).
3 Remove the rear wheel (see Chapter 7).
4 Remove the chain guard and the drive sprocket (see Chapters 8 and 7).
5 On California models, remove the evaporative emission control system canister (see Chapter 4).
6 Remove the coolant reservoir (see Chapter 3).
7 Remove the shock absorber lower mounting nut and bolt and disengage the lower end of the shock absorber from the swingarm (see Section 7).
8 Remove the swingarm pivot bolt and nut **(see illustrations)**.
9 Remove the swingarm. If you're replacing the swingarm, unbolt

10.10a Remove the left side pivot bushing and the dust seals (arrow) from the swingarm (outer dust seal not visible in this photo)

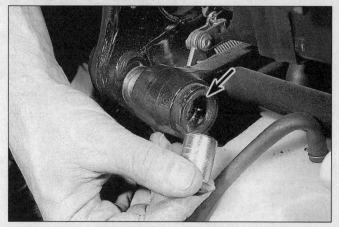

10.10b Remove the right side pivot collars and the dust seals (arrow) from the swingarm (outer dust seal not visible in this photo)

the stopper arm (the arm between the swingarm and the rear brake) and detach the drive chain protector (it's attached by two bolts: one on top, one on bottom).

Inspection

Refer to illustrations 10.10a, 10.10b, 10.11 and 10.12
10 Remove the bushing from the left swingarm pivot **(see illustration)** and remove the two collars from the right pivot **(see illustration)**.

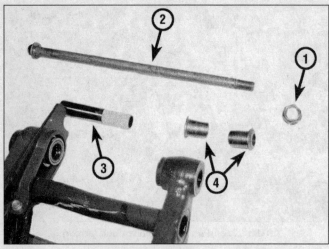

10.11 Inspect the swingarm pivot nut (1), bolt (2), the left side pivot bushing (3) and right side pivot collars (4)

10.12 Inspect the swingarm bearings; if they're dry, lubricate them with multi-purpose grease and if they're worn, replace them

11.8a Use this tool to loosen and tighten the swingarm locknut

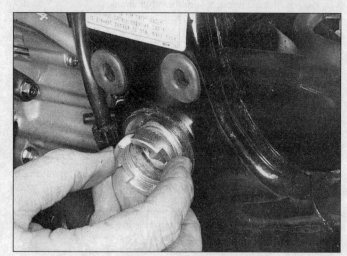

11.8b Unscrew the locknut from the pivot bolt

11   Inspect the swingarm pivot bolt, the left pivot bushing and the right pivot collars **(see illustration)** for scoring and excessive wear. If any of these parts are damaged or worn, replace them.

12   Inspect the swingarm bearings **(see illustration)** for dryness, damage and excessive wear. If they're dry, lubricate them; if they're damaged or worn, replace them (see Section 12).

Installation

13   Installation is the reverse of removal. Tighten the pivot bolt and the shock absorber lower mounting nut and bolt to the torque listed in this Chapter's Specifications.

14   Adjust the drive chain when you're done (see Chapter 1).

---

11 Swingarm (VT750 models) - removal, inspection and installation

---

Warning: *Tightening the swingarm pivot bolt safely on these models requires special tools for which there are no adequate substitutes. If you don't have the correct tools, take the bike to a Honda dealer or other properly equipped shop to have the bolt removed and installed. Refer to illustrations 11.8a, 11.8b and 11.9*

1   The bike must be supported with the rear wheel off the ground for this procedure. Raise the bike on a hydraulic lift or shop stand, or put it

on a milk crate or some other suitable support. Make sure that whatever you use is strong enough to support the bike securely.

2   Remove the exhaust pipe (see Chapter 4).

3   Remove the rear wheel (see Chapter 7).

4   Remove the rear shock absorbers (see Section 8).

5   Remove the two chain guard bolts and remove the chain guard.

6   Remove the swingarm pivot bolt caps.

7   Remove the swingarm pivot bolt nut.

8   Hold the pivot bolt and remove the swingarm pivot bolt locknut **(see illustrations)**.

9   Loosen the swingarm adjusting bolt by turning the pivot bolt **(see illustration)**.

10   Pull out the pivot bolt and remove the swingarm. If you're replacing the swingarm, unbolt the stopper arm (the arm between the swingarm and the rear brake) and detach the drive chain protector (it's attached by two bolts: one on top, one on bottom).

Inspection

11   Remove the two collars from the left and right pivots **(see illustration 10.10b)**.

12   Inspect the swingarm pivot bolt and the left and right pivot collars for scoring and excessive wear. If any of these parts are damaged or worn, replace them.

13   Inspect the swingarm bearings **(see illustration 10.12)** for dryness, damage and excessive wear. If they're dry, lubricate them with

11.9 Unscrew the pivot bolt with an Allen bolt bit

multi-purpose grease. If they're damaged or worn, replace them (see Section 12).

Installation

14   Place the swingarm in position and install the swingarm adjusting bolt. Make sure that the tip of the bolt doesn't protrude in too far (if the end of the bolt *does* protrude in too far, you won't able to install the swingarm).

15   Apply a coat of grease to the swingarm pivot bolt and install the pivot bolt.

16   Screw in the adjusting bolt by hand.

17   Push the hex shank of the pivot bolt into the socket head of the adjusting bolt.

18   Tighten the pivot bolt and adjusting bolt to the torque listed in this Chapter's Specifications.

19   Install the swingarm pivot adjusting bolt locknut and tighten it by hand, then tighten the locknut to the torque listed in this Chapter's Specifications. A special tool (07GMA-KT70200, or a suitable equivalent) is needed to hold the pivot bolt while torquing the locknut. If you're unable to obtain this special tool or a suitable equivalent (consult your dealer parts department), take the bike to a dealer and have the locknut tightened to the correct torque by the service department. **Warning:** *Don't ride the bike until the locknut has been properly tightened to the specified torque.*

20   Installation is otherwise the reverse of removal. Be sure to tighten the shock absorber mounting bolts to the torque listed in this Chapter's Specifications.

21   Adjust the drive chain when you're done (see Chapter 1).

12   Swingarm bearings - replacement

1   Remove the swingarm (VT600 models, see Section 10; VT750 models, see Section 11).

2   Special tools are needed to press out the old bearings and press in new ones. Take the swingarm to a dealer service department or to a motorcycle machine shop with the right tools and have the old bearings replaced.

3   Install the swingarm.

Notes

Chapter 7
Brakes, wheels, tires and final drive

Contents

Specifications

Brakes

Brake fluid type	See Chapter 1
Front brake disc thickness	
VT600	
Standard	5.0 mm (0.20 inch)
Minimum*	4.0 mm (0.16 inch)
VT750	
Standard	5.8 to 6.2 mm (0.23 to 0.24 inch)
Minimum*	5.0 mm (0.2 inch)
Disc runout limit	0.30 mm (0.012 inch)
Front brake pad minimum thickness	To bottom of wear groove
Rear brake drum inside diameter	
VT600	
Standard	160 mm (6.30 inches)
Maximum	161 mm (6.34 inches)*
VT750	
Standard	180 to 180.3 mm (7.09 to 7.10 inches
Maximum	181 mm (7.13 inches)*
Rear brake shoe lining thickness	
Standard	5 mm (0.20 inch)
Minimum	2 mm (0.08 inch)

*Refer to marks on the disc or drum (they supersede information printed here)

Wheels and tires

Wheel runout	
Radial (up-and-down)	2.0 mm (0.08 inch)
Axial (side-to-side)	2.0 mm (0.08 inch)
Tire pressures	See Chapter 1
Tire sizes	
Front	
VT600	100/90-19 57S
VT750	120/90-17 64S
Rear	170/80-15 M/C 77S

Torque specifications

Brake disc mounting bolts	
VT600	
1988 through 1998	39 Nm (29 ft-lbs)
1999 on	42 Nm (31 ft-lbs)
VT750	42 Nm (31 ft-lbs)

Torque specifications (continued)

Brake caliper bracket mounting bolts	
1988, 1989, 1991 through 1993 VT600...	27 Nm (20 ft-lbs)
1994 on VT600, VT750...	30 Nm (22 ft-lbs)
Brake hose banjo bolt...	34 Nm (25 ft-lbs)
Brake lever pivot bolt nut..	6 Nm (53 in-lbs)
Brake pad pin	18 Nm (159 in-lbs)
Drive sprocket bolts...	10 Nm (7 ft-lbs)
600 driven sprocket nuts..	65 Nm (47 ft-lbs)
700 driven sprocket nuts..	88 Nm (65 ft-lbs)
Front axle	
VT600	74 Nm (55 ft-lbs)
VT750	59 Nm (44 ft-lbs)
Front axle pinch bolts	22 Nm (16 ft-lbs)
Master cylinder mounting bolts	12 Nm (108 in-lbs)
Rear axle nut	
VT600	
1988 and 1989, 1991 through 1996..	90 Nm (66 ft-lbs)
1997 on...	88 Nm (65 ft-lbs)
VT750	93 Nm (69 ft-lbs)
Rear brake stopper arm bolts/nuts	
VT600	22 Nm (16 ft-lbs)
VT750	20 Nm (15 ft-lbs)

1   General information

The models covered in this Chapter are equipped with a hydraulic disc brake at the front and a mechanical drum brake at the rear. All models are equipped with wire spoke wheels and tube-type tires. And all models are chain-driven. **Caution:** *Disc brake components rarely require disassembly. Do not disassemble components unless absolutely necessary. If any hydraulic brake line connection in the system is loosened, the entire system should be disassembled, drained, cleaned and then properly filled and bled upon reassembly. Do not use solvents on internal brake components. Solvents will cause seals to swell and distort. Use only clean brake fluid, brake cleaner or alcohol for cleaning. Use care when working with brake fluid as it can injure your eyes and it will damage painted surfaces and plastic parts.*

2   Brake pads - replacement

Warning: *The dust created by the brake system may contain asbestos, which is harmful to your health. Never blow it out with compressed air and don't inhale any of it. An approved filtering mask should be worn when working on the brakes.*

Refer to illustrations 2.3, 2.4, 2.5, 2.7, 2.9 and 2.12

1   Turn the handlebar so that the brake master cylinder is level, then remove the master cylinder reservoir cover, set plate and diaphragm (see Section 5).

2   Depress the caliper pistons by pushing the caliper in (toward the disc) with your thumbs. Watch the level of the brake fluid in the master cylinder reservoir; it will rise as you depress the caliper pistons. If it gets too close to the top, siphon off a little fluid from the reservoir. If you can't depress the pistons with thumb pressure, try using a C-clamp. If the pistons stick, remove the caliper and overhaul it (see Section 3).

3   Remove the pad pin plug **(see illustration)**.

4   Remove the pad pin **(see illustration)**.

5   Remove the brake pads **(see illustration)**.

6   If the pads have removable shims, remove the shims from the old pads.

7   Note whether the friction material on the pads has been worn down to the bottom of the wear grooves, *i.e.* if the wear grooves have disappeared, or are about to disappear **(see illustration)**. If so, replace the pads, as a pair. If the pads are fouled with oil or are damaged, replace them.

8   Inspect the condition of the brake disc (see Section 4). If it needs to be machined or replaced, follow the procedure in that Section to remove it. If the disc is okay, deglaze it with sandpaper or emery cloth, using a swirling motion.

2.3 Unscrew and remove the pad pin plug

2.4 Unscrew the pad pin

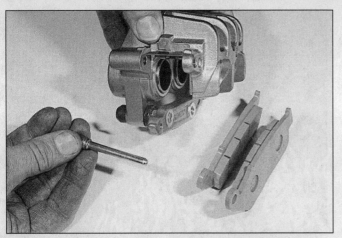

2.5 **Pull out the pad pin plug and remove the brake pads; the holes for the pad pin at the lower end of the caliper**

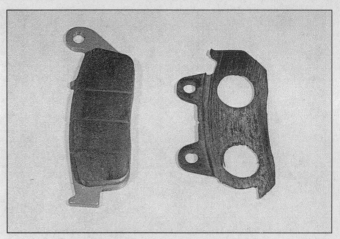

2.7 **There are grooves in new pads (left); if they're worn away (right), replace the pads immediately**

9   Inspect the condition of the pad retainer and the pad spring (**see illustration**). If either of them is distorted or damaged, replace it. If you remove the retainer or the spring, make sure that the new part fits into the caliper exactly as shown. If either of these parts is incorrectly installed, the pads will not fit into the caliper correctly.

10   Install the shims on the new brake pads.

11   Install the pads in the caliper so that their upper ends rest against the pad retainer.

12   Push the pads against the pad spring, align the holes in the lower ends of the pads with the hole in the caliper, insert the pad pin (**see illustration**) and tighten it to the torque listed in this Chapter's Specifications.

13   Install the pad pin plug and tighten it securely.

14   Refill the master cylinder reservoir (see Chapter 1) and install the diaphragm and cover.

15   Operate the brake lever several times to bring the pads into contact with the disc. Check the operation of the brakes carefully before riding the motorcycle.

3   Brake caliper - removal, overhaul and installation

Warning: *The dust created by the brake system may contain asbestos, which is harmful to your health. Never blow it out with compressed air and don't inhale any of it. An approved filtering mask should be worn when working on the brakes. Do not, under any circumstances, use petroleum-based solvents to clean brake parts. Use brake cleaner or denatured alcohol only!*

2.9 **Replace the pad retainer (left arrow) and pad spring (right arrow) if they're damaged or worn**

Removal

Refer to illustrations 3.2a, 3.2b and 3.3

1   Remove the cover, set plate and diaphragm from the master cylinder and siphon out all of the old brake fluid.

2   Detach the brake hose from the fork slider (**see illustration**). Disconnect the brake hose from the caliper (**see illustration**). Remove the

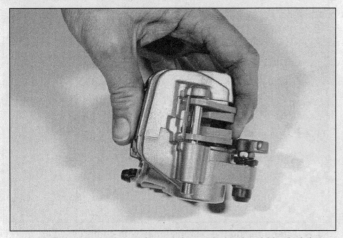

2.12 **This is how the pads and the pad pin should look right before the pad pin is screwed into the caliper**

3.2a **Brake hose clamp (upper arrow); the neck of the hose must be in this notch (lower arrow)**

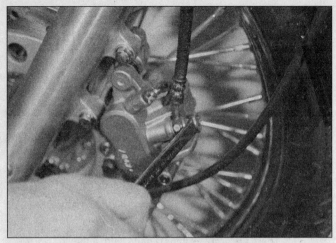

3.2b To disconnect the brake hose from the caliper, remove the banjo bolt; discard the old sealing washers

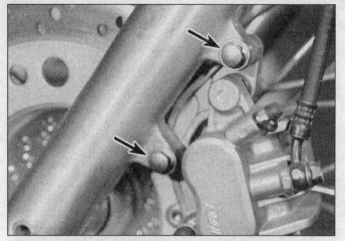

3.3 To detach the brake caliper from the fork slider, remove these two bolts (arrows)

brake hose banjo bolt and discard the sealing washers. Place the end of the hose in a container and operate the brake lever to pump out the rest of the brake fluid. After all the fluid has been expelled, wrap a clean shop rag tightly around the hose fitting to soak up any drips and prevent contamination.

3   Remove the caliper bracket mounting bolts **(see illustration)** and separate the caliper from the fork slider.

Overhaul

Refer to illustrations 3.6, 3.11, 3.12 and 3.13

4   Clean the exterior of the caliper with denatured alcohol or brake system cleaner.

5   Remove the brake pad pin and the brake pads (see Section 2).

6   Separate the caliper bracket from the caliper **(see illustration)**.

7   Remove the caliper pin dust boot and the pad retainer from the caliper bracket. Inspect the dust boot for cracks, tears and deterioration; replace it if it's damaged or worn. Make sure the retainer is neither bent nor damaged; if it is, replace it.

8   Remove the caliper bracket pin dust boot and the pad spring from the caliper. Inspect the boot for cracks, tears and deterioration; replace it if it's damaged or worn. Make sure the pad spring is neither bent nor damaged; if it is, replace it.

9   Place a few rags between the piston and the caliper frame to act as a cushion, lay the caliper on the work bench so that the pistons are facing down, toward the work bench surface, then use compressed

air, directed into the fluid inlet, to remove the pistons. Use only small quick blasts of air to ease the pistons out of the bore. If a piston is blown out with too much force, it might be damaged. **Warning:** *Never place your fingers in front of the pistons in an attempt to catch or protect them when applying compressed air. Doing so could result in serious injury.*

10   If compressed air isn't available, reconnect the caliper to the brake hose and pump the brake lever until the piston is free. (You'll have to put brake fluid in the master cylinder reservoir and get most of the air out of the hose to use this method.)

11   Once the pistons are protruding from the caliper, remove them **(see illustration)**.

12   Using a wood or plastic tool, remove the dust seals and the piston seals **(see illustration)**.

13   Clean the pistons and the piston bores with denatured alcohol, fresh brake fluid or brake system cleaner and dry them off with filtered, unlubricated compressed air. Inspect the surfaces of the pistons **(see illustration)** and the piston bores for nicks and burrs and loss of plating. If you find defects on the surface of either piston or piston bore, replace the caliper assembly (the pistons are matched to the caliper). If the caliper is in bad shape, inspect the master cylinder too.

14   Lubricate the new piston seals and dust seals with clean brake fluid and install them in their grooves in the caliper bore. Make sure they're not twisted and are fully and correctly seated.

15   Lubricate the pistons with clean brake fluid and install them into their bores in the caliper. Using your thumbs, push each piston all the

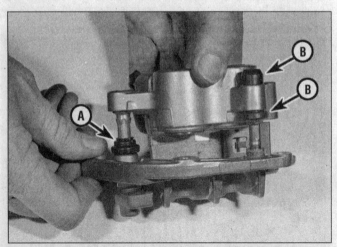

3.6 Pull the caliper and bracket apart; inspect the caliper pin dust boot (A) and the bracket pin boot (B)

3.11 After popping the pistons loose with compressed air, insert a pair of pliers inside each piston and pull them out of their bores

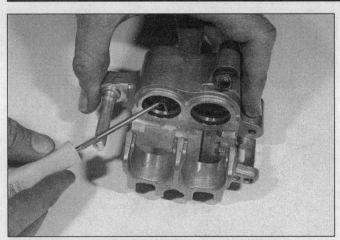

3.12 Remove the dust (outer) seals and the piston (inner) seals from both bores; be careful not to scratch the surface of the bores

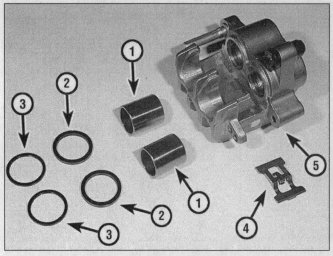

3.13 Front brake caliper assembly

1	Pistons	3	Piston seal	5	Caliper
2	Dust seal	4	Pad springs		

way in; make sure it doesn't become cocked in the bore.

16   The caliper body should be able to slide in relation to its mounting bracket. If it was seized or operated stiffly prior to disassembly, inspect the slider pins on the caliper and the bracket for excessive wear. Minor blemishes can be cleaned up with crocus or emery cloth. If either pin shows signs of serious damage, replace it. The pins can be unscrewed from the bracket and caliper. If you remove either pin, be sure to tighten the new pin to the torque listed in this Chapter's Specifications. Coat the pins with high-temperature disc brake grease.

17   Reassemble the caliper and the caliper bracket. Make sure that the two parts slide smoothly in and out on the pins.

18   If the pad retainer or pad spring was removed, install it now **(see illustration 2.9)**.

19   Install the brake pads (see Section 2).

Installation

20   Install the caliper on the fork slider, install the caliper bracket mounting bolts and tighten them to the torque listed in this Chapter's Specifications.

21   Connect the brake hose to the caliper, using new sealing washers on each side of the banjo bolt.

22   Fill the master cylinder with the recommended brake fluid (see Chapter 1) and bleed the system (see Section 7). Check for leaks.

23   Check the operation of the brakes carefully before riding the motorcycle.

4   Brake disc - inspection, removal and installation

Inspection

Refer to illustrations 4.3, 4.4a and 4.4b

1   Support the bike securely so it can't be knocked over during this procedure.

2   Visually inspect the surface of the disc for score marks and other damage. Light scratches are normal after use and won't affect brake operation, but deep grooves and heavy score marks will reduce braking efficiency and accelerate pad wear. If the disc is badly grooved it must be machined or replaced.

3   To check disc runout, mount a dial indicator to the fork leg with the plunger on the indicator touching the surface of the disc about 1/2-inch from the outer edge **(see illustration)**. Slowly turn the wheel and watch the indicator needle, comparing your reading with the limit listed in this Chapter's Specifications or stamped on the disc itself. If the runout is greater than allowed, replace the disc.

4   The disc must not be machined or allowed to wear down to a thickness less than the minimum allowable thickness, listed in this Chapter's Specifications. The thickness of the disc can be checked with a micrometer **(see illustration)**. If the thickness of the disc is less

4.3 Set up a dial indicator with the probe touching the surface of the disc, turn the wheel slowly and measure runout

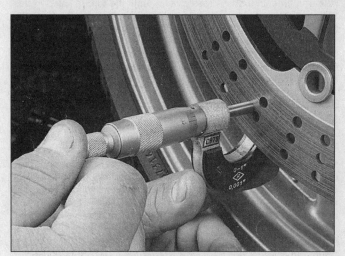

4.4a Use a micrometer to measure the thickness of the disc at several points

4.4b The minimum thickness is also stamped into the disc (if it differs from the value listed in this Chapter's Specifications, the information here supersedes the specs)

4.6 To detach the disc from the wheel, remove these five Allen bolts in a criss-cross fashion

than the minimum allowable, it must be replaced. The minimum thickness is also stamped into the disc **(see illustration)**.

Removal

Refer to illustration 4.6

5   Remove the wheel (see Section 11).

6   Mark the relationship of the disc to the wheel, so it can be installed in the same position. Remove the bolts that retain the disc to the wheel hub **(see illustration)**. Loosen the bolts a little at a time, in a criss-cross pattern, to avoid distorting the disc. Once all the bolts are loose, take the disc off.

7   Take note of any paper shims that may be present where the disc mates to the hub. If there are any, mark their position and be sure to include them when installing the disc.

Installation

8   Position the disc on the wheel, aligning the previously applied match marks (if you're reinstalling the original disc). Make sure the arrow (stamped on the disc) marking the direction of rotation is pointing in the correct direction (the direction that the wheel rotates when the bike is moving forward).

9   Apply a non-hardening thread locking compound to the threads of the bolts. Install the bolts with new lockwashers, tightening them a little at a time, in a criss-cross pattern, until the torque listed in this Chapter's Specifications is reached. Clean off all grease from the brake disc using acetone or brake system cleaner.

10   Install the wheel (see Section 11).

11   Operate the brake lever several times to bring the pads into contact with the disc. Check the operation of the brakes carefully before riding the motorcycle.

5   Front brake master cylinder - removal, overhaul and installation

1   If the master cylinder is leaking fluid, or if the lever does not produce a firm feel when the brake is applied, and bleeding the brakes does not help, master cylinder overhaul is recommended. Before disassembling the master cylinder, read through the entire procedure and make sure that you have the correct rebuild kit. Also, you will need some new, clean brake fluid of the recommended type, some clean rags and internal snap-ring pliers. **Note:** *To prevent damage to the paint from spilled brake fluid, always cover the top cover or upper fuel tank when working on the master cylinder.*

2   **Caution:** *Disassembly, overhaul and reassembly of the brake*

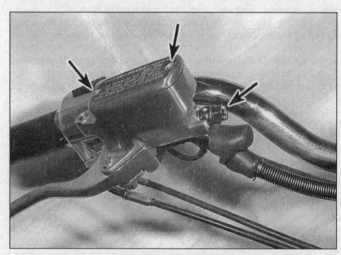

5.4 Reservoir cover screws (left arrows) and brake hose banjo bolt (right arrow)

master cylinder must be done in a spotlessly clean work area to avoid contamination and possible failure of the brake hydraulic system components.

Removal

Refer to illustrations 5.4 and 5.7

3   Remove the rear view mirror.

4   Remove the reservoir cover retaining screws **(see illustration)**. Remove the reservoir, the set plate and the rubber diaphragm. Siphon as much brake fluid from the reservoir as you can to avoid spilling it on the bike.

5   Unplug the electrical connectors from the brake light switch (see Chapter 9).

6   Pull back the rubber dust boot, loosen the brake hose banjo bolt **(see illustration 5.4)** and separate the brake hose from the master cylinder. Wrap the end of the hose in a clean rag and suspend the hose in an upright position or bend it down carefully and place the open end in a clean container. The objective is to prevent excessive loss of brake fluid, fluid spills and system contamination.

7   Remove the master cylinder mounting bolts **(see illustration)** and separate the master cylinder from the handlebar. **Caution:** *Do not tip the master cylinder upside down or any brake fluid still in the reservoir will run out.*

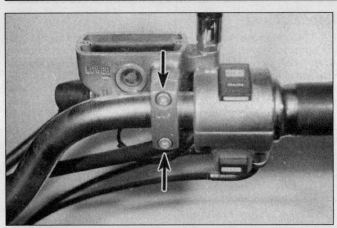

5.7 Detach the master cylinder mounting bolts (arrows); the UP mark must be upright when the master cylinder is installed

5.9a Remove the rubber dust boot (arrow) . . .

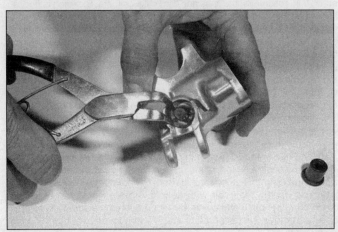

5.9b . . . and remove the snap-ring from the bore

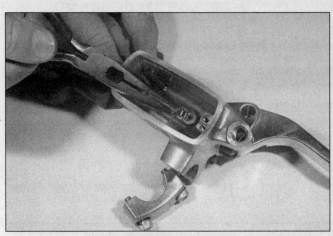

5.9c Pry the baffle plate from the bottom of the reservoir

Overhaul

Refer to illustrations 5.9a, 5.9b, 5.9c, 5.10 and 5.15

8   Remove the brake lever pivot bolt nut, remove the pivot bolt and remove the lever.

9   Carefully remove the rubber dust boot from the end of the piston **(see illustration)**. Using snap-ring pliers, remove the snap-ring **(see illustration)** and slide out the piston assembly and the spring. Remove the baffle from the bottom of the reservoir **(see illustration)**.

10   Lay the parts out in the order in which they're removed to prevent confusion during reassembly **(see illustration)**.

11   Clean all of the parts with brake system cleaner (available at motorcycle dealerships and auto parts stores), isopropyl alcohol or clean brake fluid. **Caution:** *Do not, under any circumstances, use a petroleum-based solvent to clean brake parts. If compressed air is available, use it to dry the parts thoroughly (make sure it's filtered and unlubricated). Check the master cylinder bore for corrosion, scratches, nicks and score marks. If damage is evident, the master cylinder must be replaced with a new one. If the master cylinder is in poor condition, then the calipers should be checked as well.*

12   The dust seal, piston assembly and spring are included in the rebuild kit. Use all of the new parts, regardless of the apparent condition of the old ones.

13   Before reassembling the master cylinder, soak the piston and the rubber cup seals in clean brake fluid for ten or fifteen minutes. Lubricate the master cylinder bore with clean brake fluid, then carefully insert the piston and related parts in the reverse order of disassembly. Make sure the lips on the cup seals do not turn inside out when they are slipped into the bore.

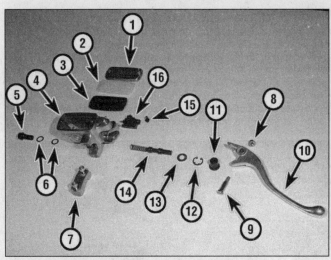

5.10 Master cylinder assembly

1	Reservoir cover	9	Brake lever pivot bolt
2	Set plate	10	Brake lever
3	Rubber diaphragm	11	Rubber dust boot
4	Master cylinder body	12	Snap-ring
5	Brake hose banjo bolt	13	Washer
6	Sealing washers	14	Piston/spring assembly
7	Master cylinder mounting bracket	15	Brake light switch mounting screw
8	Brake lever pivot bolt nut	16	Brake light switch

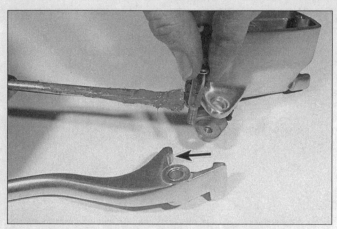

5.15 Lubricate the brake lever pivot bolt and the part of the lever (arrow) that pushes against the piston assembly

14 Depress the piston, then install the snap-ring (make sure the snap-ring is properly seated in the groove). Install the rubber dust boot (make sure the lip is seated properly in the piston groove).
15 Lubricate the brake lever pivot bolt and the friction surface on the lever that pushes against the piston assembly **(see illustration)**.

Installation

16 Attach the master cylinder to the handlebar and tighten the bolts to the torque listed in this Chapter's Specifications.
17 Connect the brake hose to the master cylinder, using new sealing washers. Tighten the banjo bolt to the torque listed in this Chapter's Specifications.
18 Fill the master cylinder with the recommended brake fluid (see Chapter 1), then bleed the air from the system (see Section 7).

6   Brake hose - inspection and replacement

Inspection

1 Once a week or, if the motorcycle is used less frequently, before every ride, check the condition of the brake hose.
2 Twist and flex the rubber hoses while looking for cracks, bulges and seeping fluid. Check extra carefully around the areas where the hoses connect with the banjo bolts, as these are common areas for hose failure.
3 Inspect the metal banjo fittings connected to the brake hoses. If the fittings are rusted, scratched or cracked, replace them.

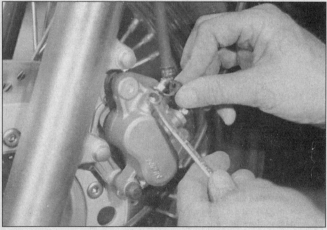

7.5a Remove the rubber dust boot from the bleed valve, place a box wrench over the bleed valve . . .

Replacement

4 The brake hose has a banjo fitting on each end of the hose. Cover the surrounding area with plenty of rags and unscrew the union bolt on either end of the hose. Detach the hose from any clips that may be present and remove the hose.
5 Position the new hose, making sure it isn't twisted or otherwise strained, between the two components. Install the union bolts, using new sealing washers on both sides of the fittings, and tighten them to the torque listed in this Chapter's Specifications.
6 Flush the old brake fluid from the system, refill the system with the recommended fluid (see Chapter 1) and bleed the air from the system (see Section 7). Check the operation of the front brake carefully before riding the motorcycle.

7   Brake system bleeding

Refer to illustrations 7.5a and 7.5b

1 Bleeding the brake system removes all the air bubbles from the brake fluid reservoirs, the lines and the brake calipers. Bleeding is necessary whenever a brake system hydraulic connection is loosened, when a component or hose is replaced, or when the master cylinder or caliper is overhauled. Leaks in the system may also allow air to enter, but leaking brake fluid will reveal their presence and warn you of the need for repair.
2 To bleed the brakes, you will need some new, clean brake fluid of the recommended type (see Chapter 1), a length of clear vinyl or plastic tubing, a small container partially filled with clean brake fluid, some rags and a wrench to fit the brake caliper bleeder valves.
3 Cover the fuel tank and any other painted surfaces near the reservoir to prevent damage in the event that brake fluid is spilled.
4 Remove the reservoir cover screws and remove the cover, set plate and diaphragm. Slowly pump the brake lever a few times, until no air bubbles can be seen floating up from the holes at the bottom of the reservoir. Doing this bleeds the air from the master cylinder end of the line. Top up the reservoir with new fluid, then install the reservoir diaphragm, set plate and cover, but don't tighten the screws; you may have to remove the cover, plate and diaphragm several times during the procedure.
5 Remove the rubber dust cover from the bleeder valve **(see illustration)** and slip a box wrench over the caliper bleed valve. Attach one end of the clear vinyl or plastic tubing to the bleed valve **(see illustration)** and submerge the other end in the brake fluid in the container.
6 Carefully pump the brake lever three or four times and hold it while opening the caliper bleeder valve. When the valve is opened, brake fluid will flow out of the caliper into the clear tubing and the lever will move toward the handlebar. Retighten the bleed valve, then release the brake lever gradually.
7 Repeat this procedure until no air bubbles are visible in the brake

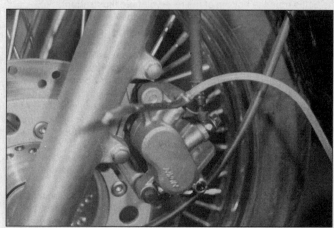

7.5b . . . then connect a length of clear plastic tubing to the valve and submerge the other end of the tubing in a jar of clean brake fluid

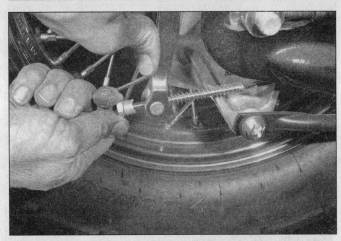

8.2 Push the brake arm forward, unscrew the adjuster nut from the brake rod and disengage the rod from the clevis pin

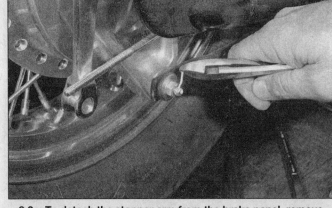

8.3a To detach the stopper arm from the brake panel, remove the cotter pin . . .

fluid leaving the caliper and the lever is firm when applied. **Note:** *Remember to add fluid to the reservoir as the level drops. Use only new, clean brake fluid of the recommended type. Never re-use the fluid lost during bleeding.*

8   Keep an eye on the fluid level in the reservoir, especially if there's a lot of air in the system. Every time you crack the bleed valve open, the fluid level in the reservoir drops a little. Do not allow the fluid level to drop below the lower mark during the bleeding process. If the level looks low, remove the reservoir cover, set plate and diaphragm and add some fluid.

9   When you're done, inspect the fluid level in the reservoir one more time, add some fluid if necessary, then install the diaphragm, set plate and reservoir cover and tighten the screws securely. Wipe up any spilled brake fluid and check the entire system for leaks. **Note:** *If bleeding is difficult, it may be necessary to let the brake fluid in the system stabilize for a few hours (it may be aerated). Repeat the bleeding procedure when the tiny bubbles in the system have settled out.*

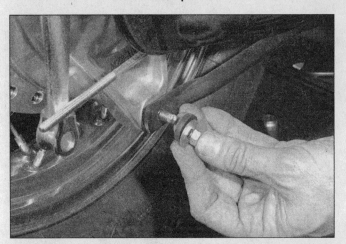

8.3b . . . remove the nut and the metal and rubber washers from the bolt, slide off the stopper arm and remove the bolt

8   Drum brake - removal, inspection and installation

Removal and disassembly

Refer to illustrations 8.2, 8.3a, 8.3b, 8.5, 8.6a, 8.6b, 8.7a, 8.7b and 8.7c

1   Before you start, inspect the rear brake wear indicator (see Chapter 1). If the shoes are excessively worn, replace them.

2   Disconnect the brake rod from the brake arm **(see illustration)**. Store the adjuster nut, the clevis pin and the brake rod spring in a plastic bag.

3   Disconnect the rear brake stopper arm **(see illustrations)**. Store the nut, bolt and metal and rubber washers in a plastic bag.

4   Remove the rear wheel (see Section 12).

5   Remove the brake panel from the wheel **(see illustration)**.

6   Remove the brake arm pinch bolt **(see illustration 12.3b)** and remove the brake arm from the splined spindle end of the brake cam. Note the punch mark on the end of the brake cam spindle **(see illus-**

8.5 Remove the brake panel from the wheel

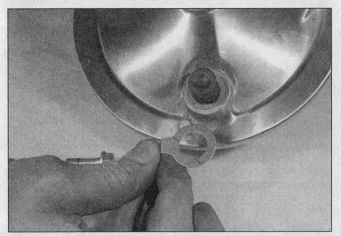

8.6a Remove the indicator plate from the brake cam spindle

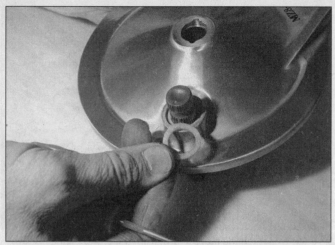

8.6b Remove the felt seal from the brake cam spindle

8.7a Remove the cotter pins from the anchor pins and remove the set plate (arrow)

8.7b Pull the upper ends of the shoes apart and pull the shoes off the anchor pins

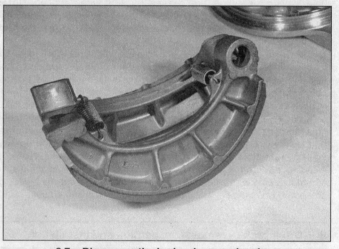

8.7c Disengage the brake shoes and springs

tration 12.3b); this mark indicates the location of the wider spline on the spindle. This wider spline must be aligned with the corresponding wider spline on the brake arm when the arm is installed. Remove the indicator plate and the felt seal **(see illustrations)**. Pull the brake cam out of the brake panel.

7   Remove the cotter pins from the anchor pins **(see illustration)** and remove the set plate (the oblong-shaped spacer that fits over the ends of both anchor pins). To remove the shoes from the brake panel, spread them apart slightly to clear the ridges on the brake cam, then slide them up and off the anchor pins **(see illustration)**. Disengage the shoes and springs **(see illustration)**.

Inspection

Refer to illustration 8.12

8   Inspect the linings for wear, damage and signs of contamination from road dirt and water. If the linings are visibly defective, replace them.

9   Measure the thickness of the lining material (just the lining material, not the metal backing) and compare your measurements to the minimum thickness listed in this Chapter's Specifications. If the lining material is worn to less than the minimum, replace the shoes.

10   Inspect the ends of the shoes, where they contact the brake cam and where they slip over the anchor pins. If there's visible wear, replace the shoes.

11   Check the fit of the brake cam in the brake panel hole. If it feels loose, replace the brake cam or the panel, depending on which part is

worn. Inspect the anchor pins for wear and damage. If the anchor pins are worn, replace the brake panel.

12   Inspect the brake drum (inside the wheel) for wear or damage. Measure the diameter at several points with a brake drum micrometer (or

8.12 The maximum diameter of the brake drum is cast into the drum; if it differs from that listed in this Chapter's Specifications, use the specification on the drum

8.14a When installing the brake shoes, make sure the upper ends of the shoes are correctly seated against the brake cam . . .

8.14b . . . and the lower ends are correctly seated against the shoulders at the lower ends of the anchor pins

8.14c Once the shoes are correctly positioned on the brake panel, install the set plate and secure the plate with a pair of new cotter pins in the anchor pins

8.17 To attach the brake rod to the brake arm clevis pin, push the brake arm forward and install the adjuster nut

have this done by a Honda dealer). If the measurements are uneven (the brake drum is "out-of-round") or if there are scratches deep enough to snag a fingernail, have the drum turned by a dealer service department or a motorcycle machine shop to correct the surface. If the drum has to be turned beyond the wear limit to remove the defects, replace it. You'll find the maximum diameter of the drum cast into the wheel **(see illustration)**. If the specified maximum diameter on the wheel is different from the maximum diameter listed in this Chapter's Specifications, the spec on the wheel supersedes the value in the Specifications.

Installation

Refer to illustrations 8.14a, 8.14b, 8.14c and 8.17

13   Apply high-temperature brake grease to the ends of the springs, the brake cam and the anchor pins. Install the brake cam, the felt seal and the indicator plate. Install the brake arm. Make sure the punch marks on the brake arm and the brake cam spindle are aligned. Install the brake arm pinch bolt and tighten it securely.

14   Hook the springs to the shoes. Position the shoes over the brake panel, slide the lower ends of the shoes onto the ends of the anchor pins, spread the upper ends of the shoes apart far enough to clear the ridges on the brake cam, push the shoes down onto the anchor pins and release the upper ends of the shoes. Make sure the upper ends of

the shoes fit correctly against the brake cam and the lower ends are fully seated on the anchor pins **(see illustrations)**. Install the set plate and install new cotter pins on the anchor pins **(see illustration)**.

15   Install the brake panel and brake shoe assembly in the wheel.

16   Install the wheel (see Section 12).

17   To reattach the brake rod to the brake arm clevis pin, install the spring on the rod, insert the rod in the hole in the clevis, push the brake arm forward and install the adjuster nut **(see illustration)**.

18   Align the wheels (see Section 15).

19   Adjust the rear brake pedal freeplay (see Chapter 1).

20   Adjust the rear brake light switch (see Chapter 1).

9   Rear brake pedal and linkage - removal and installation

1   If you're planning to service either the middle brake rod or the brake pedal assembly, remove the exhaust system (see Chapter 4).

Middle brake rod

Refer to illustration 9.2

2   Remove the cotter pins, nuts and bolts from both ends of the

9.2   The middle brake rod connects the brake shaft arm (left arrow) and brake pedal arm (right arrow)

9.4 Disconnect the middle brake rod from the brake pedal arm (lower arrow) and remove the footpeg bracket bolts (arrows) (VT600 shown; VT750 similar)

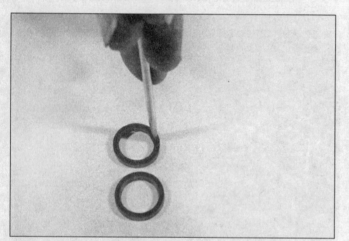

9.8 The open side of each seal faces inward

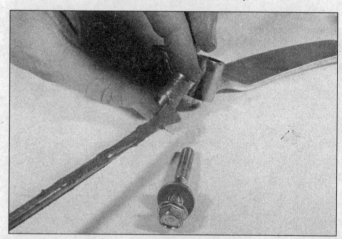

9.9 Grease the collar and the inside of the pivot bore in the pedal before reassembling them

middle brake rod and disconnect the rod from the rear brake pedal and from the brake shaft arm (VT600 models) **(see illustration)** or the middle rod joint (VT750 models). On VT750 models, note the return spring for the rod (at the middle rod joint) and the return spring for the rear brake light switch (at the pedal). Disengage both springs from the rod.

3   Installation is the reverse of removal. Tighten the nuts securely and install new cotter pins. Check and, if necessary, adjust the brake pedal height and the rear brake light switch (see Chapter 1).

Brake pedal

Refer to illustrations 9.4, 9.8, 9.9 and 9.10

4   Disconnect the middle brake rod from the rear brake pedal **(see illustration)**.

5   Unbolt the right footpeg bracket from the frame **(see illustration 9.4)**.

6   On VT600 models, remove the brake pedal, the pivot collar (bushing) and the dust seals from the footpeg bracket. On VT750C/CD models, remove the pedal pivot bolt, pedal and washer. On VT750DC models, remove the snap-ring and bushing washer. Clean the parts thoroughly and dry them off for inspection. Clean out the pivot bore of the pedal (that fits over the collar or pivot bolt) with a cylindrical wire brush.

7   Inspect the collar or pivot bolt for scoring and other damage. If it's worn or damaged, replace it.

8   On VT600 models, inspect the dust seals **(see illustration)**. If they're torn, cracked or deteriorated, replace them.

9   Grease the collar **(see illustration)** or pivot bolt. Make sure the surface of the bore in the pedal that fits over the collar or pivot bolt is

9.10 The assembled footpeg bracket and rear brake pedal should look like this (VT600 shown)

clean and free of debris and old grease.

10   On VT600 models, reassemble the collar, dust seals and brake pedal **(see illustration)**. On VT750 models, install the washer, pedal and pivot bolt; tighten the pivot bolt securely.

9.14 Disconnect the middle brake rod from the brake shaft arm (arrow)

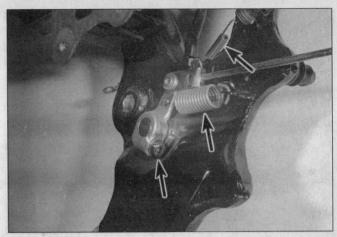

9.18 Middle brake arm pinch bolt (lower arrow), middle brake arm return spring (middle arrow) and brake light switch return spring (upper arrow)

11   Installation is the reverse of removal. Tighten the footpeg bracket bolts securely.
12   Reconnect the middle brake rod to the brake pedal and install a new cotter pin.
13   Check and, if necessary, adjust the rear brake pedal height and the rear brake light switch (see Chapter 1).

Brake rod

VT600

Refer to illustrations 9.14 and 9.18

14   Disconnect the middle brake rod from the brake shaft arm **(see illustration)**.
15   Disconnect the brake rod from the brake arm (see Section 8).
16   Remove the rear wheel (see Section 12).
17   Remove the swingarm (see Chapter 6).
18   Remove the pinch bolt from the middle brake arm **(see illustration)** and slide the middle brake arm off the brake shaft arm spindle. Note the punch marks on the brake shaft arm spindle and on the middle brake arm. These marks must be aligned when the middle brake arm is reinstalled on the brake shaft arm spindle.
19   Disengage the middle brake arm return spring and the brake light switch return spring and remove the middle brake arm.
20   Pull the brake shaft arm out of the frame.

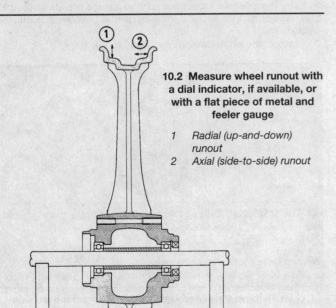

10.2 Measure wheel runout with a dial indicator, if available, or with a flat piece of metal and feeler gauge

1   *Radial (up-and-down) runout*
2   *Axial (side-to-side) runout*

VT750 models

21   Disconnect the brake rod from the brake arm (see Section 8).
22   Remove the cotter pin, pull out the clevis pin and disconnect the brake rod from the middle rod joint.

All models

23   Clean and inspect the parts for wear and damage. Replace worn or damaged parts. Be sure to clean out the bore in the frame for the brake shaft arm spindle.
24   Installation is the reverse of removal. Grease the brake shaft arm spindle before inserting it through the frame. Make sure that the punch marks on the brake shaft arm spindle and on the middle brake arm are aligned. Don't forget to install the middle brake arm return spring and the brake light switch arm.
25   Check and, if necessary, adjust the rear brake pedal height and freeplay and the rear brake light switch (see Chapter 1).

10   Wheels - inspection and repair

Refer to illustrations 10.2 and 10.5

1   Clean the wheels thoroughly to remove mud and dirt that may interfere with the inspection procedure or mask defects. Make a general check of the wheels and tires as described in Chapter 1.
2   Support the bike securely so it can't be knocked over during this procedure. Place a jack beneath the engine to raise the front wheel off the ground, or beneath the frame to raise the rear wheel off the ground. Attach a dial indicator to the fork slider or the swingarm and position the stem against the side of the rim. Spin the wheel slowly and check the side-to-side (axial) runout of the rim, then compare your readings with the value listed in this Chapter's Specifications **(see illustration)**. In order to accurately check radial runout with the dial indicator, the wheel would have to be removed from the machine and the tire removed from the wheel. With the axle clamped in a vise, the wheel can be rotated to check the runout.
3   An easier, though slightly less accurate, method is to attach a stiff wire pointer to the fork or the swingarm and position the end a fraction of an inch from the wheel (where the wheel and tire join). If the wheel is true, the distance from the pointer to the rim will be constant as the wheel is rotated. Repeat the procedure to check the runout of the rear wheel. **Note:** *If wheel runout is excessive, refer to the appropriate Section in this Chapter and check the wheel bearings very carefully before replacing the wheel or paying to have it trued.*
4   The wheels should also be visually inspected for cracks, flat spots on the rim, bent spokes and other damage.
5   Tap the spokes with a metal screwdriver blade or similar tool and

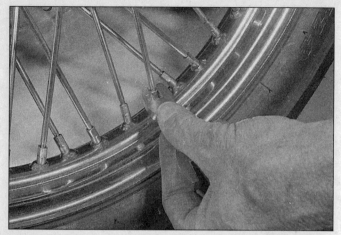

10.5 If a spoke is loose, tighten the spoke nipple with a spoke wrench (available at any motorcycle dealership or accessory store)

11.3a Pry out the pinch bolt plugs . . .

11.3b . . . loosen the axle pinch bolts . . .

11.3c . . . and unscrew the axle

listen to the sound. If the spoke makes a "clunk" or low-pitched sound, it's loose. Tighten the spoke **(see illustration)**.

6   If damage is evident, or if runout in either direction is excessive, the wheel will have to be trued or, if damage is severe, replaced with a new one.

11   Front wheel - removal and installation

Removal

Refer to illustrations 11.3a, 11.3b, 11.3c, 11.5a and 11.5b

1   Support the bike securely so it can't be knocked over during this procedure. Raise the front wheel off the ground by placing a floor jack, with a wood block on the jack head, under the engine.

2   Disconnect the speedometer cable from the speedometer gearbox (see Chapter 9).

3   Loosen the axle pinch bolts and unscrew the axle **(see illustrations)**.

4   Support the wheel, then pull out the axle and carefully lower the wheel from the forks.

5   Remove the speedometer gearbox unit from the left side of the wheel and remove the collar from the right side **(see illustrations)**. Set the wheel aside. **Caution:** *When you lay down the wheel and allow it to rest on the brake disc - the disc could become warped. Set the wheel on wood blocks so the disc doesn't support the weight of the wheel.* **Note:** *Don't operate the front brake lever with the wheel removed.*

Inspection

6   Roll the axle on a flat surface such as a piece of plate glass. If it's bent, replace it. If the axle is corroded, remove the corrosion with fine emery cloth.

7   Inspect the wheel bearings (see Section 13).

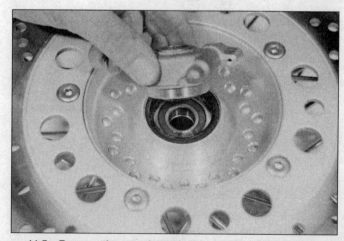

11.5a Remove the speedometer drive unit from the left side of the wheel . . .

11.5b ... and remove the collar from the right side

11.8 When installing the speedometer drive unit, make sure the tangs align with the slots

12.3a Hold the rear axle bolt ...

12.3b ... and remove the axle nut (right arrow); the punch mark on the end of the brake cam spindle (left arrow) is used for brake arm and spindle alignment

Installation

Refer to illustration 11.8

8   Installation is the reverse of removal. Apply a thin coat of grease to the seal lip, then slide the axle into the hub. Slide the wheel into place. Make sure the lugs in the speedometer drive clutch line up with the notches in the speedometer drive unit **(see illustration)**. Make sure the protrusion on the inner side of the left fork fits into the notch in the speedometer drive unit.

9   Slip the axle into place, then tighten the axle to the torque listed in this Chapter's Specifications. Tighten the axle pinch bolts to the torque listed in this Chapter's Specifications.

10   Apply the front brake, pump the forks up and down several times and check for binding and proper brake operation.

12 Rear wheel - removal and installation

Removal

Refer to illustrations 12.3a, 12.3b and 12.4a through 12.4e

1   Support the bike securely so it can't be knocked over during this procedure.

2   Detach the brake rod from the brake arm and the stopper arm from the brake panel (see Section 8).

3   Remove the axle nut **(see illustrations)** and unscrew the drive chain adjusters from the adjuster collars (see "Drive chain and sprock-

12.4a Remove the left side collar ...

ets - check, adjustment and lubrication" in Chapter 1).

4   Support the wheel, pull out the axle and remove the adjuster collars and the spacers **(see illustrations)**. Pull the wheel to the right and

12.4b . . . remove the left spacer . . .

12.4c . . . remove the right side collar . . .

12.4d . . . remove the right spacer . . .

12.4e . . . disengage the driven sprocket from the drive chain
and remove the wheel

13.3a Pry out the left side seal from the front wheel hub with a
seal removal tool

disengage the drive chain from the sprocket **(see illustration)**.

5   Before installing the wheel, check the axle for straightness by rolling it on a flat surface such as a piece of plate glass (if the axle is corroded, first remove the corrosion with fine emery cloth). If the axle is bent, replace it.

6   Inspect the sprocket (see Section 17) and inspect the driven

flange and the rubber dampers (see Section 18).

7   Inspect the seals and the wheel bearings (see Section 13).

Installation

8   Installation is the reverse of removal. Apply a light coat of multi-purpose lithium-based grease to the lips of the oil seals. Tighten the axle nut to the torque listed in the Chapter 1 Specifications.

9   Adjust the drive chain (see "Drive chain and sprockets - check, adjustment and lubrication" in Chapter 1).

10   Adjust the rear brake pedal (see Chapter 1).

11   Carefully check the operation of the brake before riding the motorcycle.

13   Wheel bearings - inspection and maintenance

1   Support the bike securely so it can't be knocked over during this procedure and remove the wheel. Remove the front wheel (see Section 11) or remove the rear wheel (see Section 12).

2   Set the wheel on blocks so as not to allow the weight of the wheel to rest on the brake disc or hub.

Front wheel bearings

Refer to illustrations 13.3a, 13.3b, 13.5a, 13.5b, 13.5c and 13.10

3   From the left side of the wheel, remove the speedometer gearbox unit **(see illustration 11.5a)**, then pry out the grease seal **(see illustration)** and remove the speedometer clutch **(see illustration)**.

13.3b Remove the speedometer clutch

13.5a Bearing remover head (right) and wedged shaft (left)

13.5b Tap the head into place (the slotted end goes into the bearing)

13.5c From the other side of the wheel, tap the wedge end of the shaft into the head's slot and drive out the bearing

13.10 Install the new bearings with a seal driver or socket

13.17a Install the 17 mm bearing remover head . . .

4   From the right side of the wheel, remove the collar **(see illustration 11.5b)**.

5   The usual method of removing wheel bearings is to insert a brass punch through one side of the hub, place it against the inner race of the opposite bearing, then tap on the punch to drive the bearing out. There may not be enough clearance for this method; if not, you'll need Honda special tools or equivalents **(see illustration)**. The remover head goes inside the bearing to be removed. The wedge part of the remover rod is then tapped into the slot of the remover head from the opposite side of the hub. This expands the remover head and locks it to the bearing. Tapping some more on the rod will drive the remover head and bearing out of the hub **(see illustrations)**.

6   Turn the wheel over and pry out the right side grease seal.

7   Remove the right side bearing the same way you removed the left one.

8   Clean the bearings with a high flash-point solvent (one which won't leave any residue) and blow them dry with compressed air (don't let the bearings spin as you dry them). Apply a few drops of oil to the bearing. Hold the outer race of the bearing and rotate the inner race - if the bearing doesn't turn smoothly, has rough spots or is noisy, replace it with a new one.

9   If the bearing checks out okay and will be re-used, wash it in solvent once again and dry it, then pack the bearing with high-quality bearing grease.

10   Thoroughly clean the hub area of the wheel. Install the left side bearing into the recess in the hub, with the marked or sealed side fac-

ing out. Using a bearing driver or a socket large enough to contact the outer race of the bearing, drive in the bearing until it's completely seated **(see illustration)**.

11   Install the speedometer gearbox retainer on top of the new bearing. Make sure the tangs on the retainer are aligned with the slots in the hub. Install a new left side grease seal with its closed side out. It should be possible to push the seal in with even finger pressure but, if necessary, use a seal driver, a large socket or a flat piece of wood to drive the seal into place.

12   Turn the wheel over and install the right side bearing as described in Step 10. Install a new right side seal as described in Step 11.

13   Install the speedometer gearbox unit, making sure the tangs on the speedometer gearbox are aligned with the slots in the retainer **(see illustration 11.8)**.

14   Clean off all grease from the brake disc using acetone or brake system cleaner.

15   Make sure the right side collar is in place **(see illustration 11.5b)** and install the wheel (see Section 11).

Rear wheel bearings

Refer to illustrations 13.17a, 13.17b and 13.17c

16   Remove the sprocket, driven flange and rubber dampers (see Section 18).

17   The rear wheel bearings are removed the same way as the front wheel bearings, in Steps 5 through 10 above **(see illustrations)**.

13.17b . . . from the other side of the wheel, install the bearing remover shaft and drive out the left side bearing

13.17c Install the new bearings with a seal driver or socket

18   While the rear wheel is removed, inspect the drive chain (see Section 16), the driven sprocket (see Section 17) and the driven flange (see Section 18). The driven flange has an outer dust seal, a bearing, an O-ring and a collar that should be inspected for wear and, if necessary, replaced.

14 Tires - general information

1   Tires with tubes are used as standard equipment on this motorcycle. They are generally easier to change than tubeless tires.
2   Before changing a tire yourself, check with your local dealership or repair shop to find out the labor charge for changing a tire. Although the procedure is not complicated, it is time-consuming, and for safety, it must be done correctly. For these reasons, it may be more practical to have the job done. Watching a professional technician do the job before attempting it yourself can provide valuable information.
3   The accompanying illustrations can be used to replace a tube-type tire in an emergency.

15 Wheels - alignment check

1   Misalignment of the wheels, which may be due to a cocked rear wheel or a bent frame or triple clamps, can cause strange and possibly serious handling problems. If the frame or triple clamps are at fault, repair by a frame specialist or replacement with new parts are the only alternatives.
2   To check the alignment you will need an assistant, a length of string or a perfectly straight piece of wood and a ruler graduated in 1/64 inch increments. A plumb bob or other suitable weight will also be required.
3   Support the motorcycle in a level position, then measure the width of both tires at their widest points. Subtract the smaller measurement from the larger measurement, then divide the difference by two. The result is the amount of offset that should exist between the front and rear tires on both sides.
4   If a string is used, have your assistant hold one end of it about half way between the floor and the rear axle, touching the rear sidewall of the tire.
5   Run the other end of the string forward and pull it tight so that it is roughly parallel to the floor. Slowly bring the string into contact with the front sidewall of the rear tire, then turn the front wheel until it is parallel with the string. Measure the distance from the front tire sidewall to the string.
6   Repeat the procedure on the other side of the motorcycle. The distance from the front tire sidewall to the string should be equal on both sides.

7   As was previously pointed out, a perfectly straight length of wood may be substituted for the string. The procedure is the same.
8   If the distance between the string and tire is greater on one side, or if the rear wheel appears to be cocked, make sure the swingarm pivot bolt and nut are tight ("Swingarm bearings - check" in Chapter 6).
9   If the front-to-back alignment is correct, the wheels still may be out of alignment vertically.
10   Using the plumb bob, or other suitable weight, and a length of string, check the rear wheel to make sure it is vertical. To do this, hold the string against the tire upper sidewall and allow the weight to settle just off the floor. When the string touches both the upper and lower tire sidewalls and is perfectly straight, the wheel is vertical.
11   Once the rear wheel is vertical, check the front wheel in the same manner. If both wheels are not perfectly vertical, the frame and/or major suspension components are bent.

16 Drive chain - removal, cleaning and installation

Removal

Refer to illustrations 16.2a, 16.2b, 16.2c and 16.2d

1   Loosen the rear axle nut and back off the axle adjuster bolts to loosen the drive chain (see "Drive chain and sprockets - check, adjustment and lubrication" in Chapter 1). Push the rear wheel forward as far as possible to create as much chain slack as possible.
2   Remove the Allen bolt from the left rear cover, remove the retaining clip (VT600 models only) and pull off the left rear cover **(see illustrations)**. After removing the cover on VT750 models, remove the col-

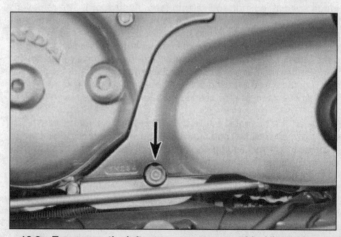

16.2a To remove the left rear cover, remove this Allen bolt . . .

TIRE CHANGING SEQUENCE - TUBED TIRES

 A Deflate tire. After pushing tire beads away from rim flanges push tire bead into well of rim at point opposite valve. Insert tire lever next to valve and work bead over edge of rim.

Use two levers to work bead over edge of rim. Note use of rim protectors **B**

 C Remove inner tube from tire

When first bead is clear, remove tire as shown **D**

 E To install, partially inflate inner tube and insert in tire

Work first bead over rim and feed valve through hole in rim. Partially screw on retaining nut to hold valve in place. **F**

 G Check that inner tube is positioned correctly and work second bead over rim using tire levers. Start at a point opposite valve.

Work final area of bead over rim while pushing valve inwards to ensure that inner tube is not trapped. **H**

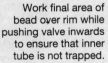

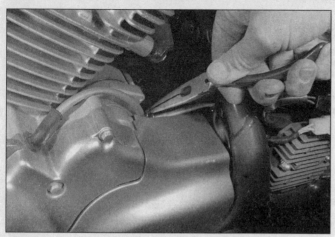

16.2b ... pull off this retaining clip (only on VT600 models) ...

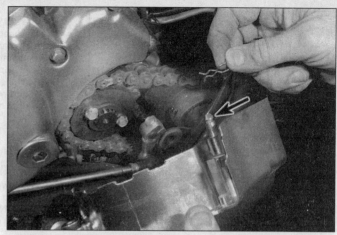

16.2c ... and remove the cover (VT600 model shown; on VT750 models, don't forget to retrieve the collar for the bolt); the post (arrow) ...

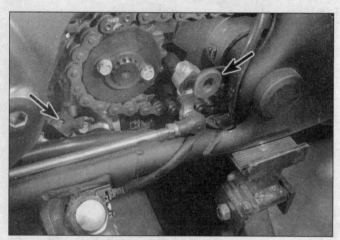

16.2d ... engages this grommet

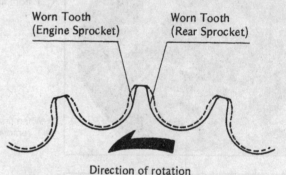

17.3 Inspect the teeth on both sprockets in the indicated areas to determine whether they are excessively worn

lar for the bolt.

3   Remove the gearshift lever from the gearshift spindle (see "Gearshift linkage - removal, inspection and installation" in Chapter 1).

4   Remove the rear wheel and lift the chain off the driven sprocket (see Section 12).

5   Detach the swingarm from the frame (see Chapter 6). Pull the swingarm back far enough to allow the chain to slip between the frame and the front of the swingarm. Lift the chain off the drive sprocket and remove it.

Cleaning

6   Soak the chain in kerosene or diesel fuel for approximately five or six minutes. **Caution:** Don't use gasoline or other cleaning fluids. Remove the chain, wipe it off then dry it with compressed air immediately. The entire process shouldn't take longer than ten minutes - if it does, the O-rings in the chain rollers could be damaged.

Installation

7   Installation is the reverse of removal. Be sure to tighten the suspension fasteners to the torque listed in the Chapter 6 Specifications. Tighten the rear axle nut to the torque listed in this Chapter's Specifications.

8   On VT750 models, don't forget to install the collar before installing the left rear cover. To install the left rear cover, place it in position, push the cover positioning pin into the grommet and align the bolt hole in the cover with the threaded hole in the bracket on the engine **(see illustration)**. Install the left rear cover Allen bolt and

tighten it securely. On VT600 models, install the retaining clip.

9   Lubricate and adjust the chain (see Chapter 1).

17   Sprockets - check and replacement

Check

Refer to illustration 17.3

1   Whenever the drive chain is inspected, the sprockets should be inspected also. If you are replacing the chain, replace the sprockets as well. Likewise, if the sprockets are in need of replacement, install a new chain also.

2   Remove the left rear cover from the engine **(see illustrations 16.2a through 16.2c)**.

3   Inspect the wear pattern on the sprockets **(see illustration)**. If the sprocket teeth are worn excessively, replace the chain and sprockets.

Replacement

Drive sprocket

Refer to illustration 17.4

4   With the chain installed and the rear tire on the ground, have an assistant apply the rear brake while you loosen the sprocket retaining bolts **(see illustration)**. Remove the bolts and remove the sprocket setting plate.

5   Disengage the drive sprocket from the chain and remove the sprocket.

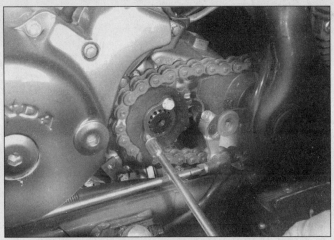

17.4 Remove the sprocket bolts and retaining plate

17.8 To remove the driven sprocket, remove these nuts (arrows) . . .

18.2 . . . and lift the sprocket/driven flange assembly from the wheel

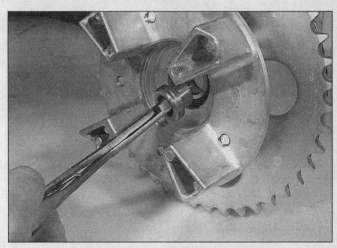

18.3 Remove the collar from the driven flange

6   Installation is the reverse of removal. Be sure to tighten the sprocket retaining bolts to the torque listed in this Chapter's Specifications.

Driven sprocket

Refer to illustration 17.8

7   If you're going to remove the drive sprocket, do it before removing the chain. Remove the rear wheel (see Section 12).

8   Remove the sprocket retaining nuts **(see illustration)** and detach the driven sprocket from the driven flange.

9   While the rear wheel is removed, inspect the wheel bearings (see Section 13) and inspect the driven flange seal, collar, bearing and rubber dampers (see Section 18).

10   Installation is the reverse of removal. Be sure to apply a non-hardening thread locking compound to the threads of the studs and tighten the sprocket retaining nuts to the torque listed in this Chapter's Specifications.

18   Driven flange and rubber dampers - removal, inspection and installation

Refer to illustrations 18.2 and 18.3

1   Remove the rear wheel (see Section 12).

2   Lift the sprocket/driven flange off the wheel **(see illustration)** from the wheel and check it for cracks, hardening and general deterioration. Replace it with a new one if necessary.

3   Remove the collar from the driven flange **(see illustration)**.

4   Inspecting and replacing the driven flange bearing and seal is just like checking and replacing a wheel bearing and seal (see Section 13).

5   Inspect the rubber dampers inside the wheel hub. If they're cracked, torn, dried out or deteriorated, replace them.

6   Installation is the reverse of removal. **Caution:** *Don't forget to install the collar, or the coupling bearing will be damaged when the axle nut is tightened.*

Notes

Chapter 8
Frame and bodywork

Contents

1 General information

The models covered in this manual use a steel frame of round-section tubing. The front fender is steel; the rear fender and side covers are plastic.

2 Frame - inspection and repair

1   The frame should not require attention unless accident damage has occurred. In most cases, frame replacement is the only satisfactory remedy for such damage. A few frame specialists have the jigs and other equipment necessary for straightening the frame to the required standard of accuracy, but even then there is no simple way of assessing to what extent the frame may have been overstressed.

2   After the machine has accumulated a lot of miles, the frame should be examined closely for signs of cracking or splitting at the welded joints. Corrosion can also cause weakness at these joints. Loose engine mount bolts can cause elongation of the bolt holes or fracturing of the mounting tabs. Minor damage can often be repaired by welding, depending on the extent and nature of the damage.

3   Remember that a frame which is out of alignment will cause handling problems. If misalignment is suspected as the result of an accident, it will be necessary to strip the machine completely so the frame can be thoroughly checked.

3 Footpegs - removal and installation

Refer to illustrations 3.3 and 3.4

1   The front footpegs are mounted on brackets that also serve as the mounting brackets for the gearshift linkage on the left side (see Chap-ter 2) and the rear brake pedal linkage on the right side (see Chapter 7). The rear footpegs are mounted on brackets bolted to the frame.

2   To replace a footpeg pad on a VT600 model, work the rubber pad off the end of the footpeg. The pad is a tight fit, so this may be difficult. Cutting off the old pad, then heating the new pad in hot water and lubricating it with soap, will make the job easier. (The footpegs and pads on VT750 models are a single assembly.)

3   To replace a footpeg, remove the cotter pin and the washer **(see illustration)**, pull out the clevis pin and separate the footpeg from the bracket. On VT750 models, note how the spring is installed, with one end hooked over the rear clevis pin boss on the footpeg and the other end hooked into the bracket. Installation is the reverse of removal. Grease the footpeg clevis pin before installing it.

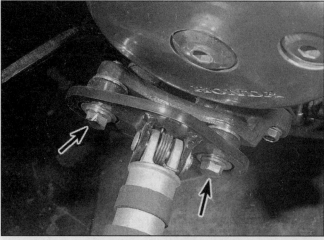

3.3 To replace a footpeg, remove the cotter pin and washer and pull out the pivot pin; the spring is used only on VT750 models

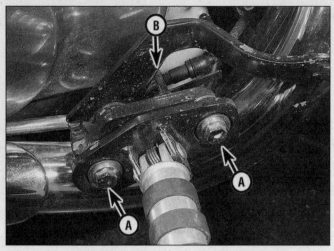

3.4 VT750 right footpeg and brake pedal assembly

A   *Mounting bolts*   B   *Brake light switch*

4   To replace a front footpeg assembly (footpeg and bracket), remove the bolts that secure the bracket to the frame **(see illustration)**. If you're removing the left footpeg assembly on a VT600 model, detach the gearshift pedal from the back of the bracket (see "Gearshift linkage - removal, inspection and installation" in Chapter 2). If you're removing the right footpeg assembly on a VT600 model, detach the brake pedal from the back of the bracket (see "Rear brake pedal and linkage - removal and installation" in Chapter 7). (On VT750 models, the footpeg brackets can be removed separately; they're not connected to the gearshift pedal or brake pedal.) Installation is the reverse of removal. Tighten the bracket bolts securely.

4   Sidestand - maintenance

Refer to illustration 4.1

1   The sidestand is attached to a bracket on the frame. A return spring anchored to a bracket on the frame ensures that the stand remains in the extended or retracted position **(see illustration)**.
2   Make sure the pivot bolt is tight and the return spring is not fatigued. An accident could occur if the stand extends while the machine is in motion, and damage to the machine could occur if the stand retracts while the machine is resting on the stand.

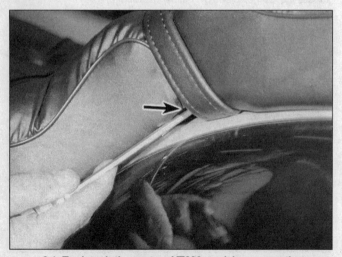

6.1 To detach the seat on VT600 models, remove the Allen bolt from each side (arrow)

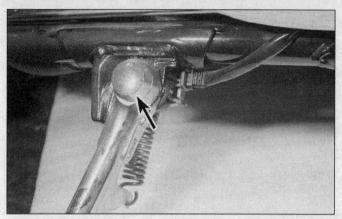

4.1 Make sure the sidestand spring is in good condition and correctly installed; the sidestand pivot bolt is under this cap (arrow)

5   Sidestand - removal and installation

1   Support the bike securely so it can't be knocked over during this procedure.
2   Unhook the sidestand spring **(see illustration 4.1)**.
3   Remove the sidestand switch (see Chapter 9).
4   Remove the dust cap **(see illustration 4.1)**.
5   Remove the sidestand switch pivot bolt and nut.
6   Installation is the reverse of removal. Be sure to grease the pivot bolt and tighten the nut securely.

6   Seat - removal and installation

VT600 models

Refer to illustrations 6.1, 6.2, 6.3a and 6.3b
1   Remove the two Allen bolts (one on each side) from under the seat **(see illustration)**.
2   Grasp the seat firmly and slide it to the rear **(see illustration)**.
3   To install the seat, place it in position, then slide it forward. Make sure that the lug under the forward end of the seat slides under the small crossmember on the frame **(see illustration)** and the two smaller lugs under the rear end of the seat slide under the two retainers on the fender **(see illustration)**.
4   Install the two retaining bolts and tighten them securely.

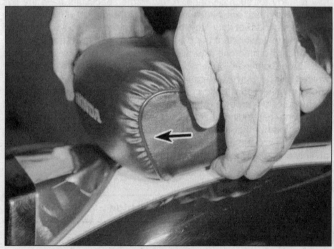

6.2 Grasp the seat firmly and slide it to the rear to disengage the retaining lugs

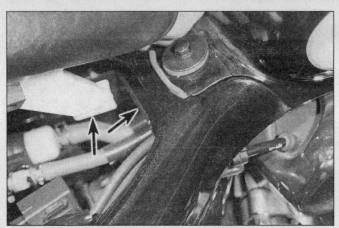

6.3a To install the VT600 seat, insert the forward retaining lug under this crossmember in the frame (arrow) . . .

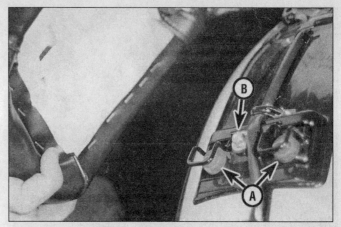

6.3b . . . and insert the two rear lugs under their retainers, then slide the seat forward and install the two mounting bolts

A   Seat retainers   B   Rear fender upper
                                  mounting bolt

VT750C/CD models

Refer to illustration 6.5

5   Remove the passenger seat retaining bolt **(see illustration)**.

6   To remove the rear seat, slide it forward and lift it up.

7   Remove the front seat mounting bolt.

8   To remove the front seat, slide it back and lift it up.

9   To install the front seat, place it in position, then slide it forward. Make sure that the lug on the forward end of the seat slides under the small crossmember on the frame **(see illustration 6.3a)**.

10   Align the hole in the front seat retaining bolt flange with the hole in the fender, install the bolt and tighten it securely.

11   To install the rear seat, insert the lug on the forward end of the seat over the front seat mounting bolt, then slide the seat to the rear.

12   Align the hole in the rear seat retaining bolt flange with the hole in the fender, install the bolt and tighten it securely.

VT750DC models

13   Remove the bolt and washer on each end of the passenger grab strap. Remove the strap.

14   Slide the seat readward to disengage its front hook from the bracket. Lift the seat off the bike.

15   Installation is the reverse of the removal steps.

6.5 To remove the rear seat on VT750C/CD models, remove this bolt (arrow), slide the seat forward and lift it up (there's another bolt just like this at the rear of the front seat)

and connectors in the area between the steering head and the fuel tank.

2   Remove the fuel tank (see Chapter 4).

VT600 models

Refer to illustrations 7.3a, 7.3b, 7.4, 7.5a, 7.5b and 7.5c

3   To remove the joint cover **(see illustrations)**, carefully pry it out.

7   Steering head covers (VT600 and VT750C/CD models) - removal and installation

1   The steering head covers conceal and protect wiring harnesses

7.3a To remove the joint cover (arrow) from the steering covers on VT600 models . . .

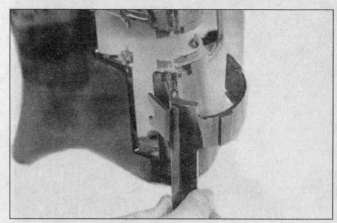

7.3b . . . carefully pry it off (joint cover and steering covers removed for clarity)

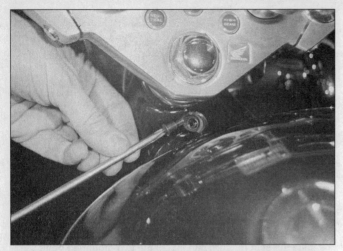

7.4 On VT600 models, remove the steering cover retaining screw (arrow)

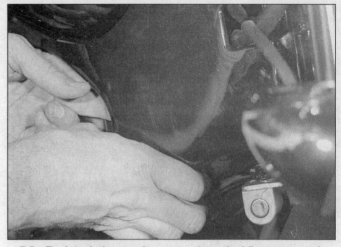

7.5a To detach the steering covers from the bike, grasp each cover half at the rear and pull it off . . .

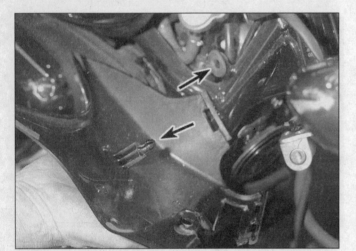

7.5b . . . to disengage each mounting lug and grommet (arrows)

7.5c On VT600 models, the steering cover halves are hinged at the front; lift the left cover up slightly and pull the tangs out of the slots (steering covers removed for clarity)

4   Remove the retaining screw (**see illustration**).
5   Pull the two steering cover halves apart from the rear to disengage their mounting lugs from the grommets on the frame (**see illustrations**), disengage the tangs and slots of the two cover halves at the steering head (**see illustration**) and remove the covers.
6   Installation is the reverse of removal. Make sure that neither cover half interferes with any wiring harnesses or connectors.

VT750C/CD models

7   Remove the two trim clips, one per side, from each steering cover half.
8   Pull the two steering cover halves apart to disengage their mounting lugs from the grommets on the frame (**see illustrations 7.5a and 7.5b**).
9   Remove the joint clip and remove the covers.
10   Installation is the reverse of removal. Make sure that neither cover half interferes with any wiring harnesses or connectors.

---

8   Side covers - removal and installation

VT600 models

Refer to illustrations 8.1a, 8.1b, 8.1c and 8.2
1   To remove a side cover, put your fingers under the lower edge of the side cover (**see illustration**) and pull out, disengaging the two mounting bosses on the side cover (**see illustration**) from their respective grommets on the frame (**see illustration**).

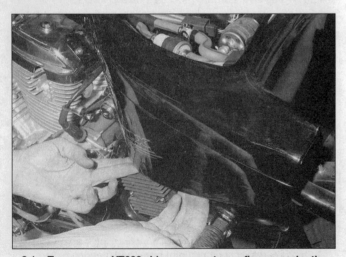

8.1a To remove a VT600 side cover, put your fingers under the lower edge of the side cover and pull out . . .

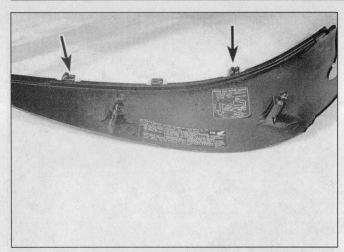

8.1b . . . disengaging the two mounting bosses (side cover removed for clarity). . .

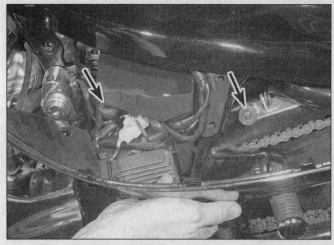

8.1c . . . from the two grommets (arrows) on the frame

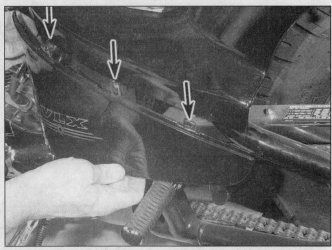

8.2 To install a VT600 side cover, insert these three tabs under the lower edge of the rear fender bodywork, then push in the lower edge of the cover and pop the two mounting bosses into their grommets

9.1 Remove the front chain guard mounting bolt (VT600 model shown)

2   To install a side cover, insert the three positioning tabs across the top of the side cover under the lower edge of the rear fender bodywork **(see illustration)**, then push in the lower edge of the side cover and pop the two bosses into their grommets.

VT750 models

3   To remove a side cover, grasp the side cover with both hands and pull it off, disengaging the three mounting bosses (one on top, one near the front end, one near the lower rear corner) from their respective grommets on the frame.
4   Installation is the reverse of removal. Simply position the side cover with the three mounting bosses aligned with their corresponding grommets and push in the cover.

9   Chain guard - removal and installation

Refer to illustrations 9.1 and 9.2
1   Remove the front chain guard mounting bolt **(see illustration)**.
2   Remove the rear chain guard mounting bolt and, on VT600 models, disengage the guard from the grommet on the swingarm **(see illustration)**.
3   Installation is the reverse of removal. Tighten the bolts securely.

9.2 Remove the rear chain guard mounting bolt and, on VT600 models, disengage the guard from the grommet on the swingarm (arrows)

10.2 To detach the fender from the forks, remove these two bolts from the left side and the two bolts from the other side

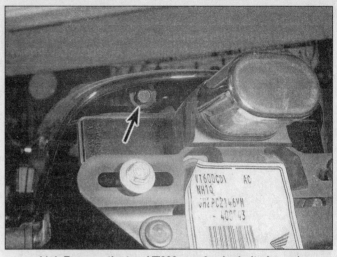

11.4 Remove the two VT600 rear fender bolts (arrow) (left bolt shown)

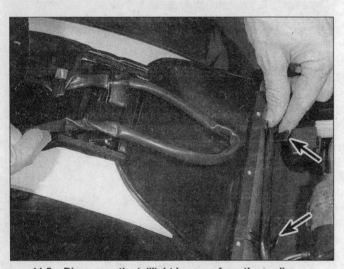

11.5a Disengage the taillight harness from these clips . . .

11.5b . . . and unplug the electrical connectors (arrows) for the taillights

10 Front fender - removal and installation

Refer to illustration 10.2

1   Remove the front wheel (see Chapter 7).
2   Unbolt the fender from the forks **(see illustration)**.
3   Installation is the reverse of the removal steps. Tighten the bolts securely. Don't forget to route the speedometer cable through the loop on the left side of the fender.

11 Rear fender - removal and installation

1   On VT600 models, remove the seat; on VT750 models, remove the front and rear seat (see Section 6).
2   On VT600 models, remove the left and right side covers; on VT750 models, remove the right side cover (see Section 8).

VT600

Refer to illustrations 11.4, 11.5a and 11.5b

3   Remove the fuel tank (see Chapter 4).
4   Remove the rear fender mounting bolts **(see illustration)**.
5   Disengage the taillight wiring harness from its clips **(see illustra-**

tion) and unplug the electrical connectors for the harness **(see illustration)**.
6   Remove the taillight assembly from the rear fender (see Chapter 9).
7   Remove the rear fender mounting bolt **(see illustration 6.3b)** and nut (see "Taillight assembly - removal and installation" in Chapter 9).
8   Installation is the reverse of removal.

VT750 models

Refer to illustration 11.10

9   Unplug the electrical connectors for the taillight.
10   Remove the fender mounting bolts **(see illustration)**.
11   Remove the fender. If you're replacing the fender, the taillight assembly or the license plate/turn signal assembly, remove the taillight assembly and the license plate light/turn signal assembly (see Chapter 9).
12   Installation is the reverse of removal.

12 Rear sub-frame (VT600 models) - removal and installation

Refer to illustration 12.3

1   Remove the rear fender (see Section 11).

11.10 To detach a VT750 rear fender from the grab rails, remove the fender mounting bolts (arrows) (right side shown)

12.3 To detach the VT600 rear sub-frame from the frame, remove the two sub-frame mounting bolts (arrow) (left bolt shown)

13 Rear grab rails (VT750 models) - removal and installation

1   Remove the rear fender (see Section 11).
2   To remove the left fender grab rail, loosen the mounting nut located at the upper end of the left shock absorber, then remove the grab rail mounting bolt and washer. Remove the left grab rail.
3   To remove the right fender grab rail, remove the right shock absorber (see Chapter 6), then remove the grab rail mounting bolts. Remove the right grab rail.
4   Installation is the reverse of removal.

2   Unplug the electrical connectors for the left and right turn signal lights **(see illustration 11.5b)**. The wires for the left turn signal are green and orange; the wires for the right turn signal are green and light blue.
3   Remove the two rear sub-frame mounting bolts **(see illustration)**.
4   Remove the rear sub-frame from the frame.
5   Installation is the reverse of removal. Be sure to tighten the rear sub-frame mounting bolts securely.

Notes

Chapter 9
Electrical system

Contents

Specifications

Battery type
VT600	12 V, 8 Ah
VT750C/CD	12 V, 14 Ah
VT750DC	12 V, 12 Ah

Fuse specifications
Main fuse	30 amps
All others	
1988 and 1989 VT600 models	Six 10-amp and one 15-amp
1990-on VT600 models	Three 10-amp and one 15-amp
VT750 models	Four 10-amp and one 15-amp

Bulb specifications
Headlight bulb	60/55W
Brake light/taillight bulbs	
1988, 1989, 1991 through 1996 VT600	32/3 cp or 27/8W
1997 on VT600	32/3 cp
VT750C/CD	32/3 cp
VT750DC	21/5W
Front turn signal bulbs	
1988, 1989, 1991 through 1996 VT600	32/3 cp or 23/8W
1997 and 1998 VT600	32/3 cp
1999-on VT600, VT750	21/5W
Rear turn signal bulbs	
1988, 1989, 1991 through 1996 VT600	32 cp or 23W
1997 and 1998 VT600	32 cp
1999-on VT600, VT750	21W
License plate bulb	
VT600	4cp
VT750	5W
Speedometer light bulb	3.4W
Indicator bulbs (turn signal, high beam, neutral)	
VT600	1.7W
VT750C/CD	3.4W
VT750D	LED

Charging system

Stator coil resistance	
VT600, VT750DC	0.1 to 1.0 ohms
VT750C/CD	0.1 to 0.3 ohms
Charging system output	
VT600, VT750C/CD	345 watts at 5,000 rpm
VT750DC	333 watts at 5,000 rpm
Regulated voltage output	
1988, 1989, 1991 through 1996 VT600	14.3 to 15.1 volts at 5,000 rpm
1997 on VT600	13.5 to 14 volts at 5,000 rpm
VT750C/CD	14 to 15 volts at 4,000 rpm
VT750DC	Less than 15.5 volts
Maximum current leakage	
VT600	1.3 mA
VT750	1.0 mA

Starter

Starter brush length	
Standard	12.5 mm (0.49 inch)
Minimum	6.5 mm (0.26 inch)
Starter driven gear hub	
VT600	
Inside diameter	37.10 mm (1.461 inches)
Outside diameter	57.60 mm (2.268 inches)
VT750	
Inside diameter	40.10 mm (1.579 inches)
Outside diameter	57.73 mm (2.273 inches)

Torque specifications

Neutral switch	12 Nm (108 in-lbs)
Oil pressure switch	10 Nm (84 in-lbs)
Sidestand switch retaining bolt	
VT600	9 Nm (78 in-lbs)
VT750	10 Nm (84 in-lbs)
Rotor (rotor) bolt	128 Nm (94 ft-lbs)
Stator assembly retaining bolts	12 Nm (108 in-lbs)
Left crankcase cover bolts	12 Nm (108 in-lbs)
Rotor-to-clutch housing bolts	29 Nm (22 ft-lbs)

1   General information

The machines covered by this manual are equipped with a 12-volt electrical system.

The charging system uses an alternator consisting of a rotor (rotor) with permanent magnets that rotates around a stator coil of copper wire. The alternator produces alternating current, which is converted to direct current by the regulator/rectifier. The regulator/rectifier also controls the charging system output.

An electric starter mounted behind the rear cylinder is standard equipment. The starter has four brushes. The starting system includes the motor, the battery, the starter relay switch and the wiring harnesses and switches. When the engine kill switch and the ignition switch are both in the On position, the starter relay switch allows the starter motor to operate only if the transmission is in Neutral (Neutral switch on) or the clutch lever is pulled in (clutch switch on) and the sidestand is up (sidestand switch on). **Note:** *Keep in mind that electrical parts, once purchased, can't be returned. To avoid unnecessary expense, make very sure the faulty component has been positively identified before buying a replacement part.*

2   Electrical troubleshooting

A typical electrical circuit consists of an electrical component, the switches, relays, etc. related to that component and the wiring and connectors that hook the component to both the battery and the frame. To aid in locating a problem in any electrical circuit, complete wiring diagrams of each model are included at the end of this Chapter.

Before tackling any troublesome electrical circuit, first study the appropriate diagrams thoroughly to get a complete picture of what makes up that individual circuit. Trouble spots, for instance, can often be narrowed down by noting if other components related to that circuit are operating properly or not. If several components or circuits fail at one time, chances are the fault lies in the fuse or ground connection, as several circuits often are routed through the same fuse and ground connections.

Electrical problems often stem from simple causes, such as loose or corroded connections or a blown fuse. Prior to any electrical troubleshooting, always visually check the condition of the fuse, wires and connections in the problem circuit. Intermittent failures can be especially frustrating, since you can't always duplicate the failure when it's convenient to test. In such situations, a good practice is to clean all connections in the affected circuit, whether or not they appear to be good. All of the connections and wires should also be wiggled to check for looseness which can cause intermittent failure.

If testing instruments are going to be utilized, use the diagrams to plan where you will make the necessary connections in order to accurately pinpoint the trouble spot.

The basic tools needed for electrical troubleshooting include a test light or voltmeter, a continuity tester (which includes a bulb, battery and set of test leads) and a jumper wire, preferably with a circuit breaker incorporated, which can be used to bypass electrical components. Specific checks described later in this Chapter may also require an ohmmeter.

Voltage checks should be performed if a circuit is not functioning properly. Connect one lead of a test light or voltmeter to either the negative battery terminal or a known good ground. Connect the other lead to a connector in the circuit being tested, preferably nearest to the battery or fuse. If the bulb lights, voltage is reaching that point, which means the part of the circuit between that connector and the battery is problem-free. Continue checking the remainder of the circuit in the same manner. When you reach a point where no voltage is present, the problem lies between there and the last good test point. Most of the time the problem is due to a loose connection. Keep in mind that some circuits only receive voltage when the ignition key is in the On position.

One method of finding short circuits is to remove the fuse and connect a test light or voltmeter in its place to the fuse terminals. There should be no load in the circuit (it should be switched off). Move the wiring harness from side-to-side while watching the test light. If the bulb lights, there is a short to ground somewhere in that area, probably where insulation has rubbed off a wire. The same test can be performed on other components in the circuit, including the switch.

A ground check should be done to see if a component is grounded properly. Disconnect the battery and connect one lead of a self-powered test light (continuity tester) to a known good ground. Connect the other lead to the wire or ground connection being tested. If the bulb lights, the ground is good. If the bulb does not light, the ground is not good.

A continuity check is performed to see if a circuit, section of circuit or individual component is capable of passing electricity through it. Disconnect the battery and connect one lead of a self-powered test light (continuity tester) to one end of the circuit being tested and the other lead to the other end of the circuit. If the bulb lights, there is continuity, which means the circuit is passing electricity through it properly. Switches can be checked in the same way.

Remember that all electrical circuits are designed to conduct electricity from the battery, through the wires, switches, relays, etc. to the electrical component (light bulb, motor, etc.). From there it is directed to the frame (ground) where it is passed back to the battery. Electrical problems are basically an interruption in the flow of electricity from the battery or back to it.

---

3 Battery - removal, inspection, maintenance and installation

1 Most battery damage is caused by heat, vibration, and/or low electrolyte levels, so make sure the battery is securely mounted, check the electrolyte level frequently (if the battery is a conventional unit) and make sure the charging system is functioning properly.

Removal and installation

VT600 models

Refer to illustrations 3.3, 3.4a and 3.4b
2 Remove the left and right side covers (see Chapter 8).
3 On the right side, peel back the protective rubber cover from the fuse box (see Section 5), pull off the fuse box and remove the battery

3.3 To remove the battery case cover on VT600 models, remove these two screws (arrows)

case cover screws **(see illustration)**.
4 Lift up the cover and disconnect the battery cables from the battery terminals, negative cable (left terminal) first, then positive **(see illustrations)**.
5 Remove the battery from the battery case and inspect it (see below).
6 Installation is the reverse of removal. Be sure to attach the positive cable (right terminal) first, then negative. Tighten the cables securely. Don't forget to put the protective cap back on the positive terminal.

VT750 models

7 Remove the seat (see Chapter 8).
8 Remove the ignition control module from the battery case cover (see Chapter 5).
9 Remove the three battery case cover screws.
10 Disconnect the battery cables from the battery terminals, negative cable (right terminal) first, then positive.
11 Lift the battery out of the battery case and inspect it (see below).
12 Installation is the reverse of removal. Be sure to attach the positive cable (left terminal) first, then negative. Tighten the cables securely. Don't forget to put the protective cap back on the positive terminal.

Inspection and maintenance

13 All machines covered in this manual are originally equipped with maintenance-free batteries. However, if you or a previous owner have installed a conventional battery, check the electrolyte level and specific gravity (see Chapter 1).

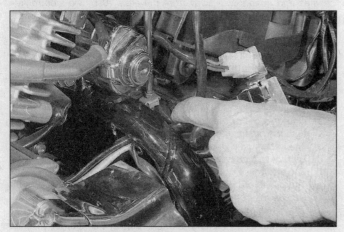

3.4a On VT600 models, disconnect the negative cable (left terminal) first . . .

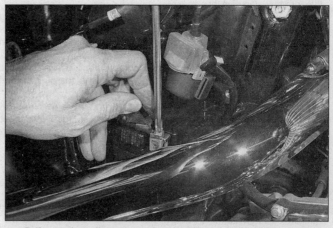

3.4b . . . then disconnect the positive cable (right terminal)

14 Check around the base inside of the battery for sediment, which is the result of sulfation caused by low electrolyte levels. These deposits will cause internal short circuits, which can quickly discharge the battery. Look for cracks in the case and replace the battery if either of these conditions is found.

15 Check the battery terminals and cable ends for tightness and corrosion. If corrosion is evident, remove the cables from the battery and clean the terminals and cable ends with a wire brush or knife and emery paper. Reconnect the cables and apply a thin coat of petroleum jelly to the connections to slow further corrosion.

16 The battery case should be kept clean to prevent current leakage, which can discharge the battery over a period of time (especially when it sits unused). Wash the outside of the case with a solution of baking soda and water. Do not get any baking soda solution in the battery cells. Rinse the battery thoroughly, then dry it.

17 If acid has been spilled on the frame or battery box, neutralize it with the baking soda and water solution, dry it thoroughly, then touch up any damaged paint. If the battery is equipped with a vent tube, make sure it's correctly routed and is not kinked or pinched.

18 If the motorcycle sits unused for long periods of time, disconnect the cables from the battery terminals. Charge the battery about once a month (see Section 4).

4 Battery - charging

1 If the machine sits idle for extended periods or if the charging system malfunctions, the battery can be charged from an external source.

Maintenance-free batteries

Refer to illustration 4.5

2 Charging the maintenance-free battery used on these models requires a digital voltmeter and a variable-voltage charger with a built-in ammeter.

3 When charging the battery, always remove it from the machine and be sure to check the electrolyte level by looking through the translucent battery case before hooking up the charger. If the electrolyte level is low, the battery must be discarded; never remove the sealing plug to add water.

4 Disconnect the battery cables (negative cable first), then connect a digital voltmeter between the battery terminals and measure the voltage.

5 If terminal voltage is 12.6 volts or higher, the battery is fully charged. If it's lower, recharge the battery. Refer to the accompanying illustration for charging rate and time **(see illustration)**.

6 A quick charge can be used in an emergency, provided the maximum charge rates and times are not exceeded (exceeding the maximum rate or time may ruin the battery). A quick charge should always be followed as soon as possible by a charge at the standard rate and time.

7 Hook up the battery charger leads (positive lead to battery positive terminal, negative lead to battery negative terminal), then, and only then, plug in the battery charger. **Warning:** *The hydrogen gas escaping from a charging battery is explosive, so keep open flames and sparks well away from the area. Also, the electrolyte is extremely corrosive and will damage anything it comes in contact with.*

8 Start charging at a high voltage setting (no more than 25 volts) and watch the ammeter for about 5 minutes. If the charging current doesn't increase, replace the battery.

9 When the charging current increases beyond the specified maximum, reduce the charging voltage to reduce the charging current to the rate listed in this Chapter's Specifications. Do this periodically as the battery charges.

10 Allow the battery to charge for the specified time listed in this Chapter's Specifications. If the battery overheats or gases excessively, the charging rate is too high. Either disconnect the charger or lower the charging rate to prevent damage to the battery.

11 After the specified time, unplug the charger first, then disconnect the leads from the battery.

12 Wait 30 minutes, then measure voltage between the battery terminals. If it's 12.6 volts or higher, the battery is fully charged. If it's

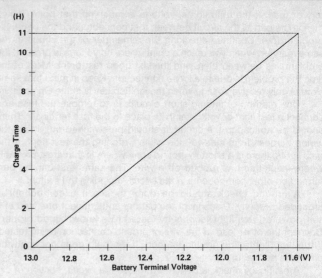

4.5 Battery charge-time table (maintenance-free batteries)

between 12.0 and 12.6 volts, charge the battery again (refer to this Chapter's Specifications and illustration 4.5 for charge rate and time). If it's less than 12.0 volts, it's time for a new battery.

13 When the battery is fully charged, unplug the charger first, then disconnect the leads from the battery. Wipe off the outside of the battery case and install the battery in the bike.

Conventional batteries

14 To properly charge the battery, you will need a charger of the correct rating, a hydrometer, a clean rag and a syringe for adding distilled water to the battery cells.

15 The maximum charging rate for any battery is 1/10 of the rated amp/hour capacity. As an example, the maximum charging rate for a 12 amp/hour battery would be 1.2 amps and the maximum charging rate for a 14 amp/hour battery would be 1.4 amps. If the battery is charged at a higher rate, it could be damaged.

16 Do not allow the battery to be subjected to a so-called quick charge (high rate of charge over a short period of time) unless you are prepared to buy a new battery.

17 When charging the battery, always remove it from the machine and be sure to check the electrolyte level before hooking up the charger. Add distilled water to any cells that are low.

18 Loosen the cell caps, hook up the battery charger leads (red to positive, black to negative), cover the top of the battery with a clean rag, then, and only then, plug in the battery charger. **Warning:** *Remember, the gas escaping from a charging battery is explosive, so keep open flames and sparks well away from the area. Also, the electrolyte is extremely corrosive and will damage anything it comes in contact with.*

19 Allow the battery to charge until the specific gravity is as specified (refer to Chapter 1 for specific gravity checking procedures). The charger must be unplugged and disconnected from the battery when making specific gravity checks. If the battery overheats or gases excessively, the charging rate is too high. Either disconnect the charger or lower the charging rate to prevent damage to the battery.

20 It's time for a new battery if:

a) *One or more of the cells is significantly lower in specific gravity than the others after a long slow charge.*
b) *The battery as a whole doesn't seem to want to take a charge.*
c) *Battery voltage won't increase.*
d) *The electrolyte doesn't bubble.*
e) *The plates are white (indicating sulfation) or debris has accumulated in the bottom of a cell.*
f) *The plates or insulators are warped or buckled.*

21 When the battery is fully charged, unplug the charger first, then disconnect the leads from the battery. Install the cell caps and wipe any electrolyte off the outside of the battery case.

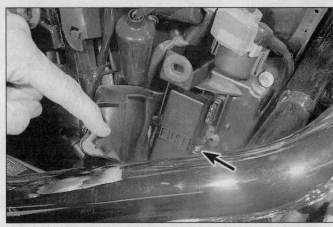

5.2 The VT600 fuse box is located behind the right side cover; to open the fuse box, remove this screw (arrow); the main (30A) fuse is located right above the fuse box

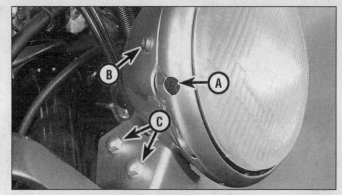

7.1 VT600 headlight assembly

A)   *Headlight adjusting screw (1 of 2)*
B)   *Headlight retaining screw (1 of 2)*
C)   *Headlight assembly nuts and bolts*

5   Fuses - check and replacement

Refer to illustration 5.2
1   Some fuses are located in the fuse block, which is located on the right side of the bike, behind the right side cover. Remove the right side cover (see Chapter 8).
2   On VT600 models, peel back the protective rubber cover **(see illustration)** and remove the fuse cover screw. The fuse box houses six 10-amp fuses and one 15-amp fuse (1988 and 1989 models) or three 10-amp fuses and one 15-amp fuse (1990 and later VT600 models). The main (30-amp) fuse is located right above the fuse box.
3   On VT750 models, remove the cover from the fuse box. The fuse box houses four 10-amp fuses (headlight, ignition-starter and fan motor) and one 15-amp fuse (front turn signal lights, rear brake light, speedometer). The main (30-amp) fuse is on the left side. To check or replace it, remove the left side cover (see Chapter 8).
4   Other fuses (turn signal/dimmer/horn switch, fan motor switch, oil pressure switch, neutral switch, sidestand switch, brake light switches, fuel pump, etc.) are installed inline, often near the electrical connector for each circuit device. Most of these fuses are easy to find when troubleshooting a circuit. For further help in locating inline fuses, refer to the wiring diagrams at the end of this Chapter.
5   If you have a test light, all of the fuses can be checked without removing them. Turn the ignition key to the On position, connect one end of the test light to a good ground, then probe each terminal on top of the fuse. If the fuse is good, there will be voltage available at both terminals. If the fuse is blown, there will only be voltage present at one of the terminals.
6   The fuses can also be tested with an ohmmeter or self-powered test light. Remove the fuse and connect the tester to the ends of the fuse. If the ohmmeter shows continuity or the test lamp lights, the fuse is good. If the ohmmeter shows infinite resistance or the test lamp stays out, the fuse is blown.
7   The fuses can be removed and checked visually. If you can't pull the fuse out with your fingertips, use a pair of needle-nose pliers. A blown fuse is easily identified by a break in the element.
8   If a fuse blows, be sure to check the wiring harnesses very carefully for evidence of a short circuit. Look for bare wires and chafed, melted or burned insulation. If a fuse is replaced before the cause is located, the new fuse will blow immediately. Occasionally a fuse will blow or cause an open circuit for no obvious reason. Corrosion of the fuse ends and fuse block terminals may occur and cause poor fuse contact. If this happens, remove the corrosion with a wire brush or emery paper, then spray the fuse end and terminals with electrical contact cleaner.
9   Fuse ratings are listed in this Chapter's Specifications. Fuse ratings are also marked on the fuses themselves. Never, under any circumstances, use a higher rated fuse or bridge the fuse block terminals, as damage to the electrical system could result.

6   Lighting system - check

1   The battery provides power for operation of the headlight, taillight, brake light, license plate light, instrument and warning lights. If none of the lights operate, always check battery voltage before proceeding. Low battery voltage indicates either a faulty battery, low battery electrolyte level or a defective charging system. If the bike has a conventional battery, check the battery electrolyte level and the specific gravity (see Chapter 1). Inspect the battery; make sure it's fully charged (see Sections 3 and 4). Check the condition of the fuses and replace any blown fuses (see Section 5). Check the charging system (see Sections 29 and 30).

Headlight

2   If the headlight is out when the engine is running, check the fuse first with the key or switch On (see Section 5), then unplug the electrical connector for the headlight and use jumper wires to connect the bulb directly to the battery terminals (see Section 7). If the light comes on, the problem lies in the wiring (see the wiring diagrams at the end of this Chapter).

Turn signal lights/brake light/taillight/license plate light

3   If a light fails to work, check the bulb and the bulb terminal first, then check for battery voltage at the electrical connector. If voltage is present, check the ground circuit for an open or poor connection.
4   If no voltage is indicated, check the wiring between the taillight and the ignition switch, then check the switch.

Brake light switches

5   See Section 12 for the brake light switch checking procedure.

Speedometer light and indicator lights

6   If the speedometer light fails to operate when the key switch is On, check the fuse (see Section 5) and the bulb (see Section 16). If the bulb and fuses are in good condition, check for battery voltage at the connector. If the turn signal indicator light fails to operate when the turn signal switch is in the LEFT or RIGHT position, or if the high-beam indicator light fails to operate when the dimmer switch is in the HI position, see Section 18. If the neutral indicator light fails to operate when the transmission in Neutral, see Section 20.

7   Headlight bulb - replacement

Refer to illustrations 7.1, 7.2, 7.3, 7.4 and 7.5
Warning: *If the bulb has just burned out, allow it to cool. It will be hot enough to burn your fingers.*
1   Remove the headlight retaining screws **(see illustration)**.

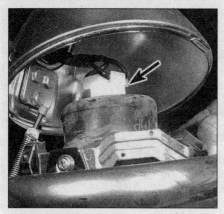

7.2 Tilt the headlight out and disconnect the wiring connector (arrow)

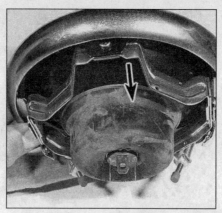

7.3 The TOP mark on the dust cover (arrow) goes upward

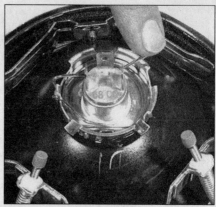

7.4 Remove the headlight bulb retainer

7.5 Lift out the bulb; don't touch the glass on the new bulb

8.3 The headlight adjusting screws are located on either side of the headlight assembly (headlight removed for clarity; the screws can be adjusted without removing the headlight)

2   Tilt the headlight forward out of the headlight housing and unplug the electrical connector **(see illustration)**.
3   Remove the dust cover **(see illustration)**.
4   Remove the bulb retainer **(see illustration)**.
5   Remove the bulb **(see illustration)**.
6   Installation is the reverse of removal. Be sure not to touch the bulb glass with your fingers - oil from your skin will cause the bulb to overheat and fail prematurely. If you do touch the bulb, wipe it off with a clean rag dampened with rubbing alcohol.

8   Headlight aim - check and adjustment

Refer to illustration 8.3
1   An improperly adjusted headlight may cause problems for oncoming traffic or provide poor, unsafe illumination of the road ahead. Before adjusting the headlight, be sure to consult with local traffic laws and regulations.
2   The headlight beam can be adjusted both vertically and horizontally. Before performing the adjustment, make sure the fuel tank is at least half full and have an assistant sit on the seat.
3   The adjusting screws are located in the lower edge of the headlight **(see illustration)**.

9   Headlight assembly - removal and installation

1   Remove the headlight (see Section 7).
2   Clearly label, then disconnect, all electrical connectors inside the headlight housing, then remove the wiring from the housing. Be careful not to cut any wires when pulling them through the holes in the housing.

VT600 models

Refer to illustrations 9.3, 9.4 and 9.5
3   If you just want to remove the headlight housing itself, remove the bracket-to-housing nuts **(see illustration)** and bolts **(see illustration 7.1)** and remove the housing.
4   If you want to remove the headlight housing bracket from the lower triple clamp, remove the nuts **(see illustration)** from the bracket

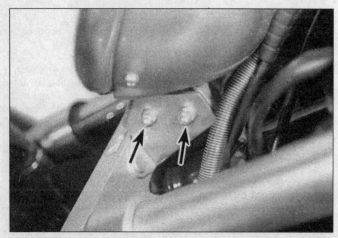

9.3 To detach the headlight housing from the bracket, remove these two nuts (arrows) and pull out the bolts (VT600 models)

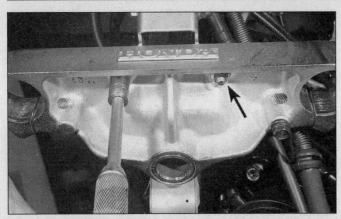

9.4 To detach the headlight housing bracket from the lower triple clamp, remove these two nuts (VT600 models)

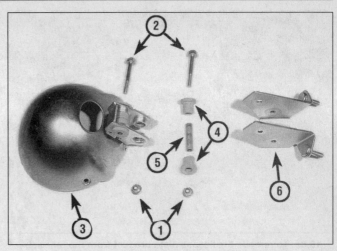

9.5 Headlight housing assembly (VT600 models)

1	Nuts	4	Collars
2	Bolts	5	Bushing
3	Headlight housing (with one bushing and set of collars assembled)	6	Headlight housing bracket

10.1 Remove the turn signal lens retaining screws (arrows) and remove the lens

studs on the underside of the lower triple clamp.

5   Remove the collars and bushings from the bracket **(see illustration)**, clean and inspect them, remove any corrosion, lubricate them lightly and reassemble.

6   Installation is the reverse of removal.

VT750 models

7   Remove the handlebar and the upper triple clamp (see Chapter 6).

8   Remove the headlight and turn signal assembly. Lift the assembly's mounting posts out of the grommets in the lower triple clamp.

9   If you're replacing a turn signal assembly, or if you're replacing the headlight assembly itself, remove the turn signal(s).

10   Installation is the reverse of removal.

10   Turn signal, tail/brake light and license plate bulbs - replacement

Turn signal bulbs

Refer to illustration 10.1

1   To replace a turn signal bulb, remove the lens retaining screws **(see illustration)**.

2   Push the bulb in and turn it counterclockwise to remove it.

3   Check the socket terminals for corrosion and clean them if necessary. Line up the pins on the new bulb with the slots in the socket, push in and turn the bulb clockwise until it locks in place.

4   Position the lens on the housing and install the screws. Be careful not to overtighten them or the lens will crack.

Tail/brake light bulbs

Refer to illustrations 10.5 and 10.6

5   Remove the lens screws **(see illustration)** and take the lens off.

6   To remove a brake or taillight bulb, push the bulb in and turn it

10.5 Remove the brake/taillight lens screws (arrows) (VT600 shown) and take off the lens

10.6 To remove a brake or taillight bulb, press the bulb into its socket and turn it counterclockwise

10.8a To remove the license plate bracket from the rear subframe on VT600 models, remove these two bolts (arrows) . . .

10.8b . . . and remove this nut from the back

10.9 License plate lens and housing bolts (VT600; VT750 uses two nuts)

10.10 Remove the license plate lens and housing from the license plate bracket

counterclockwise **(see illustration)**.

7   Install the bulb (see Steps 3 and 4).

License plate bulb

VT600 models

Refer to illustrations 10.8a, 10.8b, 10.9, 10.10 and 10.11

8   Remove the license plate bracket **(see illustrations)**.

9   Remove the two license plate lens/housing retaining bolts from

10.11 To remove the license plate bulb, push it in and turn it counterclockwise; to install it, push it in and turn it clockwise

the back of the license plate bracket **(see illustration)**.

10   Remove the lens and the housing **(see illustration)**.

11   Push the bulb in, turn it counterclockwise and remove it **(see illustration)**.

12   Installation is the reverse of removal.

VT750C/CD models

13   Remove the license light cover screws and remove the license light cover.

14   License plate bulb replacement on a VT750 model is otherwise identical to the procedure for replacing the bulb on a VT600 model (except that the lens and housing are retained by two nuts instead of two bolts). Refer to Steps 9, 10 and 11 above.

15   Installation is the reverse of removal.

---

11   Turn signal circuit and relay - check

Circuit

1   Battery voltage powers the turn signal lights, so if they don't operate, check battery voltage first and, on bikes with a conventional battery, the electrolyte level and specific gravity (see Chapter 1). Low battery voltage indicates either a defective battery (see Sections 3 and 4) or a malfunction in the charging system (see Sections 29 and 30). Also, check the fuses (see Section 5).

2   Most turn signal problems are the result of a burned out bulb or corroded socket. This is even more likely when the turn signal lights

11.4 The turn signal relay is located under the seat
on VT600 models

12.5 Disconnect the two electrical leads from the front brake light
switch (VT600 shown, VT750 similar)

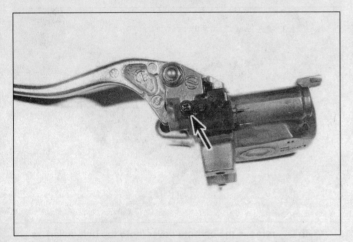

12.6 To detach the front brake light switch from the master
cylinder, remove this retaining screw (arrow)
(VT600 shown, VT750 similar)

12.7 Make sure that the positioning pin on the brake switch is
aligned with the hole (arrow) in the master cylinder
(VT600 shown, VT750 similar)

flash correctly on one side but not on the other. Check the bulbs and
the sockets (see Section 10).

3   If the bulbs and sockets check out okay, check the turn signal relay.

Turn signal relay

Refer to illustration 11.4

4   On VT600 models, remove the seat (see Chapter 8) and detach
the turn signal relay **(see illustration)**.

5   On VT750 models, remove the headlight (see Section 7) and
remove the turn signal relay from the headlight housing.

6   Locate the terminals of the turn signal relay connector for the
black/brown wire (fuse side of circuit) and the gray wire (switch side of
circuit) (on 1988 and 1989 VT600 models, there's a white/green wire,
instead of a black/brown wire). Connect the two terminals together
with a jumper wire.

7   Turn the ignition switch to ON and operate the turn signal switch.

8   If the turn signal lights *don't* come on, check the turn signal
switch for an open circuit (see Section 18). If the turn signal switch is
okay, look for an open circuit in the black/brown (green/white) wire or
in the gray wire.

9   If the turn signal lights *do* come on, check for continuity between
the terminal for the green wire and the ground terminal at the connector. If there is no continuity, there is an open circuit in the green wire. If
there is continuity, either there's a loose (intermittent) or poor contact
in the turn signal relay connector, or the turn signal relay is defective.

12 Brake light switches - check and replacement

Circuit check

1   Before checking any electrical circuit, check the fuses (see Section 5).

2   Using a test light connected to a good ground, check for voltage
at the brake light switch. If there's no voltage present, check the wire
between the switch and the fuse box (see the wiring diagrams at the
end of this Chapter).

3   If voltage is available, touch the probe of the test light to the other
terminal of the switch, then pull the brake lever or depress the brake
pedal - if the test light doesn't light up, replace the switch.

4   If the test light does light, check the wiring between the switch and
the brake lights (see the wiring diagrams at the end of this Chapter).

Switch replacement

Front brake lever switch

Refer to illustrations 12.5, 12.6 and 12.7

5   Disconnect the two electrical leads from the switch **(see illustration)**.

6   Remove the switch retaining screw **(see illustration)**.

7   Installation is the reverse of removal. Make sure that the positioning pin on the switch is aligned with the hole in the master cylinder **(see
illustration)**.

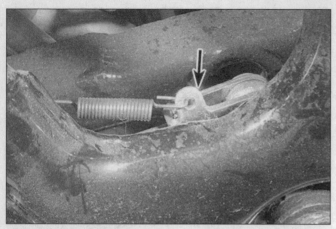

12.10 On VT600 models, disengage the rear brake light switch return spring from the middle brake arm (arrow)

12.11 To remove the rear brake light switch, turn the adjusting nut (arrow), not the switch, and take the switch out of the bracket

13.4a To detach a VT600 front turn signal assembly from the fork tube, remove this pinch bolt (arrow) . . .

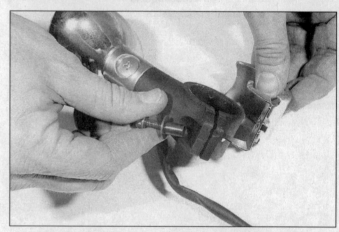

13.4b . . . remove the chrome cover (note the bolt collar). . .

Rear brake pedal switch

VT600 models

Refer to illustrations 12.10 and 12.11

8   Remove the right side cover (see Chapter 8).
9   Unplug the switch electrical connector (it can be identified by its wire colors, referring to wiring diagrams at the end of the book).
10   Unhook the switch spring **(see illustration)**.
11   Back off the switch locknut and slide the switch out of its mounting bracket **(see illustration)**.
12   Installation is the reverse of removal.
13   Adjust the switch (see Chapter 1).

VT750 models

14   The switch used on VT750 models is identical in design to the switch used on VT600 models, except that it's located up front, next to the rear brake pedal **(see illustration 3.4 in Chapter 8)**.
15   To replace the switch on a VT750 model, follow the procedure outlined above for VT600 models. The electrical connector for the switch is a black two-pin connector. On VT750C/CD models, it's behind the seat. On VT750DC models, remove the right side radiator mounting bolt and pull the grille forward for access to the connector.

13   Turn signal assembly - removal and installation

Front turn signals

Refer to illustrations 13.4a, 13.4b and 13.4c

1   On VT600 models, the front turn signal wires and connectors are

13.4c . . . and pull off the turn signal assembly

located right behind the steering head. Remove the fuel tank (see Chapter 4) and the steering head covers (see Chapter 8).
2   On VT750 models, the front turn signal wires and connectors are located inside the headlight housing. Remove the headlight from the housing (see Section 7).
.3   Locate the electrical leads for the front turn signals. On all models, the three left turn signal wires are green, orange and orange/white; the three right turn signal wires are green, light blue and light blue/white. Unplug the leads for the turn signal you are removing.
4   On VT600 models, remove the turn signal assembly pinch bolt,

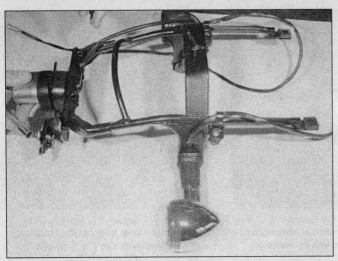

13.10a To detach a VT600 rear turn signal assembly, detach the wiring harness from all clips and clamps . . .

13.10b . . . and remove the turn signal assembly mounting nut (note how the harness is routed through the hole in the bracket)

14.4a To detach the VT600 brake light/taillight assembly from the rear fender, remove these two nuts (arrows) . . .

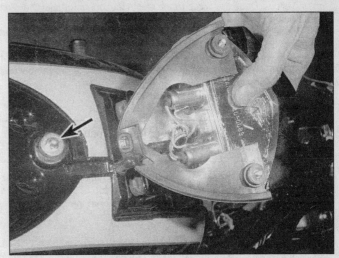

14.4b . . . lift the assembly out of the fender and carefully pull the wire harness out (pull on the harness, not the taillight) (there's a fender mounting nut (arrow) under the taillight)

remove the chrome cover and pull the turn signal assembly from the fork tube **(see illustrations)**.
5   On VT750 models, remove the turn signal assembly together with the headlight assembly (see Section 9).
6   Installation is the reverse of removal.

Rear turn signals

Refer to illustrations 13.10a and 13.10b
7   On VT600 models, the rear turn signal wires and connectors are located on under the seat. Remove the seat (see Chapter 8).
8   On VT750 models, the rear turn signal wires and connectors are located behind the right side cover. Remove the right side cover (see Chapter 8).
9   Locate the electrical leads for the rear turn signals. On all models, the two left turn signal wires are green and orange; the two right turn signal wires are green and light blue. Unplug the leads for the turn signal you are removing.
10   On VT600 models, trace the routing of the harness back to the turn signal, detach the harness from all clips and clamps on the frame, then remove the turn signal assembly mounting nut **(see illustrations)**.
11   On VT750 models, remove two screws from the underside of the license light cover and lift the cover off. Disconnect the wires running to each turn signal stalk and remove the stalk mounting nut.

12   Installation is the reverse of removal.

14   Brake light/taillight assembly - removal and installation

VT600 models

Refer to illustrations 14.4a and 14.4b
1   Remove the seat (see Chapter 8).
2   The wires for the brake light and tail light are brown, green and green/yellow. Trace the wires to the electrical connector(s) in the dust boot to the right of the fuel pump. Unplug the connector.
3   Trace the harness back to the brake light/taillight assembly and detach all clips and clamps.
4   From underneath the fender, remove the brake light/taillight assembly mounting nuts **(see illustration)** and remove the brake light/taillight assembly **(see illustration)** and pull out the harness.
5   Installation is the reverse of removal.

VT750 models

6   Remove the right side cover (see Chapter 8).

15.1 Speedometer (VT600 shown; VT750 similar)

A *Speedometer housing screws*
B *Speedometer cable nut*

15.2 To disconnect the lower end of the speedometer cable from the speedometer gearbox, remove this screw and pull out the cable

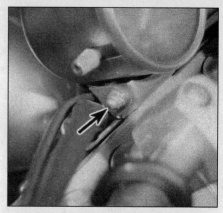

15.11 To detach the speedometer assembly from its mounting bracket, remove this nut (arrow) and pull out the bolt

7   The wires for the brake light and tail light are brown, green and green/yellow. Trace the wires to the electrical connector(s) in the dust boot behind the right side cover. Unplug the connector.
8   Trace the harness back to the brake light/taillight assembly and detach all clips and clamps.
9   From underneath the fender, remove the brake light/taillight assembly mounting nuts, remove the brake light/taillight assembly and pull out the harness.
10   Installation is the reverse of removal.

15   Speedometer and cable or speed sensor - removal and installation

1   Depending on model, the speedometer is either mounted on the upper triple clamp and driven by a cable, or on top of the fuel tank and connected by a wiring harness to a speed sensor at the front wheel.

Speedometer cable

Refer to illustrations 15.2 and 15.3
2   Unscrew the upper speedometer cable end from the speedometer **(see illustration)** and detach the cable from the speedometer.
3   Note how it's routed, then unscrew the speedometer cable from the speedometer gear box at the front fork **(see illustration)**.
4   Installation is the reverse of the removal steps. Be sure the speedometer cable is routed so that it doesn't cause the steering to bind or interfere with other components. The squared-off ends of the cable must fit into their spindles in the speedometer and gearbox.

Speed sensor

5   Remove the mounting screw at the bottom of the speed sensor and take it off the front fork leg.
6   To test the speed sensor, follow the wiring harness to the connector and disconnect it (it's inside the headlight housing on VT750DC models). Connect a voltmeter to the terminals in the speed sensor side of the connector. Place a screwdriver in the sensor slot and spin it. The voltmeter should indicate pulsing voltage between zero and 5 volts. If not, and if the wires are good, replace the sensor.
7   Installation is the reverse of the removal steps.

Speedometer

Mounted on triple clamp

Refer to illustration 15.11
8   Disconnect the cable from the speedometer **(see illustration 15.2)**.
9   On VT600 models, remove the fuel tank (see Chapter 4) and the steering head covers (see Chapter 8). Follow the speedometer wires to the black six-pin connector behind the steering head and unplug the

connector. Also, unplug the connector for the yellow/black wire.
10   On VT750 models, remove the headlight (see Section 7). Follow the speedometer wires to the black six-pin connector behind the steering head and unplug the connector.
11   Remove the bolt and nut **(see illustration)** and detach the speedometer from the mounting bracket.

Mounted on fuel tank

12   If you're working on a VT750C/CD model, unbolt the fuel tank, lift it up and disconnect the speedometer connector. Remove two bolts from the front of the speedometer cover and two bolts from the top rear. Remove the fuel tank cap and lift the speedometer off.
13   If you're working on a VT750DC model, remove the two bolts at the top rear of the speedometer cover. Slide the speedometer forward to disengage its front retainer from the tank, then lift the speedometer and disconnect its electrical connector.
14   Installation is the reverse of the removal steps. If you're working on a VT750DC model, be sure the rubber mounting pad is in position on the tank bracket.

16   Speedometer light and indicator lights - replacement

Speedometer light bulb

Refer to illustrations 16.4a and 16.4b
1   The speedometer illumination bulb on VT600 and VT750C/CD models can be replaced. On VT750DC models, speedometer illumination is provided by a light-emitting diode that can't be replaced.

16.4a To replace the light bulb that illuminates the speedometer face, pull the bulb socket out of the speedometer assembly . . .

16.4b . . . then pull the bulb out of the socket

16.8 The bulbs for the indicator lights (arrows) are accessible from the underside of the triple clamp

17.9 To remove the ignition switch cover, remove its retaining screw (arrow)

2   Remove the speedometer (see Section 15).
3   Remove the speedometer cover screws **(see illustration 15.2)** and remove the cover.
4   Remove the bulb socket **(see illustration)**, then pull the bulb out of the socket **(see illustration)**. If the socket contacts are dirty or corroded, they should be scraped clean and sprayed with electrical contact cleaner before new bulbs are installed.
5   Carefully push the new bulb into position, then push the socket into the speedometer.
6   Installation is otherwise the reverse of removal.

Indicator lights

Refer to illustration 16.8
7   The indicator lights (turn signal, neutral and high beam) on VT600 and VT750C/CD models are located in the upper triple clamp. The bulbs can be replaced. On VT750DC models, the indicator lights are light emitting diodes that can't be replaced.
8   To replace an indicator light bulb on a VT600, pull down the socket for the bulb you wish to replace **(see illustration)**, pull out the bad bulb from the socket, install a new bulb in the socket and install the new bulb and socket into its receptacle in the triple clamp. Make sure it's firmly seated.
9   To replace an indicator light bulb on a VT750C/CD, remove the indicator light lens and pull the socket out of the triple clamp and replace the bulb as described in the previous step.

17   Ignition main (key) switch - check and replacement

Check

1   Remove the left side cover (see Chapter 8).
2   Trace the wiring harness from the ignition switch to the four-pin white connector and disconnect it. The wires between the ignition switch are red, red/black and blue/orange (these are, respectively, the battery, ignition and fan motor wires). On 1988 and 1989 VT600 models, there's also a brown/white wire to this connector, and two more wires, brown and yellow/blue, lead to a black two-pin connector which must be disconnected (the extra wires on these models are for the Park position, which was eliminated after 1989).
3   Using an ohmmeter, check the continuity of the terminal pairs indicated in the following steps. Connect the ohmmeter to the *switch* side of the connector, not the wiring harness side.
4   In the OFF position, there should be no continuity between any of the wires.
5   In the ON position, there should be continuity between the red, red/blue and blue/orange wires (and, on 1988 and 1989 VT600 models, between the brown/white and brown wires).

17.10 To detach the ignition switch from its mounting bracket, drill out these two "break-off bolts"

6   In the PARK position, on 1988 and 1989 VT600 models, there should be continuity between the red and yellow/blue wires.
7   If the switch fails any of the tests, replace it.

Replacement

Refer to illustration 17.9 and 17.10
8   Disconnect the electrical connector, if you haven't already done so. Free the wiring harness from any clips or retainers.
9   Remove the ignition switch cover screw **(see illustration)** and remove the cover.
10   Drill out the two "break-off bolts" **(see illustration)** and remove the ignition switch.
11   Installation is the reverse of removal. Be sure to use new break-off bolts (available at the dealer parts department). Tighten them until their heads snap off.

18   Handlebar switches - check

1   Most handlebar switch problems are caused by dirty or corroded contacts, or by worn or broken internal parts. If some part of a switch breaks, the switch assembly must be replaced. Individual parts are not available.
2   If a handlebar switch malfunctions, check it for continuity with an ohmmeter or a continuity test light. Be sure to disconnect the battery negative cable to prevent a short circuit, before making the checks.
3   On VT600 models, remove the fuel tank (see Chapter 4) and the steering head covers (see Chapter 8).
4   On VT750 models, remove the headlight (see Section 7).

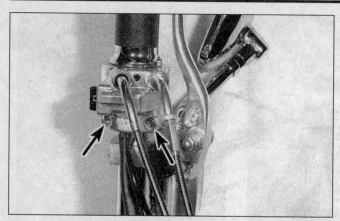

19.1a The handlebar switches are held together by screws (arrows); this is the throttle side . . .

19.1b . . . the clutch side switches are also held together by screws (arrows)

5   Trace the wiring harness from the suspect switch and unplug the electrical connector(s). All models use nine-pin connectors for the handlebar switches. The left handlebar switch has an extra two-pin connector for the horn. On 1988, 1989 and 1991 through 1996 VT600 models, all left handlebar switches use white connectors and the right switches use red connectors. On other models, the color may vary.

6   Using an ohmmeter, check the continuity of the terminal pairs indicated in the following steps. Connect the ohmmeter to the *switch* side of the connector, not the wiring harness side.

Left handlebar switches

7   The wire colors for the **left** handlebar switches are as follows:

a) The **dimmer switch** wires are blue/white, blue and white on all models.

b) The **turn signal switch** wires on 1988, 1989 and 1991 VT600 models are green, light blue, orange, brown/blue, orange/white and light blue/white.

c) The **turn signal switch** wires on all other models are green, light blue, orange, brown/blue, light blue/white and orange/white (yes, they're the same colors, but the last two wire colors are switched, which is important to remember when making the following continuity tests).

d) The **horn switch** wires on 1988, 1989 and 1991 VT600 models are white/green and light green.

e) The **horn switch** wires on all other models are black/brown and light green.

Dimmer switch

8   LO position - continuity between blue/white and white.
9   HI position - continuity between blue/white and blue.

Turn signal switch

1988, 1989 and 1991 VT600 models

10   LEFT - continuity between green and orange, and between brown/black and orange/white.
11   RIGHT - continuity between green and light blue, and between brown/black and light blue/white.

All other models

12   LEFT - continuity between green and orange, and between brown/black and light blue/white.
13   RIGHT - continuity between green and light blue, and between brown/black and orange/white.

Horn switch

1988, 1989 and 1991 VT600 models

14   RELEASED - no continuity.
15   DEPRESSED - continuity between white/green and light green.

All other models

16   RELEASED - no continuity.
17   DEPRESSED - continuity between black/brown and light green.

Right handlebar switches

18   The wire colors for the **right** handlebar switches are as follows:

a) The **starter switch** wires on 1988, 1989 and 1991 through 1993 VT600 models are black, yellow/red, black/red and blue/white.

b) The **starter switch** wires on 1994 through 1996 VT600 models are black/white, yellow/red, black/red and blue/white.

c) The **starter switch** wires on all other models are black/white and yellow/red.

d) The **kill switch** wires on 1988, 1989 and 1991 through 1993 VT600 models are black and black/white.

e) The **kill switch** wires on all other models are black/green and black/white.

Starter switch

1988, 1989 and 1991 through 1993 VT600 models

19   RELEASED - continuity between black/red and blue/white.
20   DEPRESSED - continuity between black and yellow/red.

1994 through 1996 VT600 models

21   RELEASED - continuity between black/red and blue/white.
22   DEPRESSED - continuity between black/white and yellow/red.

All other models

23   RELEASED - no continuity.
24   DEPRESSED - continuity between black/white and yellow/red.

Kill switch

1988, 1989 and 1991 through 1993 VT600 models

25   OFF - no continuity.
26   RUN - continuity between black and black/white.

All other models

27   OFF - no continuity.
28   RUN - continuity between black/green and black/white.
29   If any continuity check indicates a problem, remove the switch (see Section 19), spray the switch contacts with electrical contact cleaner, then retest. The contacts can also be scraped clean with a knife or polished with crocus cloth, if they're accessible. If the switch still fails to check out as described above, or if it's obviously damaged or broken, replace the switch.

19   Handlebar switches - removal and installation

Refer to illustrations 19.1a, 19.1b and 19.1c

1   The handlebar switches are composed of two halves that clamp around the bars. They are easily removed for cleaning or inspection by taking out the clamp screws and pulling the switch halves away from the handlebars **(see illustrations)**.

2   To completely remove the switches, the electrical connectors in the wiring harness should be unplugged.

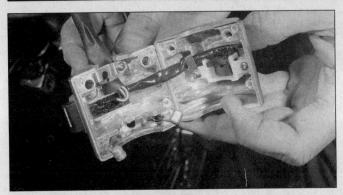

19.1c Separate the switch halves for access to the individual switches

3   When installing the switches, make sure the wiring harnesses are properly routed to avoid pinching or stretching the wires.

20 Neutral switch - check and replacement

Check

Refer to illustrations 20.3 and 20.5

1   Make sure the transmission is in neutral.
2   On VT600 models, remove the left side cover; on VT750 models, remove the right side cover (see Chapter 8).
3   The neutral switch connector has two pins and is black (VT600 and VT750C/CD) or red (VT750DC) **(see illustration)**. On most VT600 models, it's located right on top of the voltage regulator/rectifier; on some VT600 models, it's behind the regulator/rectifier, so you may have to remove the regulator/rectifier to get to it (see Section 32). On VT750C/CD models, the connector is sandwiched between the white two-pin fuel pump connector and the three-pin sidestand connector. On VT750DC models, the connector is located inside a rubber boot behind the rear engine cylinder. There are two wires to the connector; the light green or light green/red wire is for the neutral switch.
4   Ground the terminal on the harness side of the connector to bare metal on the motorcycle frame with a short length of wire. The neutral indicator light on the upper triple clamp should come on.
5   If the light doesn't come on, check the bulb (if equipped) (see Section 16) and the wiring between the ignition switch and the neutral switch (see wiring diagrams at the end of this Chapter). Remove the left rear cover (see "Drive chain - removal, cleaning and installation" in Chapter 7) and locate the switch, right in front of the drive sprocket **(see illustration)**. Make sure that the electrical lead is connected to the switch.

6   If the neutral indicator light comes on, the neutral switch might be bad. Connect an ohmmeter between the terminal on the switch side of the connector and ground. Shift through the gears. The ohmmeter should indicate continuity in neutral and no continuity in all other gears.
7   If the neutral switch doesn't operate as described, replace it.

Replacement

8   Remove the left rear cover (see "Drive chain - removal, cleaning and installation" in Chapter 7).
9   Locate the neutral switch, right in front of the drive sprocket **(see illustration 20.5)** and disconnect the electrical lead.
10   Some oil is going to come out when you unscrew the switch and remove it from the crankcase, so be prepared to catch it with a drain pan.
11   Apply thread sealant to the threads of the new switch and tighten it to the torque listed in this Chapter's Specifications.
12   Installation is otherwise the reverse of removal. Be sure to route the wire harness for the oil pressure switch and the neutral switch correctly so that it's not damaged by the drive chain.

21 Oil pressure switch - check and replacement

Check

Refer to illustration 21.3

1   When the ignition switch is turned to ON, the oil pressure warning light on the speedometer should come on. This verifies that the oil pressure switch and circuit are functioning normally.
2   If the oil pressure warning light doesn't come on when the ignition switch is turned to ON, remove the left rear cover (see "Drive chain - removal, cleaning and installation" in Chapter 7).
3   Locate the oil pressure switch **(see illustration 20.5)**, right behind the water pump. Remove the dust boot, remove the electrical lead retaining screw **(see illustration)** and detach the lead from the switch.
4   Short the switch lead to ground with a jumper wire. Turn the ignition switch to ON. The oil pressure warning indicator light should now come on.
5   If the oil pressure warning light still doesn't come on, check the 10A inline mini-fuse and check the switch circuit for an open circuit somewhere.
6   Start the engine and verify that the oil pressure warning light goes out.
7   If the oil pressure warning light doesn't go out, have the oil pressure checked by a Honda dealer service department.
8   If the oil pressure is normal, replace the oil pressure switch.

Replacement

9   On VT600 models, remove the left side cover; on VT750 models,

20.3 VT600 neutral switch connector (this is also the connector for the oil pressure switch)

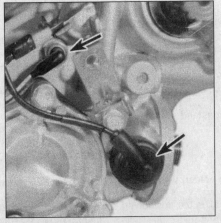

20.5 Neutral switch (left arrow) and oil pressure switch (right arrow)

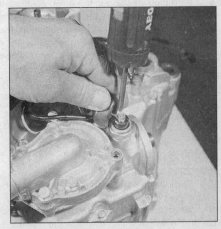

21.3 Remove the screw to disconnect the oil pressure switch wire

22.9 VT600 sidestand switch

22.13 To remove the VT750 sidestand switch, remove this bolt (arrow) and pull off the switch

24.1 Unplug the electrical connectors from the horn and remove its mounting bolt (arrow)

remove the right side cover (see Chapter 8).

10 Unplug the electrical connector for the oil pressure switch. It's the same electrical connector the neutral switch uses (see Section 20).

11 Remove the left rear cover (see "Drive chain - removal, cleaning and installation" in Chapter 7).

12 Locate the oil pressure switch **(see illustration 20.5)**, right behind the water pump. Remove the dust boot, remove the electrical lead retaining screw and disconnect the lead from the switch.

13 Some oil is going to come out when you unscrew the switch, so be prepared to catch it with a drain pan.

14 Apply thread sealant to the threads of the new switch, install the switch and tighten it to the torque listed in this Chapter's Specifications.

15 Installation is otherwise the reverse of removal. Be sure to route the wire harness for the oil pressure switch and the neutral switch correctly so that it's not damaged by the drive chain.

22 Sidestand switch - check and replacement

Check

1 On VT600 models, remove the left side cover; on VT750 models, remove the right side cover (see Chapter 8).

2 The wires in the sidestand switch circuit are green/white, yellow/black and green. Follow the wiring harness from the switch (at the upper end of the sidestand) to the green three-pin electrical connector, then unplug the connector.

3 Connect the leads of an ohmmeter to the terminals for the indicated wire colors.

4 With the sidestand in the down position, there should be continuity between the terminals for the yellow/blue and green wires.

5 With the sidestand in the up position, there should be continuity between the terminals for the green/white and green wires.

6 If the sidestand switch fails either of these tests, replace it.

Replacement

7 On VT600 models, remove the left side cover; on VT750 models, remove the right side cover (see Chapter 8).

8 Unplug the electrical connector for the sidestand switch (see Step 2).

VT600 models

Refer to illustration 22.9

9 Remove the sidestand switch bolt, switch holder, washer and switch **(see illustration)**.

10 When installing the new sidestand switch, align the positioning pin on the switch with the hole in the sidestand and align the groove in the switch with the pin on the sidestand.

11 Install the sidestand switch holder, install the retaining bolt and

tighten it to the torque listed in this Chapter's Specifications.

12 Installation is otherwise the reverse of the removal procedure. Be sure to route the electrical lead correctly.

VT750 models

Refer to illustration 22.13

13 Remove the sidestand switch bolt **(see illustration)** and remove the switch.

14 When installing the new sidestand switch, align the positioning pin on the switch with the hole in the sidestand and align the groove in the switch with the pin on the sidestand.

15 Install the sidestand switch retaining bolt and tighten it to the torque listed in this Chapter's Specifications.

16 Installation is otherwise the reverse of the removal procedure. Be sure to route the electrical lead correctly.

23 Clutch switch - check and replacement

Check

1 Disconnect the electrical connectors from the clutch switch **(see illustration 19.1b)**.

2 Connect an ohmmeter to the terminals of the clutch switch. With the clutch lever pulled in, the ohmmeter should show continuity. With the lever out, the ohmmeter should show no continuity.

3 If the switch doesn't check out as described, replace it.

Replacement

4 Disconnect the electrical connectors from the clutch switch **(see illustration 19.1b)**.

5 Remove the clutch switch from the handlebar bracket.

6 Installation is the reverse of removal.

24 Horn - check and replacement

Check

Refer to illustration 24.1

1 Disconnect the electrical connectors from the horn **(see illustration)**. Using two jumper wires, apply battery voltage directly to the terminals on the horn. If the horn sounds, check the switch (see Section 18) and the wiring between the switch and the horn (see the wiring diagrams at the end of this Chapter). The horn wiring harness is connected to the main harness at a black two-pin connector (same connector as the fan motor) behind the steering head. To get to it, remove the steering head covers (see Chapter 8).

2 If the horn doesn't sound, replace it.

25.4 The starter relay (arrow) is mounted in a rubber holder

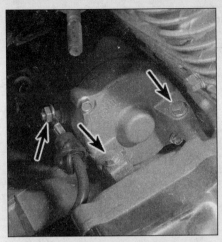

27.2 Starter cable nut and mounting bolts (arrows); the left bolt secures a ground wire

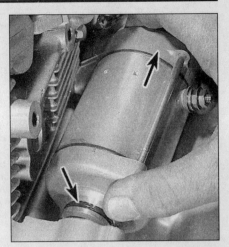

27.4 Lift the right end of the starter slightly and slide it out to the right; inspect the O-ring (arrow)

Replacement

3   Disconnect the electrical connectors and unbolt the horn **(see illustration 24.1)**.
4   Installation is the reverse of removal.

---

25 Starter relay switch - check and replacement

Check

Refer to illustration 25.4

1   Make sure the battery is fully charged.
2   Remove the right side cover (see Chapter 8).
3   **Warning:** *Make sure the transmission is in neutral for this step.* Turn the ignition switch to ON and the engine kill switch to RUN. When you push the starter button, the starter relay switch should click.
4   If the starter relay switch doesn't click, unplug the starter relay switch 4-pin electrical connector **(see illustration)** and check for continuity between the terminal for the green/red wire (on the harness side of the connector) and ground.
5   If there is continuity when the transmission is in Neutral or when the clutch is disengaged and the sidestand is up (sidestand switch closed), the ground circuit is okay (you will note a slight resistance in the circuit because of the clutch diode).
6   Reconnect the starter relay switch electrical connector, shift the transmission into Neutral and, using a voltmeter, measure the voltage between the terminal for the yellow/red wire (backprobe the connector) and ground. Battery voltage should be indicated when the starter button is pushed with the ignition switch ON.
7   Unplug the starter relay switch connector again, remove the cable attaching bolts or nuts and disconnect the cables from the relay. Using jumper wires, hook up the positive terminal of a 12-volt battery to the starter relay switch terminal for the yellow/red wire and hook up the negative terminal of the battery to the starter relay terminal for the green/red wire. Using an ohmmeter hooked up to the starter relay cable terminals, verify that there is continuity when the battery is connected to the relay. Disconnect the battery from the relay and verify that there is no continuity across the relay terminals.
8   If the starter relay switch fails any of these tests, replace it.

Replacement

9   Disconnect the battery negative cable.
10   Remove the right side cover (see Chapter 8).
11   Unplug the starter relay switch electrical connector **(see illustration 25.4)**.
12   Remove the cable attaching bolts or nuts and disconnect the

cables from the starter relay switch.
13   Remove the starter relay switch.
14   Installation is the reverse of removal. Reconnect the negative battery cable after all the other electrical connections are made.

---

26 Clutch diode - check and replacement

1   The clutch diode on VT600 models is located in the wiring harness and covered with tape. On VT750 models, it's mounted in the fuse box.
2   The clutch diode has three terminals, one for the green/red wire, one for the light green/red wire and one for the light green wire. The clutch diode allows current to flow through the first two terminals and out the third terminal, but it does not allow current the flow the other way. Think of the first two terminals (green/red wire and light green/red wire) as the "in" terminals; think of the third terminal (light green wire) as the "out" terminal.
3   Using an ohmmeter, verify that there is continuity between each of the "in" terminals and the "out" terminal in one direction, but NOT in the other direction.
4   If the clutch diode fails either of these tests, replace it.
5   Installation is the reverse of removal.

---

27 Starter motor - removal and installation

Removal

Refer to illustrations 27.2 and 27.4

1   Disconnect the cable from the negative terminal of the battery.
2   Pull back the rubber cover, remove the nut retaining the starter cable to the starter and disconnect the cable **(see illustration)**.
3   Remove the starter mounting bolts.
4   Lift the end of the starter slightly and disengage the starter from the crankcase by pulling it out to the right **(see illustration)**.
5   Inspect the O-ring on the end of the starter and replace it if necessary. Also inspect the teeth on the starter pinion gear and on the reduction gear; make sure the gear teeth are neither chipped nor excessively worn. (With a flashlight, you can inspect the reduction gear teeth through the hole in the case for the starter.)

Installation

6   Apply a little engine oil to the O-ring. Installation is otherwise the reverse of removal. Tighten the starter mounting bolts to the torque listed in this Chapter's Specifications.

28   Starter motor - disassembly, inspection and reassembly

1   Remove the starter motor (see Section 27).

Disassembly

Refer to illustration 28.2

2   Mark the position of the housing to each end cover. Remove the two through-bolts and their lockwashers and detach both end covers **(see illustration)**.

3   Remove the nut and push the terminal bolt through the starter housing, then reinstall the washers and nut on the bolt so you don't forget how they go. Pull the armature out of the housing and remove the brush plate.

4   Remove the two brushes with the plastic holder from the housing.

Inspection

Refer to illustrations 28.5, 28.6, 28.7a, 28.7b, 28.8 and 28.9

5   The parts of the starter motor most likely to require attention are the brushes. Measure the length of the brushes and compare the results to the brush length listed in this Chapter's Specifications **(see illustration)**. If any of the brushes are worn beyond the specified limits, replace the brush holder assembly. If the brushes are not worn excessively, cracked, chipped, or otherwise damaged, they may be re-used.

6   Inspect the commutator **(see illustration)** for scoring, scratches and discoloration. The commutator can be cleaned and polished with crocus cloth, but do not use sandpaper or emery paper. After cleaning, wipe away any residue with a cloth soaked in an electrical system cleaner or denatured alcohol. Measure the commutator diameter and compare it to the diameter listed in this Chapter's Specifications. If it is less than the service limit, the motor must be replaced.

7   Using an ohmmeter or a continuity test light, check for continuity between the commutator bars **(see illustration)**. Continuity should exist between each bar and all of the others. Also, check for continuity between the commutator bars and the armature shaft **(see illustration)**. There should be no continuity between the commutator and the shaft. If the checks indicate otherwise, the armature is defective.

8   Check for continuity between the brush plate and the brushes **(see illustration)**. The meter should read close to 0 ohms. If it doesn't, the brush plate has an open and must be replaced.

9   Using the highest range on the ohmmeter, measure the resistance between the brush holders and the brush plate **(see illustration)**. The reading should be infinite. If there is any reading at all, replace the brush plate.

10   Check the starter pinion gear for worn, cracked, chipped and broken teeth. If the gear is damaged or worn, replace the starter motor.

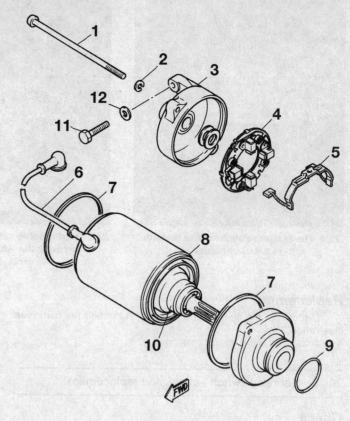

28.2 Starter - exploded view

1	*Through-bolt*	6	*Cable*
2	*Lockwasher*	7	*O-rings*
3	*Brush end cover*	8	*Starter housing*
4	*Brush plate*	9	*O-ring*
5	*Plastic brush housing*	10	*Armature*

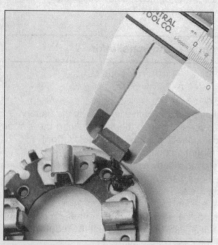

28.5 Measure the length of the brushes and compare the length of the shortest brush with the length listed in this Chapter's Specifications

28.6 Check the commutator for cracks and discoloring, then measure the diameter and compare it with the minimum diameter listed in this Chapter's Specifications

28.7a Continuity should exist between the commutator bars

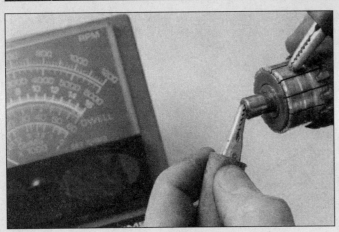

28.7b There should be no continuity between the commutator bars and the armature shaft

28.8 There should be almost no resistance (0 ohms) between the brushes and the brush plate

Reassembly

Refer to illustration 28.14

11 Install the brush holder into the housing. Make sure the terminal bolt and washers are assembled in their original order. Tighten the terminal nut securely.

12 Detach the brush springs from the brush plate (this will make armature installation much easier). Install the brush plate into the housing, routing the brush leads into the notches in the plate. Make sure the tongue on the brush plate fits into the notch in the housing.

13 Install the brushes into their holders and slide the armature into place. Install the brush springs.

14 Install any washers that were present on the end of the armature shaft **(see illustration)**.

15 Install the end covers, aligning the previously applied match marks (be sure to install the large O-rings between the starter housing and end covers). Install the O-rings and washers (if equipped) on the two through-bolts, then install the through-bolts and tighten them securely.

28.9 There should be no continuity between the brush plate and the brush holders (the resistance reading should be infinite)

29 Charging system testing - general information and precautions

1 If the performance of the charging system is suspect, the system as a whole should be checked first, followed by testing of the individual components (the alternator and the voltage regulator/rectifier). **Note:** *Before beginning the checks, make sure the battery is fully charged and that all system connections are clean and tight.*

2 Checking the output of the charging system and the performance of the various components within the charging system requires the use of special electrical test equipment. A voltmeter or a multimeter are the absolute minimum tools required. In addition, an ohmmeter is generally required for checking the remainder of the system.

3 When making the checks, follow the procedures carefully to prevent incorrect connections or short circuits, as irreparable damage to electrical system components may result if short circuits occur. Because of the special tools and expertise required, it is recommended that the job of checking the charging system be left to a dealer service department or a reputable motorcycle repair shop.

30 Charging system - check

Caution: *Never disconnect the battery cables from the battery while the engine is running. If the battery is disconnected, the alternator and regulator/rectifier will be damaged.*

1 To check the charging system output, you will need a voltmeter or a multimeter with a voltmeter function.

28.14 Be sure the shims and washers are in place on both ends of the armature shaft

2 On VT600 models, remove both side covers; on VT750 models, remove the front seat (see Chapter 8).

3 The battery must be fully charged (charge it from an external source if necessary) and the engine must be at normal operating temperature to obtain an accurate reading.

Regulated voltage output test

4 Attach the positive (red) voltmeter lead to the positive (+) battery terminal and the negative (black) lead to the battery negative (-) terminal. The voltmeter selector switch (if equipped) must be in a DC volt

31.2a Alternator wire harness routing

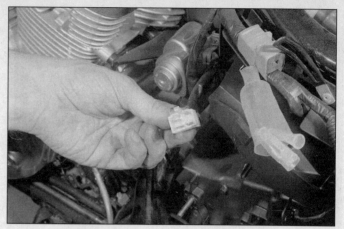

31.2b The alternators on all models use a white, three-pin connector located on the left side of the bike, in the area covered by the left side cover

range greater than 15 volts.

5　Start the engine and allow it to warm up to its normal operating temperature. With the headlight on LOW beam and the engine running at the rpm indicated in this Chapter's Specifications, note the regulated voltage output of the charging system and compare your measurement to the regulated output listed in this Chapter's Specifications. Turn off the engine.

6　If the charging system fails to produce the specified regulated voltage output, there could be an open or a short circuit, or a loose, corroded or shorted connector, somewhere in the charging system wire harness; there could be an open or short in the alternator (see Section 31); or the voltage regulator/rectifier could be defective (see Section 32).

7　If the charging system produces a higher-than-specified voltage output, the regulator/rectifier is either poorly grounded or it's defective (see Section 32), or the battery is defective (see Section 3).

8　If the indicated regulated voltage output is within the specified range, but the battery is frequently discharged, this is an indication that the battery is probably worn out. But it's also possible that there's a current leak.

Current leakage test

9　To test for a current leak, disconnect the negative battery cable (see Section 3) and hook up a digital ammeter capable of readings in the milliampere range. Connect the positive probe of the ammeter to the battery negative cable and the negative probe to the battery negative terminal. With the ignition switch turned to OFF, note whether

there is any current leakage. If there is, compare your reading to the permissible current leakage listed in this Chapter's Specifications.

10　If the indicated current leakage exceeds the specified allowable maximum, there's a short circuit somewhere. To locate the circuit where the short is occurring, unplug the harness electrical connectors one by one until the leak stops.

11　If the indicated current leakage is less than the specified allowable maximum, but the battery is frequently discharged, replace the battery (see Section 3).

31　Alternator - check and replacement

Check

Refer to illustrations 31.2a and 31.2b

1　Remove the left side cover (see Chapter 8) and the engine sprocket cover (see Chapter 7).

2　Trace the three-wire harness (all three wires are yellow on all models) from the alternator, on the left side of the engine, to the three-pin white electrical connector and disconnect the connector **(see illustrations)**.

3　Using an ohmmeter, measure the resistance between each terminal and each of the other two terminals of the connector (on the alternator side of the connector, not the wiring harness side). Compare your measurements to the stator coil resistance listed in this Chapter's Specifications.

4　If the reading between any two terminals is outside the range listed in this Chapter's Specifications, replace the stator.

5　If the reading is within the Specifications, refer to the wiring diagrams at the end of the book and check the charging circuit for breaks or poor connections. If the wiring is good, check the voltage regulator/rectifier (see Section 32).

Replacement

Stator

Refer to illustrations 31.8a, 31.8b and 31.15

6　Remove the left side cover (see Chapter 8).

7　Trace the three-wire harness (all three wires are yellow on all models) from the alternator, on the left side of the engine, to the three-pin white electrical connector and disconnect the connector **(see illustrations 31.2a and 31.2b)**.

8　Loosen the left crankcase cover mounting bolts **(see illustration)** evenly in a criss-cross pattern and remove the cover. Remove the dowel pins **(see illustration)**.

9　Remove the two stator wire holder retaining bolts **(see illustration 31.8b)** and remove the stator wire holder. Note how the wire har-

31.8a To remove the left crankcase cover, remove these 11 bolts (arrows) evenly, in a criss-cross fashion

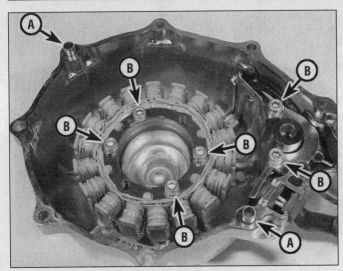

31.8b The stator is mounted inside the left crankcase cover

A   Cover dowels   B   Stator Allen bolts

31.15 Note the harness routing under the cover; place the alternator harness in its clip (arrow)

31.17 To detach the rotor (flywheel) from the crankshaft, remove this (reverse-thread) bolt arrow . . .

ness is routed in the cover, then disengage it from the cover. Remove the stator retaining bolts and remove the stator assembly.

10   Thoroughly clean the left engine cover with solvent and blow it dry with compressed air.

11   Insert the wire harness and grommets in the cover, install the stator wire holder and the holder bolts, and tighten the holder bolts securely. Install the stator retaining bolts and tighten them to the torque listed in this Chapter's Specifications.

12   Clean all traces of old gasket sealer from the cover and its mating surface on the engine.

13   Make sure there are no metal particles stuck to the rotor magnets.

14   Install the dowel pins. Position a new gasket over the dowels.

15   Install the cover and tighten the cover bolts evenly, in a criss-cross pattern, to the torque listed in this Chapter's Specifications. Route the wiring harness across the top of the crankcase and through the guide attached to the left rear cover bracket (see illustration). Connect the electrical connector.

Rotor (flywheel)

Refer to illustrations 31.17, 31.18a, 31.18b and 31.18c

16   Remove the left crankcase cover (see Steps 6, 7 and 8).

17   Install a rotor holder tool (Honda 07725-0040000, or equivalent) to lock the rotor in place. If you don't have a suitable rotor holder tool, shift the transmission into gear and have an assistant apply the rear

brake. Remove the rotor bolt and washer (see illustration). Note: *The rotor bolt is reverse thread; turn it clockwise to loosen it.*

18   Thread a rotor puller (Honda 07733-0020001, or 07933-3290001, or equivalent) into the rotor (see illustration). Remove the rotor from the end of the crankshaft and take the Woodruff key out of its slot (see illustrations).

31.18a . . . use a tool like this one to separate the rotor from the crankshaft . . .

31.18b . . . then take the rotor off . . .

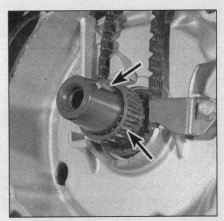

31.18c . . . and lift the Woodruff key (arrow) out of its slot; as long as the rotor is removed, this is a good time to inspect the starter clutch needle bearing (arrow)

32.2 On VT600 models, remove the regulator/rectifier mounting nuts (arrows) . . .

32.7 . . . and remove the unit

33.2a Remove the starter reduction gear (arrow) . . .

33.2b . . . remove the reduction gear shaft . . .

19 Remove and inspect the starter clutch assembly, if necessary (see Section 33).
20 Installation is the reverse of the removal steps. Be sure to reinstall the Woodruff key. **Caution:** *Make sure no metal objects have stuck to the magnets inside the rotor.* Tighten the rotor bolt to the torque listed in this Chapter's Specifications.

32 Voltage regulator/rectifier - check and replacement

Check

Refer to illustration 32.2

1 On VT600 models, remove the left side cover; on VT750 models, remove the right side cover (see Chapter 8).
2 Trace the wiring harness from the regulator/rectifier to the connector **(see illustration)**. VT600 models use a four-pin connector. VT750C/CD models use a six-pin connector. VT750DC models use two connectors, one with two pins and one with three.
3 Using a voltmeter, verify that there is voltage between the terminals for the red/white and green wires. There shouldn't be any voltage between them (if there is voltage between them, there is a short in the connector).
4 If there is no voltage between the terminals for the red/white and green wires, verify that there *is* voltage between the terminal for the red/white wire and ground. If there is, then you know that there is power to the regulator/rectifier. Finally, using an ohmmeter, verify that

there is continuity between the terminal for the green wire and ground. If there is, then you know that the regulator/rectifier output line is good. Replace the voltage regulator/rectifier.

Replacement

Refer to illustration 32.7

5 On VT600 models, remove the left side cover; on VT750 models, remove the right side cover (see Chapter 8).
6 Trace the wiring harness from the regulator/rectifier to the connector(s) (see Step 2).
7 Remove the regulator/rectifier mounting nuts **(see illustration 32.2 and the accompanying illustration)**.
8 Installation is the reverse of removal.

33 Starter clutch assembly - removal, inspection and installation

Refer to illustrations 33.2a, 33.2b, 33.2c, 33.4, 33.6a and 33.6b

1 Remove the left engine cover (see Section 31).
2 Remove the reduction gear and shaft, and the idle gear and shaft **(see illustrations)**. Inspect the reduction gear and idle gear for wear and chipped teeth. Inspect the gear shafts for scoring and excessive wear. Replace any worn or damaged parts.
3 Remove the rotor (see Section 31). Remove the needle bearing from the crankshaft **(see illustration 31.18c)**.

33.2c . . . and remove the idle gear and shaft

33.4 The starter driven gear should turn in one direction only

33.6a Remove the starter driven gear from the rotor, remove the big washer (A) and inspect the sprag (B)

33.6b To detach the clutch housing from the rotor, remove these six Torx bolts

4   Holding the rotor in one hand, with the rotor facing down and the starter clutch facing toward you, verify that the starter clutch turns freely in a counterclockwise direction (see illustration), but not at all in a clockwise direction.

5   If the starter clutch turns in both directions, or will not turn in either direction, remove it from the rotor and inspect the starter clutch assembly.

6   Remove the starter driven gear and the big washer from the rotor (see illustration). Remove the six Torx bolts from the rotor (see illustration) and detach the clutch housing and one-way clutch from the rotor. Remove the washer. Caution: *On VT750 models, do NOT separate the one-way clutch from the clutch housing unless you are definitely planning to replace it.*

7   Clean all parts thoroughly in clean solvent and blow them dry with compressed air.

8   Inspect the needle bearing, the one-way clutch sprag (see illustration 33.6a) and the clutch housing for scoring or other signs of excessive wear. Replace all worn or damaged parts.

9   Measure the inside diameter (I.D.) and outside diameter (O.D.) of the starter driven gear and compare your measurements to the I.D. and O.D. listed in this Chapter's Specifications. If the starter gear hub I.D. is greater than the specified I.D., or if the hub O.D. is less than the speci-

fied O.D., replace the starter gear.

10   Apply clean engine oil to the one-way clutch sprags and install the one-way clutch unit into the clutch housing. Install the housing with its flange toward the rotor, install the six Torx bolts and tighten them to the torque listed in this Chapter's Specifications.

11   Lubricate the big washer and install it on the backside of the rotor.

12   Lubricate the outer surface of the starter driven gear hub and install the gear into the clutch housing.

13   The remainder of installation is the reverse of removal.

34 Wiring diagrams

Prior to troubleshooting a circuit, check the fuses to make sure they're in good condition. Make sure the battery is fully charged and check the cable connections.

When checking a circuit, make sure all connectors are clean, with no broken or loose terminals or wires. When unplugging a connector, don't pull on the wires - pull only on the connector housings themselves.

Refer to the table in Chapter 9 for the wire color codes.

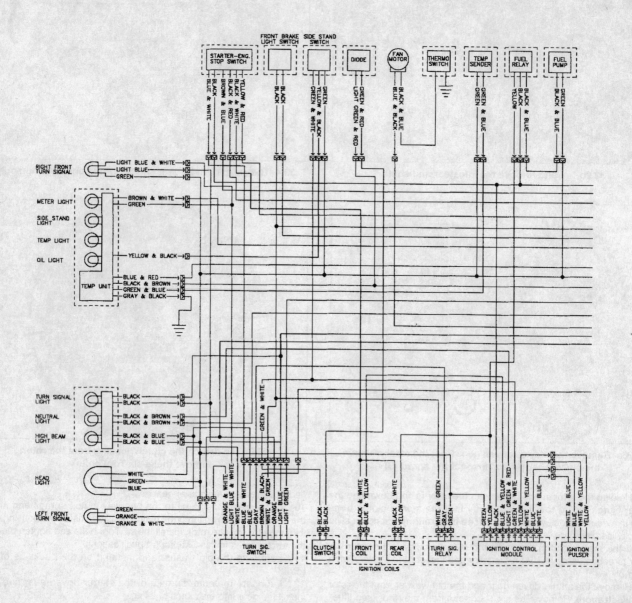

Wiring diagram - 1988 and 1989 VT600 models (1 of 2)

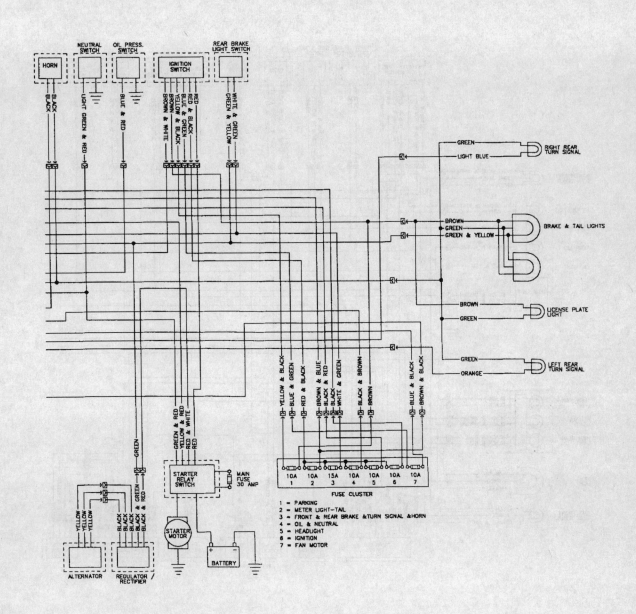

Wiring diagram - 1988 and 1989 VT600 models (2 of 2)

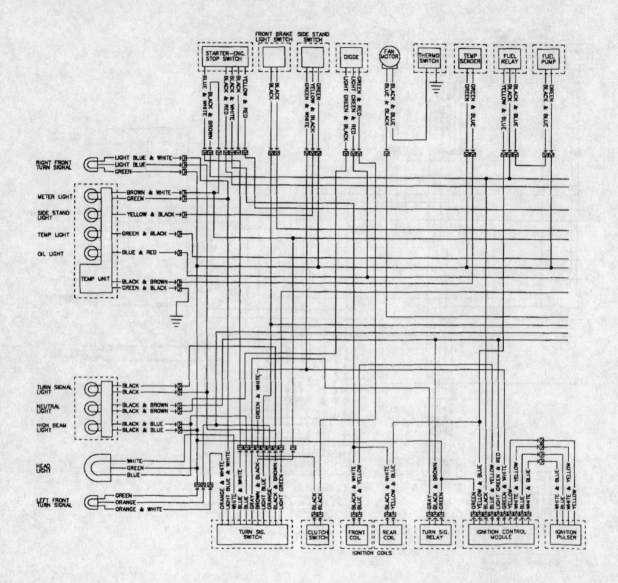

Wiring diagram - 1991 and later VT600 models (1 of 2)

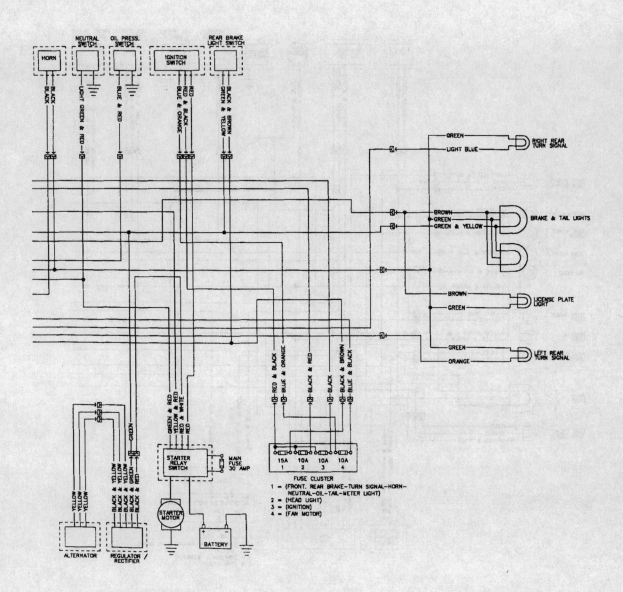

Wiring diagram - 1991 and later VT600 models (2 of 2)

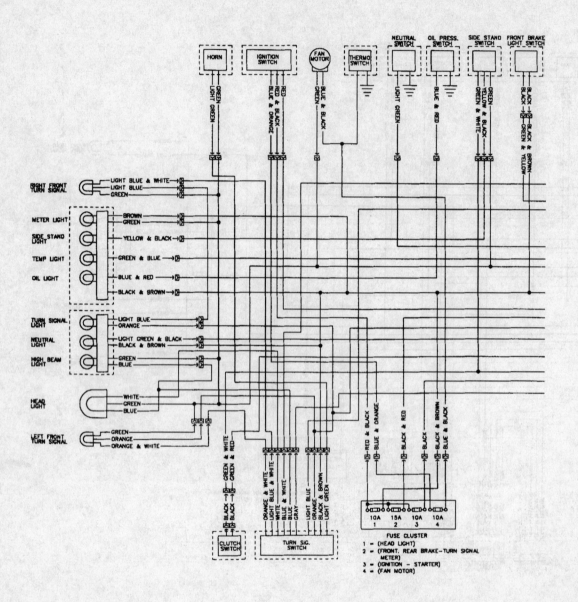

Wiring diagram - Typical VT750 model (1 of 2)

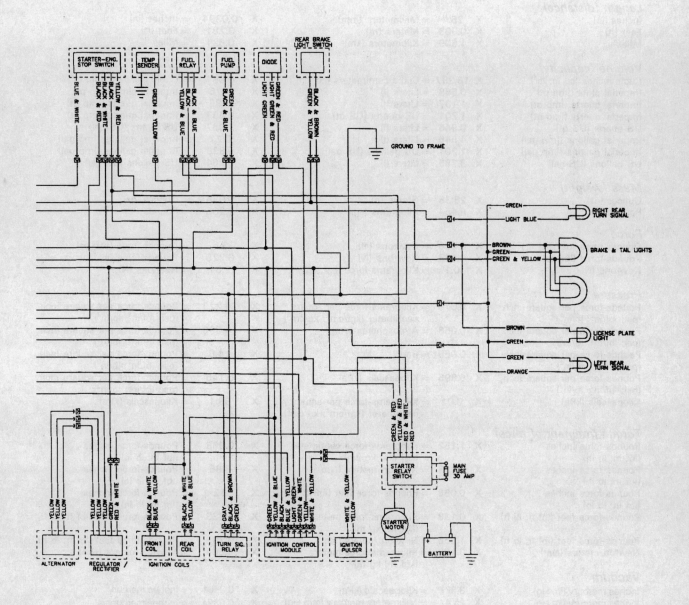

Wiring diagram - Typical VT750 model (2 of 2)

Conversion factors

Length (distance)
Inches (in)	X	25.4	= Millimeters (mm)	X 0.0394	= Inches (in)
Feet (ft)	X	0.305	= Meters (m)	X 3.281	= Feet (ft)
Miles	X	1.609	= Kilometers (km)	X 0.621	= Miles

Volume (capacity)
Cubic inches (cu in; in³)	X	16.387	= Cubic centimeters (cc; cm³)	X 0.061	= Cubic inches (cu in; in³)
Imperial pints (Imp pt)	X	0.568	= Liters (l)	X 1.76	= Imperial pints (Imp pt)
Imperial quarts (Imp qt)	X	1.137	= Liters (l)	X 0.88	= Imperial quarts (Imp qt)
Imperial quarts (Imp qt)	X	1.201	= US quarts (US qt)	X 0.833	= Imperial quarts (Imp qt)
US quarts (US qt)	X	0.946	= Liters (l)	X 1.057	= US quarts (US qt)
Imperial gallons (Imp gal)	X	4.546	= Liters (l)	X 0.22	= Imperial gallons (Imp gal)
Imperial gallons (Imp gal)	X	1.201	= US gallons (US gal)	X 0.833	= Imperial gallons (Imp gal)
US gallons (US gal)	X	3.785	= Liters (l)	X 0.264	= US gallons (US gal)

Mass (weight)
Ounces (oz)	X	28.35	= Grams (g)	X 0.035	= Ounces (oz)
Pounds (lb)	X	0.454	= Kilograms (kg)	X 2.205	= Pounds (lb)

Force
Ounces-force (ozf; oz)	X	0.278	= Newtons (N)	X 3.6	= Ounces-force (ozf; oz)
Pounds-force (lbf; lb)	X	4.448	= Newtons (N)	X 0.225	= Pounds-force (lbf; lb)
Newtons (N)	X	0.1	= Kilograms-force (kgf; kg)	X 9.81	= Newtons (N)

Pressure
Pounds-force per square inch (psi; lbf/in²; lb/in²)	X	0.070	= Kilograms-force per square centimeter (kgf/cm²; kg/cm²)	X 14.223	= Pounds-force per square inch (psi; lbf/in²; lb/in²)
Pounds-force per square inch (psi; lbf/in²; lb/in²)	X	0.068	= Atmospheres (atm)	X 14.696	= Pounds-force per square inch (psi; lbf/in²; lb/in²)
Pounds-force per square inch (psi; lbf/in²; lb/in²)	X	0.069	= Bars	X 14.5	= Pounds-force per square inch (psi; lbf/in²; lb/in²)
Pounds-force per square inch (psi; lbf/in²; lb/in²)	X	6.895	= Kilopascals (kPa)	X 0.145	= Pounds-force per square inch (psi; lbf/in²; lb/in²)
Kilopascals (kPa)	X	0.01	= Kilograms-force per square centimeter (kgf/cm²; kg/cm²)	X 98.1	= Kilopascals (kPa)

Torque (moment of force)
Pounds-force inches (lbf in; lb in)	X	1.152	= Kilograms-force centimeter (kgf cm; kg cm)	X 0.868	= Pounds-force inches (lbf in; lb in)
Pounds-force inches (lbf in; lb in)	X	0.113	= Newton meters (Nm)	X 8.85	= Pounds-force inches (lbf in; lb in)
Pounds-force inches (lbf in; lb in)	X	0.083	= Pounds-force feet (lbf ft; lb ft)	X 12	= Pounds-force inches (lbf in; lb in)
Pounds-force feet (lbf ft; lb ft)	X	0.138	= Kilograms-force meters (kgf m; kg m)	X 7.233	= Pounds-force feet (lbf ft; lb ft)
Pounds-force feet (lbf ft; lb ft)	X	1.356	= Newton meters (Nm)	X 0.738	= Pounds-force feet (lbf ft; lb ft)
Newton meters (Nm)	X	0.102	= Kilograms-force meters (kgf m; kg m)	X 9.804	= Newton meters (Nm)

Vacuum
Inches mercury (in. Hg)	X	3.377	= Kilopascals (kPa)	X 0.2961	= Inches mercury
Inches mercury (in. Hg)	X	25.4	= Millimeters mercury (mm Hg)	X 0.0394	= Inches mercury

Power
Horsepower (hp)	X	745.7	= Watts (W)	X 0.0013	= Horsepower (hp)

Velocity (speed)
Miles per hour (miles/hr; mph)	X	1.609	= Kilometers per hour (km/hr; kph)	X 0.621	= Miles per hour (miles/hr; mph)

Fuel consumption*
Miles per gallon, Imperial (mpg)	X	0.354	= Kilometers per liter (km/l)	X 2.825	= Miles per gallon, Imperial (mpg)
Miles per gallon, US (mpg)	X	0.425	= Kilometers per liter (km/l)	X 2.352	= Miles per gallon, US (mpg)

Temperature
Degrees Fahrenheit = (°C x 1.8) + 32

Degrees Celsius (Degrees Centigrade; °C) = (°F - 32) x 0.56

*It is common practice to convert from miles per gallon (mpg) to liters/100 kilometers (l/100km),
where mpg (Imperial) x l/100 km = 282 and mpg (US) x l/100 km = 235

Index